Market Services and the Productivity Race, 1850–2000

Now that services account for such a dominant part of economic activity, it has become apparent that achieving high levels of productivity in the economy requires high levels of productivity in services. This book offers a major reassessment of the United Kingdom's comparative productivity performance over the last 150 years. Whereas, in the mid-nineteenth century, Britain had higher productivity than the United States and Germany, by 1990 both countries had overtaken Britain. The key to achieving high productivity was the 'industrialisation' of market services, which involved both the serving of business and the provision of mass-market consumer services in a more businesslike fashion. Comparative productivity varied with the uneven spread of industrialised service sector provision across sectors. Stephen Broadberry provides a quantitative overview of these trends, together with a qualitative account of developments wihtin individual sectors, including shipping, railways, road and air transport, telecommunications, wholesale and retail distribution, banking, and finance.

STEPHEN BROADBERRY is Professor of Economics at the University of Warwick. His recent books include *The Productivity Race: British Manufacturing in International Perspective, 1850–1990* (1997) and, as editor with Mark Harrison, *The Economics of World War I* (2005).

Cambridge Studies in Economic History

Editorial Board

Paul Johnson
London School of Economics and Political Science
Sheilagh Ogilvie
University of Cambridge
Avner Offer
All Souls College, Oxford
Gianni Toniolo
Università di Roma 'Tor Vergata'
Gavin Wright
Stanford University

Cambridge Studies in Economic History comprises stimulating and accessible economic history which actively builds bridges to other disciplines. Books in the series will illuminate why the issues they address are important and interesting, place their findings in a comparative context, and relate their research to wider debates and controversies. The series will combine innovative and exciting new research by younger researchers with new approaches to major issues by senior scholars. It will publish distinguished work regardless of chronological period or geographical location.

Titles in the series include:
Robert Millward *Private and Public Enterprise in Europe: Energy, Telecommunications and Transport, 1830–1990*
S. D. Smith *Slavery, Family and Gentry Capitalism in the British Atlantic: The World of the Lascelles, 1648–1834*

Market Services and the Productivity Race, 1850–2000

British Performance in International Perspective

Stephen Broadberry

CAMBRIDGE
UNIVERSITY PRESS

CAMBRIDGE UNIVERSITY PRESS
Cambridge, New York, Melbourne, Madrid, Cape Town, Singapore,
São Paulo, Delhi, Dubai, Tokyo

Cambridge University Press
The Edinburgh Building, Cambridge CB2 8RU, UK

Published in the United States of America by Cambridge University Press, New York

www.cambridge.org
Information on this title: www.cambridge.org/9780521123143

© Stephen Broadberry 2006

This publication is in copyright. Subject to statutory exception
and to the provisions of relevant collective licensing agreements,
no reproduction of any part may take place without the written
permission of Cambridge University Press.

First published 2006
This digitally printed version 2009

A catalogue record for this publication is available from the British Library

ISBN 978-0-521-86718-4 Hardback
ISBN 978-0-521-12314-3 Paperback

Cambridge University Press has no responsibility for the persistence or
accuracy of URLs for external or third-party internet websites referred to in
this publication, and does not guarantee that any content on such websites is,
or will remain, accurate or appropriate.

Contents

List of figures	*page* ix
List of tables	x
Preface	xix

1 Introduction and overview   1

Part I Measuring comparative productivity performance   17

2 The contribution of services to the productivity performance of the whole economy   19

3 Comparative productivity performance in market services   28

4 A sectoral database: Britain, the United States and Germany, 1870–1990   36

Part II Explaining comparative productivity performance   79

5 Technology, organisational change and the industrialisation of services   81

6 Investment in physical and human capital   107

7 Competition and the institutional framework   127

Part III Reassessing the performance of British market services   145

8 The 'golden age' of British commerce, 1870–1914   147

9 The collapse of the liberal world economic order, 1914–1950   216

10	Completing the industrialisation of services, 1950–1990	281
11	British services in the 1990s: a preliminary assessment	357
12	Summary and conclusions	369

Bibliography 377
Index 404

Figures

1.1 Comparative US/UK labour productivity levels by sector	page 3
1.2 Comparative Germany/UK labour productivity levels by sector	4
1.3 Comparative US/UK labour productivity levels in services	4
1.4 Comparative Germany/UK labour productivity levels in services	5
2.1 Comparative labour productivity in manufacturing	22
5.1 Customised venture	101
5.2 Standardised venture	102
5.3 Interactions between scale and organisation	103
5.4 Adjustment costs	105
8.1 Production function per million ton-miles of shipping services, for steam and sail voyages of 1,000, 5,000 and 10,000 miles length, 1872	155
8.2 Production functions per million ton-miles of shipping services, for steam and sail voyages of 5,000 miles length, 1855–1891	157

Tables

2.1	Comparative US/UK labour productivity levels by sector, 1869/71–1990	page 20
2.2	Comparative Germany/UK labour productivity levels by sector, 1871–1990	21
2.3	Sectoral shares of employment in the United States, the United Kingdom and Germany, 1870–1990	25
3.1	Comparative US/UK labour productivity levels in market services, 1869/71–1990	29
3.2	Benchmark estimates of comparative US/UK labour productivity levels in market services, 1870–1993	30
3.3	Comparative Germany/UK labour productivity levels in market services, 1871–1990	31
3.4	Benchmark estimates of comparative Germany/UK labour productivity levels in market services, 1935–1993	32
3.5	Sectoral shares of employment in market services in the United States and the United Kingdom, 1870–1990	33
3.6	Sectoral shares of employment in market services in Germany and the United Kingdom, 1870–1990	34
4.1	Time series projections of comparative US/UK labour productivity levels by sector	37
4.2	Benchmark estimates of comparative US/UK labour productivity levels by sector	40
4.3	Sectoral shares of employment	42
4.4	Time series projections of comparative Germany/UK labour productivity levels by sector	48
4.5	Benchmark estimates of comparative Germany/UK labour productivity levels by sector	49
4.6	Growth rates of labour productivity, 1869–1990	52
4.7	GDP per capita, 1870–1992	53
A4.1	US real output by sector	57
A4.2	US employment by sector	58
A4.3	UK real output by sector	59

A4.4	UK employment by sector	60
A4.5	German real output by sector	61
A4.6	German employment by sector	62
A4.7	Growth rates of US real output by sector	63
A4.8	Growth rates of US employment by sector	63
A4.9	Growth rates of UK real output by sector	64
A4.10	Growth rates of UK employment by sector	64
A4.11	Growth rates of German real output by sector	65
A4.12	Growth rates of German employment by sector	65
5.1	Employment in the largest 100 employers in Britain, 1907–1955	89
5.2	Largest 125 employers in the United Kingdom and Germany, circa 1907	97
6.1	Comparative US/UK and Germany/UK total factor productivity levels by sector, 1869/71–1990	109
6.2	Comparative US/UK and Germany/UK labour productivity levels by sector, 1869/71–1990	110
6.3	Telephones per 100 population, 1900–1980	112
6.4	Office machine sales per 1,000 population, 1908–1968	113
6.5	Educational enrolment rates per 1,000 population under age twenty, 1870–1990	115
6.6	Apprentices as a percentage of persons engaged in Britain, Germany and the United States, 1895–1991	119
6.7	Professionals in Britain, the United States and Germany, 1880–1991	121
6.8	Qualified accountants in Britain, Germany and the United States, 1882–1991	122
7.1	Customs revenue as a share of import values in the United Kingdom, the United States and Germany, 1870–1989	131
7.2	Multilateral tariffs in selected commodities, 1913	133
7.3	Shares of world commodity exports, 1899–1950	135
7.4	Shares of world merchant fleet, 1860–1950	135
7.5	International trade in services, 1970–1990	136
7.6	Clerical standards of the Systems and Procedures Association of America	138
7.7	Union density in services and the whole economy, 1901–1971	139
8.1	Benchmark estimates of comparative labour productivity in market services, 1870–1910	148
8.2	Productivity in the British aggregate economy, 1871–1913	149
8.3	Comparative US/UK and Germany/UK productivity levels for the aggregate economy, 1871–1911	150

8.4	Productivity in the British transport and communications sector, 1871–1911	151
8.5	Comparative US/UK and Germany/UK labour productivity levels for the transport and communications sector, 1871–1911	152
8.6	World merchant fleet, 1860–1911	152
8.7	Competition on the North Atlantic passenger routes	153
8.8	Productivity in British shipping, 1871–1911	154
8.9	Contribution to the UK balance of payments from shipping, 1841–1913	155
8.10	Ninety-nine steamships registered in West Hartlepool, 1878–1883	158
8.11	Concentration in the German shipping fleet, 1914	160
8.12	Consolidation among British shipowners, 1880–1920	161
8.13	Concentration in the British shipping fleet, 1910–1918/19	162
8.14	British share of entrances and clearances at ports in selected countries, 1880–1911	164
8.15	Length of railway line open, 1831–1911	165
8.16	Railway operating statistics, Great Britain, 1871–1911	166
8.17	Productivity trends on British railways, 1871–1911	167
8.18	Productivity trends on US railroads, 1870–1910	167
8.19	Telecommunications statistics, United Kingdom, 1871–1913	171
8.20	Telegraph messages per 1,000 persons, 1851–1913	171
8.21	Telephones per 100 population before World War I	171
8.22	Labour productivity in the telegraph service, circa 1868	172
8.23	Productivity in the British distribution sector, 1871–1911	174
8.24	Comparative US/UK and Germany/UK labour productivity levels for the distribution sector, 1871–1911	174
8.25	Membership and retail sales of Co-operative Societies, Great Britain, 1881–1915	176
8.26	Number of multiple shop firms and branches in the United Kingdom, 1875–1915	177
8.27	Estimated maximum shares of large-scale retailers in the total retail trade of the United Kingdom, 1900–1915	178
8.28	Number and density of residential shops in Great Britain, 1869/72–1909/11	179
8.29	Visible trade of the United Kingdom, 1871–1911	180
8.30	Volume of visible trade, United Kingdom, 1871–1911	181
8.31	Price indices for exports, imports and the aggregate output of the United Kingdom, 1871–1911	181

List of tables   xiii

8.32 Principal visible imports and exports of the United
     Kingdom, 1871–1911   183
8.33 UK visible imports and exports by continent, 1871–1911   184
8.34 The role of the British Empire in British visible trade,
     1871–1911   184
8.35 Capital of some major US and UK raw cotton merchants
     in the early twentieth century   186
8.36 Merchants in the Lancashire cotton export trade,
     1860–1911   187
8.37 Principal sources of UK imports of wheat, 1873–1914   189
8.38 Shares of world exports of manufactures, 1881–1913   190
8.39 Productivity in the British financial services sector,
     1871–1911   192
8.40 Total assets and total liabilities of UK financial
     institutions, 1881–1911   193
8.41 Number of banks and branches, England and Wales,
     1825–1913   195
8.42 Combined balance sheets of UK banks, 1881–1911   197
8.43 Capital of some leading London merchant banks,
     circa 1900   202
8.44 Geographical distribution of foreign branches of British
     overseas banks, 1860–1913   204
8.45 City of London banking networks, 1890–1914   205
8.46 Fire insurance business of UK offices, 1881–1913   208
8.47 Foreign premiums as a share of total premiums, three
     British fire offices, 1856–1910   209
8.48 Life assurance business of UK offices, 1850–1914   209
8.49 Contribution to the UK balance of payments from marine
     insurance, 1841–1913   212
8.50 Accident insurance business of UK offices, 1884–1914   212
9.1 Benchmark estimates of comparative labour productivity
     levels in market services, 1910–1950   217
9.2 Productivity in the British aggregate economy, 1911–1951   218
9.3 Comparative US/UK and Germany/UK productivity levels
     for the aggregate economy, 1911–1950   219
9.4 Productivity in the British transport and communications
     sector, 1911–1951   221
9.5 Comparative US/UK and Germany/UK labour
     productivity levels for the transport and communications
     sector, 1911–1950   221
9.6 Output and productivity in British shipping, 1911–1951   222
9.7 World merchant fleet, 1913–1950   224

9.8	World trade, shipping and freight rates, 1913–1938	224
9.9	Shares of seaborne trade carried in British ships, 1912–1936	226
9.10	Proportion of merchant tonnage using diesel propulsion, 1923–1939	226
9.11	Dividends of British shipping companies, 1932–1935	227
9.12	Net receipts of British shipping, 1913–1947	228
9.13	Length of railway line open, 1913–1950	230
9.14	Railway operating statistics, Great Britain, 1913–1951	231
9.15	Productivity trends on British railways, 1913–1951	232
9.16	Motor vehicles per 1,000 inhabitants and motorisation indicator, 1922–1950	236
9.17	Output of the British public passenger road transport sector, 1911–1951	237
9.18	Output of the British road haulage sector, 1911–1951	238
9.19	Productivity in British road transport, 1911–1951	239
9.20	British civil aviation, 1920–1951	241
9.21	Aircraft flights and passengers carried between the United Kingdom and abroad, 1920–1951	241
9.22	Post Office mail traffic, United Kingdom, 1913–1951	243
9.23	Telecommunications statistics, United Kingdom, 1913–1951	244
9.24	Telephones per 100 population, 1913–1932	244
9.25	Productivity in the British distribution sector, 1911–1951	246
9.26	Comparative US/UK and Germany/UK productivity levels for the distribution sector, 1911–1950	247
9.27	Membership and retail sales of Co-operative Societies, Great Britain, 1910–1950	248
9.28	Number of multiple shop firms and branches in the United Kingdom, 1910–1950	249
9.29	Estimated maximum shares of large-scale retailers in the total retail trade of the United Kingdom, 1910–1950	250
9.30	Visible trade of the United Kingdom, 1911–1951	253
9.31	Volume of visible trade, United Kingdom, 1911–1951	254
9.32	Price indices for exports, imports and aggregate output of the United Kingdom	254
9.33	Principal visible imports and exports of the United Kingdom, 1911–1951	255
9.34	The role of the British Empire in British visible trade, 1911–1951	256
9.35	Merchants in the Lancashire cotton export trade, 1900–1939	258

List of tables   xv

9.36	Productivity in the British financial services sector, 1911–1951	260
9.37	Total assets and total liabilities of UK financial institutions, 1911–1951	261
9.38	Number of banks and branches, United Kingdom, 1911–1950	263
9.39	Combined balance sheets of UK banks, 1911–1951	264
9.40	Commercial bills outstanding in the London market, 1913/14–1936/37	270
9.41	New capital issues in the United Kingdom, 1913–1937	271
9.42	Total assets of British overseas banks, 1890–1955	272
9.43	Geographical distribution of foreign branches of British overseas banks, 1913–1955	272
9.44	Interest rates on British building society shares and the yield on consols, 1922–1938	273
9.45	Fire insurance business of UK offices, 1911–1951	275
9.46	Life assurance business of UK offices, 1911–1951	275
9.47	Accident insurance business of UK offices, 1914–1951	277
10.1	Benchmark estimates of comparative labour productivity levels in market services, 1950–1993	282
10.2	Productivity in the British aggregate economy, 1951–1990	283
10.3	Comparative US/UK and Germany/UK productivity levels for the aggregate economy, 1950–1990	284
10.4	Productivity in the British transport and communications sector, 1951–1990	285
10.5	Comparative US/UK and Germany/UK labour productivity levels for the transport and communications sector, 1950–1990	286
10.6	World merchant fleet, 1950–1990	287
10.7	Productivity in British shipping, 1951–1990	288
10.8	Freight rates and the general price level in Britain, 1948–1969	289
10.9	UK-owned and British-registered shipping in 1989	292
10.10	UK shipping earnings and the balance of payments, 1952–1990	294
10.11	Length of railway line open, 1950–1990	295
10.12	Railway operating statistics, Great Britain, 1951–1990	296
10.13	Productivity trends on British railways, 1951–1990	297
10.14	Passenger and freight transport by mode	298
10.15	Financial results of British Railways	299
10.16	Motor vehicles per 1,000 inhabitants, 1950–1990	303
10.17	Mileage of roads in Great Britain, 1950–1990	303

xvi List of tables

10.18	Output of the British road transport sector, 1951–1990	303
10.19	Productivity trends in the British road transport sector, 1951–1990	304
10.20	Labour productivity in the British road transport sector, 1951–1990	307
10.21	Traffic on UK airlines, 1951–1990	309
10.22	Productivity trends in the British air transport sector, 1951–1990	310
10.23	Aircraft flights and passengers carried between the United Kingdom and abroad, 1951–1990	310
10.24	UK civil aviation earnings and the balance of payments, 1952–1990	311
10.25	Postal services and television licences, United Kingdom, 1951–1990	315
10.26	Telecommunications statistics, United Kingdom, 1951–1990	315
10.27	Telephones per 100 inhabitants, 1950–1990	316
10.28	Productivity trends in the British communications sector, 1951–1990	317
10.29	Productivity in the British distribution sector, 1951–1990	320
10.30	Comparative US/UK and Germany/UK labour productivity levels for the distribution sector, 1950–1990	321
10.31	Wholesaling and dealing turnover in Great Britain by method of trading, 1950–1974	322
10.32	Shares of retail sales in Great Britain by form of organisation, 1950–1990	322
10.33	Shares of large-scale retailers in retail sales in Great Britain by main commodity groups, 1950–1990	325
10.34	Visible trade of the United Kingdom, 1950–1990	327
10.35	Volume of visible trade, United Kingdom, 1951–1990	328
10.36	Price indices for exports, imports and the aggregate output of the United Kingdom, 1951–1990	328
10.37	Principal visible imports and exports of the United Kingdom, 1951–1990	330
10.38	Shares of British visible exports to 'British countries' and the 'EEC6', 1951–1990	331
10.39	Productivity in the British financial services sector, 1951–1990	333
10.40	Total assets and total liabilities of UK financial institutions, 1951–1990	334
10.41	Balance of payments net credits of UK financial services, 1964–1990	336

10.42	Combined balance sheets of the London clearing banks, 1951–1973	341
10.43	Combined balance sheets of all UK banks, 1973–1990	344
10.44	Home ownership in Britain, 1914–1991	347
10.45	Life assurance business of UK offices, 1951–1990	349
10.46	General insurance business of UK offices, 1951–1990	349
10.47	Three-firm concentration ratio in the UK insurance sector, 1950–1984	352
10.48	Overseas earnings of the UK insurance market, 1965–1989	354
11.1	Comparative GDP per hour worked and GDP per capita, total economy, 1990–2001	359
11.2	Comparative labour productivity levels by sector: output per hour worked, 1990–2001	360
11.3	Productivity in the British aggregate economy, 1990–1999	362
11.4	Productivity in the British transport and communications sector, 1990–1999	363
11.5	Productivity in the British distribution sector, 1990–1999	364
11.6	Productivity in the British financial and business services sector, 1990–1999	365
11.7	Decomposition of comparative labour productivity levels in market services, 1999	366
11.8	Growth rates of real GDP per hour worked, 1950–2003	367

Preface

One way or another, I have been engaged in writing this book ever since I completed the manuscript of *The Productivity Race: British Manufacturing in International Perspective, 1850–1990*, and in many ways this book can be thought of as the second volume of a sectoral study of Britain's productivity performance. It has been a long journey, and I have incurred many debts along the way. I thank all the patient listeners at seminar and conference presentations, and all those who offered constructive criticisms. In particular, I wish to thank without in any way implicating Gerben Bakker, Martin Campbell-Kelly, Nick Crafts, Charles Feinstein, Alex Field, Rainer Fremdling, Sayantan Ghosal, Les Hannah, Angus Maddison, Andrew Marrison, Bob Millward, Mary O'Mahony, Albrecht Ritschl and Peter Wardley. The chapters in part III have benefited from the reactions of undergraduate students at Warwick taking the third-year module on 'The British Economy in the Twentieth Century'.

Parts of the book draw upon joint work with Carsten Burhop, Nick Crafts, Rainer Fremdling, Sayantan Ghosal, Douglas Irwin, Andrew Marrison and Mary O'Mahony. Other parts use unpublished material kindly made available by Charles Feinstein and Andrew Hilditch, and by Mary O'Mahony.

I owe a particular debt of gratitude to my wife, Mary O'Mahony, and to the forbearance of our children, Laura and Edward, to whom the book is dedicated.

1 Introduction and overview

1.1 Introduction

In a previous book, I argued that there was little change in the comparative productivity performance of UK manufacturing between the mid-nineteenth century and the late twentieth century (Broadberry, 1997a). In both 1870 and 1990 US labour productivity in manufacturing was about twice the British level, while German labour productivity in manufacturing was about the same as in Britain. I also noted that value added per employee varied between manufacturing and the rest of the economy, and that the size of the manufacturing sector differed across countries and over time. This meant that it was still possible for manufacturing to have contributed to Britain's relative economic decline, through, for example, greater de-industrialisation than in Germany (Broadberry and Crafts, 2003). Nevertheless, the central message of *The Productivity Race* was surely that, to understand the relative decline in British productivity and living standards since the mid-nineteenth century, it is necessary to understand what happened in services.

This book is an attempt to set out the story of Britain's productivity performance in services, focusing in particular on market services. Part I begins by establishing the comparative productivity trends in services, and fitting them into the patterns for the whole economy. I show that comparative productivity trends in services, unlike those in manufacturing, do mirror comparative productivity trends in the whole economy. In about 1870 Britain had a labour productivity lead in services over both the United States and Germany, and this was an important factor in explaining Britain's overall labour productivity leadership at this time. However, the United States overtook Britain in both services and the whole economy before World War I and continued to forge ahead until after World War II, since when Britain has been narrowing the gap slowly. Germany overtook Britain in both services and the whole economy during the 1960s, and continued to forge ahead until the 1980s. Furthermore, Britain's loss of labour productivity leadership in services was not due to trends in public or non-market services, where it is difficult to measure output independently of inputs. Rather, it reflected US and German overtaking in private or market services.

Providing a framework to explain this comparative productivity performance in services is the task of Part II. The central theme concerns the 'industrialisation' of market services, which involved the transition from customised, low-volume, high-margin business organised on the basis of networks to standardised, high-volume, low-margin business with hierarchical management. As with the related introduction of 'mass production' in manufacturing, the industrialisation of services led to sustained growth of labour productivity. However, the gains from the introduction of the technology and organisation of industrialised service provision varied by sector and over time. Understanding the differential spread of industrialised service provision in the United Kingdom, the United States and Germany is crucial to understanding the patterns of comparative productivity performance in services. High-volume methods were quick to diffuse in sectors where (1) the level of demand was sufficiently high to permit a high degree of specialisation, (2) consumers were prepared to accept a high degree of standardisation of provision, (3) the labour force had appropriate levels of education and skill, (4) workers were willing to accept the required intensification of effort and monitoring and (5) the sector was sufficiently open to competition.

Part II is concerned largely with trends in the market service sector as a whole. However, since there was a great deal of variation in comparative productivity performance across different parts of the service sector, it is important to see how the explanation works at a finer level of disaggregation. The detailed sectoral studies in Part III help to provide a sense of balance to the issue of British relative decline, since it includes success stories as well as failures. There seems little doubt that the literature on Britain's long-run economic performance had become excessively pessimistic by the 1980s, and that writers such as Supple (1994) were correct to note that Britain has clearly remained part of the rich world. However, it is important not to overstate this point, as in the work of Rubinstein (1993) or Booth (2001). At the end of the twentieth century Britain still had a lower level of GDP per employee than either the United States or Germany, and this reflected lower labour productivity in services, which dominated economic activity.

1.2   Comparative productivity in services

Chapter 2 examines the contribution of services to the productivity performance of the whole economy in an international comparative framework. Comparative labour productivity figures are provided for

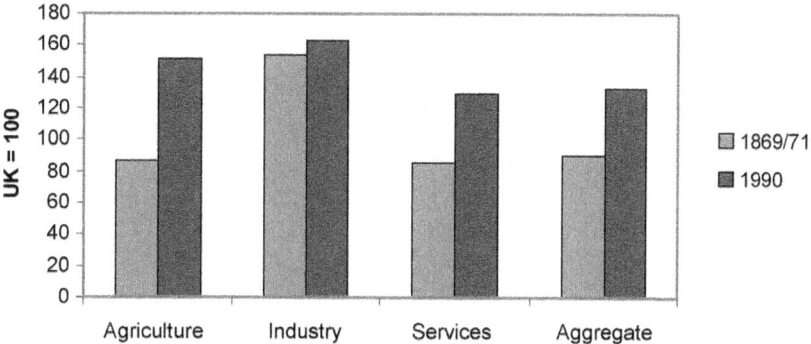

Figure 1.1 Comparative US/UK labour productivity levels by sector.
Source: Derived from table 2.1.

the economy as a whole and for a three-sector breakdown into agriculture, industry and services. Dealing first with the US/UK comparison in figure 1.1, whereas around 1870 US aggregate labour productivity stood at approximately 90% of the British level, by 1990 this had risen to 133%. Turning to the sectoral breakdown, it is clear that this owed little to developments in industry, where the US/UK comparative labour productivity level remained relatively unchanged between 1870 and 1990. Furthermore, although comparative labour productivity in agriculture changed in the right direction and by a substantial amount, it is important to remember that, whereas agriculture accounted for 50% of US employment in 1870, it accounted for less than 3% in 1990. The most important development in understanding Britain's loss of overall labour productivity leadership was, therefore, the US overtaking in services.

Similarly, figure 1.2 shows the importance of developments in services to the German overtaking of Britain. In 1871 German aggregate labour productivity was approximately 60% of the British level, but by 1990 this had risen to approximately 125%. Although there was some increase in Germany's comparative labour productivity position in industry, from about 92% of the British level in 1871 to 111% in 1990, the most important factor in the German overtaking of Britain was the much greater increase in Germany's comparative labour productivity position in services, from approximately 63% of the British level in 1871 to 135% in 1990. As in the US/UK case, there was a dramatic decline in the share of the labour force employed in agriculture in Germany, so that the increase in Germany's comparative labour productivity position in agriculture was of relatively minor significance for Germany's improving comparative labour productivity position in the economy as a whole.

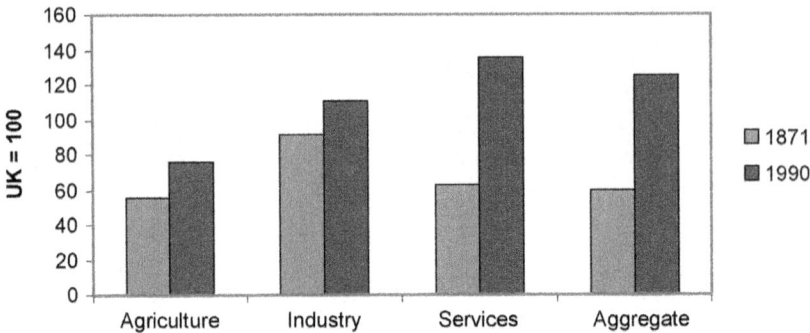

Figure 1.2 Comparative Germany/UK labour productivity levels by sector.
Source: Derived from table 2.2.

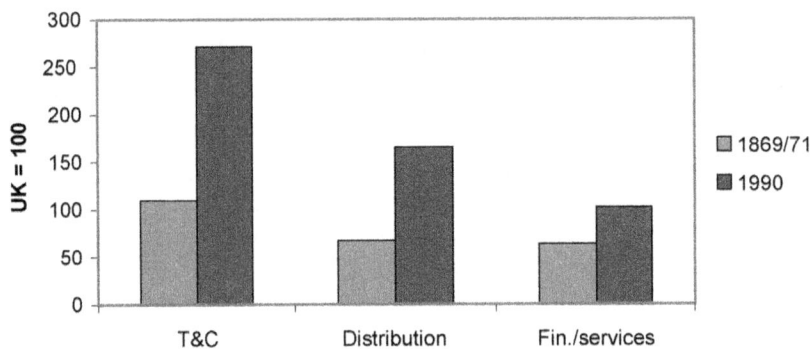

Figure 1.3 Comparative US/UK labour productivity levels in services.
Source: Derived from table 3.1.

Chapter 3 provides a breakdown of the comparative labour productivity performance of services, focusing attention on the key market service sectors. British performance tended to be worst in transport and communications and best in finance, with performance in distribution between the two. Figure 1.3 shows this situation for the US/UK case around 1870 and 1990. For the Germany/UK case, in figure 1.4, the picture is complicated by the fact that the historical data for distribution and finance in Germany are available only on a combined basis. The German performance was better in transport and communications than in distribution and finance combined.

Part I is rounded off in chapter 4 with the provision of a complete sectoral data set for the UK, US and German economies covering the

Introduction and overview

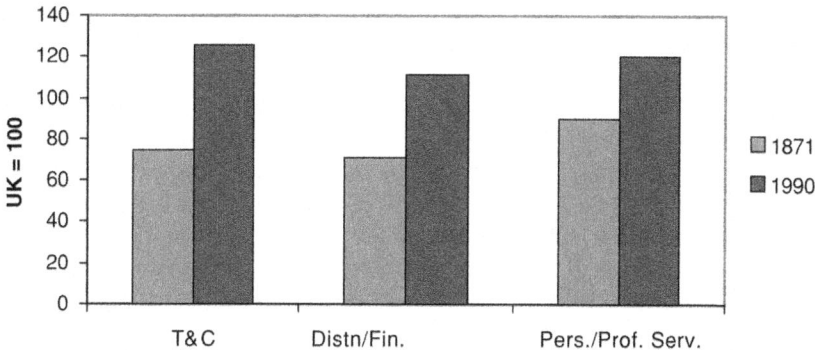

Figure 1.4 Comparative Germany/UK labour productivity levels in services.
Source: Derived from table 3.3.

period 1870 to 1990. Whereas the data in chapters 2 and 3 are presented on the basis of comparative levels of labour productivity, chapter 4 allows an investigation of the growth of labour productivity in each country. This provides a helpful reminder that, although Britain has undergone relative decline since the mid-nineteenth century, this has nevertheless been accompanied by a dramatic rise in labour productivity and living standards. Although the United States and Germany have achieved an even more dramatic growth of labour productivity, Britain's performance has been relatively successful when compared against the labour productivity performance of Asian countries such as India or China, or once rich nations such as Argentina (McCloskey, 1990: 47).

1.3 Technology and organisation

1.3.1 Innovation and the industrialisation of services

Part II provides an analytical framework to explain the patterns of comparative productivity performance outlined in Part I. Chapter 5 draws upon the work of Broadberry and Ghosal (2002, 2005) to examine the 'industrialisation' of services. This involved the transition from a world of customised, low-volume, high-margin business organised on the basis of networks to a world of standardised, high-volume, low-margin business with hierarchical management. This transformation from the world of the 'counting house' to the world of the 'modern office' depended on technologies to improve communications and information processing. The transition began in the United States, and was slower to diffuse in Britain, largely as a result of lower levels of education and stronger labour force resistance to the intensification of the labour process that the efficient utilisation of the new technologies required.

This explanation is consistent with the observed pattern of comparative US/UK labour productivity levels, since these high-volume methods diffused more rapidly in the sectors where Britain's productivity gap was largest. These methods were first developed on the railways, then spread quickly to other parts of the transport and communications sector, including steamship lines, urban traction systems and the telegraph and telephone systems (Chandler, 1977: 189–203). However, in distribution, there were limits to the degree of centralisation and standardisation that consumers found acceptable, and there were also constraints on competition which acted to support small retail outlets (Hall et al., 1961: 131–8; Field, 1996: 27; McCraw, 1996). In banking and finance, there were obvious dangers in adopting a high-volume, impersonal, standardised approach, since asymmetric information and trust are very important in this sector, while regulation also restrained the growth of large-scale banking (White, 2000: 749).

Although this book focuses on transport and communications, distribution and finance, Bakker's (2001) study of the entertainment sector is suggestive of how the approach can be applied to other personal services, where output is often less well measured in the national accounts. The industrialisation of the entertainment sector via recorded music and films dramatically raised the productivity of individual entertainers by extending the audience that could hear or see a performance. Achieving this high productivity, however, required the use of new technology and massive reorganisation of the entertainment sector. The large homogeneous home market held out the prospect of high returns to such a transformation in the United States.

The issue of market demand is also helpful in understanding the contrast between Britain and Germany in the late nineteenth century – and, indeed, much of the twentieth century. For, although the population of Germany was a little higher than that of the United Kingdom for much of this period, large parts of the German service sector remained more spread out in a much more rural society with a large agricultural sector. Britain's relatively high level of urbanisation, together with a more international orientation in much of the commercial service sector, generated external economies of scale, which underpinned high levels of productivity.

1.3.2   Investment in physical and human capital

Chapter 6 examines the investment in physical and human capital required to reap the benefits of the industrialisation of services. Sectoral data on physical capital are available for services on only a very limited basis before World War II, particularly on an internationally comparable basis. The available data utilised here suggest some role for physical capital in explaining the sectoral labour productivity gaps, but still leave substantial total factor productivity (TFP) gaps that require explanation. A closer look at sales of office machinery suggests a substantial US superiority in this crucial aspect of investment in high-volume service provision.

Turning to human capital, it is important to consider both education and vocational training, and to distinguish between higher-level (university degree) and intermediate-level (between secondary school leaving and degree) vocational training (Prais, 1995: 17). Both Germany and the United States had a general educational advantage over Britain for most of the nineteenth century, with the laggard Britain achieving universal primary education only towards the end of the century. Between the wars the United States moved to universal secondary education, which was only achieved in Britain and Germany after World War II. At this point, the United States moved to mass higher education, a point arrived at in Britain and Germany only in very recent years. It may be expected that differences in education would be more significant for services than industry, since the 'three Rs', of reading, (w)riting and (a)rithmetic, are of more direct relevance to the clerical work typical of commercial services throughout this period. There may also be a general advantage arising from high levels of education that goes beyond the specific knowledge taught in class, with pupils learning social skills, teamwork and flexibility (Goldin, 2001). This appears to be what Abramovitz (1986) had in mind when seeing education as a key measurable indicator of the 'social capabilities' of nations.

However, the apparent British and German disadvantage in formal education for much of the twentieth century was offset by a much greater provision of vocational training than in the United States (Broadberry, 2004a). Here, however, there was a difference of emphasis between the higher and intermediate levels in the two countries. Britain led in the provision of higher-level training through membership of professional organisations, particularly before World War II, and many of these professionals worked in the service sector. Germany developed an impressive system of intermediate-level training through apprenticeship, and, although this was initially focused on industry, it was extended into service sectors, particularly after World War II.

Putting together the different types of human capital formation, it is likely that Britain suffered little human capital disadvantage relative to either Germany or the United States before World War II, especially in services. However, after World War II any higher-level advantage that Britain had enjoyed over the United States in services from the large number of qualified members of professional associations was offset by the spread of mass higher education in the United States. In the comparison between Britain and Germany, by contrast, the crucial development was the spread of intermediate-level qualifications in German services, leading to the emergence of a substantial German human capital advantage by the 1970s.

1.3.3 Competition and the institutional framework

Chapter 6 focuses on the proximate causes of the changing comparative productivity performance in services, highlighting relatively low rates for the accumulation of physical and human capital in Britain. This, however, merely raises the issue of why rates of accumulation were low, and chapter 7 examines competition and the institutional framework. To see the importance of these factors, consider first why changing comparative productivity in services has contributed more than changing comparative productivity in industry to the explanation of changing comparative productivity performance overall. The reason for this is that services have typically been more sheltered from competitive pressures than industry. Although there have also been periods when protection and regulatory policies have slowed down the exit of inefficient firms in industry, in the long run competitive forces have acted more effectively in industry than in services. In much of the service sector, competition from providers located abroad is impossible, while, in other parts, firms typically have to obtain licences to operate and are required to submit to a high degree of official regulation. In these heavily regulated sectors, collusion between providers has been common. Whereas British manufacturers that failed to keep up with productivity growth abroad were ultimately replaced by imports, there was no such possibility of replacing the bulk of Britain's service providers. Hence, poor performance by service sector firms tends to show up in the productivity figures, while poor performance by industrial firms tends to show up in the sectoral composition of economic activity.

Different approaches to the competitive environment can also be seen as having an important effect on the relative size of sectors in the different economies, with knock-on effects for productivity performance. The different attitudes of Britain and Germany to the protection of agriculture before World War II illustrate this point effectively. Tariff protection in late nineteenth-century Germany was designed to slow down the decline of agriculture and accelerate the development of heavy industry. The alliance of 'rye and iron' in the newly formed German Reich meant that proportionally, at least, services had to be the loser. While German agricultural tariffs staved off a 'grain invasion' from the United States, and retained workers in a low-value-added activity, British free trade meant that consumers benefited from cheap imported food and had more income to spend on services, which could be provided more efficiently on a larger scale.

More fundamentally, different institutional frameworks affect the incentives to accumulate and innovate. Whereas US governments have generally taken a strongly pro-competitive stance since the emergence of large-scale modern business enterprise in the late nineteenth century, British and German governments have been more equivocal. Before World War II cartels were widely accepted in Germany, and British policy can at times be described as pro-trust rather than anti-trust, particularly during the inter-war period (Lucas, 1937; Broadberry and Crafts, 1990). After World War II corporatist post-war settlements provided very different incentives for the accumulation of physical and human capital in Germany and Britain (Eichengreen, 1996; Bean and Crafts, 1996). Although both Britain and Germany were more 'corporatist' than the United States, the greater centralisation of unions and employers' organisations in Germany provided stronger incentives for the accumulation of human and physical capital than in Britain (Carlin, 1996). First, the greater degree of centralisation in Germany facilitated a collective solution to the free-rider problem in vocational training. Second, decentralised labour market organisations in Britain made it harder to deliver on agreements concerning investment in new technology and wage restraint (Bean and Crafts, 1996; Olson, 1982; Crouch, 1993).

During the 1980s the institutional framework in Britain shifted decisively in the direction of promoting competition, with a toughening of anti-trust policy, the privatisation and deregulation of a number of important services, and limitations on trade union immunities. Britain's relative economic decline was at last stemmed, though not yet decisively reversed.

1.4 Sectoral studies

Part III provides a more detailed study of the individual sectors. As well as examining the time series evidence on the growth of output, inputs and productivity by sector, and the cross-sectional benchmark estimates of comparative productivity at a highly disaggregated level, this section surveys the substantial secondary literature and offers a reinterpretation of the performance of British market services by integrating the different types of evidence. This section is divided into three main chapters, covering the periods 1850–1914, 1914–1950 and 1950–1990, together with a shorter preliminary assessment of the 1990s.

1.4.1 The 'golden age' of British commerce, 1850–1914

Chapter 8 presents a systematic assessment of the performance of the major British market service sectors in international perspective between the mid-nineteenth century and World War I. In the mid-nineteenth century Britain had the highest level of per capita income in the world, and this was underpinned by a high level of labour productivity, particularly in services (Broadberry and Irwin, 2006). Although productivity growth in services was more rapid in the United States and Germany before World War I, this can be seen in many sectors as part of a process of catching up. To some extent the process of catching up was inevitable, as the release of labour from the agricultural sector in rapidly developing countries such as the United States and Germany led to a catching up in the extent of urbanisation, with concentrated urban demands allowing a high degree of specialisation in market services (Smolensky, 1972). Since services also made a substantial positive contribution to the British balance of payments, and the services of the City of London dominated world trade and payments, the period between 1850 and 1914 can be seen as the 'golden age' of British commerce (Imlah, 1958; Kynaston, 1995).

However, there were clearly some developments in the United States which threatened Britain's dominant position in internationally traded services, and Britain's productivity leadership across a broad spectrum of services. These developments have been labelled the 'industrialisation' of services, with a move from customised, low-volume, high-margin business organised on the basis of networks to standardised, high-volume, low-margin business organised on the basis of hierarchy. This approach to business originated in the United States, and has been identified as a major source of US competitive advantage by Chandler (1980). However, whereas in his later work Chandler (1990) concentrates on the emergence of the large-scale, hierarchical corporation in manufacturing, his earlier work emphasises the role of a number of service sectors, including the railways and distribution (Chandler, 1977). The key factors underlying the growth of hierarchical forms of organisation in the service sector before World War I were (1) developments in information and communications technology (ICT), reducing problems of asymmetric information and allowing much closer contact

Introduction and overview 11

between principal and agent in merchant/financial operations, and (2) the growing volume of economic activity, permitting greater specialisation in services, and hence allowing task simplification and easier monitoring of employee performance. Nevertheless, the extent to which the provision of a more customised service on the basis of networks remained competitive varied between sectors, and British performance tended to be better in sectors where conditions continued to favour networks over hierarchy.

To the extent that British networks failed to adapt to the threat from more hierarchically organised overseas competitors, it was necessary that they should be sheltered from international competition. One way in which this was achieved was through the growing strength of links between Britain and her empire in internationally traded services, as in international economic relationships more generally (Schlote, 1952). A second way in which competition was restricted was through the growing cartelisation of the market and the spread of restrictive practices. The conference system in shipping and agreements on interest rate setting in banking are well-known examples here (Deakin, 1973; Griffiths, 1973).

The sectoral analysis shows a variety of comparative productivity and wider performance outcomes during the period 1850–1914. However, in general, British performance was better in the service sectors less suited to industrialisation, where the network form of organisation remained dominant. In sectors where networks remained important, such as tramp shipping, wholesale distribution, international banking and non-life insurance, Britain continued to do well. However, in other sectors which required large-scale hierarchical organisation, such as railways and telecommunications, Britain began to fall behind.

1.4.2 The collapse of the liberal world economic order, 1914–1950

Chapter 9 examines the development of the major market services between 1914 and 1950. Although there were signs of growing pressures from protection and restrictions on the free migration of labour before 1914, most economic historians see World War I as marking a watershed, ushering in a period of retreat from the liberal world economic order that had characterised the period since the mid-nineteenth century (O'Rourke and Williamson, 2000). The fragile recovery from World War I during the 1920s was soon followed by the Depression of the 1930s with a further retreat into autarkic policies before the outbreak of World War II. Despite the disturbed nature of this period, it is nevertheless possible to identify trends in the comparative performance of the major market service sectors. Although labour productivity growth was faster in the United States than in Britain, the British market service sectors kept pace with their German counterparts. Since the United States had largely caught up with Britain by World War I in services, faster US labour productivity growth in these sectors after 1914 led to the United States forging ahead, although it was only in parts of the transport and communications sector that the US labour productivity lead became very large.

The US forging ahead in transport and communications, together with the absence of large Anglo-American labour productivity gaps in distribution and finance, is most easily explained by the increasing 'industrialisation' of much of the transport and communications sector in the United States, together with the continued suitability of large parts of the distribution and finance sectors for organisation on the basis of flexible networks, a traditional British strength. Furthermore, the continued employment of around 30% of the German labour force in agriculture between the wars meant that Germany's service sector remained underdeveloped, so that Britain continued to enjoy a substantial labour productivity advantage over Germany in most services. Although Germany achieved higher labour productivity than Britain on the railways, the pioneering sector of industrialised services, this was exceptional. Whereas Germany's universal banks are often praised for their developmental role by economic historians of the pre-1914 period, there is no attempt to see Germany's banks in a positive light between the wars (Gerschenkron, 1962; Collins, 1998).

The disruption to international economic relations caused by the two world wars and the increasingly autarkic environment of the inter-war period would be expected to have had a much greater impact on the highly globalised British economy than on either the domestically oriented US economy or the more highly protectionist German economy of the pre-1914 period. Nevertheless, growing integration within the empire to some extent cushioned the British economy from the hostile international environment, providing secure supplies of vital food and raw materials in wartime and providing export markets on preferential terms, in services as well as industrial goods. Although in the short run this may have been beneficial, and at times perhaps even vital for survival, there were also some long-run costs. As the world economy reintegrated after World War II, trade with far-flung Commonwealth countries was bound to decline, and called for a major reorientation of marketing investments. Also, it may be argued that the strengthening of the Imperial Preference system had unfavourable effects for the economic and social system more generally, perpetuating incentives for rent seeking at the expense of wealth creation.

The collusive behaviour and restrictive practices that had begun to be formalised in a number of British market service sectors during the Edwardian period were strengthened during the inter-war period, as protectionism limited international competition and as governments encouraged domestic collusion as a means to stabilise falling prices. As with Imperial Preference, it is possible to see these policies as having beneficial effects in the short run, but with adverse consequences in the long run (Broadberry and Crafts, 1992). In the short run preventing prices from falling helped to preserve employment by muting real wage increases in the face of sticky nominal wages, but in the long run collusion also reduced competitive pressures for change, with adverse consequences for productivity growth.

1.4.3 Completing the industrialisation of services, 1950–1990

Chapter 10 examines the development of the major market services between 1950 and 1990. By the early 1950s the US labour productivity lead over all European countries, including both Britain and Germany, had reached its peak. This was true in market services, as well as in the economy as a whole, and reflected in part, at least, the much greater degree of disruption caused by World War II in Europe. Between 1950 and 1990 Britain narrowed the productivity gap with the United States, in services and in the economy as a whole, but at a slower pace than Germany. As a result, Germany overtook Britain in terms of labour productivity during the mid-1960s, again in both services and the economy as a whole.

As during the inter-war period, Britain's performance was generally poorer in sectors suitable for large-scale, hierarchical organisation, such as the railways, and rather better in sectors that retained a suitability for organisation on the basis of networks, such as parts of the financial service sector. However, general technological trends continued to favour standardisation and large-scale organisation, and more and more services became increasingly industrialised. Britain had little choice but to embrace these developments, but the transition to industrialised services was difficult, since social capabilities remained oriented towards the network form of organisation.

In considering the three-way contrast between Britain, the United States and Germany since World War II, it is important to consider the institutional framework. During the early post-war period, the contrast appears strongest between a 'corporatist' institutional framework in Britain and Germany on the one hand and a 'competitive' framework in the United States on the other hand. The corporatist framework in Europe was centred on a post-war settlement involving unions, employers' organisations and government. However, the system was much better at encouraging the accumulation of human and physical capital in Germany, where unions and employers' organisations were centralised, than in Britain, where the equivalent labour market organisations were highly fragmented and decentralised. In the accumulation of human capital, Germany's more centralised framework was also better able to solve the free-rider problem of the poaching of skilled workers than Britain's decentralised framework. While Germany was able to establish an effective system of vocational training in services after World War II, Britain's apprenticeship system went into decline, even in industrial sectors. Although a similar poaching problem existed in the United States, this was offset by the greater reliance on general education than vocational training. Turning to physical capital accumulation, again it is the case that the more centralised German unions and employers' organisations were better able to deliver on agreements concerning investments in new technology and wage restraint than the more fragmented British labour market organisations.

A major change of direction occurred in Britain during the 1980s, with the adoption of a more vigorous anti-trust policy, the privatisation of a number of important services in the transport and communications sector, a policy of deregulation, particularly in financial services, and legislation to limit the immunities of trade unions. By the end of the 1980s the major contrast in the institutional frameworks was therefore between the competitive approach of Britain and the United States on the one hand and the corporatist approach of Germany on the other hand. After more than a century, Britain's relative economic decline began to be stemmed, if not yet decisively reversed.

1.4.4 *British services in the 1990s: a preliminary assessment*

Chapter 11 provides a preliminary assessment of developments in the major market service sectors during the 1990s. Whereas technological change during most of the twentieth century tended to favour standardisation and hierarchical organisation, the ICT revolution of the 1990s has tended to favour customisation and networks, whilst preserving the high volume and high productivity of industrialised services. In earlier periods the trend towards standardisation and hierarchy occurred unevenly between sectors, and, similarly, the information revolution has

Introduction and overview 15

had an uneven impact on different sectors. To the extent that these changes tap into social capabilities that have remained strong in Britain, this should lead to an expectation of improved relative performance. To some extent, this expectation has been borne out, with Britain beginning to catch up with continental European countries during the 1990s (O'Mahony and de Boer, 2002). However, with the new technology coming largely from the United States, Anglo-American productivity gaps have been slow to narrow.

As Brynjolfsson and Hitt (2000: 26) note, a fall of more than 99.9% in the cost of automated information processing since the 1960s has had a dramatic impact on efficient work practices, restoring autonomy to individual workers. However, this has happened within an 'industrialised' environment characterised by the high-volume and low-margin provision of services. In the 'New Economy', many routine tasks have been automated, most workers perform their own clerical tasks using personal computers and email, and most workers have access through the use of networked computers and the internet to information that was previously only available centrally. It is in the technology-intensive service sectors that the impact has been greatest. However, as with the earlier innovations favouring standardisation and hierarchical forms of organisation, conditions have varied between sectors, affecting the pace at which the new ICTs have been adopted. Bresnahan et al. (2002) argue that investment in information technology has been greater in organisations that are decentralised and have a greater investment in human capital, while Brynjolfsson et al. (1994) argue that greater levels of investment in information technology are also associated with smaller firms and less vertical integration.

1.5 Conclusions

Chapter 12 provides a brief summary of the argument. Britain's loss of overall productivity leadership between the mid-nineteenth century and the late twentieth century owes more to developments in services than in industry. Britain's position in the mid-nineteenth century was more precarious than is usually realised. As the first industrial nation, Britain had a small agricultural sector, and a correspondingly high share of the labour force in the relatively high-value-added industrial and service sectors. However, British industry was labour-intensive, and industrial labour productivity was substantially higher in the United States and just as high in Germany. Only in services did Britain have a labour productivity lead over both Germany and the United States, and this owed much to the high levels of urbanisation in Britain, allowing the development of a large and highly specialised service sector. This British advantage was bound to disappear once other countries industrialised and urbanised.

However, there was more to Britain's loss of productivity leadership in services than catching up by the United States and Germany. Britain also fell behind during the industrialisation of services. The adoption of a standardised, high-volume, low-margin approach to business, with hierarchical management, began on the US railroads and spread out to other parts of the market service sector at varying rates. The institutional framework conditioned the response of British and German services to these developments, affecting the speed of adoption of the new technology and organisation. Before World War II the earlier industrialisation of services in Britain than in Germany reflected the contrast between the decline of agriculture in Britain and its protection in Germany, which seriously delayed the development of services in Germany. After World War II, although Germany as well as Britain adopted a corporatist institutional framework, Germany's more centralised system provided a better set of incentives for the accumulation of human and physical capital. Britain's relative economic decline has been stemmed since the adoption of a more competitive institutional framework in the 1980s and a return to a technological system favouring a more customised approach to service provision during the 1990s.

Part I

Measuring comparative productivity performance

2 The contribution of services to the productivity performance of the whole economy

2.1 Introduction

Although data on comparative labour productivity at the aggregate level have been used widely by economists and economic historians since they were brought together in an important series of publications by Maddison (1964, 1982, 1991, 1995, 2001), there has been much less systematic quantitative work on how this aggregate productivity performance can be broken down by sector. This absence of comparative productivity level data on a sectoral basis has allowed a number of serious misunderstandings about Britain's comparative economic performance since the mid-nineteenth century to persist. One of the aims of this book is to correct these misperceptions and to establish firmly the sectoral patterns of Britain's comparative productivity performance during this period.

Before outlining the sectoral breakdown, it is important to establish the patterns of Britain's comparative labour productivity performance at the aggregate level. For the US/UK and Germany/UK cases, the aggregate picture is widely agreed. The figures in tables 2.1 and 2.2 refer to GDP per person engaged, but the levels and trends are very similar to Maddison's (1995) well-known comparative data on GDP per hour worked. Around 1870 aggregate labour productivity in the United States was about 90% of the British level, but US overtaking occurred in the 1890s. The United States then forged ahead, reaching a peak labour productivity lead around 1950, after which Britain slowly narrowed the gap. In 1871 aggregate labour productivity in Germany was less than 60% of the British level. Although this had risen above 75% before World War I, the war provided a significant setback to Germany. By the late 1930s German labour productivity had reached about 80% of the British level, but World War II provided another setback. After World War II Germany returned to the catching-up path, overtaking Britain during the 1960s. Germany continued to forge ahead until 1979, and during the 1980s comparative aggregate labour productivity fluctuated without trend until German reunification.

Table 2.1 *Comparative US/UK labour productivity levels by sector, 1869/71–1990 (UK = 100)*

	Agriculture	Industry	Services	Aggregate economy
1869/71	86.9	153.6	85.9	89.8
1879/81	98.1	149.8	87.9	95.9
1889/91	102.1	164.1	84.2	94.1
1899/01	106.3	174.7	104.0	108.0
1909/11	103.2	193.2	107.4	117.7
1919/20	128.0	198.0	118.9	133.3
1929	109.7	222.7	121.2	139.4
1937	103.3	190.6	120.0	132.6
1950	126.0	243.5	140.8	166.9
1960	153.1	250.4	137.7	167.9
1968	156.7	248.1	139.6	164.2
1973	131.2	214.8	137.4	152.3
1979	156.1	186.0	137.2	145.5
1985	146.9	161.1	134.1	134.8
1990	151.1	163.0	129.6	133.0

Note:
Benchmark estimates of comparative productivity levels for 1937 are projected to other years using time series for output and employment from historical national accounting sources. Details of the construction of the data set are given in chapter 4.

Source: Derived from Broadberry (1997b).

The natural starting point for the sectoral analysis of Britain's comparative productivity performance is the widely acknowledged fact that comparative productivity trends in manufacturing have differed from trends in the aggregate economy (Broadberry, 1993). The US/UK and Germany/UK cases are shown here in figure 2.1. In contrast to the situation at the aggregate level, in manufacturing there has been no long-run trend in comparative labour productivity. In 1870 US labour productivity in manufacturing was roughly twice the UK level, and this remained the case in the late twentieth century. Although there have been periods of sustained deviation from this two-to-one US labour productivity advantage, particularly following major wars, in the long run there has always been a return to this ratio. Similarly, there has been no long-run change in the Germany/UK comparative labour productivity ratio, with Germany roughly on a par with Britain in both 1870 and 1990.

Since manufacturing was the biggest industrial sector, and since agriculture had shrunk in importance to around 2 or 3% of the labour force in all three countries by the late 1980s, reconciling the trends and levels

Table 2.2 *Comparative Germany/UK labour productivity levels by sector, 1871–1990 (UK = 100)*

	Agriculture	Industry	Services	Aggregate economy
1871	55.7	91.7	62.8	59.5
1881	54.7	93.7	61.3	57.3
1891	53.7	99.3	64.4	60.5
1901	67.2	105.0	71.9	68.4
1911	67.3	127.7	73.4	75.5
1925	53.8	92.3	76.5	69.0
1929	56.9	97.1	82.3	74.1
1935	57.2	99.1	85.7	75.7
1937	59.0	96.9	89.4	79.2
1950	41.2	91.8	83.2	74.4
1960	47.8	117.9	102.6	94.5
1968	48.6	121.9	115.9	107.1
1973	50.8	121.1	120.1	114.0
1979	65.5	132.8	131.8	126.5
1985	62.1	114.8	131.6	120.9
1990	75.4	111.0	134.9	125.4

Note:
Benchmark estimates of comparative productivity levels for 1935 are projected to other years using time series for output and employment from historical national accounting sources. Details of the construction of the data set are given in chapter 4.

Source: Derived from Broadberry (1997c).

of comparative productivity performance in manufacturing and the whole economy seemed to require a loss of British productivity leadership in services. This was first established by Broadberry (1997b, 1997c, 1998) using a nine-sector breakdown. However, to bring out the crucial importance of services for understanding Britain's comparative productivity performance since 1870, it is helpful first to consider the results on the basis of a three-sector breakdown, covering agriculture, industry and services. Having considered the trends in these three major branches, a further disaggregation of services will then be offered in chapter 3.

2.2 Methodological issues

2.2.1 *Time series projections and benchmark checks*

Before setting out the sectoral breakdown of comparative productivity performance, it will be useful to address some important methodological issues, beginning with the basic method of time series projection and the

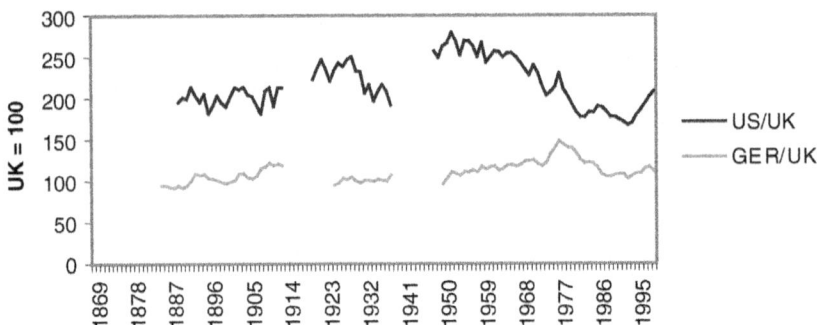

Figure 2.1 Comparative labour productivity in manufacturing.
Source: Broadberry (1997a), updated from O'Mahony (2002)

use of benchmark checks. As with Maddison's (1995) aggregate data set, the methodology involves time series projection from a benchmark. Time series for output and employment can be used to construct indices of labour productivity for each country, and these indices can then be combined to provide a time series for comparative labour productivity. To pin down the comparative level of labour productivity then requires a cross-sectional benchmark. This involves comparing the levels of labour productivity in the two countries at a point in time, either by comparing physical output per employee or by converting value added per employee at a (sector-specific) price ratio adjusted in line with purchasing power parity (PPP).

Maddison's (1995) methodology involves picking a benchmark as close as possible to the present and using time series projection over very long periods. However, since there are potentially many index number problems involved in time series projections over long periods, it is important to provide some additional corroboration. To address these problems Broadberry (1993) has proposed a modification of the basic Maddison approach. This involves picking a benchmark as close as possible to the centre of the period covered by the time series as the base from which time series projections are made. The approach also involves using additional benchmark estimates for earlier and later years to corroborate the time series projections. This deals with the basic objections to what Ward and Devereux (2003) call 'long-span' estimates of comparative productivity (Broadberry, 2003).

2.2.2 Measurement problems in services

Most studies of comparative productivity are carried out either for the economy as a whole or for the manufacturing sector. This appears to reflect a widespread perception that it is not possible to measure output and hence productivity in services. However, a moment's reflection shows that this is not a sustainable position. If it were not possible to measure productivity in services then it would not be possible to say anything about aggregate labour productivity in rich countries in recent decades, when the bulk of the labour force has been employed in services. The approach taken in this book is to acknowledge that there are measurement difficulties in services, just as there are in industry. But, again, as in industry, the appropriate response is not to abandon the analysis but to scrutinise the available data, assess their fitness for purpose and look for corroboration.

One conclusion, which becomes obvious from a close scrutiny of the data, is that there are parts of the service sector where output can, in fact, be measured fairly well. Whilst in the national accounting framework there are undoubtedly parts of the non-market service sector where output is measured largely by inputs, this is not generally true of the main market service sectors. The early post-war guide to the UK national accounts, for example, takes seven pages just to list the primary indicators used in tracking real output in market services (UK Central Statistical Office, 1956: 359–65). In transport the key indicators are ton-miles and passenger miles for freight and passengers, respectively, whereas for communications there are indicators such as items of mail, telegraph messages and telephone calls. For distribution the volume of goods produced and consumed in all the main branches can be tracked, while in finance the number of key transactions, such as cheque clearings, stock exchange transactions, the number and real value of loans and the number and real value of insurance policies, can be measured. Many of these indicators are available on a comparative basis.

These measures of output and productivity are far from perfect in market services, just as they are in industry. However, they do appear to be good enough to establish the basic trends of comparative productivity in services. And these trends in services do appear to be consistent with what is known about trends in industry and in the whole economy. However, to be really convincing, they have to be related to experience in the individual sectors, and this is the task of Part III of this book. Again, the results are reassuring, with the quantitative picture being confirmed by the detailed case studies based on a wider range of evidence.

2.3 The US/UK comparison

The importance of services to the changing US/UK comparative labour productivity level in the aggregate economy over the period 1870–1990 can be seen in the sectoral breakdown of comparative productivity levels in table 2.1. To get the full picture, however, requires adding to this the sectoral breakdown of employment in the two countries, shown in Table 2.3. The first point to note is that the long-run trends in comparative labour productivity for the aggregate economy owe rather less to trends in industry performance than is usually assumed in accounts of comparative productivity performance. Hence, for example, between circa 1890 and 1990, the US labour productivity lead in industry declined slightly, while the United States went from a position of lower aggregate labour productivity to a 33% lead over Britain. This is not to say that industry did not matter, particularly in shorter-run fluctuations of comparative labour productivity. Indeed, Broadberry (1997a) notes that the US labour productivity lead in manufacturing increased significantly across World War I and again across World War II, but, in each case, the increase was not sustained.

Note, second, that, although the trend of comparative labour productivity in agriculture was in the same direction as in the aggregate economy, with the United States overtaking Britain, this was not the really significant contribution of agriculture to changing comparative productivity performance at the aggregate level. The greater significance of agriculture was in its declining share of the labour force, which can be seen for both countries in table 2.3. The decline in agriculture's share of employment had a significant impact on aggregate labour productivity because agriculture is a relatively low-value-added activity. Shifting labour from agriculture into higher-value-added industrial and service sectors hence acted to boost aggregate labour productivity. Note, however, that this shift out of agriculture occurred rather later in the United States than in Britain, thus contributing to the US catch-up. Whereas in about 1870 agriculture accounted for just 22.2% of employment in Britain, it still accounted for a full half of the US labour force. By 1990, however, agriculture accounted for less than 3% of employment in both countries.

The most important point to note in table 2.1 is that comparative labour productivity trends in services broadly mirror comparative labour productivity trends for the economy as a whole. The US overtook Britain in services during the 1890s, and forged ahead up to the 1950s. Furthermore, since services grew in importance throughout the period in both countries, it is this loss of British productivity leadership in services that largely explains Britain's loss of overall productivity leadership. Services also dominated in shorter-run fluctuations; the correlation coefficient R between comparative productivity levels in the aggregate economy and services is 0.98, compared with 0.85 between the aggregate economy and industry, or 0.65 between the aggregate economy and agriculture.

Table 2.3 *Sectoral shares of employment in the United States, the United Kingdom and Germany, 1870–1990 (%)*

A. United States

	Agriculture	Industry	Services
1870	50.0	24.8	25.2
1910	32.0	31.8	36.2
1920	26.2	33.2	40.6
1930	20.9	30.2	48.9
1940	17.9	31.6	50.5
1950	11.0	32.9	56.1
1973	3.7	28.9	67.4
1990	2.5	21.8	75.7

B. United Kingdom

	Agriculture	Industry	Services
1871	22.2	42.4	35.4
1911	11.8	44.1	44.1
1924	8.6	46.5	44.9
1930	7.6	43.7	48.7
1937	6.2	44.5	49.3
1950	5.1	46.5	48.4
1973	2.9	41.8	55.3
1990	2.0	28.5	69.5

C. Germany

	Agriculture	Industry	Services
1871	49.5	29.1	21.4
1913	34.5	37.9	27.6
1925	31.5	40.1	28.4
1930	30.5	37.4	32.1
1935	29.9	38.2	31.9
1950	24.3	42.1	33.6
1973	7.2	47.3	45.5
1990	3.4	39.7	56.9

Note:
Details of the construction of the data set are given in chapter 4.

Source: Derived from Broadberry (1997b, 1997c, 1998).

2.4 The Germany/UK comparison

The importance of services to the changing Germany/UK comparative labour productivity level in the aggregate economy over the period 1870–1990 can be seen in the sectoral breakdown of comparative productivity levels in table 2.2, together with the sectoral employment data in table 2.3. Again, the first point to note is that the long-run trends in comparative productivity levels for the aggregate economy owe rather less to trends in industry than is usually assumed in accounts of comparative productivity performance. Thus, for example, between 1911 and 1990, the German labour productivity lead in industry declined while for the aggregate economy Germany went from three-quarters of the British level to a lead of more than 25%. However, over shorter periods there have been substantial movements in comparative Germany/UK labour productivity levels in industry. Broadberry (1997a) emphasises the German forging ahead in manufacturing during the 1970s, with Germany attaining close to a 50% labour productivity lead by the end of the decade. This was not sustained, however, and by the end of the 1980s most of the German lead had been eliminated (Broadberry and Crafts, 2003).

Second, although Germany's comparative productivity position in agriculture has improved since the late nineteenth century, agricultural labour productivity remained much lower in Germany than in Britain in 1990. The real significance of agriculture for comparative productivity performance in the aggregate economy was its declining importance as a share of the labour force in both countries. Since the shift of labour out of low-value-added agriculture occurred much later in Germany than in Britain, and even substantially later than in the United States, this had important implications for the lateness of German catching up at the aggregate economy level. With such a large share of the German labour force tied up in low-productivity agriculture before World War II, the overall labour productivity level was bound to be much lower in Germany than in Britain. On the other hand, once Germany shifted decisively out of agriculture after World War II, overall catching up was rapid.

For the Germany/UK case in table 2.2, the most important point to note is that comparative labour productivity trends in services broadly mirror comparative labour productivity trends for the economy as a whole, as for the US/UK case in table 2.1. Again, the key to understanding Germany's overtaking of Britain at the aggregate level was the loss of British productivity leadership in services. Services also apparently dominated the shorter-run fluctuations; the correlation coefficient R between comparative productivity levels in the aggregate economy and services is 0.99, compared with 0.74 between the aggregate economy and industry, and just 0.29 between the aggregate economy and agriculture.

2.5 Conclusions

Services played a dominant role in explaining variation in comparative labour productivity performance at the aggregate level in both the US/UK and Germany/UK cases. We are interested mainly in the long-run change in overall comparative labour productivity levels, and the basic story here is of Britain being overtaken at the aggregate level by both the United States and Germany primarily as a result of the loss of labour productivity leadership in services. Services also played a dominant role in the shorter-run fluctuations of comparative labour productivity, although industry played an important secondary role here. The key contribution of agriculture was its declining importance, with the later shift out of this low-value-added activity in the United States and Germany contributing to the process of catching up and overtaking.

3 Comparative productivity performance in market services

3.1 Introduction

Chapter 2 has established that services played a dominant role in the changing patterns of comparative labour productivity performance at the aggregate level. In particular, over the long run, Britain was overtaken at the aggregate level because of a loss of labour productivity leadership in services. It was also pointed out in chapter 2, however, that many economists and economic historians worry about measurement issues in services. This chapter therefore takes a more disaggregated look at productivity performance in services, focusing on market services, where the problems of measuring output independently of inputs are less important. The patterns are reassuring, showing that the British loss of productivity leadership in services reflects changes within the main market sectors, and is not just some statistical artefact arising from changes in the importance of non-market services, where measurement problems are most severe.

3.2 The US/UK comparison

Table 3.1 provides time series projections of comparative US/UK labour productivity levels in the key market service sectors of transport and communications, distribution, and finance with professional and personal services. These projections are based on 1937 benchmarks, which are shown at a more disaggregated level in table 3.2, together with benchmarks for additional years. These benchmarks for other years can be used as additional cross-checks on the time series projections, as well as providing a more disaggregated picture of comparative productivity levels.

In the time series projections of table 3.1, we see that the United States had already built up a substantial labour productivity lead in transport and communications before World War I, and the US lead in this sector remained substantial during the inter-war period. Despite

Table 3.1 *Comparative US/UK labour productivity levels in market services, 1869/71–1990 (UK = 100)*

	Transport and communications	Distribution	Finance, professional and personal services
1869/71	110.0	66.9	64.1
1879/81	146.9	107.9	58.4
1889/91	167.1	97.0	53.2
1899/01	226.8	107.1	71.6
1909/11	217.4	120.0	77.9
1919/20	250.6	109.0	103.6
1929	231.5	121.9	101.5
1937	283.4	119.8	96.1
1950	348.4	135.2	111.5
1960	318.8	143.2	112.3
1968	336.8	147.9	121.3
1973	303.3	149.6	118.0
1979	302.7	153.8	118.3
1985	294.8	177.3	103.6
1990	270.5	166.0	101.0

Note:
Benchmark estimates of comparative productivity levels for 1937 are projected to other years using time series for output and employment from historical national accounting sources. Details of the construction of the data set are given in chapter 4.

Source: Derived from Broadberry (1997b).

a reduction in the US lead since World War II, British productivity remained much lower in transport and communications in 1990. In the disaggregated benchmark data of table 3.2, these trends can also be seen on the railways, which accounted for nearly a quarter of employment in Britain's transport and communications sector at the peak of their importance before World War I, and still 20% at the end of World War II (Mitchell, 1988: 104–5). Note that a substantial US/UK labour productivity gap had also opened up in communications before World War I, and in road transport, shipping and air transport after World War II.

Returning to the time series projections in table 3.1, although the United States had overtaken Britain by World War I in distribution, the lead was relatively small and remained so between the wars. This is confirmed by the benchmark estimates in table 3.2. Only since World War II has the US lead in distribution been decisive.

Returning again to the time series projections in table 3.1, in finance with professional and personal services, although the United States

Table 3.2 *Benchmark estimates of US/UK comparative labour productivity levels in market services, 1870–1993 (UK = 100)*

	1870	1890	1910	1924	1930	1937
Railways	76.2	158.2	215.5	342.2	447.9	390.6
Communications			143.5	136.1	166.5	270.0
Total transport and communications			196.1	287.9	362.0	283.4
Distribution			118.7			119.8
Finance	43.3	68.9	119.9	155.8	103.0	86.4
Total finance, professional and personal services			79.1	92.6	90.0	96.1

	1950	1968	1993
Railways	620.7	395.0	370.3
Road transport		167.2	
Shipping		170.0	
Air transport		152.0	
Communications	144.6	302.0	152.9
Total transport and communications	358.9	250.0	
Distribution	148.4		143.6
Finance	138.7		117.7
Total finance, professional and personal services	95.5		

Note:
Benchmark estimates are based on direct observation for the years stated.

Source: Broadberry (1997b); railway estimates – 1870 and 1890: derived from Fishlow (1966), Mitchell (1988), Cain (1980), Hawke (1970); additional figures – 1968: derived from Pryke (1971), Smith et al. (1982); 1993: derived from O'Mahony et al. (1998).

pulled ahead across World War I, the British lead was restored during the financial crisis of the 1930s, and the US lead in this sector has remained relatively small since World War II. Using the benchmark data of table 3.2, it is possible to build up a picture of comparative productivity in finance more narrowly defined. The comparative productivity trend in finance more narrowly defined was similar to that in the wider sector over the long run, but with some important differences in the short run. First, the United States had pulled slightly ahead of Britain in finance before rather than during World War I, and built up a bigger lead during the 1920s. Second, however, the US financial collapse of the 1930s restored the British lead in finance as well as in professional and personal services. And third, the US lead in finance narrowly defined has been

Table 3.3 *Comparative Germany/UK productivity levels in market services, 1871–1990 (UK = 100)*

	Transport and communications	Distribution and finance	Professional and personal services
1871	74.4	70.7	89.7
1881	97.4	38.6	83.4
1891	113.5	45.9	77.0
1901	150.0	49.7	76.6
1911	166.8	52.5	76.3
1925	140.0	47.1	86.7
1929	151.2	50.3	99.8
1935	132.4	54.3	105.6
1937	136.3	56.8	113.0
1950	122.0	50.7	94.2
1960	117.0	64.2	85.7
1968	130.0	75.4	101.3
1973	119.5	88.0	98.4
1979	135.0	106.4	103.1
1985	132.7	109.2	105.3
1990	125.7	111.2	120.5

Note:
Benchmark estimates of comparative productivity levels for 1935 are projected to other years using time series for output and employment from historical national accounting sources. Details of the construction of the data set are given in chapter 4.

Source: Derived from Broadberry (1997c).

substantially higher than in the broader finance and professional and personal services sector since World War II.

3.3 The Germany/UK comparison

Despite Germany's generally poor productivity performance in services before World War I, the time series projections in table 3.3 indicate that Germany had already overtaken Britain in transport and communications by 1891. However, the scale of the German lead in this sector at this time owed much to the relative importance of the railways and was subsequently reduced as other forms of transport and communications accounted for a growing share of economic activity.[1] In distribution and

---

[1] The scale of the German lead in transport and communications before World War I is lower here than suggested in Broadberry (1997c), due to a correction for pre-war employment on the German railways. Hoffmann (1965: 191, 201) allocated all technical

Table 3.4 *Benchmark estimates of comparative Germany/UK labour productivity levels in market services, 1935–1993 (UK = 100)*

	1935	1968	1973	1993
Railways	178.9	108.2		107.2
Road transport		129.8		
Shipping		190.0		
Air transport		113.0		
Communications	34.5	106.4		67.7
Total transport and communications	132.4	121.0		
Distribution			127.0	112.1
Finance	{54.3}			109.9
Professional and personal services	105.6			

Note:
Benchmark estimates are based on direct observation for the years stated.

Source: Broadberry (1997c); additional figures – 1968: Pryke (1971); 1973: Smith and Hitchens (1985); 1993: O'Mahony et al. (1998).

finance, German productivity levels remained a long way behind British productivity levels before World War II. This part of the service sector remained relatively underdeveloped in Germany at this time, and German overtaking occurred only during the 1970s. German catching up occurred earlier in personal and professional services than in distribution and finance.

Benchmark estimates of comparative Germany/UK labour productivity are available in Table 3.4. Although there are no estimates for the period prior to 1935 to provide additional benchmark checks on the time series projections back to the nineteenth century, disaggregated benchmark estimates do exist for the period after World War II. These estimates suggest a German labour productivity lead in all major branches of transport and communications by the late 1960s.

3.4 Sectoral employment shares

It is worth noting some similarities and differences in the structure of the service sector in the different countries, drawing on tables 3.5 and 3.6. Dealing first with the US/UK comparison in table 3.5, both countries have devoted similar shares of the labour force to transport and communications, with the share rising to a peak of 8 to 9% in 1930,

personnel to industry before World War I, and a correction can be made for this using the later proportional breakdown between industry and the railways.

Table 3.5 *Sectoral shares of employment in market services in the United States and the United Kingdom, 1870–1990 (% of total labour forces)*

A. United States

	Transport and communications	Distribution	Finance, professional and personal services
1870	4.6	6.1	12.2
1910	8.3	9.1	17.1
1920	9.2	9.3	15.5
1930	8.6	11.7	21.4
1940	6.9	13.4	26.3
1950	6.0	18.7	21.3
1973	4.4	20.2	31.8
1990	4.0	22.0	40.2

B. United Kingdom

	Transport and communications	Distribution	Finance, professional and personal services
1871	5.4	7.5	19.5
1911	7.7	12.1	20.2
1924	8.5	12.0	19.3
1930	8.3	14.3	20.9
1937	7.9	14.4	21.6
1950	7.9	12.2	19.5
1973	6.4	17.8	23.3
1990	5.5	19.5	37.5

Note:
Details of the construction of the data set are given in chapter 4.
Source: Derived from Broadberry (1997b, 1998).

before falling back to around 5% by 1990. Although the United States started in 1870 with smaller shares of the labour force in distribution and in finance, professional and personal services, the US share was larger in both sectors by 1990.

Turning to the Germany/UK comparison in table 3.6, note first that it is necessary to reorganise the UK data to include finance with distribution rather than professional and personal services. Whereas the levels and trends of the employment shares are quite similar in the United States and Britain, the differences are more striking in the comparison between Britain and Germany. Transport and communications accounted for a much smaller share of employment in Germany than in

Table 3.6 *Sectoral shares of employment in market services in Germany and the United Kingdom, 1870–1990 (% of total labour forces)*

A. Germany

	Transport and communications	Distribution and finance	Professional and personal services
1875	2.4	6.0	10.0
1913	4.9	11.2	8.3
1925	4.8	12.5	7.9
1930	5.0	14.7	8.4
1935	4.8	13.5	8.8
1950	5.6	13.2	16.3
1973	5.5	15.3	12.2
1990	5.6	16.3	19.9

B. United Kingdom

	Transport and communications	Distribution	Finance, professional and personal services
1871	5.4	7.8	19.2
1911	7.7	13.2	19.1
1925	8.4	14.5	17.5
1930	8.3	16.4	18.8
1935	7.9	17.1	19.8
1950	7.9	14.1	17.6
1973	6.4	24.0	17.1
1990	5.5	31.4	25.6

Note:
Details of the construction of the data set are given in chapter 4.
Source: Derived from Broadberry (1997b, 1997c, 1998, 2004b).

Britain until the 1970s. Although Germany constructed a productive railway system in the nineteenth century and built up an efficient liner fleet on the North Atlantic route before World War I, the rest of the German transport and communications sector was relatively small and unproductive. For the entire period distribution and finance have accounted for a smaller share of employment in Germany than in Britain. Other services have also remained substantially smaller in Germany, which has had a correspondingly large agricultural sector before the 1970s, and a large industrial sector since the 1970s.

3.5 Conclusions

This chapter has provided a more disaggregated look at Britain's comparative productivity performance in services. The loss of Britain's labour productivity leadership in services, identified in chapter 2 as a key factor behind Britain's loss of productivity leadership in the aggregate economy, has been shown here to reflect developments in market services. In 1870 Britain had higher labour productivity than the United States in distribution and in finance, professional and personal services, and, although the United States had slightly higher labour productivity in transport and communications as a whole, Britain was still ahead on the railways. By 1990 the United States was ahead in all three major sectors, with a substantial labour productivity lead in transport and communications. In 1870 Britain had a labour productivity lead over Germany in transport and communications, in distribution and finance, and in professional and personal services. By 1990 Germany was ahead in all three major market service sectors.

The patterns revealed also point helpfully to the key explanatory framework behind Britain's loss of productivity leadership in services. This appears to be associated with a process which has been labelled the 'industrialisation' of services. This has involved the adoption of a standardised, high-volume, low-margin approach to service provision with hierarchical management, replacing an earlier approach to business based on customisation, low volumes and high margins, organised through networks. This transformation began on the US railroads in the late nineteenth century, and spread rapidly to other parts of the transport and communications sector before World War I, but was much slower to spread to distribution and financial services. US overtaking of Britain in market services followed this pattern. In the Germany/UK case, cross-sectional comparative productivity levels followed a similar pattern, with British performance better in sectors where a more customised approach to business remained viable. In the German case, however, the overall level of productivity in services was held down before World War II by the protective institutional framework, which kept a large proportion of the labour force in low-productivity agriculture. The low level of demand for services which resulted from this, and its spreading out over the countryside in contrast to the concentrated urban demands in Britain, limited the degree of specialisation and lowered the level of productivity in German market services before World War II.

4 A sectoral database: Britain, the United States and Germany, 1870–1990

4.1 Introduction

This chapter provides a full guide to the sectoral database underlying the quantitative information on comparative labour productivity levels presented in chapters 2 and 3. In addition to the main tables of comparative labour productivity levels for nine sectors in agriculture and industry as well as services, I have taken the opportunity to make available here the underlying data. This consists of the sectoral time series in appendix 4.1 and cross-sectional benchmarks in appendix 4.2. Having presented the time series data, it is natural to proceed to an analysis of productivity growth to complement the focus on comparative productivity levels. This helps to underline the fact that, although Britain has undoubtedly undergone a relative economic decline since the mid-nineteenth century, this has occurred within the context of growth. Indeed, in absolute terms, and even relative to most countries, there can be little doubt that Britain has been very successful in raising productivity and living standards throughout the period under review. Nevertheless, Germany and the United States have been even more successful, and Britain has been overtaken.

4.2 Comparative US/UK labour productivity levels

4.2.1 Time series projections

The starting point for the time series projections of comparative US/UK labour productivity levels in table 4.1 is the set of historical national accounts for the two countries. Full sources are listed in appendix 4.1, but, in general, time series for British output and employment are taken from Feinstein (1972) to 1948, and updated to 1990 from the official UK national accounts and OECD labour force estimates. For the United States, the basic source is Kendrick (1961) to 1948, updated to 1990 using the official US national accounts and OECD labour force estimates.

Table 4.1 Time series projections of comparative US/UK labour productivity levels by sector (UK = 100)

	1869/71	1879/81	1889/91	1899/01	1909/11	1919/20	1929	1937	1950	1960	1968	1973	1979	1990
Agriculture	86.9	98.1	102.1	106.3	103.2	128.0	109.7	103.3	126.0	153.1	156.7	131.2	156.1	151.1
Mineral extraction	103.1	99.3	109.0	147.3	162.0	228.2	248.9	232.1	376.5	618.4	700.9	668.0	156.6	119.1
Manufacturing	182.5	170.7	193.8	196.5	202.7	205.6	250.0	208.3	262.7	243.0	242.8	215.0	202.6	175.2
Construction	95.5	138.8	164.3	139.7	198.5	234.2	133.7	107.8	177.6	235.5	204.5	146.6	129.7	98.5
Utilities	55.8	74.5	113.5	128.1	149.5	295.5	335.9	359.3	573.4	719.9	767.9	590.8	523.9	389.8
Transport and communications	110.0	146.9	167.1	226.8	217.4	250.6	231.5	283.4	348.4	318.8	336.8	303.3	302.7	270.5
Distribution	66.9	107.9	97.0	107.1	120.0	109.0	121.9	119.8	135.2	143.2	147.9	149.6	153.8	166.0
Finance and services	64.1	58.4	53.2	71.6	77.9	103.6	101.5	96.1	111.5	112.3	121.3	118.0	118.3	101.0
Government	114.3	108.6	102.6	111.2	95.8	97.9	99.4	100.0	116.2	110.2	104.4	101.7	96.5	93.2
Total of above	92.0	94.5	96.3	110.6	120.6	137.9	142.7	132.6	167.2	163.4	159.1	144.3	139.4	128.3
Aggregate GDP	89.8	95.8	94.1	108.0	117.7	133.3	139.4	132.6	166.9	167.9	164.2	152.3	145.5	133.0

Note:
Time series projections of output per person engaged from 1937 benchmarks.

Source: See text and appendix 4.1.

For the pre-1950 period, I have stuck fairly closely to the national accounts sources. The main exception is the use of Balke and Gordon's (1989) output series for total GDP in the United States during the period 1869–1889, in line with Maddison (1991). Kendrick (1961) was clearly unhappy with the cyclical pattern of his own total GDP series during this period, and generally reported figures for the decade averages, 1869–1878 and 1879–1888. Note also that the US output series for agriculture is Kendrick's (1961) series for real gross output of the farm segment, which moves more closely in line with the series used in previous industry-of-origin studies of agriculture by Clark (1951) and Hayami and Ruttan (1985). In finance, professional and personal services, it was not possible to use Kendrick's (1961) output index for the United States for the period 1869–1889 since this was obtained as a residual, and I have preferred Balke and Gordon's (1989) aggregate GDP for this period. Rather, for the period 1869–1889 the US output index is assumed to grow in line with employment. Finally, for the pre-1950 period, the British index of construction output before World War I is a preliminary estimate compiled by Feinstein and Andrew Hilditch as part of a study of the pre-1914 national accounts.[1] This has the effect of smoothing out some rather extreme fluctuations in output and labour productivity.

For the post-1950 period, I have made two important changes to the standard national accounts sources. In the first place, I have continued to use the output and employment series constructed for my earlier manufacturing estimates, reported in Broadberry (1993). These estimates are taken from production censuses. Although they do not change the long-run growth of output or employment in the United States, or of employment in the United Kingdom, they do increase the growth of British output over the period 1950–1970. This appears to reflect an under-recording of output growth in the official British index of industrial production, which was used in the national accounts during this period. Lomax (1959: 198) corrects a similar under-recording of growth in the pre-war Board of Trade index of industrial production, noting 'the tendencies of a currently published, quickly available index to under-estimate the rate of growth in output trend'. The other major change is in agriculture, where for the United States I have used the Food and Agriculture Organisation (FAO) series for real output in agriculture and the national accounts series for farm employment. This then yields a picture that is broadly consistent with other

---

[1] I am grateful to Charles Feinstein and Andrew Hilditch for making this index available.

industry-of-origin studies of productivity comparisons in agriculture over the long-run (Hayami and Ruttan, 1985; O'Brien and Prados de la Escosura, 1992; Federico and Malanima, 2004).

These changes in the component series lead to some small changes in the aggregates. Hence, in addition to the 'aggregate GDP' series taken from the original sources, I also report in table 4.1 a 'total of above' series, where new implicit aggregate output and employment series have been constructed. The discrepancies between the whole economy productivity figures obtained using the 'total of above' and 'aggregate GDP' series are within the usual margins of error for this kind of work. The differences between the two series should be regarded as residual error, and the aggregates from the original sources are to be preferred.

The choice of sectors follows fairly naturally from the available data. The commodity sectors covering agriculture, mineral extraction, manufacturing, construction and the utilities have been well documented by production censuses going back to the nineteenth century in the United States and to the early twentieth century in Britain. Reliable estimates are also available for transport and communications, while distribution has been covered by censuses in both countries since the mid-twentieth century. Although it is possible to separate out finance from other services in Britain for the whole period, this cannot be done for the United States before 1929. Hence, finance is grouped with professional and personal services. For the case of government (public administration and defence), and also some non-market personal services, output is largely proxied by employment, which inevitably creates some difficulties of interpretation in a study of productivity. In a single-country context, it is usual to assume that the real output of non-marketed services rises in line with employment. In a cross-country comparison, the equivalent assumption is that comparative real output is proxied by comparative employment, which yields comparative labour productivity equal to 100 by construction.

4.2.2 Benchmark cross-checks

The time series projections in table 4.1 depend on benchmarks for comparative productivity levels in each sector in 1937. These estimates are provided in table 4.2, together with additional benchmarks for other years, which can be used to provide cross-checks on the time series projections. Detailed sources of the benchmarks are given in appendix 4.2. The key source for the 1937 benchmarks is the pioneering study by Rostas (1948), which relies heavily on physical indicators of real output, and his methods have been used to provide additional

Table 4.2 *Benchmark estimates of comparative US/UK labour productivity levels by sector (UK = 100)*

	1910	1924	1930	1937	1950	1968	1990
Agriculture	108.5	116.2	103.8	103.3	117.3	186.3	181.7
Mineral extraction	161.3	290.7	280.1	232.1	396.9	525.7	
Manufacturing	201.9	252.6	241.9	208.3	273.4	263.7	186.6
Construction	133.6	150.9	98.9	107.8	168.6	193.9	
Utilities	142.7	200.3	239.6	359.3	435.6	618.6	
Transport and communications	196.1	287.9	362.0	283.4	358.9	250.0	
Distribution	118.7			119.8	148.4		
Finance and services	79.1	92.6	90.0	96.1	95.5		
Government	100.0	100.0	100.0	100.0	100.0	100.0	100.0
Whole economy	108.8			132.6	162.5		

Source: See text and appendix 4.2.

benchmarks for the period prior to World War II. For 1950 there is the important study by Paige and Bombach (1959), which also uses information on sectoral value added compared at sector-specific purchasing power parities. The study by Smith et al. (1982) provides the basis for the benchmarks for 1968. There is a good deal of approximation involved here, since the benchmark estimates inevitably have a less complete coverage of the sub-sectors in each major sector grouping than the time series, and are often based on comparisons across slightly different years. Nevertheless, the broad picture is reasonably reassuring, with tables 4.1 and 4.2 telling the same basic story.

4.2.3 Sectoral aspects of the US overtaking

It is helpful to consider comparative productivity performance in terms of the three major sectors – agriculture, industry and services. One of the main results is that labour productivity gaps have been larger in industry than in agriculture or services throughout the period 1870–1990. At the same time, however, it is important to bear in mind that comparative labour productivity levels have been stationary in manufacturing, mineral extraction and construction. Although there were periods when the manufacturing labour productivity gap increased substantially, these periods were always followed by a return to the long-run two-to-one level. In mineral extraction, similarly, although Britain's comparative labour productivity position has not deteriorated over the long-run, this masks considerable swings associated with changes in the composition of output. This reflects in particular the growing importance of the high-value-added oil industry in the US mineral extraction sector through much of the twentieth century and the rise of the North Sea oil industry in Britain since 1973, together with the rundown of the low-productivity deep-mined coal industry in Britain over the same period. Construction exhibits inverse long swings, or Kuznets cycles, in the two countries, with British labour productivity approaching US levels during British building booms.

The one part of the industrial sector in which there was a long-run deterioration of Britain's labour productivity position was in the utilities. Here, as in mineral extraction, there were significant effects arising from changes in the composition of output and natural resource discoveries. The shift away from manufactured gas to electricity and natural gas greatly increased the scale of the US labour productivity lead in much of the twentieth century. In 1910, for example, census figures suggest a US/UK labour productivity ratio of only 115.7 in manufactured gas, but a ratio of 194.4 in electricity (Broadberry, 1997b). Hence, the growing importance of electricity, together with the growing use of natural gas in the gas industry, led to a surge in the US labour productivity lead in the utilities sector. The discovery of North Sea gas has allowed Britain to close the gap since the early 1970s. The small share of employment in utilities in both Britain and the United States, shown here in table 4.3, means that, in industry as a whole, comparative labour productivity was stationary.

As noted in chapter 2, changes in overall comparative labour productivity performance mirrored changes in comparative labour productivity performance in services, and, as noted in chapter 3, this in turn reflected real developments in market services. The United States overtook Britain in distribution and in finance, professional and personal services, and forged further ahead in transport and communications. Hence, although British comparative labour productivity performance appears better in services than in industry in terms of levels, it is also true that, in terms of changes, the deterioration of Britain's labour productivity performance over the long-run has been heavily concentrated in services. Whereas in 1870 Britain had a labour productivity lead in a number of service sectors, by 1990 there was a small labour productivity shortfall in these sectors.

In agriculture, Britain's performance also looks better than in industry when viewed in terms of comparative labour productivity levels. However, as in services, there was also a deterioration in Britain's position over time. The high labour productivity level of British agriculture during the nineteenth century has also been noted by Crafts

Table 4.3 *Sectoral shares of employment (%)*

A. United States

	1870	1910	1930	1950	1990
Agriculture	50.0	32.0	20.9	11.0	2.5
Mineral extraction	1.5	2.8	2.2	1.5	0.6
Manufacturing	17.3	22.2	21.3	25.0	15.3
Construction	5.8	6.3	5.9	5.5	5.2
Utilities	0.2	0.5	0.8	0.9	0.7
Transport and communications	4.6	8.1	8.6	6.0	4.0
Distribution	6.1	9.1	11.7	18.7	22.0
Finance and services	12.2	17.1	21.4	21.3	40.2
Government	2.3	1.9	7.2	10.1	9.5
Total	100.0	100.0	100.0	100.0	100.0

B. United Kingdom

	1871	1911	1930	1950	1990
Agriculture	22.2	11.8	7.6	5.1	2.0
Mineral extraction	4.0	6.3	5.4	3.7	0.6
Manufacturing	33.5	32.1	31.7	34.9	20.1
Construction	4.7	5.1	5.4	6.3	6.7
Utilities	0.2	0.6	1.2	1.6	1.1
Transport and communications	5.4	7.7	8.3	7.9	5.5
Distribution	7.5	12.1	14.3	12.2	19.5
Finance and services	19.5	20.2	20.9	19.5	37.5
Government	3.0	4.1	5.2	8.8	7.0
Total	100.0	100.0	100.0	100.0	100.0

C. Germany

	1875	1913	1935	1950	1990
Agriculture	49.5	34.5	29.9	24.3	3.4
Mineral extraction	1.5	2.8	1.7	2.8	0.6
Manufacturing	24.7	29.5	30.0	31.4	31.4
Construction	2.8	5.3	5.9	7.2	6.7
Utilities	0.1	0.3	0.6	0.7	1.0
Transport and communications	1.9	3.8	4.8	5.6	5.6
Distribution and finance	6.0	11.2	13.5	13.2	16.3
Professional and personal services	10.0	8.3	8.8	7.9	19.9
Government	3.5	4.3	4.8	6.9	15.1
Total	100.0	100.0	100.0	100.0	100.0

Source: United States – derived from Carson (1949), Lebergott (1966), US Department of Commerce (1983, *Survey of Current Business*, various years); United Kingdom – derived from Feinstein (1972), OECD (*Labour Force Statistics*, various years), UK Central Statistical Office (*Annual Abstract of Statistics*, various years); Germany – derived from Hoffmann (1965), Statistisches Bundesamt (1991).

(1985: 60–9), who argues that Britain's achievement during the Industrial Revolution was to shift labour out of agriculture to create an unusually large industrial sector, which was actually quite labour-intensive and not characterised by particularly high labour productivity. It should also be borne in mind that the high labour productivity of British agriculture reflected both the composition of output and the degree of capital intensity. The composition effect arose from the mid-nineteenth-century shift of the product mix away from grain towards pastoral products with the growth of grain imports from the New World, while the high capital intensity reflected the moves towards 'high farming' in response to the increased competition (Jones, 1968). As with services, the good performance of agriculture in levels does not alter the fact that there has been a trend deterioration in Britain's comparative labour productivity position in this sector.

The really crucial contribution of agriculture to comparative productivity performance, however, was as a source of labour for the higher-value-added industrial and service sectors. In table 4.3, we see that the most important trend in sectoral employment shares was the decline in the importance of agriculture in all three countries. However, whereas agriculture still accounted for about a half of total employment in the United States in 1870, in Britain it already accounted for less than a quarter. Given the lower value added per employee in agriculture, the later structural shift out of agriculture contributed to the US overtaking of Britain.

4.2.4 Methodological considerations

It will be noted that the above analysis has been predicated on the need to keep separate the time series projections and the benchmark estimates, and to use the latter as a check on the former. This imposes quite a strong consistency check on the data, ensuring that growth rates do not stray too far from benchmark levels. This is important to bear in mind when considering the recent work of Ward and Devereux (2003, 2004). Inspired by the early work of the Income Comparisons Project (ICP) for the post-1950 period, Ward and Devereux (2003) use a series of benchmarks based on comparative price levels to try to cast doubt on the time series projections of Maddison (1995) for US/UK comparative per capita income levels over the period 1870–1990. The scale of the disagreement in the late nineteenth century is enormous, with Ward and Devereux (2003: 840) claiming US per capita incomes in 1872 to be 18% higher than in the United Kingdom, compared with Maddison's

44   Measuring comparative productivity performance

result of the United States at 78% of the UK level – a discrepancy of 40 percentage points, or more than 50% of the Maddison estimate.[2]

Having initially used their set of benchmarks to cast doubt on the time series projections of Maddison (1995), Ward and Devereux (2004: 884) now cite Heston and Summers (1993) in support of a weaker claim that there are inevitably large index number problems in creating consistency across both space and time. However, although Heston and Summers did originally provide a set of benchmarks that conflicted with time series projections for the post-war period, they have subsequently acknowledged that this is unsatisfactory. Heston et al. (2001: 2) state the problem in the following terms:

> If per capita GDP in India relative to Korea is 40% in a 1970 benchmark and 35% in a 1975 benchmark, then one inference is that the growth rate per capita in Korea must have been about 5% more than in India between 1970 and 1975. Often such an implied result is not consistent with the national growth rates in the two countries, posing a problem to users.

In the current context, the problem is that Ward and Devereux's (2003: 840) benchmarks show the United States to have roughly the same per capita income lead over the United Kingdom in 1905 as in 1872, while the standard historical national accounts sources show the per capita growth rate between these years to be 1.8% per annum in the United States compared with just 0.9% in the United Kingdom (Kendrick, 1961; Feinstein, 1972).

One solution offered by Summers and Heston (1988) to the problem of inconsistency between benchmarks and time series projections is to change the national growth rates as well as the benchmarks, in a process known as 'consistentization'. However, as Heston et al. (2001: 6) now acknowledge, in an understated way:

> It was hard to sell the idea of modifying country growth rates to countries, international organizations and to men or women of affairs. Therefore in our recent uses of consistentization we have not modified country growth rates, but only the different benchmark estimates.

Since Ward and Devereux are not in a position to replace the time series of Feinstein (1972) and Kendrick (1961), consistency requires modification of their multiple benchmarks to bring them back into line with the time series projections. In fact, this would merely involve going back to the original US and UK price data, which Ward and Devereux (2003: 831) modify to allow for rural–urban price differences. As Broadberry

---

[2] $118/78 = 151.3\%$.

and Irwin (2006) show, using the unadjusted price data for an 1850 benchmark yields a benchmark result very close to the time series projection.

There exists a large body of work which finds a higher price level in the United States, including the UK Board of Trade (1908, 1911, 1913c), Allen (1994) and Williamson (1995). There is also widespread acceptance that, contrary to the claims of Ward and Devereux (2003: 835), the US/UK real exchange rate (or relative price level) was stationary during the nineteenth century (Friedman and Schwartz, 1982; Lothian and Taylor, 1996; US Congress, 1893: 15–16, 335). Note further that if Ward and Devereux's (2003) rural–urban price adjustment were valid it would also require changes to the level of nominal income, leaving real income unchanged, since nineteenth-century nominal GDP data were to a large extent obtained by reflating volumes, rather than real GDP data being obtained by deflating nominal values (Broadberry, 2003).

If the aggregate pattern of per capita income and labour productivity suggested by Ward and Devereux (2003) is incorrect, so must be the sectoral pattern set out in Ward and Devereux (2004: 888). One problem here is that these data cannot really be considered to be benchmark estimates, since they include time series projections from Broadberry (1998) for a number of sectors. Where Ward and Devereux (2004) do provide new estimates, there is gross inconsistency between the pattern of comparative productivity implied by the multiple benchmarks and the productivity growth rates in the two countries obtained from historical national accounting sources. Thus, in 'trade' (or distribution), Ward and Devereux (2004: 888) claim that US labour productivity rose from 141% of the UK level in 1870 to 159% by 1910, which would require labour productivity in the United States to be growing just 0.3% per annum faster than in the United Kingdom. However, standard sources from Kendrick (1961) and Feinstein (1972) show labour productivity in the United States to be growing 1.5% per annum faster than in the United Kingdom between these years.

The biggest difference, however, concerns agriculture, where Ward and Devereux (2004: 880–1) argue for a huge two-to-one US output per worker advantage in the nineteenth century. Broadberry and Irwin (2006) show how their finding of broad equality in agricultural output per worker fits into the existing literatures on both UK performance and US performance. One important point to be borne in mind here is that equal output per worker implies an advantage in US output per hour worked of the order of two to one in agriculture. This is because the number of full-time equivalent man-hours per gainful worker in US agriculture was little more than half the level in the rest of the economy. As David (1996) notes, this helps to explain the coexistence of separate literatures emphasising, on the one hand, how agriculture was a backward sector from which surplus labour needed to be extracted to effect development and, on the other hand, how land abundance in the United States led to labour shortages in industry by creating a high opportunity cost for labour outside agriculture.

It should also be noted that the Broadberry and Irwin (2006) view is consistent with the existing body of literature on international comparisons of output per worker in agriculture, including the widely accepted work of Clark (1951), Hayami and Ruttan (1971) and Yamada and Ruttan (1980). For example, Yamada and Ruttan (1980, table 10.A, 5–6) have the US relative output per worker in agriculture as 92 in 1910, quite close to the 108.9 relative output per worker benchmark in Broadberry (1997b). This is significantly different from Ward and Devereaux's (2004: 880) benchmark of 192 in that year. The Broadberry and Irwin (2006) view of broad equality in US and UK agricultural output per worker is also endorsed in the recent study by Federico and Malanima (2004). An important point to bear in mind is that, although the United States had a favourable land/labour ratio, this was offset by low land productivity (Yamada and Ruttan, 1980: 516–17). Thus, for example, wheat yields have been estimated within the range of 13 to 15 bushels per acre in the United States during the nineteenth century, compared with 30 to 50 bushels per acre in England and Wales (US Department of Commerce, 1975, series K448; Afton and Turner, 2000: 1788).

4.3   Comparative Germany/UK labour productivity levels

4.3.1   Time series projections

The British time series data are taken from the same sources as for the US/UK comparison. For Germany, the basic time series are also taken from standard historical national accounts sources, primarily Hoffmann (1965), updated from 1959 using the official national accounts of the Federal Republic of Germany. Boundary changes have been treated as in Hoffmann (1965) and Feinstein (1972). Thus, for the United Kingdom, overlapping estimates for 1920 including and excluding the Irish Republic are spliced together, while, for Germany, output and employment both vary with the changing territories of the Reich and the Federal Republic. Details are given in appendix 4.1. It should be noted that the discontinuities of labour productivity are much smaller than the discontinuities of output and employment considered separately. Furthermore, it is clear that, despite the geographical and political discontinuities, there is a fundamental economic continuity in the German territories considered here, which were perceived as a major force in international trade.

For Germany, as with the case of Britain (discussed above), deviations from the standard sources were kept to a minimum, but some changes have been made to incorporate new information and to iron out inconsistencies. For German agriculture, I have used Hoffmann's (1965) real gross output series through to 1959, as there seem to be serious problems with the value-added data (Fremdling, 1988; O'Brien and Prados de la Escosura, 1992). Given the changes in the component series for the two countries, I have reported in table 4.4 a 'total of above' series, where new implicit aggregate GDP and employment series have been constructed. The discrepancies between the 'total of above' and the original 'aggregate GDP' series shown in table 4.4 are within the usual margins of error for this kind of work. As in the US/UK case, the differences between the two series should be regarded as residual error and the aggregates from the original sources are to be preferred.

The choice of sectors is much as in the US/UK case, with the important difference that the German sources do not allow a separation between distribution and finance before 1960. For the sake of consistency, I have kept them together for the whole sample period.

4.3.2 Benchmark cross-checks

The time series projections in table 4.4 depend on benchmarks for comparative productivity levels in each sector in 1935. These estimates are provided in table 4.5, together with additional benchmarks for other years, which can be used to provide cross-checks on the time series projections. Detailed sources of the benchmarks are given in appendix 4.3. The 1935 benchmark was constructed by Broadberry (1997c) following the method of Rostas (1948), and estimates for some sectors are available for other years. As in the US/UK case, there is a good deal of approximation in these estimates. Nevertheless, the broad picture is again reassuring, with tables 4.4 and 4.5 telling the same basic story.

4.3.3 Sectoral aspects of the German overtaking

By far the biggest part of the industrial sector has been manufacturing throughout the period 1870–1990 in both Britain and Germany, as can be seen from the employment shares in table 4.3. Since comparative

Table 4.4 Time series projections of comparative Germany/UK labour productivity levels by sector (UK = 100)

	1871	1881	1891	1901	1911	1925	1929	1935	1950	1960	1968	1973	1979	1990
Agriculture	55.7	54.7	53.7	67.2	67.3	53.8	56.9	57.2	41.2	47.8	48.6	50.8	65.5	75.4
Mineral extraction	55.9	72.1	80.9	86.4	101.2	106.8	116.4	123.6	92.4	132.1	135.3	138.1	45.1	17.5
Manufacturing	92.6	88.7	94.0	98.8	119.3	95.2	104.7	102.0	96.0	114.8	120.0	118.6	140.3	108.3
Construction	76.1	113.7	90.1	100.3	117.7	65.7	50.2	70.6	84.2	102.0	105.5	117.7	130.2	117.9
Utilities	31.3	49.9	64.2	93.0	103.8	146.2	158.6	144.0	120.6	151.2	146.7	139.2	164.5	130.0
Transport and communications	74.4	97.4	113.5	150.0	166.8	140.0	151.2	132.4	122.0	117.0	130.0	119.5	135.0	125.7
Distribution and finance	70.7	38.6	45.9	49.7	52.5	47.1	50.3	54.3	50.7	64.2	75.4	88.0	106.4	111.2
Professional and personal services	89.7	83.4	77.0	76.6	76.3	86.7	99.8	105.6	94.2	85.7	101.3	98.4	103.1	120.5
Government	97.8	95.5	94.6	104.1	98.2	100.1	100.0	100.0	96.9	111.8	111.0	113.3	109.9	108.6
Total of above	60.8	57.4	60.7	67.9	74.6	66.6	73.0	75.7	71.5	95.0	105.5	110.1	126.1	120.4
Aggregate GDP	59.5	57.3	60.5	68.4	75.5	69.0	74.1	75.7	74.4	94.5	107.1	114.0	126.5	125.4

Note:
Time series projections of output per person engaged from 1935 benchmarks.

Source: See text and appendix 4.1.

Table 4.5 *Benchmark estimates of comparative Germany/UK labour productivity levels by sector (UK = 100)*

	1910	1935	1968	1973	1990
Agriculture	57.0	57.2		74.0	
Mineral extraction	81.7	123.6	172.8		
Manufacturing		102.0	130.4		112.7
Construction		70.6	161.0		
Utilities		144.0		189.2	
Transport and communications		132.4	121.0		
Distribution and finance		54.3			
Professional and personal services		105.6			
Government	100.0	100.0	100.0	100.0	100.0
Whole economy		75.7			

Source: See text and appendix 4.3.

labour productivity in manufacturing has been stationary, with fluctuations around broad equality, this limits the extent to which industry can be seen as responsible for the changing Germany/UK comparative labour productivity position at the whole-economy level. In construction, there have been long swings, as in the US/UK case, with British labour productivity higher when a British building boom coincided with a German building slump, and with German labour productivity higher when a British building slump coincided with a German building boom. In mineral extraction, although the comparative Germany/UK labour productivity ratio trended upwards to 1973, the subsequent British exploitation of North Sea oil and the rundown of the British deep-mined coal industry led to a dramatic reversal of this trend. In the relatively small utilities sector, the Germany/UK labour productivity ratio trended upwards until 1979, after which the British exploitation of North Sea gas reversed the trend.

As in the US/UK case, the changing pattern of comparative labour productivity performance in the aggregate economy mirrors the pattern in services. Also, this pattern in services reflects real changes in the market service sectors. The largest service sector for much of the period was distribution and finance, and here the German overtaking occurred only in the 1970s. In transport and communications, the big German gains occurred before World War I, as a result of high labour productivity on the railways. With the subsequent decline in importance of the railways, Britain narrowed the labour productivity gap in transport and communications. In professional and personal services, the upward trend in the comparative Germany/UK labour productivity level may well be dampened by the use of employment as a proxy for output in parts of this sector.

In agriculture, labour productivity in Germany remained substantially lower than in Britain throughout the period 1870–1990. Although the gap narrowed during peacetime periods, the two world wars led to setbacks for Germany. Of more significance for Anglo-German productivity differences at the aggregate level were the substantial differences in the shares of the labour force devoted to agriculture in the two countries. Whereas in the 1870s Germany still had nearly a half of its labour force in agriculture, in Britain the share was less than a quarter. Given the lower level of value added per employee in agriculture, the later structural shift out of agriculture contributed to the German catching up and overtaking of Britain. In Germany agriculture still accounted for about a quarter of employment as late as 1950, so that agricultural decline continued to play a significant part in German catching up well into the period after World War II (Kindleberger, 1967; Temin, 2002).

It is worth reflecting on the consequences of the late retention of such a large share of the labour force in German agriculture for overall productivity performance. In late nineteenth-century Germany, protection was designed to slow down the decline of agriculture and accelerate the development of heavy industry. First, there was the direct implication for agricultural productivity. Whereas, in free trade Britain, the 'grain invasion' from the New World ensured that the agriculture that remained was highly productive and able to compete internationally, in protectionist Germany the alliance of 'rye and iron' allowed the survival of low-productivity agriculture. Second, however, there was an indirect effect via the under-development of services. This follows from the fact that the protectionist policies aimed to promote heavy industry as well as to slow down agricultural decline, which meant that – proportionally, at least – services had to lose out. This necessarily limited the extent of the domestic market for services, and the German service sector was much less geared towards overseas markets than the British service sector. Low levels of specialisation led to low levels of productivity in German services.

4.3.4 Methodological considerations

For a complete sectoral breakdown of the German historical national accounts, there is currently no practical alternative to the data of Hoffmann (1965). However, these data have been subjected to much criticism over the years, which it is helpful to review here (Fremdling,

1988, 1995; Ritschl, 2002, 2004a; Spoerer, 1997; Ritschl and Spoerer, 1997; Fremdling and Stäglin, 2003). As in the US/UK comparison, benchmark estimates can be used to serve as a check on the time series projections for the Germany/UK comparison.

Ritschl (2004a, 2004b) argues that Hoffmann's (1965) series for real output are flawed, particularly for industry and agriculture. It is interesting to note, however, that his use of alternative output series from Wagenführ (1933) and von der Decken and Wagenführ (1935) does not lead to a major change in the path of aggregate output. Rather, it leads to offsetting changes in the paths of agricultural and industrial production. The key finding of Ritschl (2004a) is that Wagenführ's (1933) index of industrial production grew more slowly than Hoffmann's (1965) index before World War II, while Ritschl (2004b) argues that von der Decken and Wagenführ's (1935) measure of agricultural output grew more rapidly than Hoffmann's. Hence, projecting backwards from 1935, Ritschl (2004b) finds for the period before World War I a larger German labour productivity lead in industry and an even more backward German agricultural sector. This has the effect, then, of confirming the basic sectoral patterns of Anglo-German comparative labour productivity levels established by Broadberry (1997c), but in a more exaggerated fashion.

Hence, for example, whereas Broadberry (1997c: 251) reports a figure of 67.3 for the comparative Germany/UK labour productivity level in agriculture in 1911, Ritschl (2004b) reports a value of 53.7. Offsetting this, however, in manufacturing, whereas Broadberry (1997c: 251) reports a comparative Germany/UK labour productivity level of 119.3, Ritschl (2004b) finds a value of 137.3. The problem with this is that the exaggerated German labour productivity lead in manufacturing prior to World War I would be very hard to square with what is known about nominal incomes in industry. For example, Fremdling (1991) finds industrial value added per employee in Germany to be lower than in Britain just before World War I when converted to a common currency using a PPP-adjusted price ratio. It is likely that Hoffmann's (1965) estimates of capital income, used by Fremdling (1991), are too low, as indeed Fremdling (1988: 348-9) himself suggests. Hence, Fremdling and Stäglin (2003) accept that the Fremdling (1991) estimates understate Germany's industrial labour productivity level compared with Britain. However, whereas it is possible to see how correcting for this could be consistent with a small German labour productivity advantage in manufacturing before World War I, it is difficult to see how it could possibly be consistent with a German productivity lead of the order of magnitude suggested by Ritschl (2004b). A recent new benchmark

Table 4.6 *Growth rates of labour productivity, 1869–1990 (% per annum)*

A. United Kingdom

	1871–1911	1911–1950	1950–1990	1871–1990
Agriculture	0.6	1.8	4.4	2.3
Industry	0.9	1.4	3.2	1.9
Services	0.4	0.0	1.2	0.6
Whole economy	0.8	0.7	1.9	1.2

B. United States

	1869–1909	1909–1950	1950–1990	1869–1990
Agriculture	1.0	2.1	4.9	2.1
Industry	1.5	2.1	2.1	1.9
Services	1.1	0.7	1.0	0.9
Whole economy	1.5	1.6	1.3	1.4

C. Germany

	1871–1911	1925–1937	1950–1990
Agriculture	1.0	3.2	5.9
Industry	1.7	2.6	3.7
Services	0.9	1.1	2.4
Whole economy	1.4	2.2	3.2

Source: Appendix 4.1.

estimate by Broadberry and Burhop (2005) for 1907 confirms that Germany had a small labour productivity advantage over Britain before World War I, in line with the time series projections using the Hoffmann (1965) data.

4.4 Growth rates of labour productivity

The data in tables 4.1 to 4.5 work in terms of comparative levels of labour productivity. However, this does not on its own allow a distinction between a situation of relative and absolute economic decline. In other words, it is possible for Britain to have fallen behind the United States either because productivity growth is slower in Britain (but still positive) or because of an absolute decline in British productivity. Having presented the time series data in appendix 4.1, then, it is natural to proceed to an analysis of productivity growth to complement the focus on comparative productivity levels. Table 4.6 provides the labour

Table 4.7 *GDP per capita, 1870–1992 (dollars of 1990 purchasing power)*

	United Kingdom	United States	France	India	China	Argentina
1870	3,263	2,457	1,858	558	523	1,311
1900	4,593	4,096	2,849	625	652	2,756
1913	5,032	5,307	3,452	663	688	3,797
1950	6,847	9,573	5,221	597	614	4,987
1973	11,992	16,607	12,940	853	1,186	7,970
1992	15,738	21,558	17,959	1,348	3,098	7,616

Source: Derived from Maddison (1995: 23–4).

productivity growth rates for Britain, the United States and Germany over the period 1869–1990 and selected sub-periods. Labour productivity growth has been positive in Britain as well as in the United States and Germany in all major sectors, including services.

This is helpful in reminding us that, although Britain has undoubtedly undergone a relative economic decline since the mid-nineteenth century, this has occurred within the context of growth. Indeed, in absolute terms, and even relative to most countries, there can be little doubt that Britain has been very successful in raising productivity and living standards throughout the period under review. Nevertheless, Germany and the United States have been even more successful, and Britain has been overtaken. Table 4.7 presents data on levels of per capita income for the United Kingdom and a selection of other countries, expressed in dollars of 1990 purchasing power. The countries compared with Britain are similar to those examined by McCloskey (1990: 47). It is clear that, despite relative decline, Britain has remained a part of the rich world, represented here by the United States and France. The British economy has continued to deliver living standards massively above those experienced in poor countries such as India and China, while Britain has managed to avoid relative decline on the scale of Argentina.

4.5 Conclusions

This chapter provides a detailed sectoral database for the evaluation of comparative economic performance in Britain, the United States and Germany during the period 1870–1990. Using data on comparative labour productivity levels, the text emphasises the role of services in the US and German overtaking of Britain. The main time series of output and employment for each country are presented in appendix 4.1, along with a detailed discussion of sources and a presentation of sectoral growth rate data. Appendices 4.2 and 4.3 provide details on the derivation of the benchmark estimates of comparative labour productivity, which are used to provide cross-sectional checks on the time series extrapolations. The growth rate data provide a useful reminder that Britain's economic decline over this period was only relative, and that Britain has clearly remained a part of the rich world.

Appendix 4.1: Source and methods for sectoral time series

A. United States

1. **Output by sector**
   1869–1948: Kendrick (1961).
   1948–1979: US Department of Commerce (1983).
   1979–1990: US Department of Commerce (*Survey of Current Business*, various issues).
   Note that, although the Department of Commerce estimates are available at an aggregate level from 1929, the disaggregated figures are only available from 1947.

2. **Employment by sector**
   1869–1948: Kendrick (1961).
   1948–1979: US Department of Commerce (1983).
   1979–1990: US Department of Commerce (*Statistical Abstract of the United States*, various issues); OECD (*Labour Force Statistics*, various issues).

3. **Exceptions**
   Whole economy: output 1869–1889 from Balke and Gordon (1989).
   Agriculture: output pre-1950 real gross output rather than real net output, farm segment only; output post-1950 from Food and Agriculture Organisation (*FAO Yearbook*, various issues).
   Manufacturing: post-1950 output and employment from Broadberry (1993).
   Finance and services: output 1869–1889 assumed to move in line with employment; this is preferred to Kendrick's estimate obtained as a residual, which would not be consistent with Balke and Gordon's (1989) aggregate series.

B. United Kingdom

1. **Output by sector**
   1871–1948: Feinstein (1972).

1948–1990: UK Central Statistical Office (*National Income and Expenditure*, various issues).

2. **Employment by sector**

   1871–1965: Feinstein (1972), with links across 1911–1921 from Mitchell (1988).

   1965–1990: UK Central Statistical Office (*Annual Abstract of Statistics*, various issues); OECD (*Labour Force Statistics*, various issues). Note that series in the *Annual Abstract of Statistics* do not provide a sectoral breakdown of self-employment.

3. **Exceptions**

   Construction: output 1871–1913 is a new construction index compiled by Feinstein and Hilditch as part of a new study of the pre-1913 national accounts. This index is spliced to the post-1920 index in Feinstein (1972) using the 1907–1924 bridge from Lomax (1959), which is based on production census data.

   Manufacturing: post-1950 output and employment from Broadberry (1993).

4. **Boundary changes**

   The procedures of Feinstein (1972) have been followed, with estimates including Southern Ireland before 1920 and excluding Southern Ireland from 1920, and with an overlap in 1920.

C. Germany

1. **Output by sector**

   1871–1959: Hoffmann (1965).

   1959–1985: Statistisches Bundesamt (1991).

2. **Employment by sector**

   1871–1959: Hoffmann (1965). Employment in 1871 obtained by interpolation for construction, utilities, and distribution and finance.

   1959–1985: Statistisches Bundesamt (1991, 1988); OECD (*Labour Force Statistics*, various issues).

3. **Exceptions**

   Agriculture: output pre-1959 real gross output rather than value added, from Hoffmann (1965).

4. **Boundary changes**

   I have followed the procedure of Hoffmann (1965: 2), who presents figures for both output and employment corresponding to the following territories: 1871–1917, the territories of the German Reich, including Alsace-Lorraine; 1918–1944, the territories of the German Reich excluding Austria and the Sudetenland, but from 1934 including the Saar; 1945–1959, the territories of the German Federal

Table A4.1 US real output by sector (1929 = 100)

	Agri-culture	Mineral extraction	Manu-facture	Constr-uction	Utilities	Total industry	Transport and commun-ications	Distrib-ution	Finance and other services	Govern-ment	Total services	Whole economy
1869	28.9	5.1	7.1	11.8	0.58	7.2	4.0	7.6	9.3	16.5	8.7	10.2
1879	45.2	9.8	10.2	18.4	1.16	10.7	8.1	15.9	10.9	22.3	13.1	16.1
1889	57.2	18.7	18.3	33.4	2.26	19.4	17.7	23.9	17.9	26.1	20.4	23.7
1899	72.5	31.3	27.5	43.5	4.1	28.5	31.6	36.2	33.6	35.8	34.2	36.1
1909	78.8	55.3	43.4	75.7	13.9	46.8	52.1	53.3	56.0	50.3	54.0	54.0
1919	87.3	68.7	61.0	56.3	42.6	59.9	77.1	66.3	71.7	119.7	76.1	71.0
1929	100.0	100.0	100.0	100.0	100.0	100.0	100.0	100.0	100.0	100.0	100.0	100.0
1937	102.4	95.7	103.3	61.4	130.2	98.9	100.8	104.2	89.2	182.2	105.1	105.0
1950	141.9	134.0	201.1	147.0	344.1	195.9	192.6	188.2	141.4	238.1	175.0	180.6
1960	178.1	173.4	304.2	239.8	751.0	301.4	225.8	253.6	221.3	338.1	247.5	249.5
1968	201.3	229.6	488.7	279.6	1192.6	461.0	326.0	366.6	318.4	468.0	354.7	354.2
1973	217.8	245.6	551.8	250.5	1621.1	515.8	407.8	451.6	394.9	483.2	428.1	409.0
1979	254.7	239.4	574.2	255.0	1802.9	536.9	509.9	528.8	496.0	529.3	515.6	473.1
1985	275.0	277.3	577.7	266.1	1883.5	548.1	607.8	692.0	589.7	560.0	627.0	533.3
1990	306.7	305.6	661.8	267.7	2239.4	622.7	743.5	794.8	683.9	617.4	725.1	610.3

Table A4.2 US employment by sector (1929 = 100)

	Agriculture	Mineral extraction	Manu-facture	Constr-uction	Utilities	Total industry	Transport and communications	Distribution	Finance and other services	Govern-ment	Total services	Whole economy
1869	58.2	14.3	19.9	24.2	6.88	20.2	14.8	12.8	16.7	16.5	14.1	25.0
1879	77.1	26.6	26.6	27.0	8.44	27.2	20.0	17.1	19.6	22.3	19.4	32.8
1889	90.4	48.0	38.3	40.3	10.2	42.1	37.5	29.1	32.3	26.1	30.1	45.4
1899	99.4	62.3	50.8	55.0	17.7	52.4	50.8	40.0	42.9	35.8	40.9	56.4
1909	105.6	102.1	72.7	72.9	36.4	74.9	74.9	55.9	59.8	50.3	58.3	73.1
1919	103.8	108.3	100.3	63.4	57.9	94.6	97.6	71.6	65.9	119.7	79.2	88.9
1929	100.0	100.0	100.0	100.0	100.0	100.0	100.0	100.0	100.0	100.0	100.0	100.0
1937	93.8	91.1	101.2	75.5	96.9	96.1	79.6	104.4	98.7	182.2	107.5	101.3
1950	78.3	88.7	143.5	145.1	114.0	139.8	100.6	144.4	122.1	243.9	142.1	128.3
1960	54.3	67.3	162.9	153.6	127.7	149.8	97.4	170.2	164.4	340.8	179.0	146.0
1968	37.5	58.2	189.7	178.0	136.8	174.2	105.0	199.3	213.1	464.0	225.8	174.4
1973	34.7	60.5	192.8	211.8	152.8	182.1	112.4	231.1	250.3	482.4	253.3	190.5
1979	32.0	90.2	204.4	246.1	167.8	197.8	125.5	278.9	311.9	526.1	299.5	218.6
1985	26.5	87.6	182.6	258.6	188.6	188.2	127.5	315.2	387.4	559.0	346.4	237.5
1990	23.5	68.1	181.9	282.4	197.6	191.2	141.1	351.5	470.3	608.1	397.5	264.1

Table A4.3 UK real output by sector (1929 = 100)

	Agriculture	Mineral extraction	Manu-facture	Constr-uction	Utilities	Total industry	Transport and communications	Distrib-ution	Finance and other services	Govern-ment	Total services	Whole economy
1871	93.7	46.3	34.6	42.4	6.8	34.2	26.0	41.2	57.2	36.7	45.3	42.3
1881	89.8	59.4	41.6	51.2	11.1	42.0	33.0	49.6	71.4	42.3	55.9	50.1
1891	85.6	70.6	51.2	53.3	17.5	50.4	43.6	61.4	86.9	53.6	69.1	60.1
1901	87.3	81.9	62.1	77.6	27.1	63.1	55.3	74.4	98.3	79.0	82.2	72.1
1911	91.2	101.5	72.6	67.7	46.0	71.9	70.3	86.5	119.1	87.5	98.5	83.6
1920	83.5	86.9	81.7	46.5	69.1	78.0	74.8	91.2	95.6	146.2	95.2	87.0
1929	100.0	100.0	100.0	100.0	100.0	100.0	100.0	100.0	100.0	100.0	100.0	100.0
1937	101.3	96.2	132.9	126.0	159.3	130.0	108.4	117.4	112.3	117.0	113.4	119.5
1950	124.6	81.1	177.1	110.3	284.2	164.8	146.4	118.1	111.2	182.4	125.0	140.6
1960	158.8	75.7	296.4	142.1	465.7	250.8	181.1	152.1	143.7	171.8	152.8	180.7
1968	191.2	65.0	395.1	188.3	718.5	327.1	221.5	179.6	182.2	187.7	185.9	224.8
1973	226.6	54.0	482.4	194.5	926.6	383.2	276.9	208.9	213.5	202.3	217.5	258.4
1979	223.1	145.1	457.1	174.7	1070.7	392.9	305.1	209.0	249.4	212.7	240.7	276.4
1985	290.5	188.7	412.2	185.5	1152.6	390.5	330.9	226.1	304.9	210.6	275.7	297.5
1990	324.9	149.1	488.0	232.1	1344.0	439.3	422.9	271.5	380.7	217.0	335.8	345.7

Table A4.4 UK employment by sector (1929 = 100)

	Agriculture	Mineral extraction	Manufacture	Construction	Utilities	Total industry	Transport and communications	Distribution	Finance and other services	Government	Total services	Whole economy
1871	149.5	53.8	70.8	62.1	13.4	66.2	45.7	38.1	64.9	42.2	52.0	66.8
1881	137.0	64.3	74.1	78.0	17.9	71.8	51.7	47.2	73.9	46.2	60.0	70.2
1891	126.0	79.4	83.1	79.0	26.8	80.6	66.7	59.5	82.2	55.3	70.8	77.7
1901	116.0	96.5	90.2	102.5	44.6	91.0	87.1	72.2	88.6	88.4	84.3	87.3
1911	115.0	122.0	98.6	96.8	53.6	99.8	94.9	89.3	97.6	84.3	94.2	95.6
1920	115.9	125.6	110.5	91.7	82.6	109.5	102.5	88.1	89.7	144.0	97.2	104.2
1929	100.0	100.0	100.0	100.0	100.0	100.0	100.0	100.0	100.0	100.0	100.0	100.0
1937	87.4	85.4	108.5	124.9	126.8	108.1	104.8	115.6	117.7	117.7	114.8	109.7
1950	79.0	81.2	132.8	144.6	160.7	128.6	115.1	100.5	105.5	218.4	117.9	119.6
1960	67.6	73.0	154.3	160.3	169.7	140.1	107.6	119.9	118.2	192.0	125.5	127.4
1968	50.9	46.4	149.0	183.3	188.4	137.7	103.8	118.5	145.8	195.4	136.3	130.4
1973	43.2	35.7	145.0	180.3	153.6	130.5	100.0	131.2	157.4	206.7	145.8	131.5
1979	39.9	34.4	131.9	163.5	155.4	120.9	98.2	139.1	182.8	205.3	158.2	133.3
1985	37.5	28.0	95.1	147.9	143.3	97.0	88.4	149.8	204.5	201.3	168.5	128.2
1990	34.3	15.9	94.0	180.3	137.6	98.6	93.8	163.5	260.6	200.4	196.7	142.8

Table A4.5 German real output by sector (1929 = 100)

	Agriculture	Mineral extraction	Manufacture	Construction	Utilities	Total industry	Transport and communications	Distribution and finance	Professional and personal services	Government	Total services	Whole economy
1871	55.8	15.3	18.2	26.2	0.7	18.3	7.5	22.4	44.8	42.2	26.5	27.3
1881	64.5	25.7	23.4	37.8	1.6	24.5	13.9	27.0	48.8	49.4	31.8	33.8
1891	72.8	37.5	34.2	64.6	3.7	37.1	24.1	38.4	54.1	61.0	41.8	44.0
1901	92.8	56.5	48.6	88.4	9.8	52.7	41.7	57.1	61.7	76.4	57.6	60.5
1911	106.9	86.9	73.1	137.7	28.6	80.5	73.3	76.7	79.3	95.4	79.2	83.0
1925	85.2	80.7	84.7	87.0	74.2	84.3	80.9	85.6	84.7	84.5	84.3	86.2
1929	100.0	100.0	100.0	100.0	100.0	100.0	100.0	100.0	100.0	100.0	100.0	100.0
1935	109.5	86.7	102.3	120.3	108.4	103.7	82.2	95.9	104.9	109.2	96.7	100.5
1937	115.3	111.5	122.3	145.7	137.5	125.1	96.3	110.1	113.8	118.3	109.1	117.6
1950	60.5	66.7	77.8	92.3	114.9	80.3	74.9	72.1	65.8	93.9	74.7	74.8
1960	75.9	105.8	223.2	206.5	284.6	205.3	120.7	151.2	89.8	136.1	144.8	144.1
1968	87.1	83.0	317.7	266.2	460.6	277.8	162.2	223.7	114.4	193.9	201.5	196.8
1973	97.9	75.9	412.1	323.0	750.7	355.0	207.9	289.4	142.6	242.6	255.9	250.3
1979	97.3	60.4	461.5	311.5	1033.3	389.4	266.2	356.4	181.4	285.4	316.0	287.5
1985	108.3	51.6	468.5	280.6	1102.6	388.8	310.8	395.5	223.9	310.6	362.0	306.7
1990	129.4	41.5	528.9	310.9	1274.2	435.9	377.6	471.3	287.4	328.3	432.3	356.4

Table A4.6 German employment by sector (1929 = 100)

	Agriculture	Mineral extraction	Manufacture	Construction	Utilities	Total industry	Transport and communications	Distribution and finance	Professional and personal services	Government	Total services	Whole economy
1871	90.8	37.0	42.1	25.3	7.0	37.5	26.8	12.7	70.6	49.6	39.9	53.7
1881	102.2	44.9	49.2	25.4	8.2	43.4	33.8	29.9	73.5	56.5	45.8	61.2
1891	101.6	60.7	61.8	53.3	14.0	58.0	49.1	38.4	79.3	66.5	54.7	69.7
1901	104.4	89.7	74.8	58.4	27.5	70.3	66.2	53.7	84.5	82.1	67.6	79.4
1911	113.8	120.2	87.1	83.9	50.9	85.0	89.7	72.9	98.0	93.6	84.9	93.1
1925	103.3	108.0	98.8	76.8	88.9	95.9	94.4	85.6	95.6	82.9	89.2	96.2
1929	100.0	100.0	100.0	100.0	100.0	100.0	100.0	100.0	100.0	100.0	100.0	100.0
1935	96.0	76.3	89.7	87.4	105.3	88.8	93.7	89.8	102.9	118.8	94.7	92.7
1937	95.8	88.2	104.6	107.1	121.1	104.3	103.3	96.4	106.1	136.1	101.7	101.0
1950	52.9	84.1	63.6	72.1	85.4	66.3	73.0	59.9	62.9	116.0	69.7	63.4
1960	38.4	89.9	106.0	114.6	108.8	94.5	92.7	91.0	82.9	136.1	95.4	79.7
1968	27.1	51.0	104.5	123.2	130.6	93.2	88.4	95.3	88.6	181.8	104.9	79.0
1973	20.9	42.3	109.3	127.6	141.8	96.9	95.0	102.4	99.7	218.8	117.6	82.8
1979	15.1	37.0	99.4	112.3	144.6	87.6	96.0	104.1	120.7	250.6	129.7	81.2
1985	12.8	35.7	93.0	100.4	152.4	81.7	94.6	104.4	140.9	267.1	138.4	81.0
1990	10.3	29.5	98.5	102.7	159.1	85.6	100.8	114.2	171.0	279.3	154.5	87.0

Table A4.7 *Growth rates of US real output by sector (% per annum)*

	1869–1909	1909–1950	1950–1990	1869–1990
Agriculture	2.5	1.4	1.9	2.0
Mineral extraction	6.1	2.2	2.1	3.4
Manufacturing	4.6	3.8	3.0	3.8
Construction	4.8	1.6	1.5	2.6
Utilities	8.3	8.1	4.7	7.1
Total industry	4.8	3.6	2.9	3.8
Transport and communications	6.6	3.2	3.4	4.4
Distribution	5.0	3.1	3.7	3.9
Finance and services	4.6	2.3	4.0	3.6
Government	2.8	3.9	2.4	3.0
Total services	4.7	2.9	3.6	3.7
Whole economy	4.2	3.0	3.1	3.4

Table A4.8 *Growth rates of US employment by sector (% per annum)*

	1869–1909	1909–1950	1950–1990	1869–1990
Agriculture	1.5	−0.7	−3.0	−0.1
Mineral extraction	5.0	−0.3	−0.7	1.3
Manufacturing	3.3	1.7	0.6	1.8
Construction	2.8	1.7	1.7	2.1
Utilities	4.3	2.8	1.4	2.8
Total industry	3.3	1.5	0.8	1.9
Transport and communications	4.1	0.7	0.8	1.9
Distribution	3.7	2.3	2.2	2.8
Finance and services	3.2	1.8	3.4	2.8
Government	2.8	3.9	2.3	3.0
Total services	3.6	2.2	2.6	2.8
Whole economy	2.7	1.4	1.8	2.0

Republic excluding West Berlin and the Saar; 1960–1990, the Federal Republic including West Berlin and the Saar. Note that the 1990 data exclude the new Länder from the former German Democratic Republic.

Table A4.9 *Growth rates of UK real output by sector (% per annum)*

	1871–1911	1911–1950	1950–1990	1871–1990
Agriculture	−0.1	0.8	2.3	1.1
Mineral extraction	2.0	−0.6	1.5	1.0
Manufacturing	1.9	2.3	2.6	2.2
Construction	1.2	1.3	1.9	1.4
Utilities	4.9	4.8	4.0	4.5
Total industry	1.9	2.1	2.5	2.2
Transport and communications	2.5	1.9	2.7	2.4
Distribution	1.9	0.8	2.1	1.6
Finance and services	1.9	−0.2	3.1	1.6
Government	2.2	1.9	0.4	1.5
Total services	1.9	0.6	2.5	1.7
Whole economy	1.7	1.3	2.3	1.8

Table A4.10 *Growth rates of UK employment by sector (% per annum)*

	1871–1911	1911–1950	1950–1990	1871–1990
Agriculture	−0.7	−1.0	−2.1	−1.2
Mineral extraction	2.1	−1.0	−4.0	−1.0
Manufacturing	0.8	0.8	−0.9	0.2
Construction	1.1	1.0	0.6	0.9
Utilities	3.5	2.9	−0.4	2.0
Total industry	1.0	0.7	−0.7	0.3
Transport and communications	1.8	0.5	−0.5	0.6
Distribution	2.2	0.3	1.2	1.2
Finance and services	1.0	0.2	2.3	1.2
Government	1.7	2.5	−0.2	1.3
Total services	1.5	0.6	1.3	1.1
Whole economy	0.9	0.6	0.4	0.6

Table A4.11 *Growth rates of German real output by sector (% per annum)*

	1871–1911	1925–1937	1950–1990
Agriculture	1.6	2.6	1.9
Mineral extraction	4.3	2.7	−1.2
Manufacturing	3.5	3.1	4.9
Construction	4.2	4.4	3.1
Utilities	9.7	5.3	6.2
Total industry	3.8	3.3	4.3
Transport and communications	5.9	1.5	4.1
Distribution and finance	3.1	2.1	4.8
Professional and personal services	1.4	2.5	3.8
Government	2.1	2.8	3.2
Total services	2.8	2.2	4.4
Whole economy	2.8	2.6	4.0

Table A4.12 *Growth rates of German employment by sector (% per annum)*

	1871–1911	1925–1937	1950–1990
Agriculture	0.6	−0.6	−4.0
Mineral extraction	3.0	−1.7	−2.6
Manufacturing	1.8	0.5	1.1
Construction	3.0	2.8	0.9
Utilities	5.1	2.6	1.6
Total industry	2.1	0.7	0.6
Transport and communications	3.1	0.8	0.8
Distribution and finance	4.5	1.0	1.6
Professional and personal services	0.8	0.9	2.5
Government	1.6	4.2	2.2
Total services	1.9	1.1	2.0
Whole economy	1.4	0.4	0.8

Appendix 4.2: Sources and methods for benchmark estimates of comparative US/UK labour productivity levels

A. **Reworking rostas' circa 1937 benchmark**

Except where stated below, I have used Rostas' (1948) figures for individual industries, taking the geometric mean of the total calculated using both British and American employment weights. Wherever possible, output and employment are taken from the same source, and can thus be relied on as an indicator of labour productivity.

1. **Agriculture, forestry and fishing**
   Rostas' separate figures for farming and fishing have been used, weighted by employment for the sector total.
2. **Mining**
   Separate figures for coal and for iron ore have been obtained from the UK Board of Trade (1938) and the US Department of Commerce (1975).

	Tons per employee
US coal	670.1
UK coal	287.0
US iron ore	2,038
UK iron ore	1,303

3. **Manufacturing**
   Figures from Broadberry (1993), based on an employment-weighted average of Rostas' figures for 1937 in the United States compared with 1935 in the United Kingdom, with a cyclical adjustment onto a 1937 basis at the aggregate level.
4. **Construction**
   Number of houses built per employee in 1935. For the United Kingdom, the number of houses built from Mitchell (1988: 390) and the value of housing investment from Feinstein (1972: table 39) are related to the total value of construction work and employment from the UK Board of Trade (1938). For the United States, the number of houses and construction costs from the US Department

of Commerce (1966) are related to expenditure for new construction and employment in construction from the US Department of Commerce (1975).

	Houses per Employee
United States	0.984
United Kingdom	0.913

5. **Utilities**
   Rostas' figures for electricity, manufactured gas and total gas (manufactured plus natural) are combined using employment weights.

6. **Transport and communications**
   Rostas' figures for railways, other transport and communications (post, telegraph and telephone) are combined using employment weights. Note that Rostas' transport figures allowing for distances are used, which raises the US productivity lead considerably. Geographical factors thus play a large role in the American productivity lead in this sector.

7. **Distribution**
   The inverse of distribution employees per 100 of population is used as a crude indicator of labour productivity, following the suggestion of Rostas (1948: 87). British figures for 1937 from Feinstein (1972), US figures for 1940 from Carson (1949).

	Distribution employees per 100 of total population
United States	5.45
United Kingdom	6.53

8. **Finance and services**
   For finance I follow Pilat (1994: 250) in taking the ratio of the money supply to national income as a measure of the degree of financial intermediation. M_2 and net national product (NNP) for the United Kingdom and the United States are taken from Friedman and Schwartz (1982). The relative quantity of financial services is obtained as the relative size of NNP (converted at the exchange rate) multiplied by the relative degree of financial intermediation. This is then related to the relative size of employment in the financial sector.

	United States	United Kingdom
Degree of financial intermediation (M_2/NNP)	0.608	0.712
Quantity of financial services (UK = 100)	284.8	100.0
Employment (thousands)	1,549	470

68   Measuring comparative productivity performance

Education sector productivity is measured by pupils per teacher in primary and secondary schools. British data from Mitchell (1988), American data from US Department of Commerce (1975).

	Pupils per teacher
United States	25.4
United Kingdom	26.1

9. **Government**

If output is measured by employment, as is usual in the system of national accounts, this implies equal labour productivity by construction in an international benchmark comparison.

10. **Aggregate economy**

Aggregation requires making an allowance for differences in income per employee between sectors, rather than simply aggregating with employment shares. Both the method of aggregation and the data on income per employee by sector are taken from Rostas (1948: 91).

B.   **A new benchmark for 1910**

I have constructed a complete benchmark for 1910, using as far as possible the sources and methods used by Rostas (1948), supplemented by the sources noted above. Below, I note some of the details.

1. **Agriculture**

For Britain, net output and employment are taken from the agricultural census of 1908, reported by the UK Ministry of Agriculture and Fisheries (1912). For the United States, net output and employment for the census year 1909 are taken from the US Department of Commerce (1975). The US figure is converted into pounds using a purchasing power parity based on seventeen commodities, with British prices from the agricultural census and American prices from Barger and Landsberg (1942). The commodities covered are: wheat, barley, oats, rye, buckwheat, potatoes, hops, hay, apples, pears, horses, cattle and calves, sheep and lambs, pigs, wool, milk, butter.

US net output per employee ($)	346.96
GB net output per employee (£)	77.60
PPP ($ per £)	4.12

2. **Mining**

Figures for coal and iron ore from the UK Board of Trade (1912) and from the US Department of Commerce (1913c).

US coal	Tons per employee
US coal	530.41
UK coal	325.84
US iron ore	915.6
UK iron ore	604.5

3. **Manufacturing**

Figures from Broadberry (1994), based on employment-weighted average of 29 industries from the UK Board of Trade (1912) and the US Department of Commerce (1913a), with a cyclical adjustment onto a common-year basis.

4. **Construction**

Same method as for 1937.

	Houses per employee
United States 1909	0.7406
United Kingdom 1907	0.7414

5. **Utilities**

British data for electricity and manufactured gas from the UK Board of Trade (1912). American output and employment data for the electricity industry in 1907 from the US Department of Commerce (*Statistical Abstract of the United States*, 1932: table 366). American data on manufactured gas from the US Department of Commerce (1913b).

Manufactured gas (m. cu. ft.):	
US output per employee	3.559
UK output per employee	3.077
Electricity (kWh):	
US output per employee	123,068
UK output per employee	63,317

6. **Transport and communications**

For railways, British data for 1911 are taken from Munby and Watson (1978) and American data for 1910 from the US Department of Commerce (1975). American freight traffic data are available in ton-miles and passenger traffic in passenger-miles. British freight data are only available in tons carried and passenger data in number of passengers carried. However, these have been multiplied by the average length of freight haul and the average length of passenger journey in 1920, the first year for which distance data are available. Allowing for distance in this way makes a considerable difference to freight traffic, since the shorter-haul journeys in Britain require a much greater terminal service component. Although Rostas also presents figures for transport that do not allow for distance, it is clear that, in a national accounting framework, sending goods further distances does constitute higher output.

	United States	United Kingdom
Freight ton-miles (millions)	255,017	29,841
Passenger-miles (millions)	32,338	15,372
Weighted average output (UK = 100)	698.5	100.0
Employment (persons)	1,670,000	515,130

For communications, employment in Britain cannot be obtained separately for the mail, telegraph and telephone sections of the Post Office. Hence, it is only possible to obtain a single figure for productivity in communications as a whole. British figures for 1913–14 are taken from the UK Board of Trade (*Statistical Abstract for the United Kingdom*, 1913 and 1924–37) while American figures for 1912 are from the US Department of Commerce (*Statistical Abstract of the United States*, 1943). Mail includes letters, parcels and money orders. Output of the communications sector as a whole is calculated using unit price weights for the three sectors.

	United States	United Kingdom
Items of mail (millions)	17,679	6,113.3
Telegrams (millions)	109.4	92.8
Telephone calls (millions)	13,736	834
Weighted output (UK = 100)	254.8	100.0
Employment (persons)	442,942	249,606

7. **Distribution**

Same method as for 1937: comparing distribution employees per 100 of the population for the United Kingdom in 1911 with the United States in 1910. The American figure has been adjusted upwards by 25% to allow for the greater extent of mail order business in the United States at this time (Barger, 1955: 35–6; Chandler, 1990: 59, 256, 259–61).

	Distribution employees per 100 of total population
United States	4.58
United Kingdom	5.43

8. **Finance and services**

For finance, same method as for 1937 benchmark: output data for both countries and UK employment data for 1911, with US employment data for 1910.

	United States	United Kingdom
Degree of financial intermediation (M_2/NNP)	0.483	0.532
Quantity of financial services (UK = 100)	269.7	100.0
Employment (persons)	517,000	230,000

For education, same method as for 1937 benchmark: data on pupils per teacher in primary and secondary schools for 1910 in both countries.

	Pupils per teacher
United States	24.5
United Kingdom	32.2

9. **Government**

As for 1937, comparative labour productivity in public administration and defence is assumed 100 by construction.

10. **Aggregate economy**

The method of Rostas (1948) is used, allowing for differences in income per employee between sectors. Data on income per employee by sector for the United States are taken from Martin (1939).

C. Other years 1870–1910

Benchmark estimates circa 1870 and 1890 are only available for agriculture, coal mining and finance. These estimates are inevitably rather speculative.

1. **Agriculture**

Estimates of national income per employee in farming are available for the United States from Gallman (1960) and for the United Kingdom from Feinstein (1972). PPPs based on wheat prices are from the US Department of Commerce (1975) and the UK Board of Trade (*Statistical Abstract for the United Kingdom*, various years).

	1869/71	1889/91
US value added per employee ($)	373.3	277.6
UK value added per employee (£)	72.4	69.3
PPP ($ per £)	4.47	4.165

2. **Coal mining**

British output and employment data for 1870 and 1890 from Mitchell (1988). American output data for 1870 and 1890 and employment data for 1890 from US Department of Commerce (1975). American employment data for 1870 from Borenstein (1954).

	Tons per employee
United States 1870	310.5
United Kingdom 1870	314.6
United States 1890	442.7
United Kingdom 1890	291.3

3. **Finance**

Same method as used for 1910 and 1937.

	United States	United kingdom
1869/71		
Degree of financial intermediation (M_2/NNP)	0.177	0.516
Quantity of financial services (UK = 100)	46.6	100.0
Employment (persons)	43,000	40,000
1889/91		
Degree of financial intermediation (M_2/NNP)	0.325	0.555
Quantity of financial services (UK = 100)	102.1	100.0
Employment (persons)	163,000	43,000

D. Other years, 1910–1950

The methods used for the 1937 and 1910 benchmarks have been applied to a number of other years where possible. A full benchmark for all sectors has also been calculated for 1950, drawing also on the work of Paige and Bombach (1959). Estimates for most sectors are also available circa 1924 and 1930 (UK production census years).

E. Other years, 1950–1990

The 1968 benchmark estimates have been taken mainly from the study by Smith et al. (1982). For utilities, however, I have replicated the Rostas (1948) approach based on quantity indicators, which has been used for the earlier estimates. The farming estimate is from Prasada Rao (1993).

The 1990 figures are from Prasada Rao (1993) for farming and from van Ark (1992) for manufacturing.

Appendix 4.3: Sources and methods for benchmark estimates of comparative Germany/UK productivity levels

A. A new benchmark for circa 1935

I have constructed a complete Anglo-German benchmark for 1935, using as far as possible the methods of Rostas (1948), who constructed the first industry-of-origin benchmark for Britain and the United States in the 1930s. Rostas also provided some Anglo-German estimates for a number of sectors, and I have built upon these estimates in constructing my economy-wide figure.

1. **Agriculture**
   Figures for income and employment in agriculture in 1937–38 converted at an agricultural sector PPP, all from Rostas (1948: 77–8).

2. **Mining**
   Separate figures for coal and iron ore production in 1935 have been obtained from the UK Board of Trade (1938) and the Statistisches Reichsamt (*Statistisches Jahrbuch für das Deutsche Reich*, 1937).

	Tons per employee
German coal	363.9
UK coal	290.4
German iron ore	507.6
UK iron ore	1,001.6

3. **Manufacturing**
   Figures for 1935 from Broadberry (1993), based on an employment-weighted average of Broadberry and Fremdling's (1990) estimates for manufacturing industries only.

4. **Construction**
   Germany/UK output ratio obtained by comparing the number of dwelling units built in 1935. This is compared with the ratio of construction employees. British and German output data from the Statistisches Reichsamt (*Statistisches Jahrbuch für das Deutsche Reich*, 1938: S.97*); British employment data from Feinstein (1972: table

59); German employment data from the Statistisches Reichsamt (1939, S.86).

	Germany	United Kingdom
Dwelling units (thousands)	263.8	350.3
Employees (thousands)	1,220	1,141

5. **Utilities**

British electricity and manufactured gas data for 1935 from the UK Board of Trade (1938). German output data for 1936 from the Statistisches Reichsamt (*Statistisches Jahrbuch für das Deutsche Reich*, various years) and employment data for 1936 from the Statistisches Reichsamt (1939).

Electricity (kWh):	
German output per employee	387,300
UK output per employee	222,300
Manufactured gas (m^3):	
German output per employee	69,897
UK output per employee	71,150

6. **Transport and communications**

For railways, German and UK passenger and freight data for 1937 from Rostas (1948: 238), weighted by average revenue.

	Germany	United Kingdom
Freight ton-miles (millions)	46,778	18,384
Passenger-miles (millions)	31,130	22,370
Weighted average output (UK = 100)	217.2	100.0
Employment (thousands)	704	580

For communications, German and British output data for 1935–36 are taken from the Statistisches Reichsamt (*Statistisches Jahrbuch für das Deutsche Reich*, 1938: S.116*–117*). German employment data are from the Statistisches Reichsamt (*Statistisches Jahrbuch für das Deutsche Reich*, 1937: S.197), while British employment data are from the UK Board of Trade (*Statistical Abstract for the United Kingdom*, 1924–38: table 242).

	Germany	United Kingdom
Items of mail (millions)	6,225.1	8,137.8
Telegrams (millions)	21.0	65.2
Telephone calls (millions)	2,435.7	1,821.7
Weighted output (UK = 100)	52.1	100.0
Employment (persons)	371,688	245,851

7. Distribution and finance

I follow Pilat (1994: 250) in taking the ratio of the money supply to national income as a measure of the degree of financial intermediation. Due to the absence of separate data on German distribution, I have assumed that differences in the degree of financial intermediation can be extended to the whole sector. Data on money (notes and coins, commercial and savings bank deposits) for 1935 from the League of Nations (1939: tables 125, 130, 131). NNP figures are taken from Friedman and Schwartz (1982: table 4.8) for the United Kingdom and from Hoffmann (1965: table 248) for Germany.

	Germany	United Kingdom
Degree of financial intermediation (M_2/NNP)	51.6	99.5
Quantity of commercial and financial services (UK = 100)	53.7	100.0
Employment (thousands)	3,381	3,417

8. Professional and personal services

Education sector productivity measures by pupils per teacher in primary schools. For 1936, British data from Mitchell (1988), German data from the Statistisches Reichsamt (*Statistisches Jahrbuch für das Deutsche Reich*, 1937: S.620).

	Pupils per teacher
Germany	42.7
United Kingdom	28.2

For personal services, data on the number of domestic servants in 1939 from Rostas (1948: 248) for the United Kingdom and from Hoffmann (1965: table 20) for Germany. There is no suggestion in the literature of international differences in productivity in this sector, so I have assumed equal labour productivity in the two countries. This also helps to capture the importance of non-marketed output in this sector more generally.

9. Government

With real output proxied by employment in the system of national accounts, this implies equal labour productivity by construction in an international benchmark comparison.

10. Aggregate economy

Aggregation requires making an allowance for differences in income per employee between sectors, rather than simply aggregating with employment shares. The method of aggregation is taken from Rostas (1948: 91). Data on income per employee by sector for the

United Kingdom in 1935 are derived from Feinstein (1972: tables 9 and 59).

B. Sectoral benchmarks for circa 1910

1. **Agriculture**
   Source: O'Brien and Prados de la Escosura (1992: 518). Final outputs in both countries have been valued in the prices of both countries, and the geometric mean taken. The figures used refer to output per member of the total agricultural labour force.
2. **Coal mining**
   Source: Broadberry and Fremdling (1990: 405), based on data from the UK Board of Trade (1912) and the Statistisches Reichsamt (*Statistisches Jahrbuch für das Deutsche Reich*, various years).

C. Sectoral benchmarks for circa 1968 and circa 1973

1. **Agriculture**
   Final output per employee in agriculture for 1970, in international dollars. Source: Prasada Rao (1993).
2. **Mining**
   Based on production census data for 1967 for Germany and 1968 for the United Kingdom. Separate estimates are available for coal mining and other mining. Source: Smith et al. (1982: 112). Geometric mean of results at UK and German prices reported.
3. **Manufacturing**
   Based on production census data for 1967 for Germany and 1968 for the United Kingdom. Source: Derived from Smith et al. (1982: 21), with a cyclical adjustment by Broadberry (1993: 774). Geometric mean of results at UK and German prices reported.
4. **Construction**
   Based on the UK Department of Industry (1973) and the Statistisches Bundesamt (1972). Net output deflated by price ratios derived from Kravis et al. (1975); source: Smith et al. (1982: 21). Geometric mean of results at UK and German prices reported.
5. **Utilities**
   Net output and employment data for 1975 are taken from the UK Department of Industry (1979) and the Statistisches Bundesamt (*Statistisches Jahrbuch für die Bundesrepublik Deutschland*, various years). Producer price ratios are obtained from the same sources and used to deflate net output per employee. However, results are reported at UK prices only, thus imparting an upward bias to the

Germany/UK results (the Gerschenkron effect). Separate estimates are available for gas, electricity and water; source: Smith et al. (1982: 136).

6. **Transport and communications**
Output figures for 1970 are obtained using methods similar to Rostas (1948), based on physical indicators. Separate estimates are produced for railways; local and road passenger transport; and road haulage; sea transport, ports and inland waterways; air transport; and posts and telecommunications. Source: Smith et al. (1982: 145, 157).

7. **Distribution**
Sales per employee are obtained from the UK Department of Industry (1975) and the Statistisches Bundesamt (1975) and deflated by price ratios from Kravis et al. (1975). An adjustment is made to bring the estimates onto a common year basis in 1971; source: Smith and Hitchens (1985: 112). Geometric mean of results at UK and German prices reported.

D. **Sectoral benchmarks for 1990**

1. **Agriculture**
Final output per employee in agriculture for 1990, in international dollars; source: Prasada Rao (1993).

2. **Manufacturing**
Gross value added and employment in manufacturing obtained from production censuses for 1987, deflated by producer price ratios obtained from the same sources; source: O'Mahony (1992). Geometric mean of results at UK and German prices reported.

Part II

Explaining comparative productivity performance

5 Technology, organisational change and the industrialisation of services

5.1 Introduction

This chapter provides the basic analytical framework for understanding the patterns of comparative productivity performance outlined in Part I. The key development has been the 'industrialisation' of services. This involved the transition from a world of customised, low-volume, high-margin business organised on the basis of networks to a world of standardised, high-volume, low-margin business with hierarchical management. This shift from the 'counting house' to the 'modern office' required technologies to improve communications and information processing as well as major organisational change from networks to hierarchies. These developments occurred initially in transport and communications in the United States and spread more slowly into distribution and finance. The transformation occurred more slowly in Britain, because of lower levels of education and stronger labour force resistance to the intensification of the labour process that the efficient utilisation of the new technologies required. Developments were initially even slower in Germany, as a result of the smaller market for services, squeezed by the protection of agriculture and industry.

After examining Britain's success in services during the nineteenth century on the basis of external economies of scale, this chapter proceeds to an analysis of the industrialisation of services in the United States. This is followed by sections on the response of British and German services to US developments. A model of technology, organisation and economic performance in services is then provided to set out more explicitly the economic argument.

5.2 External economies of scale during the 'golden age' of British commerce

Britain was highly successful in commercial services during the nineteenth century, playing a key international role in shipping, distribution and finance. For most of the nineteenth century Britain had a labour productivity lead over the United States as well as over Germany in services as a whole (Broadberry and Irwin, 2006). Similarly, British success in commercial services shows up in the balance of payments, with Imlah's (1958) figures on the net contribution of business services to the current account surplus amounting to £86.8 million in 1870, equivalent to about 8% of national income.

This British success was based largely on external rather than internal economies of scale. The City of London provided the largest agglomeration of commercial activity in the world, yet it consisted of a large number of small firms rather than a small number of giant firms. The large scale of the overall activity facilitated specialisation, and each firm could benefit from proximity to other specialised firms in classic Marshallian fashion (Marshall, 1920). Since asymmetric information was endemic in this type of activity, it was important to be able to deter opportunistic behaviour. As a result, trade often took place within networks of agents, who could be trusted. Although there is a large historical literature on merchant networks from medieval times, it is only recently that economic historians and economists have begun to analyse the economic mechanisms underpinning them. The pioneering work in this field by Greif (1989) used the *geniza* documents from old Cairo to show the importance of a reputation mechanism in sustaining trade among Maghribi traders during the eleventh century. Subsequent work, summarised in Greif (2000), puts this example of an early merchant network into a general framework, where, for individuals to enter into mutually beneficial exchange relationships, they had to be able to commit to fulfil their contractual obligations. The merchant network can be seen, then, as one way of mitigating this 'fundamental problem of exchange'.

Britain's commercial networks in the modern period can now be understood in the light of this framework. In shipping, Boyce's (1995) detailed study of share purchases in ninety-nine steamship ventures registered in West Hartlepool over the five-year period 1878–1883 captures information asymmetries by distinguishing occupational categories of shareholders and captures the building up of reputation and trust over time by examining patterns of repeat purchase. Other studies, by Ville (1987, 1989) and Cottrell (1981), document the role of networks in other ports, including London, Newcastle upon Tyne and Liverpool. In finance, Cassis (1994) uses information on bankers and bank directors from ten private banks, twenty merchant banks, seven discount houses, thirteen joint stock banks, fourteen overseas (colonial) banks and the Bank of England to provide an equally detailed study of networks in the City of London, but focusing on social as well as economic aspects. He builds up a picture of small family firms, public school and Oxbridge education, marriage into the aristocracy, and empire links. However, whereas this is sometimes used to suggest a culture of industrial decline, it is seen here to be associated with commercial success. In distribution, the study by Broadberry and Marrison (2002) emphasises the key role of merchants in the generation of external economies of scale in the Lancashire cotton industry.

In many ways the period 1850–1914 can be seen as the 'golden age' of British commerce, with London remaining firmly at the centre of the networks of world trade and payments. Nevertheless, developments had already occurred in the United States to undermine Britain's dominant position in parts of the service sector. These developments in American services will now be considered in the next section.

5.3 The industrialisation of American services: from the 'counting house' to the 'modern office'

5.3.1 *The origins of modern business enterprise*

Part I showed that in 1870, although Britain still had a labour productivity lead over the United States in services as a whole, the United States had already caught up in transport and communications. By World War I, furthermore, the United States had a substantial labour productivity lead over Britain in this sector. In distribution, the United States had just overtaken Britain by World War I, though Britain remained ahead in other services until the inter-war period. In services as a whole, therefore, the United States was already ahead by World War I and continued to forge ahead until the 1950s. Britain only narrowed the productivity gap with the United States in services (and in the economy as a whole) substantially from the 1970s.

The emergence of the US labour productivity lead in services is associated with 'service sector industrialisation' through 'modern business enterprise', beginning in transport and communications and spreading later to distribution and finance. As noted by Chandler (1977: 81–121), the modern hierarchical corporation began on the US railways during the late nineteenth century. Unlike turnpikes or canals, railways required centralised operation, since steam locomotives moved much faster than horse-drawn carriages or barges and operated on a single track. As the length of the track that a railway operated extended beyond what could be managed personally by a single superintendent, the railway was divided into geographic divisions, and each division was further subdivided by function and managerial hierarchies appeared (Chandler, 1980: 16). By the beginning of the twentieth century the modern corporate form had spread to other parts of the transport and communications sector, including steamship lines, urban traction systems and the telegraph and telephone systems (Chandler, 1977: 189–203).

These changes in transport and communications were accompanied by the emergence of modern business enterprise in distribution, with commodity dealers who bought directly from farmers and sold directly to processors replacing commission merchants in the distribution of agricultural produce, and with full-line wholesalers replacing commission merchants in the marketing of manufactures (Chandler, 1980: 19–20). Also, from the 1880s, wholesalers were beginning to lose ground to direct links between manufacturers and the new mass retailers, such as department stores, chain stores and mail-order houses (Chandler, 1980: 20). Nevertheless, distribution was slower to industrialise than transport and communications. For one thing, there were limits to the degree of centralisation and standardisation that consumers found acceptable in retailing, particularly given the relatively low levels of population density in the United States (Hall et al., 1961: 131–8; Field, 1996: 27). And, second, as Field (1996: 25–7) notes, there were restraints on competition which acted to support small retail outlets. In particular, resale price maintenance retained an ambiguous legal status until 1975 and limited price competition, making it easier for small independent retailers to survive (McCraw, 1996). In addition, state legislation aimed at supporting the independent retailers applied escalating tax rates to businesses with two or more retail outlets (Tedlow, 1996: 214–26; Perkins, 1999: 119–20).

American finance was relatively slow to industrialise, partly because of the nature of the business, but also partly because of the regulatory environment. Dealing first with the nature of the business, there are obvious dangers in adopting a high-volume, impersonal, standardised approach to banking and finance, since asymmetric information and trust are very important in this sector (Stiglitz and Weiss, 1981; Lamoreaux, 1994). Although simple routines have been developed for assessing risks on relatively small transactions, reputation and personal contact have often remained important on large transactions. Hence, it is not surprising that low-volume, high-margin business has continued to be important in financial services, particularly in international finance, where networks of personal contacts can be more important than modern business enterprise in generating high value added (Jones, 1993). Nevertheless, it seems clear that the industrialisation of banking and finance in the United States has also been limited by regulation. In particular, regulations prevented the growth of inter-state banking, keeping concentration in US banking relatively low (White, 2000: 749). Calomiris (1995) also cites the Glass–Steagall Act and Regulation Q as helping to keep American banks small by keeping apart commercial and investment banking and by setting a ceiling on interest rates that could be paid on bank deposits.

5.3.2   Technology and office organisation

The industrialisation of services can be characterised as a shift to high-volume, low-margin business, which required enormous technological and organisational change. As a result of these changes, the 'counting house' of the nineteenth century, which had been common in a range of trades covering the transport and communications, distribution and financial sectors, including banking, insurance, shipping, broking and merchant wholesaling, was transformed into the 'modern office' of the twentieth century (Anderson, 1976: 4; Lockwood, 1958: 23–4). This industrialisation of services was made possible by developments in information and communications technologies, which permitted the high-volume approach to business (Yates, 1989; Campbell-Kelly, 1992). It is useful to consider developments in three main areas: (1) telecommunications technologies, including the telegraph and the telephone; (2) written communications technologies, including the typewriter, the duplicator and the vertical filing system; and (3) data processing technologies, including the adding machine and the calculator. Rather more attention has been paid to the telegraph and the telephone than to the technologies of written communications and data processing, at least in the context of economic growth.

The telegraph and telephone opened up new possibilities for rapid exchanges of information across large distances, and hence had their biggest impact on businesses spread over large geographical distances, such as shipping companies, railways, merchant wholesalers and international banks. In terms of office management and the switch to productivity-enhancing, high-volume business, however, the impact was rather limited, since the telegraph was most often used for ad hoc communications and the telephone for informal communications (Yates, 1989: 21–2).

By contrast, the introduction of the typewriter, the duplicating machine and the vertical filing system radically changed the way that a business could produce, reproduce and store documents, which crucially affected the way that the whole business was organised (Yates, 1989: 21–64). In the counting house, written records were slowly entered into large ledger books using quill pen and ink. Copies had to be handwritten or made at the time of writing using a rudimentary letter press, and the storage of records was necessarily chronological. The typewriter speeded up the production of documents, and, together with shorthand and dictation, freed up time for managers to concentrate on executive decisions. The development of carbon paper and the duplicating machine made possible multiple copies at the time of writing, while the later introduction of photocopying separated reproduction from the production of written records. The replacement of the ledger book by the vertical filing system meant that records no longer had to be stored chronologically, and allowed incoming correspondence, outgoing correspondence and internal memoranda to be combined in a system indexed in a way that suited the record keeper.

The 1880s and 1890s saw a wave of invention of new office machinery in the United States, much of it concerned with data processing. It is not difficult to see a path from these primitive adding and calculating machines to the modern computer (Cortada, 1993: 25). Adding machines had been built before, but the addition of a keyboard for data entry, following the development of the typewriter, made an enormous difference to the possibilities of wide diffusion (Cortada, 1993: 29–30). The punched card tabulator and the cash register were further important developments in the late nineteenth century which aided the shift to high-volume business (Cortada, 1993: 44–78).

These developments all contributed to a transformation in the US office environment. Rotella (1981: 69–70) lists the following machines as commonly available in American offices by 1919: typewriters, dictating machines, stenotypes, copypresses, automatic typewriters, stencil or gelatin duplicators, typesetting machines, printing presses, photographing machines, telephones, TelAutographs, dictaphs, mechanical messenger boys (pneumatic tubes and overhead carriers), adding machines, calculating machines, billing machines, cash registers, statistical machines (card punchers and readers), mailing machines, addressing machines, letter openers, letter folders, envelope feeders, time clocks, paper cutters, padding machines, binding machines and bailing machines.

The modern office was a more intensive working environment than the counting house, with work organised on a more systematic basis and with closer supervision and monitoring. These aspects of the transformation of office work are noted by Lockwood (1958: 41–96), who argues that: (1) the modern office typically employed more clerks than the counting house; (2) there was a much higher degree of specialisation of tasks with reduced autonomy for individual clerks; (3) recruitment became more impersonal, less dependent on the personal networks of the counting house era; (4) hence there were reduced prospects of promotion to partnership within the firm as a narrower range of tasks was undertaken; and (5) the material status advantages that clerks enjoyed over the mass of manual workers were eroded in the modern office, particularly from the 1930s.

It should be noted, however, that the intensification occurred for managers as well as for workers, since the former had to monitor the latter closely. We may therefore expect resistance to the adoption of modern office technology where workers have power in the labour market, particularly where trade union density is high. However, we may also expect managers and workers to perceive a common interest in slowing the adoption of modern office technology where product market power is strong and there are rents to be shared. This bargaining approach has been applied by Broadberry and Crafts (1992) to Anglo-American productivity differences in manufacturing during the inter-war period, and it is natural to extend the approach to market services, where regulation meant that restrictions on competition were much more systematic and persistent than in manufacturing.

Although previous writers have discussed these developments in office technology and organisation, it is striking how they have been seen mainly as preconditions for the emergence of mass production in manufacturing, rather than as developments directly affecting productivity in the service sector, which was becoming the biggest sector in the economy. This has already been noted in the case of Chandler (1990), but it applies also to the work of Yates (1989), who writes explicitly within the Chandlerian framework. The argument here is that the biggest impact of the office technology revolution was in the service sector.

5.4 The growth of large-scale enterprise in British services

One defining feature of the modern business enterprise is large scale. A popular myth for a long time was that British industrial firms were smaller than their US counterparts. In fact, in sectors where mass production became the norm in the United States, British firms also consolidated, but performed relatively badly (Prais, 1981; Kinghorn and Nye, 1996; Broadberry, 1997a). Similarly, in those market services where high-volume, low-margin business became the norm, British firms consolidated. Hence, the sectoral pattern of the emergence of large-scale business in British services looks very similar to the pattern in the United States. Large firms became important first in transport and communications and spread later to distribution and finance.

However, by lagging in the adoption of modern office technology, these large British service sector firms were much slower to achieve the improved productivity performance of their US counterparts.

Table 5.1 presents data on the growth of large firms in Britain, based on lists of the hundred largest employers provided by Jeremy (1991) with corrections by Wardley (1999, 2001).[1] In Britain, large firms accounted for a high share of employment in transport and communications already before World War I, and a much lower share in distribution and finance. Equally, it is clear from table 5.1 that the numbers employed in large firms increased over time in all service sectors, although, in the case of distribution, this did not lead to an increase in the proportion employed in large firms between 1907 and 1935 because of a larger increase of employment in small firms during the depressed conditions between the wars (Foreman-Peck, 1985). Only after World War II did the share of large-scale retailers (multiples, department stores and co-operatives) in retail sales rise decisively above one-third (UK Board of Trade, 1953).[2] Chandler (1977, 1990) has focused on rankings of US firms by market capitalisation, and much less is known about employment (Wardley, 1999: 94). Jeremy and Farnie (2001: 105) note that this is odd, given the emphasis on managerial hierarchies in the Chandler paradigm. Nevertheless, Wardley's (1999: 107) data on employment in forty large US firms do suggest that Britain's large service sector firms were of a similar size to their US counterparts.

The message of table 5.1 is that the transformation from the counting house to the modern office was embarked upon in Britain with much the same sectoral pattern as in the United States, beginning in transport and communications and spreading later to distribution and finance. However, the productivity outcomes were much less successful in Britain. Clearly, there was more to the effective industrialisation of services than simply scale. One issue here is human capital, and chapter 6 examines international differences in education and training as well as differences in capital intensity and investment in modern office technology. Relatively low levels of education in Britain can be seen as one factor behind the delayed industrialisation of services. A second issue is the extent of competition and the regulatory framework. Large scale may simply confer on firms greater market power, which can be utilised to resist painful reorganisation. Chapter 7 then considers the extent of

---

[1] In fact, the corrections make little difference to the basic findings reported here on the proportions of employment in each sector accounted for by large firms.
[2] Large supermarkets with self-service appeared in Britain for the first time only after World War II (Turner, 1969: 252–3).

Table 5.1 *Employment in the largest 100 employers in Britain, 1907–1955*

A. 1907

	Employees in large firms	Large firm employment as percentage of all employment	Number of firms
Industry	660,038	7.3	66
Services			
Transport and communications	819,249	51.9	26
Distribution	48,560	19.7	6
Finance	28,625	12.4	2
Total services	896,434	10.0	34
Total economy	1,556,472	7.6	100

B. 1935

	Employees in large firms	Large firm employment as percentage of all employment	Number of firms
Industry	1,148,749	13.3	76
Services			
Transport and communications	894,488	56.6	9
Distribution	157,254	5.3	9
Finance	73,358	16.2	6
Total services	1,125,100	11.2	24
Total economy	2,273,849	11.3	100

C. 1955

	Employees in large firms	Large firm employment as percentage of all employment	Number of firms
Industry	2,878,627	24.9	68
Services			
Transport and communications	1,281,233	72.8	8
Distribution	395,926	12.7	16
Finance	98,442	19.9	6
Other services	38,500	0.6	2
Total services	1,814,101	15.5	32
Total economy	4,692,728	19.3	100

Sources: Derived from Jeremy (1991), with correction for 1907 and 1935 from Wardley (1999, 2001); sectoral employment data from Feinstein (1972).

competition in services and international differences in the regulatory framework. British service sector firms appear to have used their market power to delay the effective industrialisation of services in Britain.

5.5 Developments in German services

Although Britain began to fall behind the United States in parts of the service sector from the late nineteenth century as a result of the adoption of high-volume methods using modern office technology, British productivity in most parts of the service sector remained higher than in Germany until after World War II. In sectors where Germany was able to adopt US methods (particularly in transport and communications), productivity was relatively high, but large parts of the German service sector remained too spread out in a predominantly rural society with a large agricultural sector. Britain's high level of urbanisation, together with an international orientation in much of the commercial service sector, generated external economies of scale which underpinned high levels of productivity (Bairoch, 1976: 312).

German catching up in most parts of the service sector occurred only after World War II, with the shrinking of the agricultural sector. The shift of labour from agriculture into services was accompanied by high levels of physical and human capital accumulation in Germany, a development associated with the institutional framework of the post-war settlement (Eichengreen, 1996; Carlin, 1996). This underpinned the spread of vocational training from industry into services after World War II, coupled with high rates of investment in physical capital. As a result, Germany has achieved higher levels of labour productivity than Britain in most parts of the service sector since the 1970s.

5.5.1 *The effects of tariff protection*

Tariff protection in late nineteenth-century Germany was designed to slow down the decline of agriculture and accelerate the development of heavy industry. The alliance of 'rye and iron' in the newly formed German Reich meant that, proportionally, at least, services had to be the loser. This effective bias against services strengthened considerably after World War I with the growing scale of protection. German agricultural tariffs can be seen as an attempt to stave off a 'grain invasion' from the United States (O'Rourke, 1997). Webb (1980) argues that industrial tariffs in Wilhelmine Germany, often in combination with cartels, should be seen as an attempt to reduce the riskiness of investment in capital-intensive technologies by restricting competition. He thus sees tariffs as successfully stimulating heavy industry in Germany. To the extent that tariffs slowed down the shift of labour out of agriculture and accelerated the expansion of industrial employment, then services must have been squeezed.

The consequences of these protectionist policies for German productivity performance have often been misunderstood. Contemporaries and historians have consistently overestimated the strength of the German economy before World War II by focusing on the modern sectors which policy was designed to promote. However, it is important not to forget that these policies also had adverse consequences for the less favoured sectors.

5.5.2 The Gerschenkronian perspective reconsidered

The widespread overestimation of the performance of the German economy before World War II is dependent on a view of economic activity which privileges industry, and particularly heavy industry. In most analyses of Germany's industrialisation since the work of Gerschenkron (1962), the success of German heavy industry receives a great deal of attention (Tilly, 1991). However, there is much less acknowledgement of the costs arising from the protection of agriculture in the face of competition from the New World, and even less recognition of the underdevelopment of services in Germany. Indeed, since the Gerschenkronian analysis emphasises the role of the railways in creating a national market and the role of the universal banks in mobilising finance for heavy industry, there is even a danger that economic historians may draw the seriously misleading conclusion that Germany had a dynamic and highly productive service sector. But, in fact, although the German railway system was relatively productive, the German banking system, with its low level of specialisation, was distinctly underdeveloped compared with its British counterpart (Collins, 1988: 18). Furthermore, productivity remained relatively low in much of the German service sector, given its low level of specialisation across the board.

This lack of specialisation in the German service sector can be linked to the slow contraction of agriculture behind tariff barriers, combined with the direction of resources into industry. This necessarily limited the extent of the domestic market for services, and the German service sector was much less geared towards overseas markets than the British service sector, which had developed a global outlook with the expansion of the British Empire during the eighteenth and nineteenth centuries (Rubinstein, 1993; Cain and Hopkins, 1993). With specialisation limited by the extent of the market, the German tendencies towards autarky and a large domestic agricultural sector before World War II resulted in relatively low productivity in services, as well as in agriculture (Stigler, 1951; Smolensky, 1972).

5.5.3 Germany's railways

The German railways have received a great deal of attention because of their perceived role in creating a unified national market (Fremdling, 1975). This is traditionally seen as having been important for industrial development, and hence for industrial productivity. However, the most remarkable feature of the German railways was their role in generating high levels of productivity in the transport and communications sector. The key question is: how did Germany manage to achieve such high levels of productivity on the railways when productivity in the rest of the service sector was so low? To understand this, it is helpful to return to the origins of modern business enterprise in the United States during the nineteenth century.

Modern business enterprise, characterised by standardised, high-volume, low-margin business and multiple operating units managed by a hierarchy of salaried executives, began on the US railways during the late nineteenth century (Chandler, 1977: 81–121). The railway system that emerged in Germany was also organised on the basis of modern business enterprise, with a high-volume, low-margin approach and hierarchical management. The promotion of heavy industry, centred on iron and steel and coal, which needed to be transported in bulk, was important in generating the internal economies of scale that underpinned Germany's high productivity on the railways (Fremdling, 1975). Note that the railways were, in turn, very important users of these products, generating important backward linkages (Fremdling, 1977). It must be emphasised, however, that the high productivity of the railways was very atypical of German services.

5.5.4 Universal banking

The Gerschenkronian literature alleges that the German universal banks were better than the British clearing banks at mobilising capital for domestic industry (Gerschenkron, 1962: 13–16; Kennedy, 1987: 121–2). There are a number of problems with this view, however. First, it is clear that in Germany, as well as in Britain, most industrial investment was financed from internal rather than external funds (Edwards and Ogilvie, 1996; Fohlin, 1999). Second, it is important to recognise that the British clearing banks were part of a specialised system, with merchant banks responsible for the mobilisation of long-term capital. Third, even if defined widely to include the private banks as well as the joint-stock credit banks, the universal banks never accounted for more than about a half of the German credit market (Guinnane, 2002: 81). The public savings banks (*Sparkassen*), credit co-operatives, mortgage banks and other small institutions that made up the banking sector were often oriented more towards agriculture than industry, and pulled down the average productivity performance of the German banking sector. Fourth, in terms of short-term lending to industry, on which it is fair to judge the British clearing banks, recent archival research has revealed that they were just as supportive as their Continental counterparts (Capie and Collins, 1996; Baker and Collins, 1999). But, even if the clearing banks supported British industry with short-term funds, it is still possible that the merchant banks, with their primary responsibility for long-term funds, were biased against British industry. If that were the case, though, it should show up in relative rates of return on domestic and overseas issues. Edelstein (1971), however, has shown that rates of return on domestic and overseas assets of the same risk (measured by the variance of returns) were not significantly different.

Before being too critical of the highly specialised British banking system, it is important to remember that, even in Gerschenkron's (1962) work, the German universal banking system was seen as a result of economic backwardness. Finance was provided on a much greater overall scale in Britain than in Germany before World War I, permitting greater specialisation and sophistication. It makes little sense, then, to criticise British banks for failing to develop along German lines as if the German system were the final stage on a development path (Collins, 1998: 18). This is important once it is recognised that it is the overall level of GDP rather than just industrial output that matters, since the British financial system, with its global outlook, clearly generated high levels of GDP per person employed. Furthermore, even if attention is limited to industrial output, it is important to bear in mind that, to the extent that German banks were successful at directing funds into heavy industry, this meant that light industry was starved of funds (Neuburger and Stokes, 1974; Tilly, 1986). This matters because any productivity advantage that Germany enjoyed over Britain in heavy industry was offset by lower productivity in light industry (Broadberry and Fremdling, 1990; Broadberry and Burhop, 2005).

Arguments concerning the alleged superiority of the German universal banking system over the British specialised system rarely consider the inter-war period. Nonetheless, it is precisely during such volatile times that the disadvantages of banks tying up their assets in long-term loans to industry become most obvious. Had Britain's clearing banks become more heavily involved in industrial rationalisation, as Tolliday (1987), Best and Humphries (1986) and others have argued they ought to have done, it is likely that the stability of the financial system would have been threatened. As it was, the liquidity of the British clearing banks helped Britain to avoid the devastating collapse of the banking system that occurred in Germany, the United States and other countries, and there were no important bank failures in Britain during the 1930s (Collins, 1998: 19–20). Indeed, the experience of the financial crisis after 1929 led the United States to insist on a clear separation between commercial and investment banking in the Glass–Steagall Act of 1933 (Carosso, 1970: 371).

5.5.5 Other services

The rest of the German market service sector appears decidedly underdeveloped in the period prior to World War II, and has attracted little attention in the modern literature.[3] The most important other sector to consider is distribution, which Hoffmann (1965) groups together with finance in a general trade or commerce sector (*Handel*). As with finance, one contrast between Britain and Germany is the greater importance of international business for the former, with British merchant wholesalers at the hub of a global trading system. A recent study by Jones (2000) documents the growth of the British overseas trading companies and their continued success before World War II on the basis of the network form of organisation.

However, the quantitatively most important part of the distribution sector was domestic retailing, and here again there were important contrasts between Britain and Germany. An important trend in Britain, as in the United States, was the emergence of large-scale enterprise in retailing, in the form of multiple shops (chain stores), department stores and co-operative societies (Clapham, 1938: 238–51). Jefferys (1954: 29–30, 73–4) shows that the share of large-scale retailers in total UK retail trade increased from 13.5% in 1900 to 36.5% by 1939. Jefferys (1954: 34) sees this development as dependent on the existence of a large, steady and consistent demand from a relatively homogeneous urban working class. This provides a strong contrast with Germany,

---

[3] The organisational details can nevertheless be readily obtained from studies carried out by the German historical school of economics (Conrad et al., 1910; Aubin and Zorn, 1976; Henning, 1996).

which remained a far more agricultural and rural society until well after World War II, serviced by a large number of small general shops (Mataja, 1910: 246–7). Although the United States was also more rural than Britain, most writers have stressed the homogeneity of US demand, even among the rural population. Whereas the mail-order store provided cheap homogeneous goods to rural consumers in the United States, this occurred on a much more limited scale in Germany (Chandler, 1990: 59, 420). It must also be remembered that per capita incomes were always higher in the United States than in Germany.

When large-scale department stores, chain stores and consumer co-operatives threatened for the first time to take significant market share from Germany's small-scale *Mittelstand* retailers in the inter-war period, the latter organised buyer co-operatives and pressed for legislation to limit the growth of large retailers (Kopper, 2002: 15–19). Persuading the National Socialists that department stores and chain stores were part of a Jewish world conspiracy, the *Mittelstand* retailer activists were successful in securing legislation to tax large-scale retailers more heavily, to ban the founding or expansion of such businesses, and to limit price discounts (Kopper, 2002: 35–8). However, a voluntary 'Aryanisation' of boards saved the department stores from extinction (Homburg, 2000: 175–6). Many of the restrictions on German retailing survived well after World War II (Kopper, 2002: 75–81).[4]

It is not simply that there were more large British firms in distribution and other services, however. Just as important is the fact that the overall size of these service sector activities was greater in Britain, so that the many small firms were able to benefit from external economies of scale. This followed partly from the greater international orientation of the British economy, but it also resulted simply from the smaller share of economic activity accounted for by agriculture in Britain. In Germany, with such a large fraction of the total labour force engaged in agriculture and such a large share of the non-agricultural labour force engaged in industry, there was simply not the labour available to provide services on the same level as in Britain. There is thus a strong contrast between the small but specialised service sector firms in Britain, reaping external economies of scale, and the small, general service sector firms in Germany, operating at lower levels of productivity.[5]

---

[4] Indeed, the *Rabattgesetz* of 1933, which limited discounts to 3%, lasted until 2001 (Kopper, 2002: 75).

[5] Mataja (1910: 246) finds little more than three-quarters of the businesses in Germany's *Handel* sector in 1907 to be specialised in trade. Figures from the Statistisches Reichsamt (*Statistisches Jahrbuch für das Deutsches Reich*, 1937) show the average size in retailing in

5.5.6 Large firms in British and German services

The above analysis has suggested that German services have to be treated carefully in any international comparison, because of the way that the process of modernisation occurred in Germany. Given the importance of the railways in creating a unified market and the role of the universal banks in mobilising capital for heavy industry, the early emergence of a number of large firms should be expected in these sectors. In the rest of the service sector, however, relatively few large firms should be expected. The data on the 125 largest employers in Britain and Germany around 1907, in table 5.2, allow a comparison of the scale of employment in large firms with a breakdown between industry and services, and between the main service sectors.

Of the 125 largest employers in the two countries, just thirteen were in services in Germany, compared with thirty-two in Britain. In absolute terms, the distribution of firm size was quite similar in the two countries, although a few German firms at the top end of the distribution were larger than their British counterparts, while the British firms at the lower end of the distribution were a little larger than their German counterparts (Wardley, 1999). Because these giant German firms were largely in transport and communications (including the railways and shipping), the share of employment in this sector accounted for by large firms was extremely high. Germany's other large service sector employers in 1907 were two banks. Although no banks appeared in the list of large British employers before the amalgamations at the end of World War I, two large insurers did (Wardley, 1999; Jeremy, 1991). Six large retailers also appeared in the list of Britain's largest employers. So, although large firm employment as a share of all employment was actually larger in Germany than in Britain in services as well as in industry, this was entirely due to the transport and communications sector. The rest of the service economy in Germany was populated by small firms.

5.6 Modelling the industrialisation of services

5.6.1 The model

This section presents a model of technology, organisation and economic performance, which provides a framework of analysis for the

---

1935 to vary between two and four persons in all branches apart from electrical goods and office supplies. In wholesaling, average employment was fewer than eight in all branches apart from electrical goods and office supplies.

Table 5.2 *Largest 125 employers in the United Kingdom and Germany, circa 1907*

A. United Kingdom

	Employees in large firms	Large firm employment as percentage of all employment	Number of firms
Industry	824,093	9.2	93
Services			
Transport and communications	771,909	48.9	24
Distribution	48,560	19.7	6
Finance	28,625	12.4	2
Total services	849,094	9.4	32
Total economy	1,673,187	8.2	125

B. Germany

	Employees in large firms	Large firm employment as percentage of all employment	Number of firms
Industry	1,186,795	11.3	112
Services			
Transport and communications	994,198	76.3	11
Distribution	0	{0.3}	0
Finance	7,523		2
Total services	1,001,721	13.4	13
Total economy	2,188,516	7.7	125

Note:
Gas, electricity and water are included in industry. German employment figures are available only for distribution and finance together. German employment data in transport and communications include an allowance for technical personnel.

Source: Derived from Wardley (1999); employment by sector – derived from Feinstein (1972), Hoffmann (1965).

industrialisation of services and changing productivity leadership. The model was originally presented in Broadberry and Ghosal (2005), together with a more formal version, but here only a diagrammatic exposition is used, to convey the intuition behind the key results. An example, based on British shipping in the late nineteenth century, will help to clarify the situation being considered. As Boyce (1995) notes, shipping ventures at the time were usually conducted by networks. A group of agents would each make an initial investment, which would allow the purchase of a ship and other necessary items. The aim of the venture might be to take a cargo between two cities (say London and Buenos Aires), find a cargo for the return voyage and then sell the ship or undertake another venture. Agents might bring different skills and commercial contacts as well as initial capital. However, it might be extremely difficult to centralise decision making, since it is not really possible to monitor the actions that agents need to take and to verify that they have been carried out. This leaves scope for opportunistic behaviour by individuals. Suppose, for example, that there are difficulties in finding a return cargo in Buenos Aires, which reduces the profitability of the venture. This may not be the fault of the agent on the ground in Buenos Aires, but it is very difficult and costly for the other agents to verify this. Group reputation and the associated persistence of group membership, however, can be used to provide a solution to the incentive problem and deter opportunistic behaviour.

Now consider the case where there has been an increase in the scale of business between London and Buenos Aires and an improvement in communications, so that agents in London can keep in continuous contact with agents in Buenos Aires by telephone. It may now be feasible to establish a regular scheduled service between the two ports, requiring an investment in a fleet of ships, the establishment of a bureaucracy to run the regular service and a marketing organisation to secure sufficient demand to fill the capacity. The establishment of a shipping line can therefore be seen as requiring Chandler's (1977) three-pronged investment in production, management and marketing. The key development is the standardisation of the business and the possibility of moving to a hierarchical form of organisation. The industrialisation of services requires this dual shift in technology and organisation. The entrepreneur can now specify more closely the actions to be taken by agents and verify that they have been carried out. Wage contracts can now be used to ensure that appropriate actions are taken by venture members.

Time periods are indexed by $t = 0, 1, 2 \ldots$ and there is a collection of individuals indexed by i, each of whom is endowed in each period with a consumption good, x, and a set of actions, a. Within each period t, utility depends positively on the consumption good and negatively on the cost of matching actions to shocks. Each individual agent i has a discount factor, δ, where $0 < \delta < 1$. This discount factor is used to aggregate the utility an agent receives within each period to obtain a lifetime utility for the agent. The discount factor can be thought of as reflecting the impatience of an individual agent. When δ is low, an individual is impatient and puts a higher utility weight on current consumption relative to future consumption. When δ is close to one, an individual is patient and discounts future consumption less.

There is an entrepreneur, agent *0*, who is endowed with information about a venture. The venture can be either customised or standardised, and this will be referred to as the venture technology. In the **customised venture**, individual agents must make decisions in the light of individual information. There is a minimum venture size $K + 1$, with agent *0* and K other agents. All agents, including agent *0*, must invest their good and choose actions a to match participant-specific shocks θ. There is a highest level of venture output $\bar{q}_c^K$ if there is a match between action and shock for all agents. Output will be lower than this if even one agent does not match action and shock. In this formulation of the customised venture, the information relevant to discerning the appropriateness of individual actions is privately observed and efficient operation of the venture requires participants to choose different actions in response to their privately observed shocks. Participants are thus autonomous and have considerable discretion in choosing their actions.

The **standardised venture** is similar to the customised venture, but with one key difference. Now, each participant has to choose an action to match the corresponding common, venture-wide shock. In this formulation of the standardised venture, the information relevant to determining the appropriateness of individual actions is commonly available, and efficient operation of the venture requires participants to choose the same action. Participants are no longer autonomous and their scope for discretion is extremely limited.

The two types of venture technology (customised or standardised) can be operated by either of two organisational forms, a hierarchy or a network. A **network** involves decentralised decision making: all venture members choose actions independently, and the share of venture output of each current venture member is fixed at $(\frac{1}{K+1})$. A **hierarchy** involves centralised decision making: agent *0* invests in a monitoring technology, which allows him to verify at a fixed cost M the actions of all other agents. Agent *0* also chooses the action profile of all participants, specifies payment as a function of those actions and verifies that they have been carried out.

Within each period, there are two stages. In the first stage, common to both organisational forms, agent *0* chooses the venture technology and the set of current venture members, while new and existing members decide whether or not to participate in the venture. In the second stage, the interaction between venture members depends on the organisational set-up and the type of venture. In a **network**, individual venture members choose their actions in the light of their individual shocks. In a **hierarchy**, agent *0* invests in the monitoring technology, and specifies the actions of venture members and their payments, subject to feasibility and participation constraints.

At each period *t*, a venture has a **history,** which can be described in terms of past membership and past venture output. At each *t*, a strategy for an individual venture member specifies all current choices as a function of history and currently available information. Dynamic equilibria in strategies are studied, with the requirement that all members of a venture behave and are treated in the same way, both within and across periods.

5.6.2 Results

This section states some results which characterise the dynamic equilibria, using a simple diagrammatic exposition.

Result 1: *A network may operate a customised venture efficiently through a group reputation mechanism, while a hierarchy may not.*

With a customised venture, there are individual shocks, which cannot be observed by the entrepreneur. In a network, the share of output for each agent is fixed in proportion to his initial investment. However, each agent participating in today's venture gets a future reward from continuing to be selected for membership of the network in the future (this future reward is discounted by δ). In a network, individuals are induced to match actions to shocks through a group reputation mechanism, together with the associated persistence of membership, since, although individual effort cannot be monitored, group output can. An individual who is tempted to behave opportunistically must weigh up the short-run gains against the loss of future utility from network participation when his membership is terminated.

The essence of the result is shown diagrammatically in figure 5.1, which shows the trade-off faced by a single current venture member, given that all other current and future venture members choose appropriate actions. The benefit of deviating from the appropriate action B_c^N is a one-shot gain, and hence does not vary with the discount rate δ. On the other hand, if the current venture member deviates, venture output is reduced. Therefore, agent *0* will detect that some current member has chosen an inappropriate action. This allows agent *0* to condition future membership in the venture as a function of other agents' actions. Therefore, the cost of deviating from the appropriate action C_c^N arises from the loss of the discounted future utility as a result of membership termination. Under our assumptions, this is a linear function of the

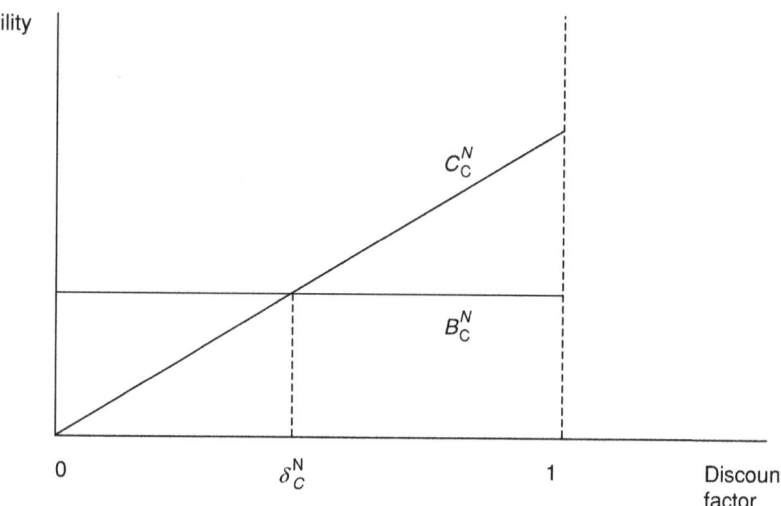

Figure 5.1 Customised venture.

discount rate δ. If the discount rate δ is too low (i.e. if individuals are too impatient) then the benefit of deviating exceeds the cost, and it is not possible to sustain a high-output equilibrium. Above the critical value δ_c^N, however, it is possible for networks to run the customised venture efficiently.

In a **hierarchy**, it is not possible to sustain the efficient outcome with high output in a customised venture, because the shocks are privately observed and agent *0* does not have sufficient information to specify from the centre the correct actions to be taken by individual venture members.

Result 2: *A hierarchy may operate a large-scale standardised venture efficiently, but a small-scale standardised venture may be operated efficiently only by a network.*

Under the standardised venture technology, investment in the monitoring technology allows agent *0* to verify whether the action chosen by an individual venture member matches the common shock and to operate the venture as a hierarchy. The problem for agent *0* is thus to condition payments to individuals on actions so that all agents choose the appropriate action. Figure 5.2 illustrates this problem for an individual venture member. Agent *0* pays each current venture member a wage (w) to compensate the utility cost of choosing the appropriate action, so that the venture member is indifferent between participating and not participating in the venture. In figure 5.2, agent *0* picks the wage w^* that

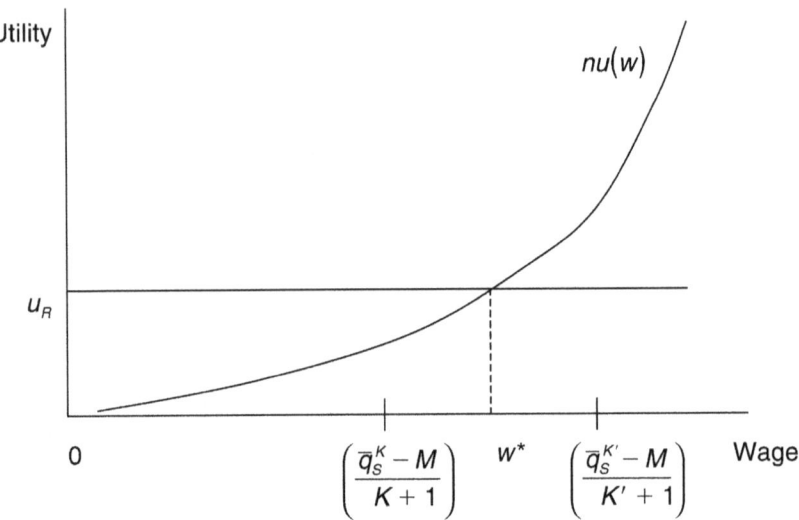

Figure 5.2 Standardised venture.

equates the utility from the outside option (u_R) to the net utility cost of choosing the appropriate action $nu(w)$, which depends on the wage. If the per capita venture output net of monitoring costs ($\frac{\bar{q}_S^K - M}{K+1}$) is lower than w^*, the hierarchy is not feasible. On the other hand, when the per capita venture output net of monitoring costs ($\frac{\bar{q}_S^{K'} - M}{K'+1}$), for a larger venture of size K', is higher than w^* then the hierarchy is feasible. Hence, a large enough standardised venture can be run efficiently by a hierarchy.

For a smaller standardised venture, a network can use a reputation mechanism to run the venture efficiently without investing in the monitoring technology. The group reputation mechanism is used as in figure 5.1.

Results 1 and 2 characterise how customised and standardised ventures may be operated efficiently by networks and hierarchies. These results suggest that, in general, customised ventures are likely to be run by networks and standardised ventures by hierarchies. Next, organisational responses to exogenous changes in venture technology are examined. Technological change that favours large-scale standardised ventures may create some difficulties of adjustment for an economy with a history of networks operating small-scale customised ventures.

Result 3: *As venture scale increases, a hierarchy is more likely to operate a standardised venture efficiently, while a network is less likely to operate a customised (or standardised) venture efficiently.*

(a) Scale and hierarchy

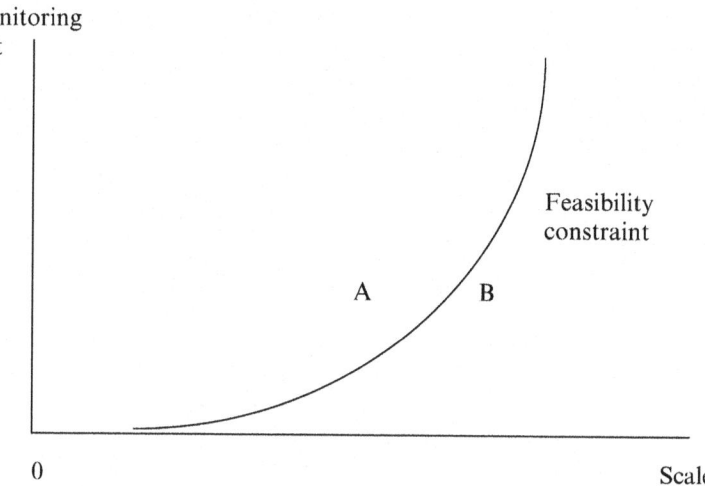

(b) Scale and networks

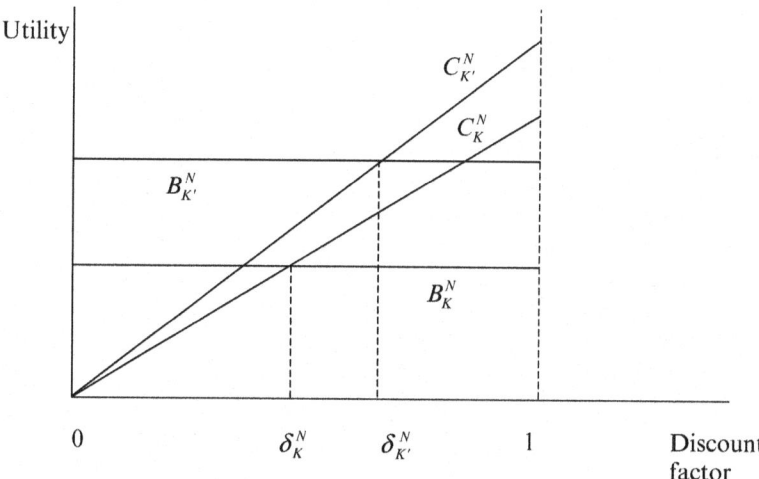

Figure 5.3 Interactions between scale and organisation:
(a) scale and hierarchy; (b) scale and networks.

A hierarchy is more likely to be feasible when the scale of the venture is large. This is illustrated in figure 5.3(a), where a point represents a particular combination of monitoring cost and scale, so that each venture technology corresponds to a point. For a hierarchy to be feasible, the venture technology must lie to the south-east of the feasibility constraint, which is upward-sloping since higher fixed costs of monitoring must be spread over a larger scale of venture output. At the venture technology given by point A, the entrepreneur will use the network form of organisation. A change in venture technology with larger scale, such as point B, makes it feasible for the entrepreneur to use the hierarchical form of organisation to run the venture. A fall in monitoring costs holding scale constant will also make a hierarchy more feasible.

The difficulties faced by a network operating a customised technology as scale increases can be illustrated using figure 5.3(b). Note that B_K^N and C_K^N are the benefits and costs of deviating from the appropriate action in a venture of size K, as in figure 5.1, while $B_{K'}^N$ and $C_{K'}^N$ are the benefits and costs of deviating from the appropriate action in a larger-scale venture of size K'. Also, note that, as in figure 5.1, the trade-off is considered for a current venture member, given that all other current and future venture members will choose the appropriate action. The crucial feature that illustrates the difficulty a network faces in adapting to the increase in scale is the fact that the minimum value of δ for which the network operates the larger-scale venture efficiently, $\delta_{K'}^N$, is higher than δ_K^N, the minimum value of δ for which the network operates the smaller-scale venture efficiently. The logic behind this result can be understood as follows. First, as scale increases, individual deviation has a smaller proportional negative effect on venture output, which means that $B_{K'}^N$ lies above B_K^N. Second, however, and offsetting this, the costs of deviating are also higher in the large-scale case because the future pay-off from continued membership is higher with the higher productivity associated with the increase in scale. Hence, $C_{K'}^N$ also lies above C_K^N. So long as the productivity increase is moderate, the first effect must dominate, and $\delta_{K'}^N$ must lie to the right of δ_K^N. This is a reasonable assumption to make when considering a moderate relative productivity decline such as Britain compared with the United States.

Result 3 suggests that networks may have to transform themselves into hierarchies to operate the standardised technology efficiently. So far, it has been assumed that the utility cost of matching an action to a shock in a hierarchy is the same as in a network. However, there are at least two reasons for thinking that this will not be the case. First, there is a loss of autonomy, as, after the transition to a hierarchy, network members submit themselves to centralised decision making. It is assumed that this loss of autonomy is reflected in an additional utility cost, G, of matching an action to a shock. The second reason for higher utility costs in the standardised venture would be if some additional education or training is required. Similarly, for the entrepreneur, G can be thought of

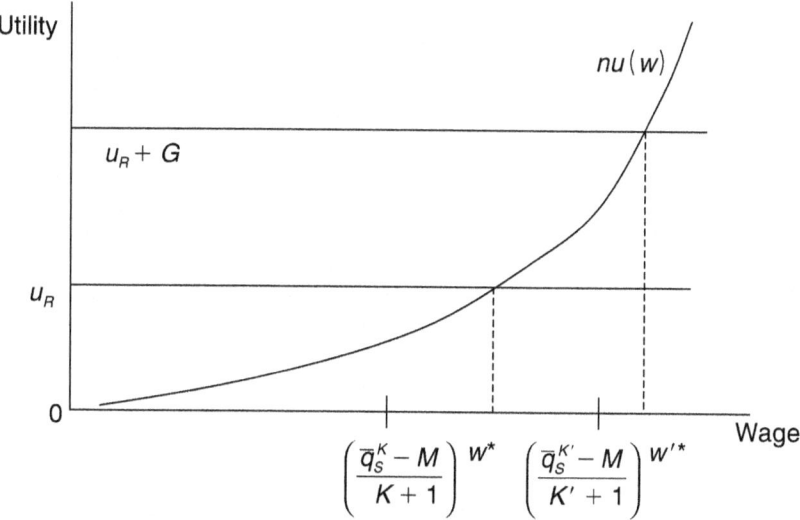

Figure 5.4 Adjustment costs.

as measuring the utility cost of the extra burden of responsibility in the transition to a hierarchy from a network.

Result 4: *A network operating a small-scale customised venture may fail to adapt successfully to an exogenous change in technology that favours large-scale standardised ventures, because network members resist the transition to hierarchy.* This is illustrated in figure 5.4, which builds on figure 5.2. Notice that, with the old technology, a hierarchy is not feasible, since the wage required to compensate venture members for their efforts (w^*) is more than per capita output net of monitoring costs ($\frac{\bar{q}_S^K - M}{K+1}$). Ignoring the extra utility costs associated with the loss of autonomy or retraining (i.e. setting $G = 0$), a hierarchy is feasible with the new technology, since the required wage is below the higher per capita output net of monitoring costs ($\frac{\bar{q}_S^{K'} - M}{K'+1}$). However, if G is positive then this additional utility cost must be added to the reservation utility (u_R), which pushes up the wage payment needed to compensate existing network members. If G is sufficiently large then the new wage needed to compensate existing network members (w'^*) may be greater than the per capita output net of monitoring costs ($\frac{\bar{q}_S^{K'} - M}{K'+1}$). Therefore, the post-transition hierarchy is no longer feasible. Hence, existing network members will face an incentive to resist transition if they care sufficiently about the loss of autonomy associated with the adoption of a hierarchical form of organisation or if they face sufficiently large education or training costs. A society with a low level of general education may therefore be expected to face a higher adjustment cost G. Note also that a low level of education may lead to a low reservation level of utility (u_R), making it easier to sustain a network, which requires the payment received by venture members to be above u_R.

5.6.3 *Implications*

Result 1 suggests a link between the provision of customised services and the network form of organisation. Britain excelled in this type of service provision during the nineteenth century, and this success depended on networks in sectors such as shipping, banking and merchant wholesaling. This theme will be developed in chapter 8. Result 2 suggests a link between the provision of standardised services and the hierarchical form of organisation, and the empirical association has been noted in the rise of modern business enterprise on the US railways and its spread to other market services. Hence, the industrialisation of services has required organisational as well as technological change.

Result 3 emphasises the role of scale in the industrialisation of services, with the growth of scale making it both easier to operate hierarchies and harder to operate networks. This accords well with the growth of large firms during the industrialisation of services noted above. Result 4 then deals with the transitional problems of adjustment from networks to hierarchies. These problems were particularly severe for Britain because of the success in market services on the basis of networks during the nineteenth century.

5.7 Conclusions

The productivity patterns in services outlined in Part I can be explained by a series of technological and organisational changes that occurred during the industrialisation of services. This involved moving from a world of low-volume, high-margin, customised business, organised on the basis of networks of trust, to a world of high-volume, low-margin, standardised business, organised on the basis of hierarchically managed corporations. This chapter has examined the origins of this transformation on the US railways and its spread to the rest of the market service sector. It has also examined the earlier success of the British market service sector on the basis of networks and the difficulties of adjusting to the rise of modern business enterprise in services. The industrialisation of services occurred even later in Germany, due to the smaller market for services, squeezed by the protection of agriculture and industry.

6 Investment in physical and human capital

6.1 Introduction

The industrialisation of services was accompanied by investments in physical and human capital, which are documented and analysed in this chapter. Sectoral data on physical capital are available for services to only a very limited extent before World War II, and there are significant problems of international comparability even after World War II. The available data nevertheless suggest a limited contribution of international differences in capital intensity to explaining international differences in labour productivity in services. However, a large part of overall capital in services consists of buildings, with at best an indirect link to labour productivity. It is therefore also useful to focus more narrowly on office machinery, which suggests a more significant role for investment in physical capital.

In human capital formation, it is important to consider both education and vocational training, and to distinguish between higher (university degree equivalent) and intermediate (between school leaving and degree equivalent) levels of vocational training (Prais, 1995: 17). Adding together the different types of human capital formation, Britain suffered little human capital disadvantage relative to either Germany or the United States before World War II, particularly in services. However, after World War II any higher-level advantage that Britain had enjoyed over the United States in services from the large number of qualified members of professional associations was offset by the spread of mass higher education in the United States. In the comparison between Britain and Germany, however, the crucial development was the spread of intermediate-level qualifications in German services, leading to the emergence of a substantial German human capital advantage by the 1970s.

6.2 Physical capital and total factor productivity

6.2.1 Comparative TFP levels

Much of the literature on international comparisons suggests that labour productivity growth rates differ at least in part because of differences in capital stock growth (Denison, 1967; Maddison, 1987). Hence, it is of some interest to consider the role of capital in explaining international differences in labour productivity levels. Working in terms of levels provides a check on the consistency and plausibility of trends in the growth rate of capital stocks in different countries. This is an important issue, because concerns have been raised about the international comparability of capital stock data derived from data on investment using official asset life assumptions that vary substantially between countries (Maddison, 1995; O'Mahony, 1996).

Detailed sources for the basic capital stock time series are given in appendix 6.1. For Britain, the key sources are Feinstein (1972, 1988) to 1965 and the official national accounts subsequently. Gross capital stock data for the aggregate economy and for individual sectors have been constructed by asset type for the whole period using the perpetual inventory method. For the United States, the capital stock estimates are rather less satisfactory, since, although perpetual-inventory-based estimates have now been published for the whole period at the aggregate level, the sectoral disaggregation must still be based largely on census stock estimates before 1950. For Germany, Hoffmann's (1965) figures for the pre-1950 period are available only at a highly aggregate level and are based in some cases on very limited information.[1]

To pin down relative levels of capital intensity and TFP by sector requires a benchmark estimate. The benchmark levels of capital intensity and TFP have been established for 1950 using the PPP price ratios for investment goods from Gilbert and Kravis (1954). Levels of comparative capital intensity and TFP for other years can then be obtained by time series projection from the 1950 benchmark. The share of capital declines from 0.4 before World War I to 0.25 after World War II. These shares are derived from Matthews et al. (1982), Kendrick (1961) and Hoffmann (1965).

For the US/UK case at the aggregate level, trends in comparative TFP in table 6.1 and labour productivity in table 6.2 are similar, but with TFP differences generally smaller than labour productivity differences.

---

[1] For example, the estimates for the industrial sector before World War I are based on data for Baden (Hoffman, 1965: 239–41).

Table 6.1 *Comparative US/UK and Germany/UK total factor productivity levels by sector, 1869/71–1990 (UK = 100)*

A. US/UK

	Agriculture	Industry	Services	Aggregate economy
1869/71	99.5	154.2	86.5	95.2
1889/91	123.0	139.6	64.3	83.3
1909/11	118.7	150.9	71.6	90.5
1919/20	133.1	158.3	92.1	108.2
1929	118.0	187.8	92.0	112.7
1937	119.2	161.2	89.1	105.9
1950	132.6	217.6	110.2	138.1
1973	125.9	202.2	120.6	137.4
1990	138.8	157.3	119.8	125.3

B. Germany/UK

	Agriculture	Industry	Services	Aggregate economy
1871	58.4	90.5	67.2	61.6
1891	59.8	91.6	65.5	63.2
1911	71.6	106.1	76.4	75.4
1925	57.0	92.9	83.6	74.3
1929	59.3	96.0	90.0	78.5
1935	59.6	97.1	88.8	78.2
1950	44.7	89.4	89.3	76.2
1973	48.1	105.7	127.6	108.6
1990	65.4	98.5	139.0	116.5

Source: Derived from Broadberry (1997b, 1997c, 1998).

This means that capital has a role to play in explaining labour productivity differences, but not enough to eliminate TFP differences altogether. One point worth noting here is that whereas the United States overtook Britain before World War I in terms of labour productivity, it was only between the wars that the United States gained a TFP advantage. This would be consistent with the emphasis of Abramovitz and David (1973, 1996) on the importance of capital rather than TFP in American economic growth during the nineteenth century. It is also consistent with McCloskey's (1970) claim that Victorian Britain did not fail, at least in the sense that the United States was still catching up in terms of aggregate TFP levels. In services, too, note that the US overtaking of Britain also occurred later in terms of TFP than in terms of labour productivity.

For the Germany/UK case, a comparison of tables 6.1 and 6.2 shows that trends are very similar for comparative TFP and labour productivity

Table 6.2 *Comparative US/UK and Germany/UK labour productivity levels by sector, 1869/71–1990 (UK = 100)*

A. US/UK

	Agriculture	Industry	Services	Aggregate economy
1869/71	86.9	153.6	85.9	89.8
1889/91	102.1	164.1	84.2	94.1
1909/11	103.2	193.2	107.4	117.7
1919/20	128.0	198.0	118.9	133.3
1929	109.7	222.7	121.2	139.4
1937	103.3	190.6	120.0	132.6
1950	126.0	243.5	140.8	166.9
1973	131.2	214.8	137.4	152.3
1990	151.1	163.0	129.6	133.0

B. Germany/UK

	Agriculture	Industry	Services	Aggregate economy
1871	55.7	91.7	62.8	59.5
1891	53.7	99.3	64.4	60.5
1911	67.3	127.3	73.4	75.5
1925	53.8	92.3	76.5	69.0
1929	56.9	97.1	82.3	74.1
1935	57.2	99.1	85.7	75.7
1950	41.2	91.8	83.2	74.4
1973	50.8	121.1	120.1	114.0
1990	75.4	111.0	134.9	125.4

Note:
The same data are available for more years in tables 2.1 and 2.2.

Source: Derived from Broadberry (1997b, 1997c, 1998).

at the aggregate level, but with differences in TFP generally smaller than differences in labour productivity. Again, as in the US/UK case, this means that capital has a role to play in explaining labour productivity differences, but not enough to eliminate TFP differences altogether. Note that, in industry, Germany had caught up with Britain in terms of TFP as well as labour productivity before World War I. In services, higher capital intensity in Britain throughout the period means that until 1950 the British TFP lead was smaller than the British labour productivity lead, but that from 1973 the German TFP lead was greater than the German labour productivity lead.

Although Maddison (1995) argues for standardisation of asset lives in international comparisons, there are serious practical objections. The first problem is that a substantial proportion of the historical capital stock data is based on direct estimates of the capital stock from fire insurance records and censuses, which are used to obtain estimates of investment, thus inverting the perpetual inventory method. To use these investment data to obtain new estimates of the capital stock would inevitably involve some circularity of argument. The second problem is that Maddison's (1995: 253–4) standardised estimates produce a US/UK capital per employee ratio of more than five to one in 1938, when the United States managed to produce less than 70% more output per employee than Britain. For the long period studied here, then, there is no real alternative to relying on the official capital stock data.[2]

6.2.2 Investment in office machinery

The total capital stock in services has been dominated by buildings, so it is useful also to examine data on the diffusion of office machinery, where the link to productivity is more direct. We begin with the diffusion of the telephone, as measured by the number of connections and extensions per 100 population, shown here in table 6.3. Although the telephone was faster to diffuse in Germany than in Britain, there was a much larger gap between the United States and both European countries. It is only possible to distinguish between business and residential telephones from the 1920s, but it is clear that before 1920 the scale of telephone ownership was so much higher in the United States than in Britain or Germany that it must have affected business usage (Hannah, 1974a: 257). After 1920, although the absolute scale of the gap between the United States and Europe continued to increase, the proportional gap narrowed. Furthermore, the gap was considerably smaller for business telephones than for total telephones. Nevertheless, it is clear that the United States retained an advantage even in business telephones, which must have affected business-to-business communications. This US advantage must also have been reinforced in business-to-consumer communications, which require high overall levels of telephone ownership. One problem here, however, is that the slow development of telephone usage in Britain may reflect simply the supply policies of the Post Office, which had a monopoly of the telephone service for much of

---

[2] But see O'Mahony (1996) for a study of the post-1950 period using standardised capital stock estimates. See also O'Mahony (1999) for an analysis using capital services, where different types of capital are weighted by their user costs rather than simply added together.

Table 6.3 *Telephones per 100 population, 1900–1980*

	Total telephones			Business telephones	
	United Kingdom	United States	Germany	United Kingdom	United States
1900	0.005	1.8	0.5		
1905	0.08	4.9	1.0		
1910	0.2	8.3	1.6		
1915	1.7	10.5	2.1		
1920	2.0	12.5	2.9		4.0
1925	2.9	14.6	3.8	2.1	4.8
1930	4.1	16.3	5.0	2.9	5.6
1935	5.1	13.7	4.9	3.4	5.0
1940	6.9	16.6	5.3	4.1	6.4
1950	10.2	28.4	4.1	6.2	8.5
1960	15.0	41.3	10.7	8.4	11.6
1970	25.1	59.0	22.7	12.3	16.2
1980	47.5	79.6	46.3	17.4	21.1

Source: United Kingdom – telephones: Mitchell (1988: 566–7), UK Post Office (various years); population: Mitchell (1988: 13–14); United States – telephones and population: US Department of Commerce (1975, *Statistical Abstract of the United States*, various years); Germany – telephones: Statistisches Reichsamt (*Statistisches Jahrbuch für das Deutsche Reich*, various years), Statistisches Bundesamt, (*Statistisches Jahrbuch für die Bundesrepublik Deutschland*, various years); population: Hoffmann (1965: 173–6), Statistisches Bundesamt (*Statistisches Jahrbuch für die Bundesrepublik Deutschland*, various years).

the period under consideration (Foreman-Peck and Millward, 1994: 252).

However, it can also be shown that Britain was slow to adopt data processing machinery and other office machinery such as the typewriter. Campbell-Kelly (1992: 126) notes that, in contrast to the vast literature on the slow adoption of mass production technology in British manufacturing, the slow adoption of office machinery in Britain has received almost no attention, and he provides a number of intriguing case studies. Table 6.4 presents some flow data on sales of office machinery in Britain, the United States and Germany from the early 1900s to the late 1960s. The starting date reflects the fact that office machinery was not recorded separately in British trade statistics before 1908, while the end date reflects the growing importance of the electronic computer. Sales have been calculated by subtracting exports from the sum of production and retained imports. In the case of typewriters, the volume of units is available, and this has been used in the comparison of sales between

Table 6.4 *Office machine sales per 1,000 population, 1908–1968*

A. Typewriters (units)

	1908	1924	1930	1935	1948	1958	1968
United Kingdom	0.50	1.29	1.32	1.78	1.74	3.65	5.70
United States	1.13	3.68	4.34	6.08	7.76	8.91	18.62
Germany					3.51	10.28	9.34

B. Cash registers, calculating machines and other office machinery (£ at constant 1929 prices)

	1930	1935	1948	1958	1968
United Kingdom	28.3	33.3	106.0	289.5	509.2
United States	128.9	187.8	252.1	757.6	2,352.6
Germany		79.4	67.5	229.0	1,016.1

Note:
Sales obtained as production minus exports plus imports. US and German values converted to £ at unit value price ratios for manufacturing; current prices in £ converted to constant prices using the UK deflator for GDP at factor cost. Dates for United States: 1900, 1925, 1929, 1937, 1947, 1958, 1967; dates for Germany: 1936, 1950, 1958, 1967.

Source: Production – US Department of Commerce (*Census of Manufactures*, various years), UK Board of Trade (*Census of Production: Final Report*, various years), Statistisches Reichsamt (1939), Statistisches Bundesamt (*Die Industrie der Bundesrepublik Deutschland*, various years); exports and imports – US Department of Commerce (*Foreign Commerce and Navigation of the United States*, various years), UK Board of Trade (*Annual Statement of the Trade of the United Kingdom*, various years), Statistisches Reichsamt (*Monatliche Nachweise über den auswärtiges Handel Deutschlands*, various years), Statistisches Bundesamt (*Der Aussenhandel der Bundesrepublik Deutschland*, various years); population – US Department of Commerce (*Statistical Abstract of the United States*, various years), Feinstein (1972), UK Central Statistical Office (*Annual Abstract of Statistics*, various years), Statistisches Reichsamt (*Statistisches Jahrbuch für das Deutsche Reich*, various years), Statistisches Bundesamt, (*Statistisches Jahrbuch für die Bundesrepublik Deutschland*, various years); manufacturing unit value price ratios – Broadberry (1997a); deflator for GDP at factor cost – Feinstein (1972), UK Central Statistical Office (*Economic Trends Annual Supplement*, various years).

the countries. However, for Britain, since production data are not available until 1930, production has been estimated for the early years using the 1930 ratio of production to exports. The results are not very sensitive to this assumption, since the sales figures were dominated by imports at this time. It is also possible to compare unit values to check that quality differences are not too large. In the case of cash registers, calculating machines and other office machinery, the lack of adequate volume data means that the value of sales must be used in the comparison between countries. Sales values are converted to a common currency using a unit value price ratio, reflecting deviations from purchasing power parity. Finally, current prices in pounds are converted to constant 1929 prices using the UK deflator for GDP at constant factor cost.

For typewriters, the US/UK comparative sales per 1,000 population ratio fluctuates around a level of about three to one, giving the United States a considerable lead. For cash registers, calculating machines and other office machinery, the ratio fluctuates rather more, but around a higher level of the order of five to one. The flow data on office machine sales, then, point clearly in the same direction as the stock data on telephone ownership, with a large US advantage. German services were generally even slower than British services to adopt the American high-volume, low-margin approach. Hence a similar lag in the adoption of modern office technology is to be expected in Germany. For typewriters, there is evidence of a rapid German investment drive during the 1950s, although this fell off again during the 1960s, suggesting a post-war reconstruction effect. For cash registers, calculating machines and other office machinery, there is no evidence of a systematic German lead over Britain before the late 1960s, and both European countries clearly lagged behind the United States.

6.3   Human capital

6.3.1   Formal education

The most basic indicator of human capital is the level of education of the labour force. Table 6.5 provides data on formal schooling in Britain, the United States and Germany. The data are presented in the form of enrolment rates per 1,000 population under the age of twenty, to facilitate international comparisons. Although there are obvious difficulties in comparing enrolment data across countries, these issues have been worked over by a number of scholars, and it is now possible to draw fairly firm conclusions in several areas (Mitchell, 1975; Flora, 1983; Mitch, 1992; Goldin, 1998; Lindert, 2004). First, it is clear that Britain lagged behind both Germany and the United States in the provision of mass primary education until about 1900, as has been widely noted in the history of education literature, and as has been demonstrated quantitatively by Easterlin (1981). However, it is widely accepted that the official data on primary enrolments in England and Wales overstate the British shortfall due to under-recording. Lindert (2004: 147–52) provides a corrected series using data on the number of child scholars from the 1871 Census of Occupations, which shows primary enrolments

Table 6.5 *Educational enrolment rates per 1,000 population under age twenty, 1870–1990*

A. Britain

	Primary	Secondary	Higher
1871	118.6		
1881	238.4		
1891	285.8		
1901	344.7		1.6
1911	374.1	11.1	
1921	371.8	24.1	3.8
1931	380.6	31.7	
1938	357.1	37.1	4.8
1951	323.1	164.4	8.7
1961	299.8	233.2	13.9
1971	337.4	258.0	26.0
1981	327.4	327.4	30.5
1991	333.1	279.1	46.8

B. United States

	Primary	Secondary	Higher
1870	390.6	4.2	
1880	404.5	4.6	
1890	492.5	10.3	
1900	478.9	18.7	
1910	475.6	26.8	
1920	472.9	56.1	15.8
1930	479.2	99.6	23.1
1938	472.2	147.1	29.8
1950	409.6	125.2	52.0
1960	436.6	138.6	62.5
1970	443.0	187.4	111.5
1980	389.0	248.7	167.0
1990	434.1	213.3	191.1

C. Germany

	Primary	Secondary	Higher
1871	364.7	9.5	0.8
1880	362.4	9.6	1.0
1890	365.5	10.1	1.3
1900	372.1	10.6	1.8
1911	372.4	10.9	2.3
1925	291.2	35.4	4.0
1933	383.2	38.3	6.4

(*continued*)

Table 6.5 (cont.)

C. Germany

	Primary	Secondary	Higher
1939	345.6	34.5	2.6
1950	410.6	52.3	6.9
1960	332.9	73.9	12.5
1970	368.2	123.1	19.7
1980	332.0	226.9	60.7
1990	286.6	191.4	99.8

Note:
For Britain, primary and secondary enrolment data refer to England and Wales only. For Germany, primary and secondary enrolment data before 1911 refer to Prussia only.

Source: Britain – primary and secondary school enrolments: Mitchell (1988: 799–810), UK Department of Education and Science (various years); higher enrolments: Halsey (1988: 270–2), UK Department of Education and Science (various years); population: Mitchell (1988: 15), UK Central Statistical Office (*Annual Abstract of Statistics*, various years); United States – primary and secondary school enrolments: US Department of Commerce (1975: 368–9, *Statistical Abstract of the United States*, various years); higher enrolments: Tyack (1967: 478); population: US Department of Commerce (1975: 15, *Statistical Abstract of the United States*, various years); Germany – primary and secondary enrolments: 1871–1911 – Königlichen Statistischen Bureau (various years) and Kaiserliches Statistisches Amt (*Statistisches Jahrbuch für das Deutsche Reich*, various years); 1911–1939 – Statistisches Reichsamt (*Statistisches Jahrbuch für das Deutsche Reich*, various years), Länderrat des Amerikanischen Besatzungsgebiets (1949); 1950–1990 – Statistisches Bundesamt (*Statistisches Jahrbuch für die Bundesrepublik Deutschland*, various years); higher enrolments: 1871–1911 – Ringer (1979: 272); 1925–1939 – Statistisches Reichsamt (*Statistisches Jahrbuch für das Deutsche Reich*, various years), Länderrat des Amerikanischen Besatzungsgebiets (1949); 1950–1990 – Statistisches Bundesamt (*Statistisches Jahrbuch für die Bundesrepublik Deutschland*, various years); population: Hoffmann (1965: 173–6), Königlichen Statistischen Bureau (various years), Statistisches Bundesamt (*Statistisches Jahrbuch für die Bundesrepublik Deutschland*, various years).

per 1,000 population in England and Wales having already reached 137.5 by 1871. This suggests that the British lag in primary education may not have been as great as suggested by the official data in table 6.5; but it does not eliminate the lag. Second, both Britain and Germany lagged behind the United States in the development of mass secondary education between the two world wars. This has been noted by historians of education such as Ringer (1979: 252–3), and has also been emphasised recently in the work of Goldin (1998). Third, both Britain and Germany lagged behind the United States in the provision of mass higher education after World War II. Tertiary enrolment ratios in Britain and Germany were still a long way behind US levels in 1990.

Two points should be borne in mind when interpreting these trends. First, the transfer from primary to secondary education has generally occurred at a later age in the United States and Germany than in Britain, affecting the breakdown between primary and secondary education. Second, however, it is not possible to give enrolment ratios for narrower age bands, as the difference between primary and secondary education was a matter of class as well as age before World War II.

Previous attempts to provide a link between education and productivity have focused on industry, where the link between the tasks that most workers actually perform on the shopfloor and the skills learned in school seems rather tenuous. In services, by contrast, the link between education and the tasks performed by most office workers seems rather closer. Although Goldin and Katz (1996) claim that the early development of mass secondary schooling in the United States was important in the development of batch and continuous-process methods in the early twentieth century, the argument goes against the grain of an earlier view, which sees the development of mass production in the United States as substituting away from skilled labour (Habakkuk, 1962; Braverman, 1974). Furthermore, Goldin's (1998) own evidence on the cross-state variation in the level of schooling shows a negative relationship between high school graduation and the share of the labour force in manufacturing. As David and Wright (1999) note, a long period of time undoubtedly elapsed before industrial employers learned to make effective use of the supply of high school graduates. The move to mass secondary schooling surely makes more sense when seen in the context of the organisational and technological changes occurring in the rapidly expanding service sector during the first half of the twentieth century. High levels of formal education can thus be seen as one factor behind the early industrialisation of services in the United States.

6.3.2 *Vocational training: intermediate-level skills*

Not all human capital is accumulated in schools, so it is important to supplement the data on formal education with data on vocational training. It is also important to draw a distinction between higher-level and intermediate-level vocational training. Higher-level training is taken to cover vocational qualifications at the standard of a university degree, including membership of professional institutions, while intermediate-level training is taken to cover craft and technician qualifications above secondary level but below degree level, including non-examined time-served apprenticeships (Prais, 1995: 17). Intermediate-level skills are examined here first, paying particular attention to developments in the service sector since World War II.

Table 6.6 provides ratios of apprentices to total employment in Britain, Germany and the United States. As well as economy-wide ratios, estimates are also provided on a sectoral basis where available. Data are taken from official sources, including occupational censuses for all three countries and various enquiries into apprenticeship training; detailed sources are provided in the table. Traditionally, apprenticeships have been concentrated in the industrial sector, and this is reflected in the table. The most striking finding is the much lower proportion of apprentices in US industry compared with both Britain and Germany throughout the period. The most important factor here is the different approaches to training in manufacturing on the two sides of the Atlantic, with US manufacturing oriented towards mass production with unskilled or semi-skilled labour, and European manufacturing more oriented towards flexible production with skilled craft workers (Broadberry, 1997a).

In services, although apprentice-to-employment ratios were also substantially lower in the United States than in Britain and Germany throughout the period, the transatlantic gap was smaller than in industry before World War II. This reflected the fact that the absolute numbers involved in service sector apprenticeship were small, even in Germany. After World War II, however, the German lead in the provision of intermediate-level vocational training in services became substantial, with the spread of apprenticeship into services. Given the importance of developments within services for the German overtaking of Britain in terms of aggregate labour productivity after World War II, this German lead in the provision of intermediate-level vocational skills in services is of major significance.

6.3.3 Vocational training: higher-level skills

An important aspect of human capital accumulation was the early development in Britain of professional bodies, a key function of which was to oversee professional training (Carr-Saunders and Wilson, 1933; Reader, 1966). The majority of these qualified professionals worked in the service sector, where Britain had a labour productivity lead over Germany and the United States in the late nineteenth century. Table 6.7 presents data on the employment of professionals in the three countries since 1881. The British data allow a distinction between higher and lower professions, and data on the higher professions are shown in panel A. The definition is taken from Routh (1965), and corresponds

Table 6.6 *Apprentices as a percentage of persons engaged in Great Britain, Germany and the United States, 1895–1991*

A. Great Britain

	Agriculture	Industry	Services	Whole economy
1906		4.19	0.65	2.48
1925		5.02	0.50	2.54
1951	0.17	3.22	0.59	1.87
1961	1.41	4.61	2.69	3.56
1966	1.34	5.08	3.18	4.01
1971	1.11	4.05	2.74	3.28
1981	0.56	3.67	1.98	2.58

B. Germany

	Agriculture	Industry	Services	Whole economy
1895		7.67	1.60	2.99
1907		6.38	1.60	2.87
1925		7.64	0.40	3.18
1933		6.48	0.48	2.28
1950	0.50	7.87	3.89	4.75
1957	0.73	6.95	6.33	5.70
1962	0.77	4.78	5.65	4.62
1969	1.60	4.99	5.50	4.89
1980	3.47	7.94	5.29	6.34
1988	3.89	7.39	5.31	6.08

C. United States

	Agriculture	Industry	Services	Whole economy
1880		0.95	0.07	0.25
1900		0.87	0.06	0.28
1920		0.91	0.06	0.34
1930		0.56	0.03	0.19
1940		0.47	0.02	0.16
1952		0.74	0.03	0.26
1960		0.72		0.24
1970		0.98		0.31
1975		1.00		0.29
1991		0.84		0.20

Source: Britain – 1906: More (1980: 98–103), based on data from the UK Board of Trade (1909a), supplemented with information from the UK Board of Trade (1915); 1925: derived from the UK Ministry of Labour (1928); 1951: UK Office of Population Censuses and Surveys (*Census of England and Wales*, industry tables, table 4); 1961: UK Office of Population Censuses and Surveys (*Census of England and Wales*, industry tables, Part I (10% sample), table 2); 1966: UK Office of Population Censuses and Surveys (*Census

broadly with the concept of higher-level skills employed here, requiring a qualification at the standard of a university degree (Prais, 1995). Although the key higher professions in the nineteenth century were in the Church, medicine and law, the twentieth century saw the growing importance of engineering, science and accounting. Increasingly, these professions have come to be restricted to graduate entry, so that in recent times information on professional associations does not substantially alter the picture of human capital levels gleaned from data on higher education.

To measure the growth of the professions on a comparative basis, it is necessary to include the lower professions as well as the higher professions, in panel B of table 6.7. Although Britain started the period with a higher share of the occupied population in the professions, the United States had pulled ahead by the start of the twentieth century. Although much of the existing literature on the professions concentrates on social aspects and eschews quantification, the idea of a leading role for Britain in the professionalisation of society during the nineteenth century and a leading role for the United States during the first half of the twentieth century does seem to be widely accepted (Perkin, 1996; Gilb, 1966). In Germany, the effects of the large agricultural sector and low per capita

Notes to Table 6.6 (*cont.*)

of Great Britain, Part I (10% sample), economic activity tables, table 14); 1971: UK Office of Population Censuses and Surveys (*Census of Great Britain*, Part II (10% sample), economic activity, table 16); 1981: UK Office of Population Censuses and Surveys (*Census eat Britain*, (10% sample), economic activity, table 9); Germany – apprentices: 1895 – Kaiserliches Statistisches Amt (1898), Berufs- und Gewerbezählung vom 14. Juni 1895: Gewerbestatistik für das Reich im Ganzen, *Statistik des Deutschen Reichs*, Neue Folge, Band 113; 1907 – Kaiserliches Statistisches Amt (1909), Berufs- und Gewerbezählung vom 12. Juni 1907: Berufsstatistik, *Statistik des Deutschen Reichs*, Band 202; 1925 – Statistisches Reichsamt (1929), Volks-, Berufs- und Betriebszählung vom 16. Juni 1925; Gewerbliche Betriebszählung: Die gewerblichen Betriebe und Unternehmungen im Deutschen Reich, *Statistik des Deutschen Reichs*, Band 413; 1933 – Statistisches Reichsamt (1936), Volks-, Berufs- und Betriebszählung vom 1933: Das Personal der gewerblichen Niederlassungen nach der Stellung im Betrieb und die Verwendung von Kraftmaschinen, *Statistik des Deutschen Reichs*, Band 462; 1950, 1957 – Statistisches Bundesamt (1957), 'Die Lehrlinge und Anlernlinge 1950 bis 1957/58', Beilage zum Heft 11/57 der *Arbeits- und sozialstatistischen Mitteilungen*; 1962, 1969 – Statistisches Bundesamt (1970), 'Auszubildende in Lehr- und Anlernberufen in der Bundesrepublik Deutschland', Beilage zum Heft 12/70 der *Arbeits- und sozialstatistischen Mitteilungen*; 1980, 1988 – Statistisches Bundesamt (*Statistisches Jahrbuch für die Bundesrepublik Deutschland*, various years); employment: Hoffmann (1965, tables 14, 15, 20), Kohler and Reyher (1988, table 5.2), Statistisches Bundesamt (*Statistisches Jahrbuch für die Bundesrepublik Deutschland*, various years); United States – Bolino (1989), US Department of Commerce (1975, *Statistical Abstract of the United States*, various years), the US Department of Labor.

Table 6.7 *Professionals in Britain, the United States and Germany, 1880–1991*

A. **Higher professionals in Britain, 1881–1991 (thousands)**

	1881	1911	1931	1951	1971	1991
Church	38	44	48	49	41	34
Medicine	21	35	46	62	80	115
Law	20	26	23	27	39	82
Engineering	24	24	51	138	343	542
Writing	7	15	21	26	51	79
Armed forces	8	14	16	46	40	34
Accounting	13	11	16	37	127	171
Science	1	7	20	49	95	114
Total	132	176	240	434	816	1,173

B: **Higher and lower professions as a percentage of total employment in Britain, the United States and Germany, circa 1880 to 1950**

	1880	1890	1900	1910	1920	1930	1950
Britain	3.6	3.7	4.0	4.1	4.3	4.4	6.1
United States	3.1	3.7	4.0	4.4	5.0	6.1	7.5
Germany			2.6	2.8	2.6	3.0	3.5

Note:
'Church' includes Anglican, Roman Catholic and Free Church clergy; 'Medicine' includes doctors and dentists; 'Law' includes barristers and solicitors; 'Engineering' includes engineers, surveyors and architects; 'Writing' includes editors and journalists; 'Armed forces' includes commissioned officers; 'Accounting' includes accountants and company secretaries; 'Science' includes pure scientists. Lower professions include: nurses; others in medicine, including veterinary surgeons, pharmacists and opticians; teachers; draughtsmen, including industrial designers; librarians; social welfare workers; navigating and engineering officers, aircrew; the arts, including painters, producers, actors and musicians. Dates for Britain are 1881, 1891, 1901, etc.; dates for Germany are 1895, 1907, 1925, 1933, 1950.

Source: Britain – 1881–1911: UK Office of Population Censuses and Surveys (*Census of England and Wales, Census of Scotland,* various years); 1911–1951: Routh (1965: 13–15); 1951–1991: UK Office of Population Censuses and Surveys (*Census of Great Britain,* various years); United States – 1880–1910: Edwards (1943); 1910–1950: Routh (1965: 13); Germany – 1895: Kaiserliches Statistisches Amt (1898), Berufs- und Gewerbezählung vom 14. Juni 1895: Gewerbestatistik für das Reich im Ganzen, *Statistik des Deutschen Reichs,* Neue Folge, Band 113; 1907: Kaiserliches Statistisches Amt (1909), Berufs- und Gewerbezählung vom 12. Juni 1907: Berufsstatistik, *Statistik des Deutschen Reichs,* Band 202; 1925, 1933: Statistishces Reichsamt (*Statistisches Jahrbuch für das Deutsche Reich,* various years); 1950: Statistisches Bundesamt (*Statistisches Jahrbuch für die Bundesrepublik Deutschland*).

Table 6.8 *Qualified accountants in Britain, Germany and the United States, 1882–1991*

A. United Kingdom

	ICAEW	Other UK bodies	Total UK membership	Professional accountants in census (000)
1882	1,193	290	1,486	
1891	1,737	1,092	2,829	9
1901	2,776	2,951	5,727	11
1911	4,391	6,950	11,341	11
1921	5,337	9,932	15,269	9
1931	9,213	16,340	25,553	16
1941	13,694	21,994	35,688	
1951	16,079	28,667	44,746	37
1961	35,228	30,174	65,402	110
1971	51,660	41,633	93,293	127
1981	72,695	67,726	140,421	142
1991	96,208	100,367	196,575	171

B. Germany

	Chartered accountants	Tax advisers	Total
1932	540		
1943		22,588	
1945	3,043		
1955		22,000	
1961	2,741	23,761	26,505
1971		26,294	
1981		39,171	
1986	4,925	43,905	48,830
1991	10,787	49,176	59,963

C. United States

	Certified public accountants
1896	56
1901	303
1911	1,780
1921	5,143
1931	13,774
1941	25,242
1951	47,224
1958	64,887

Note:
United Kingdom – ICAEW = Institute of Chartered Accountants in England and Wales; Germany – 'Chartered accountants' includes 'Wirtschaftsprüfer' and related occupations;

incomes can be seen in the restricted growth of the professions. Figures for the inter-war period suggest a substantially smaller professional sector in Germany through to 1950 (McClelland, 1991).

For some professional groups, it is possible to chart the growth of qualifications on a comparative basis. Data on the development of the accountancy profession in Britain, Germany and the United States are provided in table 6.8. In 1991 Britain had a substantially larger number of accountants than Germany, despite the similarity of the size of the labour force in the two countries.[3] Note, however, that if all accountants rather than just chartered accountants are considered, the British lead is not as great as is sometimes suggested.[4] Although the historical information is rather more sketchy for Germany, it seems that the British reliance on professional accountants is of long standing, and can be explained at least in part by the nature of the British capital market, which generated an early and growing need for independent auditors (Matthews et al., 1997). Note that the growth of professionally qualified accountants in Britain mirrors the growth of the number of accountants enumerated in the higher professional occupational group in the census.

The US data are derived from flows of Certified Public Accountant (CPA) certificates, which were established in 1896 following the British lead in professionalisation (Edwards, 1978: 69). The flow data have been converted to a stock basis using the perpetual inventory method, assuming an average working life of thirty-five years after qualifying. Allowing for the much greater population in the United States, it is clear that the density of qualified accountants was much greater in Britain, and this remains true today (Handy et al., 1988).

Although British services almost certainly had a human capital advantage over the United States during the late nineteenth century in terms of the proportion of workers with higher-level professional qualifications,

Notes to Table 6.8 (*cont.*)

'Tax advisers' includes 'Steuerberater' and related occupations; United States: numbers of certified public accountants calculated from data on CPA certificates issued.

Source: United Kingdom – Matthews et al. (1997: 408, table 11.7); Germany – Wirtschaftsprüferkammer, Düsseldorf; Bundessteuerberaterkammer, Bonn; United States – Edwards (1978: 362–3).

---

[3] The German figures refer to the former Federal Republic.
[4] Although Matthews et al. (1997: 409) note that in some countries taxation work is the province of lawyers rather than accountants, they provide figures only on the narrowest definition of charted accountants in their table 6.4.

this was increasingly offset by the rapid growth of higher education in the United States, particularly after World War II.

6.4 Conclusions

The changing comparative productivity patterns in services can be related to investment in physical and human capital. In services, as in the aggregate economy, Britain had higher physical capital intensity than both Germany and the United States in 1870. Before World War I Britain also had a relatively large supply of service sector workers with higher-level professional qualifications, offsetting any disadvantage arising from relatively low levels of formal primary education. Physical capital intensity increased more rapidly in the United States and Germany than in Britain, with the United States particularly forging ahead between 1870 and 1914. Any British human capital advantage arising from the higher-level professional qualifications was eroded by the growth of general education at the higher level in the United States, and by the spread of intermediate-level vocational qualifications in Germany, particularly after World War II.

Higher levels of investment in both physical and human capital in both Germany and the United States can be seen as proximate sources for the German and US overtaking. However, to understand why these countries invested more requires a consideration of competition, regulation and the institutional framework.

Appendix 6.1: Sources for capital stock time series

Figures refer to the real gross stock of domestic reproducible fixed assets, comprising non-residential structures and equipment, except where stated otherwise.

A. United States

1. **Sources for aggregate economy**
   1869–1899: Gallman (1987). Gross capital stock data for equipment assuming seventeen-year asset lives (pp. 249–50) and structures ('improvements') assuming fifty-year asset lives (pp. 252–3).
   1899–1929: Kendrick (1961). Public and private non-residential structures and equipment derived from table A-XVI (pp. 323–5).
   1929–1985: US Department of Commerce (1987); equipment and structures in all industries (table A6) and government (table A19).
   1985–1990: US Department of Commerce (*Survey of Current Business*, various years).

2. **Sources for agriculture, industry and services**
   1869–1929: Kendrick (1961). These figures are on a net capital stock basis.
   1929–1985: US Department of Commerce (1987).
   1985–1990: US Department of Commerce (*Survey of Current Business*, various years).

B. United Kingdom

1. **Sources for aggregate economy and individual sectors**
   1871–1920: Feinstein (1988, table XI, 448–9).
   1920–1965: Feinstein (1972, table 6.4, T99–T100).
   1965–1990: UK Central Statistical Office (*National Income and Expenditure*, various years).

C. Germany

1. Sources for aggregate economy and individual sectors
1871–1950: Hoffmann (1965, table 39, 253–4).
1950–1960: Kirner (1968, 108–9, Übersicht 29, rechteckige Überlebensfunktion).
1960–1990: Statistisches Bundesamt (1991).

7 Competition and the institutional framework

7.1 Introduction

Economic analysis suggests an ambiguous relationship between competition and economic performance. Schumpeter (1943) has pointed out that, although competition may be relied upon to bring about static efficiency, the prospect of monopoly profits may act as an incentive to investment and innovation. Hence, for Schumpeter, the existence of quasi-rents, based on temporary monopoly power, may lead to better dynamic performance. However, such a positive outcome is not guaranteed, since, as pointed out by Hicks (1935: 8), the 'best of all monopoly profits is a quiet life'. The recent influential textbook on economic growth by Aghion and Howitt (1998) models both the positive and negative effects of product market competition on economic growth, pointing out that which effect dominates is an empirical issue.

Although Aghion and Howitt (1998: 205) conclude that, on balance, the relationship between product market competition and growth is positive, they cite only evidence relating to British manufacturing during the 1970s and 1980s, from Nickell (1996) and Blundell et al. (1995). It is more difficult to draw such an unambiguous conclusion from the three-way comparison between Britain, the United States and Germany over the longer period since the mid-nineteenth century. Restricting attention to the two-way comparison between Britain and the United States, there is indeed ample evidence to support the proposition that competition has been a spur to better economic performance. Nowhere has competition been more single-mindedly pursued than in the United States since the late nineteenth century, during the period of catching up on Britain and forging ahead to sustained world productivity leadership. However, the situation looks rather more complicated once Germany is introduced into the analysis. Germany is widely perceived to have adopted a much less competitive institutional framework than Britain, let alone the United States. Whilst this can clearly be shown to have had some significant costs for Germany prior to World War II, it is hard to deny that there were also some successes, particularly in heavy industry. Furthermore, in the period since World War II, despite having a less competitive institutional framework, Germany overtook Britain in terms of labour productivity in services and in the aggregate economy. In terms of GDP per hour worked (although not in terms of GDP per employee or GDP per capita) Germany has caught up with the United States. Moreover, despite the return to a more competitive institutional framework in Britain since 1979 being more than two decades old now, productivity remains substantially higher in Germany than in Britain, and the situation is much the same in the rest of north-western Europe (UK Treasury, 2000).

To understand how the German economy did so well after World War II, it is necessary to examine the institutional framework of the post-war settlement in Europe (Eichengreen, 1996; Bean and Crafts, 1996). The idea of the post-war settlement was to stimulate investment through a commitment mechanism: unions were prepared to moderate wage claims so long as firms invested, and firms were prepared to invest so long as unions were prepared to moderate wage claims (Lancaster, 1973). Whilst this appears to have worked well in economies such as Germany, with sufficiently centralised unions and employers' organisations, it faced severe difficulties in a country such as Britain, with decentralised industrial relations (Crouch, 1993; Bean and Crafts, 1996). Although it was industry that was most directly affected by these post-war settlements, parts of the service sector were also highly unionised, and the wage moderation effects filtered through to services through wage relativities. Hence Eichengreen (1996) formulates the model at the level of the economy as a whole.

Whilst physical capital played a part in the German overtaking of Britain, human capital played a more important role, particularly in services. Germany has invested heavily in intermediate-level qualifications in services since World War II, with the spread of apprenticeship. Although there was a similar development in Britain during the 1950s, it occurred at a much lower level than in Germany, where vocational training has been accorded a very high priority (Prais, 1995). Again, the difference between the two countries can be seen as an outcome of the post-war settlement, with Germany providing a more centralised solution to the externalities posed by the possibility of 'free-rider' firms poaching trained workers whilst providing no costly training themselves (Carlin, 1996; Soskice, 1994).

7.2 Competition in product markets

7.2.1 *Competition and comparative productivity performance in industry and services*

Britain was overtaken in comparative productivity levels for the whole economy by the United States and Germany primarily as a result of trends in services rather than by trends in industry. An important permissive factor here was the sheltered nature of many services and the regulatory environment, which severely limited competition. In industry, although there were periods when protection and regulatory policies acted to slow down the exit of inefficient firms, in the long run competitive forces have operated more effectively than in services. In much of the service sector, competition from providers located abroad is impossible, while, in other parts, firms typically require licences to operate and are required to submit to a high degree of regulation. In these heavily regulated sectors, collusion between providers has been common, as is documented below. Whereas British manufacturers that failed to keep up with productivity growth abroad were ultimately replaced by imports, there was no such possibility of replacing the bulk of Britain's service providers. The survival of inefficient firms, then, is dependent on product market power. Without market power, it is not possible for the inefficient to remain in business in the long run.

A similar point has been made previously by McCloskey and Sandberg (1971) in the context of British manufacturing during the period 1870–1914. But, whereas there was a high degree of competition in most British manufacturing industries before 1914, cartelisation and restrictive practices had already begun to spread in a number of market services. The conference system in shipping and agreements on interest rate setting in banking are notorious pre-1914 examples of restrictions on competition (Deakin, 1973; Griffiths, 1973). These practices spread more widely during the inter-war period, as protectionist regulations limited international competition and governments encouraged domestic collusion. Policies of imperial integration were adopted as a response to the autarkic environment of the inter-war period, while collusion and price fixing were tolerated as a means to stabilise falling prices and so prevent real wages from rising in a world of sticky nominal wages (Drummond, 1974; Broadberry and Crafts, 1990). After World War II an anti-competitive environment persisted in many parts of the service sector, shored up by regulation and restrictive practices. Much of the transport and communications sector was nationalised, the financial service sector was highly regulated and resale price maintenance and other restrictive practices were prevalent in distribution (Hannah, 1994; Griffiths, 1973; Yamey, 1966).

7.2.2 Protection in the United States and sectoral productivity performance

The US economy is usually portrayed as being more competitive than the British or German economies since the late nineteenth century, with a tough anti-trust policy dating from the Sherman Act of 1890 (Neale, 1960). Nevertheless, manufacturing industry was highly protected in the United States before 1914, as can be seen clearly in table 7.1. Although the ratio of import duties to total imports is an imperfect measure of protection, most writers find that it captures the broad movements (Capie, 1994: 31–2). The ratio of total import duties to total import values, and also the ratio of total import duties to dutiable imports, follow similar trends in the United States, but with the latter ratio higher than the former. Although the trend was downwards between 1870 and 1913, the level of protection was high by international standards. Furthermore, on the basic measure of total duties compared to total import values, the United States remained more protectionist than either Britain or Germany until the 1930s.

The link between high levels of protection and rapid economic growth in the United States before World War I has been seen as part of a general pattern, with a number of writers claiming a systematic negative relationship between openness and growth during this period (Bairoch, 1989; O'Rourke, 2000). However, Irwin (2002) urges caution here, pointing out that the correlation does not imply causation running from protection to growth. First, Irwin argues that countries such as Argentina and Canada used tariffs largely to raise revenue, and specifically excluded machinery from duties, so as to build up export industries on the basis of processing primary products. And in the case of the United States, where domestic manufacturing clearly was protected, Irwin uses the data of Broadberry (1998) to point out that the US overtaking of Britain occurred through more rapid productivity growth in services rather than in heavily protected industry.

7.2.3 Protection and the size of the service sector in Germany

Tariff protection in late nineteenth-century Germany was designed to slow down the decline of agriculture and accelerate the development of heavy industry. The alliance of 'rye and iron' in the newly formed German Reich meant that – proportionally, at least – services had to be

Table 7.1 *Customs revenue as a share of import values in the United Kingdom, the United States and Germany, 1870–1989 (%)*

	United Kingdom		United States		Germany
	Total duties cf. total imports	Duties excl. tobacco and petrol cf. total imports	Total duties cf. total imports	Total duties cf. dutiable imports	Total duties cf. total imports
1870	7.1	5.0	44.9	47.1	
1880	4.7	2.7	29.1	43.5	5.8
1890	4.8	2.7	29.6	44.6	8.8
1900	4.6	2.6	27.6	49.5	8.1
1910	4.5	2.2	21.1	41.6	7.4
1913	4.4	2.1	17.7	40.1	6.3
1920	7.7	4.7	6.4	16.4	
1929	9.7	4.4	13.5	40.1	8.2
1935	24.5	10.2	17.5	42.9	30.1
1938	24.1	10.4	15.5	39.3	33.4
1940	22.7		12.5	35.6	
1945	38.2		9.3	28.2	
1950	31.2	2.9	6.0	13.1	5.4
1960	30.2	3.9	7.4	12.2	6.5
1970		3.1	6.5	10.0	2.6
1980		2.0	3.1	5.7	1.3
1989		1.4	3.4	5.2	1.3

Sources: United Kingdom – total customs revenue from Mitchell (1988: 581–6); total import values from Mitchell (1988: 451–4); customs revenue from tobacco and petrol from the UK Board of Trade (*Statistical Abstract for the United Kingdom*, various years), the UK Central Statistical Office (*Annual Abstract of Statistics*, various years, *National Income and Expenditure*, various years); imports of tobacco and petrol from Mitchell (1988: 474–80); United States – US Department of Commerce (1975, *Statistical Abstract of the United States*, various years); Germany – customs duties and imports from Mitchell (1980) to 1975, updated from Statistisches Bundesamt (*Statistisches Jahrbuch für die Bundesrepublik Deutschland*, various years).

the loser. This effective bias against services strengthened considerably after World War I with the growing scale of protection.

German agricultural tariffs can be seen as an attempt to stave off a 'grain invasion' from the United States. On the eve of World War I agriculture still accounted for 34.5% of employment in Germany, compared with just 11.8% in Britain. Even in the United States, a land-abundant grain exporter, agriculture accounted for a smaller share of employment. One effect of Britain's policy of free trade in agriculture following the repeal of the Corn Laws in 1846, then, was undoubtedly a further transfer of labour from agriculture into industry and services. The agriculture that remained in Britain was highly productive, and able to compete internationally. This was achieved partly by increasing capital intensity in what remained of arable farming, and partly by shifting the product mix away from grain towards higher-value-added pastoral products (Ó Gráda, 1994: 149–56; Brown, 1987: 25–6, 33). The high levels of agricultural labour productivity that already characterised British agriculture during the Industrial Revolution were raised still further, and the relatively small British agricultural sector continued to achieve output per worker levels on a par with the United States before World War I.

Webb (1980) argues that industrial tariffs in Wilhelmine Germany, often in combination with cartels, should be seen as an attempt to reduce the riskiness of investment in capital-intensive technologies by restricting competition. He thus sees tariffs as successfully stimulating heavy industry in Germany. To the extent that tariffs slowed down the shift of labour out of agriculture and accelerated the expansion of industrial employment, then services must have been squeezed. Nevertheless, the scale of the retreat from free trade in Germany before World War I must be kept in proportion. The figures in table 7.1 suggest that customs revenue as a share of import values was not dramatically higher in Germany than in Britain before World War I, although the scale of the difference is increased if the British figures are adjusted to allow for revenue-raising duties on tobacco and petrol, which were not produced domestically. Compared with the retreat into autarky during the 1930s, however, Germany remained integrated into the world economy before 1914. Table 7.2 shows multilateral tariff rates on a number of key commodities on the eve of World War I. They show Britain to be a free trade country and Germany moderately protectionist. However, it should be noted that Germany had a high tariff on wheat, the key agricultural product.

The consequences of these protectionist policies for German productivity performance have often been misunderstood. Contemporaries and historians have consistently overestimated the strength of the German economy before World War II by focusing on the modern sectors which policy was designed to promote. However, it is important to remember that these Gerschenkronian policies had adverse consequences for the less favoured sectors. The underdevelopment of these other sectors shows up not just in their low productivity but also in their low shares of economic activity. Olson (1963: 138–40) highlights the importance of these factors for the outcome of the two world wars, noting that it was Germany rather than Britain that succumbed to

Table 7.2 Multilateral tariffs in selected commodities, 1913 (German marks per 100 kilograms)

	Wheat	Cotton yarn	Cotton fabric unbleached	Cotton fabric printed	Laces	Bar iron	Sheet iron	Sewing needles
Russia	free	108.13	1,161.00	1,404.0	2,539.0	9.89	13.85	641.20
Spain	6.50	140.00	352.35	299.70	1,093.5	5.18	6.48	243.00
United States	3.95	67.20	51.87	103.74	45%	2.78	5.56	25%
Austria-Hungary	5.35	28.05	—	121.55	561.00	4.25	8.50	144.50
France	5.66	14.99	86.67	152.28	405.00	6.07	10.93	205.50
Italy	6.08	26.73	63.18	129.68	405.00	4.86	9.72	64.80
Germany	5.50	18.00	70.00	120.00	350.00	1.00	4.50	100.00
Sweden	4.16	22.50	56.25	123.75	450.00	free	4.50	45.00
Denmark	free	7.04	56.80	151.68	227.50	1.17	1.17	75.00
Belgium	free	12.15	64.80	81.00	15%	0.81	0.81	13%
Norway	4.86	13.50	28.13	123.75	674.50	free	free	84.38
Japan	2.68	22.28	62.70	87.14	69.60	2.09	2.61	175.89
Switzerland	0.24	16.20	8.10	48.60	81.00	0.24	0.49	40.50
Netherlands	free	free	5%	5%	5%	5%	5%	5%
United Kingdom	free	free	free	free	free	free	free	free

Note:
Percentage values refer to *ad valorem* rates.

Source: Grunzel (1916: 155–8).

blockade. He points to the ability of the British agricultural sector (138–9) to expand output on the stored-up fertility of grasslands brought back into arable use compared with the inability of German agriculture to maintain output at full stretch in the face of wartime disruption. However, he also argues that the decisive factor was the flexibility of the British service sector (146), which was able to draw on a wealth of experience in general administration as well as skills directly related to distribution and finance.

7.2.4 International trade in services

Systematic data on national shares of international trade in services are available only from 1970. For the period before 1950, however, it is possible to get an idea of the orders of magnitude from data on national shares of world commodity trade and the world merchant fleet. To estimate Britain's net exports of services during the century before World War I, Imlah (1958: 47–56) uses data on the value of Britain's imports, exports and re-exports to estimate profits on merchant distribution, and also on insurance and other financial services. To this he adds net shipping credits earned by the British merchant marine in the carrying trade of other countries as well as on Britain's trade, estimated on the basis of the size of the British merchant fleet. The data in table 7.3 on national shares of world commodity exports can thus be used as a guide to the relative importance of Britain, the United States, Germany and France in international distribution and finance, while the data in table 7.4 on national shares of the world merchant marine provide a guide to the relative importance of these same countries in international transport and communications.

During the nineteenth century Britain was the world's largest trading nation, and Britain's share of commodity exports was still substantially higher than America's or Germany's in 1899. By 1913 the United States had all but caught up with Britain, and by 1929 it was substantially ahead. Although Germany had also nearly caught up with Britain by 1913, there was a subsequent decline in Germany's share of world exports during the autarkic war and inter-war periods. These data reflect the rise of New York as the world's leading financial centre after World War I. The data on sailing ship and steamship net tonnage in table 7.4A show the strong dominance of Britain in shipping during the nineteenth century. Note that, in this sector, the United States lost an earlier position of dominance following the disruption of the Civil War. The decline of the US fleet was particularly marked in the international sector, seen here in the data on the US fleet excluding the Great Lakes

Table 7.3 *Shares of world commodity exports, 1899–1950 (%)*

	1899	1913	1929	1937	1950
United Kingdom	27.6	22.8	20.4	20.3	20.1
United States	20.7	22.1	26.2	23.1	31.8
Germany	17.2	21.4	16.0	16.3	6.3
France	14.0	12.1	9.8	6.6	9.8

Source: Derived from Maizels (1963: 426–7).

Table 7.4 *Shares of world merchant fleet, 1860–1950 (%)*

A. Sailing ship and steamship net tonnage

	1860	1870	1880	1890	1900	1910
United Kingdom	34.8	33.9	32.9	35.8	35.5	33.4
United States (inc. Great Lakes)	39.5	25.0	20.4	19.9	19.7	21.7
United States (exc. Great Lakes)	19.2	9.0	6.8	4.2	3.2	2.7
Germany		5.9	5.9	6.4	7.4	8.7
France	7.5	6.4	4.6	4.2	3.9	4.2

B. Steamship and motor ship gross tonnage

	1913	1920	1929	1939	1950
United Kingdom	42.4	33.6	30.2	26.1	21.5
United States (inc. Great Lakes)	9.9	26.9	20.3	16.6	32.5
Germany	11.0	0.8	6.1	6.5	0.5
France	4.2	5.5	5.0	4.3	3.8

Source: Derived from Kirkaldy (1914, appendix XVII), Svennilson (1954: 153).

tonnage. Germany became Britain's major rival in international shipping, although Germany's share of the world fleet was still less than 10% in 1910. Table 7.4B on steamship and motor ship gross tonnage shows the gains made by the United States during both world wars, with Britain as the major loser. Germany's fleet was destroyed or taken as reparations in both world wars.

By the 1970s, when systematic data on trade in services become available, Britain's tradable services sector was no longer much larger than its American and German rivals, although it remained more open. Part A of table 7.5 shows that during the first half of the 1970s Germany

Table 7.5 *International trade in services, 1970–1990*

A. Credits as a percentage of OECD total

	United Kingdom	Germany	United States
1970	12.1	10.7	20.0
1975	11.1	11.5	15.4
1980	11.3	11.8	13.8
1985	9.4	10.6	21.1
1990	8.1	10.4	19.9

B. Debits as a percentage of OECD total

	United Kingdom	Germany	United States
1970	10.7	13.5	23.0
1975	9.6	16.1	15.4
1980	9.2	16.0	14.0
1985	7.3	12.5	23.8
1990	7.2	13.2	17.7

C. Ratio of credits to debits

	United Kingdom	Germany	United States
1970	1.19	0.84	0.92
1975	1.24	0.77	1.08
1980	1.31	0.78	1.06
1985	1.36	0.90	0.94
1990	1.15	0.80	1.14

Source: Derived from OECD (*Services: Statistics on International Transactions*, various years).

overtook Britain in terms of the share of total OECD service sector credits, and retained a slightly larger share throughout the rest of the 1970s and the 1980s. However, since Germany retained a much larger share of total OECD service sector debits, shown here in part B, Germany remained a substantial net importer of services, while Britain continued to be a major net exporter of services. Hence, the ratio of credits to debits in part C of table 7.5 is persistently above unity for Britain and below unity for Germany. For the United States, the ratio has fluctuated above and below unity.

Despite the absence of systematic data on international trade in services before 1970, there can be little doubt that UK services exhibited a higher degree of openness than their German or US rivals during the nineteenth century and the first half of the twentieth century, given the importance of Britain in world commodity trade and the size of the British merchant marine. This would suggest a positive relationship between openness and economic performance, since the level of labour productivity in British services was relatively high during this period. However, it remains true that services were much less open than industry, with many parts of the service sector remaining effectively sheltered from international competition.

7.3   Competition in factor markets

7.3.1   Trade unions and labour market flexibility

The industrialisation of services meant an intensification of the labour process. This intensification of work and increased intrusiveness of monitoring are well illustrated by the data on clerical standards recommended by the Systems and Procedures Association of America in 1960, reproduced here in table 7.6. In addition to these extraordinarily precise allowances for the opening and closing of items of office furniture and the strange-sounding 'chair activity', there are detailed timings for many other activities, including 'cutting with scissors', which gives different timings for the first snip and for each additional snip (Braverman, 1974: 322). The example is extreme, but there can be no doubt about the loss of autonomy with the general trend towards intensification and monitoring in the modern office.

These developments would clearly have been unwelcome to established office workers, and led to a dramatic change in the composition of the British clerical labour force during the first half of the twentieth century. Routh's (1965: 4–5) figures show the female share of clerical employment in Britain rising from 20.2% in 1911 to 58.8% in 1951. A similar feminisation of the clerical labour force occurred a generation earlier in the United States, and is explained by Rotella (1981: 168–9) as a response to the standardisation of office work, which removed many of the firm-specific skills of the counting house. These firm-specific skills had acted as a barrier to the employment of women, who were perceived as having shorter attachments to the labour force.

As with mass production technology in manufacturing, modern office technology in services reduced the autonomy of workers, creating an army of workers performing standardised tasks and subject to close monitoring. And, as in manufacturing, the pattern of British trade union densities in table 7.7A tended to follow the pattern of big business growth, with high union densities in the transport and communications

138   Explaining comparative productivity performance

Table 7.6 *Clerical standards of the Systems and Procedures Association of America*

Activity	Minutes
Open and close	
File drawer, open and close, no selection	0.040
Folder, open or close flaps	0.040
Desk drawer, open side drawer of standard desk	0.014
Open centre drawer	0.026
Close side	0.015
Close centre	0.027
Chair activity	
Get up from chair	0.033
Sit down in chair	0.033
Turn in swivel chair	0.009
Move in chair to adjoining desk or file (4 ft. maximum)	0.050

Source: Braverman (1974: 321).

sector, and lower union densities in the distribution and financial services sectors. Although the sectoral union density data for the United States are not available at such a low level of disaggregation, they also follow the pattern of higher levels of unionisation in transport and communications. However, it should also be noted that the overall level of unionisation in the US economy was lower than in Britain. For Germany, the importance of a number of general unions precludes a sectoral breakdown, but the overall level of unionisation has generally been closer to the British than the US level, with evidence of higher levels of unionisation than in Britain before the proscribing of unions under the National Socialist regime between 1933 and 1945.

However, it is important not to see the resistance to the industrialisation of services as arising solely from the labour market power of trade unions. As in manufacturing, there is evidence that managers disliked the intensive monitoring as much as the workers who were being monitored. Thus, Campbell-Kelly (1998: 24) finds that managers in the Post Office Savings Bank were as strongly opposed as the workers to the introduction of modern office technology. The decision to retain bound ledgers, for example, was supported by management with the argument that a card-based system would be 'most troublesome and distasteful to the clerks' and would 'render their daily duties more irksome and difficult'. As Campbell-Kelly (1998: 24) notes, the concern of the managers with the welfare of the workers rings rather hollow given their previous

Table 7.7 *Union density in services and the whole economy, 1901–1971 (%)*

A. Great Britain

	1901	1911	1921	1931	1951	1961	1971
Railways	11.3	16.9	59.1	55.3	84.8	85.1	91.2
Road transport	14.6	33.3	59.2	48.8	93.0	91.8	85.4
Sea transport	10.6	83.3	73.4	55.7	80.4	84.0	89.8
Inland waterways	38.2	86.0	80.2	67.4	90.2	77.3	82.6
Air transport					56.1	49.3	68.9
Post and telecommunications	42.7	59.2	64.2	62.4	81.2	85.3	84.9
Distribution	2.7	5.4	9.0	7.2	15.0	12.3	11.6
Insurance, banking and finance	2.4	6.7	22.4	17.5	29.5	31.3	34.7
Whole economy	12.6	17.7	35.8	24.0	45.0	44.0	48.7

B. United States

	1910	1920	1930	1939	1953	1960	1970
Transport, communications and public utilities		31.4	24.0	50.0	79.9	81.2	73.0
Railways					58.3	91.2	
Government		6.2	8.4	10.5	11.3	12.8	32.5
Other services		2.9	2.5	6.0	9.5	10.2	9.9
Whole economy	9.0	16.7	8.9	14.9	31.6	26.3	27.1

C. Germany

	1901	1911	1921	1931	1951	1961	1971
Whole economy	5.7	20.0	50.4	31.5	38.1	36.7	36.8

Source: Bain and Price (1981: 37–8, 67–74, 88–9, 94–100, 133–4).

record, but there can be no doubt about their distaste for modern office technology. Thus, it is not simply that unionised workers resisted the attempts of managers to introduce new technology. Rather, workers and managers shared rents arising from a sheltered competitive environment.

7.3.2 *The financial system and capital market flexibility*

The German financial system is usually characterised as more of an 'insider' system than its more market-oriented British or American counterparts, with the distinction between the 'Rhenish' and 'Anglo-Saxon' systems having deep historical roots (Carlin, 1996: 488; Mayer and Sussman, 2001: 462). Although Gerschenkron (1962) has highlighted the role of German banks in corporate finance during the late nineteenth century, later writers have tended to play down the distinction between bank-based and stock-market-based lending, pointing out that the shares of the major sources of firm finance have not differed dramatically between Rhenish and Anglo-Saxon economies (Edwards and Ogilvie, 1996; Fohlin, 1999). However, Mayer and Sussman (2001) continue to emphasise the importance of the concentration of ownership for corporate performance, with insider systems characterised by concentrated ownership and consistently strong performance. Within this framework, the concentrated share holdings by German banks before World War II can be seen as providing an effective mechanism for disciplining poor management. By contrast, the mechanisms that emerged in Britain and the United States involved more market-oriented processes, such as the hostile takeover (Hannah, 1974b).

However, it should be noted that, whilst this insider system appears to have worked well in heavy industry, where German labour productivity was already higher than in Britain before World War I, this may have been at the expense of lighter industry and services, where Germany's labour productivity performance was substantially worse (Broadberry and Fremdling, 1990; Broadberry and Burhop, 2005). Tilly (1986) describes the German banks as providing 'development assistance for the strong'.

7.3.3 *The post-war settlement and competition*

Carlin (1996) sees the institutional framework established by the post-war settlement in Germany as underpinning high levels of investment in human and physical capital, and hence an important factor explaining the strong productivity performance. This institutional framework has enabled Germany to catch up with the United States in terms of labour productivity, despite being a long way from the textbook ideal of the competitive market economy. Carlin (1996) stresses three main elements, involving a centralised system of industrial relations, a vocational training system with both public and private elements, and an insider financial system. The centralised industrial relations system encourages high levels of investment, with unions prepared to moderate wage claims as long as firms invest, and with firms prepared to invest so long as unions deliver on wage moderation (Lancaster, 1973; Eichengreen, 1996). The centralisation of wage bargaining makes coordination easier and mitigates the free-rider problem, although Soskice

(1991) claims that there is still an element of flexibility via second-round bargaining at local level.

The vocational training system encourages high levels of human capital accumulation. The state contributes through the provision of vocational schools for apprentices and through setting national standards for qualifications. Unions and firms cooperate to establish the content of apprenticeships and to set training wages low enough to contribute to the financing of the training. Local chambers of industry and commerce monitor the standards of training provided by firms. The wage setting and monitoring of training act to mitigate the free-rider problem and reduce the extent of poaching (Soskice, 1994).

The insider financial system, with concentrated ownership, is seen by Carlin (1996: 488) as encouraging investment in physical and human intangible capital that is specific to a particular firm and its long-term relationships with other firms. These investments are seen as harder to make in a more market-oriented financial system because of the problem of realising their value in the event of a change of ownership. Nevertheless, it is important to balance this against the costs of the loss of flexibility, and the loss of international business which is attracted to the more open, market-oriented British and US financial service sectors.

Although the institutional framework ushered in by the post-war settlement in Britain was clearly less competitive than the institutional framework prevailing in the United States, it would be difficult to make the case that Britain was less competitive than Germany. This raises the issue of why the deviation from a competitive institutional framework was more damaging for Britain than for Germany. One issue stressed in the literature on corporatism is the fragmentation of interest groups in Britain (Batstone, 1986; Calmfors and Driffill, 1988). For Calmfors and Driffill (15) there is a non-linear relationship between the centralisation of the bargaining process and economic performance, with good performance in both highly decentralised and highly centralised systems, but poor performance at intemediate levels of centralisation This is related to Olson's (1982) idea that organised interests are most harmful when they are strong enough to cause major deviations from the competitive outcome but not sufficiently encompassing to bear the costs imposed on society by their actions.

Consider the incentives facing an interest group that is called upon to accept painful changes that will increase the size of the cake to be divided among all members of society, such as a trade union facing a technical change which would raise productivity but result in the redundancy of some members. The union could accept the change, but it could also resist the new technology and press instead for tariff protection or a subsidy. Rather than increasing the size of the cake for the whole society, this would redistribute a larger share of the existing cake to the union from the rest of society. From the union's point of view, the advantage of this redistributive strategy is that its members reap all the benefits of its actions. By contrast, accepting the new technology yields benefits that cannot be appropriated by the union, which nevertheless bears all the costs.

Notice, however, that the interest group can gain from the redistributive strategy only if it is not too big. In the limit, an interest group that encompasses all members of society has nobody to redistribute from. Hence, a country with a high level of union density, but strong control exercised by an encompassing central organisation, may be just as capable of avoiding distributional struggles as a country with a highly competitive labour market structure. The problems may be expected to be most severe in a country with high levels of union density but a fragmented multiple union structure. Hence, despite the fact that Britain did not have a substantially less competitive institutional framework than Germany, Britain's productivity performance was worse on account of the more fragmented nature of interest groups in Britain. Bean and Crafts (1996) emphasise the importance of multiple craft-based unions in Britain.

7.4 Concluding comments: comparative institutions

7.4.1 Before World War II

Theoretical analysis, together with an examination of the historical record, suggests an ambiguous relationship between competition and growth. It will therefore be helpful to conclude with a brief review of comparative institutions, highlighting the differences between the periods before and after World War II. Before World War II, although the United States adopted an anti-trust policy from the late nineteenth century, product markets in manufacturing were highly protected. However, since the US overtaking was stronger in services than in manufacturing, this is seen by Irwin (2002) as consistent with a positive relationship between openness and growth. In the case of Germany, furthermore, although protection and cartelisation appear to have stimulated heavy industry, they damaged services by slowing down the release of labour from agriculture.

In factor markets, Britain and Germany were both more heavily unionised than the United States, at least until 1933, when unions were proscribed in Germany. The German financial system was more of an insider system, with banks exercising strong influence over management, than the more market-oriented British and American systems. The insider system appears to have succeeded in mobilising capital for German heavy industry, but only at the expense of light industry and services. Hence, although there is evidence of some successes arising from the less competitive institutional framework in Germany, these successes were offset by substantial costs. Hence, for the period before World War II, on balance there appears to be a positive relationship between competition and productivity performance.

7.4.2 *After World War II*

For the period after World War II the relationship between competition and productivity performance appears more complex, since, although the United States has remained ahead of Britain, Germany overtook Britain despite having a less competitive institutional framework. This is broadly consistent with the findings of the literature on corporatism, which suggests a non-linear relationship between the degree of centralisation and economic performance. While Bean and Crafts (1996) point to problems arising from the fragmentation of Britain's multiple unions, Carlin (1996) highlights the positive aspects of the institutional framework arising from the post-war settlement in Germany, including the system of vocational training and the insider financial system, as well as the more centralised system of industrial relations.

Part III

Reassessing the performance of British market services

8 The 'golden age' of British commerce, 1870–1914

8.1 Introduction

This chapter presents a systematic assessment of the performance of the major British market service sectors in international perspective between the mid-nineteenth century and World War I. In the mid-nineteenth century Britain had the highest level of per capita income in the world, and this was underpinned by a high level of labour productivity, particularly in services. Although productivity growth in services was more rapid in the United States and Germany before World War I, this can be seen, in many sectors, as part of a process of catching up. This is well illustrated by the case of finance in table 8.1, which presents benchmark estimates of the level of comparative US/UK labour productivity in market services before World War I, extracted from table 3.2 To some extent, the process of catching up was inevitable, as the release of labour from the agricultural sector in rapidly developing countries such as the United States and Germany led to a catching up in the extent of urbanisation, with concentrated urban demands allowing a high degree of specialisation in market services. Since services also made a substantial positive contribution to the British balance of payments, and the services of the City of London dominated world trade and payments, the period between 1850 and 1914 can be seen as the 'golden age' of British commerce (Imlah, 1958; Kynaston, 1995).

However, there were clearly some developments in the United States which threatened Britain's dominant position in internationally traded services, and Britain's productivity leadership across a broad spectrum of services. These developments have been labelled the 'industrialisation' of services, with a move from customised, low-volume, high-margin business organised on the basis of networks to standardised, high-volume, low-margin business organised on the basis of hierarchy. This approach to business originated in the United States, and has been identified as a major source of US competitive advantage by Chandler (1980). However, whereas Chandler's (1990) later work concentrates on

Table 8.1 *Benchmark estimates of comparative labour productivity levels in market services, 1870–1910 (UK = 100)*

US/UK	1870	1890	1910
Railways	76.2	158.2	215.5
Communications			143.5
Distribution			118.7
Finance	43.3	68.9	119.9

Source: Table 3.2.

the emergence of the large-scale hierarchical corporation in manufacturing, his earlier work emphasises the role of a number of service sectors, including the railways and distribution (Chandler, 1977). Table 8.1 shows the emergence of a substantial US labour productivity lead on the railways by 1910.

The key factors underlying the industrialisation of services and the growth of hierarchical forms of organisation before World War I were: (1) developments in ICT, reducing problems of asymmetric information and allowing much closer contact between principal and agent in merchant/financial operations; and (2) the growing volume of economic activity, permitting greater specialisation in services, and hence allowing task simplification and easier monitoring of employee performance. Nevertheless, the extent to which the provision of a more customised service on the basis of networks remained competitive varied between sectors, and British performance tended to be better in sectors in which conditions continued to favour networks over hierarchy.

Although the British labour force had less general education than the US or German labour forces before World War I, this was offset by the large number of higher-level qualified professionals in the service sector. Nevertheless, the lack of general education among the bulk of the labour force hindered the adoption of new technology and new forms of organisation. To the extent that British networks failed to adapt to the threat from more hierarchically organised overseas competitors, it was necessary that they should be sheltered from international competition. One way in which this was achieved was through the growing strength of links between Britain and her empire in internationally traded services, as in international economic relationships more generally (Schlote, 1952). A second way in which competition was restricted was through the growing cartelisation of the domestic market and the spread of restrictive practices. The conference system in shipping and agreements on interest

Table 8.2 *Productivity in the British aggregate economy, 1871–1913*

A. Indices of output, inputs and productivity (1911 = 100)

	Output	Labour	Capital	Labour productivity	TFP
1871	50.5	69.9	44.6	72.2	88.0
1873	52.1	71.2	46.7	73.5	88.2
1881	59.9	73.5	56.5	81.5	91.5
1891	71.7	81.3	66.1	88.2	96.6
1901	86.1	91.4	100.3	94.2	90.4
1911	100.0	100.0	100.0	100.0	100.0
1913	106.6	102.6	103.5	103.9	103.5

B. Growth rates of output, inputs and productivity (% per annum)

	1871–1911	1873–1913
Output	1.7	1.8
Labour	0.9	0.9
Capital	2.0	2.0
Labour productivity	0.8	0.9
TFP	0.3	0.4

Note:
Factor shares are 44% for capital and 56% for labour, based on 1913 figures.

Sources: Output – Feinstein (1972: table 6); labour – Feinstein (1972: table 57); capital – Feinstein (1988: table XI); factor shares – Matthews et al. (1982: 164).

rate setting in banking are well-known examples here (Deakin, 1973; Griffiths, 1973).

The sectoral analysis shows a variety of comparative productivity and wider performance outcomes during the period 1850–1914. However, in general, British performance was better in the service sectors less suited to industrialisation, in which the network form of organisation remained dominant. In sectors in which networks remained important, such as tramp shipping, wholesale distribution, international banking and insurance, Britain continued to do well. However, in other sectors which required large-scale hierarchical organisation, such as railways and telecommunications, Britain began to fall behind.

In assessing the performance of individual sectors in the rest of this chapter, it will be convenient to have as a standard of comparison the productivity performance of the aggregate economy. Table 8.2 sets out data on output, input and productivity trends in the British economy as a whole for the period 1871–1913. Since data on labour inputs for

Table 8.3 *Comparative US/UK and Germany/UK productivity levels for the aggregate economy, 1871–1911 (UK = 100)*

	Labour productivity		TFP	
	US/UK	Germany/UK	US/UK	Germany/UK
1871	89.8	59.5	95.2	61.6
1881	95.9	57.3		
1891	94.1	60.5	83.3	63.2
1901	108.0	68.4		
1911	117.7	75.5	90.5	75.4

Note:
US/UK dates of comparison are 1869/71, 1879/81, etc.
Sources: Tables 6.1, 6.2.

individual sectors are only available at census years, we will be forced to present productivity figures at decade intervals and calculate growth rates between 1871 and 1911 rather than the cyclical peak years of 1873 and 1913. However, it can be shown that the bias introduced by working with the former dates is small, since for the aggregate economy Feinstein (1972) presents annual employment figures. In part B of table 8.2 we see that, over the period 1871–1911, real GDP grew at an annual rate of 1.7%, while labour productivity and total factor productivity grew at 0.8 and 0.3% per annum respectively. These are very close to the corresponding figures for 1873–1913, which are also given in part B of table 8.2 for comparison.[1] The figures in table 8.3 place this performance in international perspective. Whereas Britain had higher labour productivity than either Germany or the United States in 1871, by 1911 the United States had overtaken Britain and Germany had narrowed the gap. Note, however, that Britain retained a lead in total factor productivity levels until after World War I.

8.2 Transport and communications

8.2.1 Introduction

Output, input and productivity trends for the British transport and communications sector as a whole are shown in table 8.4. Although output grew more rapidly in transport and communications than in the

---

[1] See also Matthews et al. (1982: 228–9).

Table 8.4 *Productivity in the British transport and communications sector, 1871–1911*

A. Indices of output, inputs and productivity (1911 = 100)

	Output	Labour	Capital	Labour productivity	TFP
1871	37.0	48.1	42.8	76.9	81.0
1881	46.9	54.4	54.7	86.2	86.1
1891	62.1	70.3	67.7	88.3	89.9
1901	78.7	91.8	82.6	85.7	89.8
1911	100.0	100.0	100.0	100.0	100.0

B. Growth rates of output, inputs and productivity (% per annum)

	1871–1911
Output	2.5
Labour	1.8
Capital	2.1
Labour productivity	0.7
TFP	0.5

Sources: Output – Feinstein (1972: table 8); labour – Feinstein (1972: table 60); capital – Feinstein (1988: table XI).

economy as a whole, so too did labour and capital inputs. This meant that both labour productivity and TFP grew at approximately the same rates as the whole economy. The more rapid output growth of the transport and communications sector than the economy as a whole thus owed more to factor inputs than to exceptional productivity performance. Indeed, in an international context, the British productivity performance in transport and communications was decidedly disappointing, as can be seen in table 8.5. Whereas in about 1870 there was little difference in labour productivity levels between Britain and the United States, while Germany lagged clearly behind, by about 1910 labour productivity was more than twice the British level in the United States and more than 60% higher in Germany than in Britain.

8.2.2 Shipping: Britannia rules the waves

British merchant shipping retained a strong position in world markets between the mid-nineteenth century and World War I, operating about one-third of world tonnage. Nevertheless, as Aldcroft (1968a) notes, British shipping did face a major competitive threat during this period from Germany. To some extent this is reflected in table 8.6, where we

Table 8.5 *Comparative US/UK and Germany/UK labour productivity levels for the transport and communications sector, 1871–1911 (UK = 100)*

	US/UK	Germany/UK
1871	110.0	74.4
1881	146.9	97.3
1891	167.1	113.5
1901	226.8	150.0
1911	217.4	166.8

Note:
US/UK dates of comparison are 1869/71, 1879/81, etc.

Source: Tables 3.1, 3.3.

Table 8.6 *World merchant fleet, 1860–1911*

A. Thousands of net tons

	1860	1870	1880	1890	1900	1911
United Kingdom	4,658	5,690	6,574	7,978	9,304	11,698
Germany		982	1,181	1,433	1,941	3,023
Norway	558	1,022	1,518	1,705	1,508	1,646
Sweden		346	542	510	613	765
Denmark		178	249	302	408	538
Netherlands	433	389	328	255	346	565
France	996	1,072	919	944	1,037	1,462
Greece	263	404		271	319	484
United States (excl. Great Lakes)	2,546	1,516	1,352	946	826	932
World total	13,295	16,765	19,991	22,265	26,205	34,885

B. Shares of world fleet (%)

	1860	1870	1880	1890	1900	1911
United Kingdom	35.0	33.9	32.9	35.8	35.5	33.5
Germany		5.9	5.9	6.4	7.4	8.7
Norway	4.2	6.1	7.6	7.7	5.8	4.7
Sweden		2.1	2.7	2.3	2.3	2.2
Denmark		1.1	1.2	1.4	1.6	1.5
Netherlands	3.3	2.3	1.6	1.1	1.3	1.6
France	7.5	6.4	4.6	4.2	4.0	4.2
Greece	2.0	2.4		1.2	1.2	1.4
United States (excl. Great Lakes)	19.2	9.0	6.8	4.2	3.2	2.7

Sources: Kirkaldy (1914, appendix XVII), UK Board of Trade (1913b).

Table 8.7 *Competition on the North Atlantic passenger routes*

A. Number of westbound passengers

	1883		1903		1913	
	Cabin	Steerage	Cabin	Steerage	Cabin	Steerage
British/Canadian	39,838	160,634	113,553	303,769	230,071	476,119
German	10,934	119,531	62,859	321,342	111,253	393,704
Other lines	7,824	108,102	34,909	269,815	111,632	535,826
All lines	58,596	388,267	211,321	894,926	452,956	1,405,649

B. Percentages of total westbound passengers

	1883		1903		1913	
	Cabin	Steerage	Cabin	Steerage	Cabin	Steerage
British/Canadian	68.0	41.4	53.7	33.9	50.8	33.9
German	18.7	30.8	29.8	35.9	24.6	28.0
Other lines	13.3	27.8	16.5	30.2	24.6	38.1

Source: Aldcroft (1968a: 356).

see that Germany's share of the world fleet rose from 5.9% in 1870 to 8.7% by 1911. However, the German threat was heavily concentrated on the North Atlantic liner routes, and hence can be seen as fitting into the classic pattern of British business facing its strongest challenge in the 'industrialised' parts of the service sector, characterised by high volume, low margins and hierarchical organisation.[2] The scale of the German success on the North Atlantic liner routes can be seen in table 8.7. Between 1883 and 1903, in particular, British lines lost out to German lines, in both cabin and steerage class. Between 1903 and 1913, however, the British lines held their own, and indeed lines from other countries took business from the German lines.

Table 8.8 presents data on output and productivity in the British shipping sector. Output is derived from data on net tonnage, counting one steam ton as equivalent to three sail tons, since steamships could travel more miles in a year than sailing ships. Additional adjustments are made for trend improvements in speed and service and for capacity

---

[2] What is perhaps more unusual in this context is that, although German business succeeded in shipping, American business was relatively unsuccessful, and indeed the US share of the world fleet (excluding tonnage employed on the Great Lakes) continued to decline after the disruption of the Civil War decade (Pollard and Robertson, 1979: 9–12).

Table 8.8 *Productivity in British shipping, 1871–1911*

A. Indices of output, inputs and productivity (1911 = 100)

	Output	Labour	Capital	Labour productivity	TFP
1871	22.7	71.4	30.6	31.8	46.1
1881	34.1	67.9	42.7	50.2	61.6
1891	52.3	85.7	58.4	61.0	72.2
1901	70.5	89.3	73.8	78.9	85.9
1911	100.0	100.0	100.0	100.0	100.0

B. Growth rates of output, inputs and productivity (% per annum)

	1871–1911
Output	3.7
Labour	0.8
Capital	3.0
Labour productivity	2.9
TFP	1.9

Sources: Output – Lewis (1978: 260–3); labour – Lewis (1978: 265); capital – Feinstein (1988: tables 15.11, 15.16, 15.17).

utilisation (Lewis, 1978: 259). Between 1871 and 1911 shipping output grew at an annual rate of 3.7% compared with 2.5% in transport and communications as a whole. With the labour force in shipping increasing at only 0.8% per annum, labour productivity grew at the impressive rate of 2.9% per annum. With capital in shipping growing rapidly, TFP growth in shipping was less rapid than labour productivity growth, but still an impressive 1.9% per annum. Shipping made an increasingly important positive contribution to the UK balance of payments. Imlah's (1958: 70–5) data, shown here in table 8.9, suggest that, by 1913, net shipping credits amounted to more than £100 million per annum, equivalent to about 4% of GDP.

Britain's rise to dominance in shipping coincided with the switch from sail to steam. And yet sail continued to be used by British shippers on some routes well into the twentieth century. Economic historians of Victorian Britain have often tried to interpret the retention of old technology as evidence of 'entrepreneurial failure', but, given the success of the British merchant marine, such an interpretation would be difficult to sustain here. In fact, Harley (1971) succeeds in showing that British shipowners rationally switched from sail to steam at different moments on different routes because of differences in relative cost conditions.

The 'golden age' of British commerce, 1870–1914   155

Table 8.9 *Contribution to the UK balance of payments from shipping, 1841–1913 (£ million)*

	At current prices	At constant 1913 prices
1841	12.3	11.7
1851	15.0	19.0
1861	28.7	28.8
1871	47.1	47.3
1881	59.6	64.4
1891	60.4	67.7
1901	66.4	70.6
1911	93.4	97.0
1913	107.4	107.4

Sources: Balance of payments data at current prices from Imlah (1958: 70–5), converted to constant prices using the GDP deflator from Feinstein (1972: table 61) and the Rousseaux wholesale price index from Mitchell (1988: 722–3).

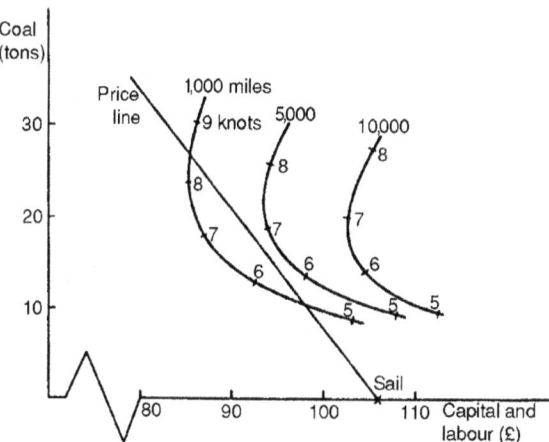

Figure 8.1 Production function per million ton-miles of shipping services, for steam and sail voyages of 1,000, 5,000 and 10,000 miles length, 1872.

Source: Harley (1971: 219).

The choice between sail and steam can be represented using a standard production function approach, as in figure 8.1. The crucial substitution is between coal and other inputs (primarily capital and labour). For steamships, there are different isoquants representing different length voyages of 1,000, 5,000 or 10,000 miles. On the 1,000 mile voyage, for example, it is possible to use different combinations of coal and other inputs by varying the speed, between five and nine knots. At high speed, more coal is used, but fewer man-hours of labour are required because the voyage is completed more quickly. Since sail does not require any coal and uses a fixed amount of capital and labour, sail technology is represented by a single point. Whether steam or sail technology is more efficient depends on the relative price of coal and other inputs, represented here by the slope of the price line that is drawn passing through the sail point. If the steam isoquant lies to the south-west of this price line, it is cheaper to use steam; if on the other hand the steam isoquant lies to the north-east of this price line, it is cheaper to use sail. In figure 8.1, which represents the situation in 1872, it is cheaper to use sail on the 5,000 and 10,000 mile voyages, but cheaper to use steam on the 1,000 mile voyages at moderate speeds.

In 1872, then, the advantage still lay with sail on long voyages, and even on some short voyages. Over time, however, technical progress in steamships meant that there were substantial savings in input requirements, moving the steam isoquants towards the origin. The main technical advance in steam technology was the reduction in coal use, which was important because steamships had to carry their own coal, which reduced the capacity for carrying freight. Refuelling along the way would not have reduced costs because most of the good-quality coal needed for steaming came from south Wales. Figure 8.2 shows the process of technical progress for the 5,000 mile voyage over the period 1855–1891. Although there was some progress in sailing ship technology, it was swamped by the much greater progress in steamship technology, so that gradually steam technology came to dominate on all routes. The actual pattern of adoption of steamships follows Harley's predicted pattern quite closely. By the early 1860s steamships were established on short British trade routes with continental Europe and were beginning to appear on voyages up to about 3,000 miles, especially in the Mediterranean, where variable wind conditions made the use of sailing ships a less attractive alternative. Steamships were established on 3,000 mile Atlantic voyages to the northern United States by the early 1870s, and on 5,000 mile voyages to New Orleans for cotton by the mid-1870s. After the opening of the Suez Canal, in 1869, the drastic reduction in the length of the trip to India and the Far East led to the

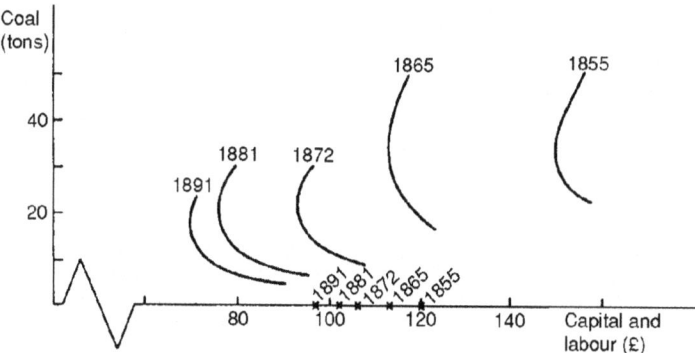

Figure 8.2 Production functions per million ton-miles of shipping services, for steam and sail voyages of 5,000 miles length, 1855–1891. Source: Harley (1971: 220).

adoption of steamers on these routes. However, on the longest routes to Australia and the west coast of America, sail remained dominant into the twentieth century (Harley, 1971: 223–5).

The success of British shipping in the mid-nineteenth century was based on networks, a point argued forcibly by Boyce (1995), who presents the most convincing micro-evidence of networks in the recent business history literature. Boyce's most detailed evidence is based on the pattern of share purchase in ninety-nine steamship ventures registered in West Hartlepool over the five-year period 1878–1883. In table 8.10, each row represents an occupational category, which attempts to capture the information asymmetries that lay at the heart of the network form of organisation. Each column represents an investment category, with repeat purchases capturing the building up of reputation and trust over time.

Boyce uses the data to distinguish between an 'active core', a 'passive fringe' and a 'public periphery'. The active core consists of the initial and repeat purchases of managing agents and partners (O and OR) for all occupational groups plus the repeat purchases (R and RV) of the maritime occupations (M1 to M3) and the elite commercial businesses (C1). The passive fringe consists of the owner's family purchases (OF) for all occupational groups plus the repeat purchases (R and RV) of the occupational groups outside the active core (P1, P2, S, and C2 to C4). The public periphery consists of non-owners who invested only once (V, SV, OFV and I). On average, the active core contributed 70.3% of the capital and the passive fringe contributed 9.2% with the remaining 20.5% coming from the public periphery. The fact that the public periphery

Table 8.10 *Ninety-nine steamships registered in West Hartlepool, 1878–1883 (pattern of share purchase by percentage)*

	O	OR	OF	R	V	RV	SV	OFV	I	Total
M1	43.19	3.86	0.11	1.20	0.13	1.03	0.63	0.00	2.04	52.19
M2	1.69	14.14	0.00	0.25	0.00	0.22	1.94	0.00	0.14	18.38
M3	1.29	0.61	0.03	0.21	0.00	0.00	0.02	0.00	0.77	2.93
P1	0.13	0.00	0.27	1.82	0.60	1.20	0.13	0.00	2.24	6.39
P2	0.00	0.00	0.00	0.28	0.08	0.00	0.00	0.00	0.49	0.85
S	0.00	0.00	0.11	1.56	0.13	0.00	1.01	0.09	1.70	4.60
C1	0.19	0.00	0.02	0.63	0.16	0.21	0.11	0.00	1.45	2.77
C2	0.90	0.00	0.00	0.30	0.00	0.16	0.24	0.00	0.69	2.29
C3	0.54	0.00	0.00	0.39	0.22	0.05	0.19	0.00	0.96	2.35
C4	0.00	0.00	0.00	1.83	0.33	1.07	0.33	0.09	3.58	7.23
Total	47.93	18.61	0.54	8.47	1.65	3.94	4.60	0.18	14.06	100

Active core	70.3	
Passive fringe	9.2	
Public periphery	20.5	
Total	100.0	

Notes:
Occupations – M1 = ship owner/managing agent; M2 = shipbuilder; M3 = master mariner, marine engineer, marine superintendent, ship agent, ship broker, ship's chandler; P1= gentleman; P2 = surgeon, doctor, solicitor, accountant, schoolmaster, architect, civil engineer; S = women and clergy; C1 = agent, Lloyds underwriter, coal factor, colliery owner, coal merchant, provision merchant, banker, licensed victualler, railway manager, railway superintendent, grocer, oil merchant; C2 = commercial agent, other broker, metal broker, other engineer, mining engineer, timber merchant, steel merchant, iron founder, iron merchant, iron/steel works manager; C3 = other merchants; C4 = others with commercial, industrial or farming ties and labourers; investment categories – O = 'owner': initial shares held by managing agent or partners; OR = 'owner's repeat': shares in a managing agent's or partner's ships, which he repurchased from investors, and/or purchased shares of ships operated by a second network in which he was an active member; OF = 'owner's family': share purchases by persons with the same last name and resident in the same town as the managing agent or partner; R = 'repeat': repeat purchases of shares in vessels operated by one network only; the shareholder has no other outside holdings

contributed more capital than the passive fringe indicates the existence of a sizeable market for shares, although this was highly localised.

The market for shares in steamship ventures in West Hartlepool was clearly not an anonymous market, then, but rather one where local knowledge and reputations played an important role. Although this evidence is highly specific geographically, a similar picture emerges from the work of Ville (1987, 1989) and Cottrell (1981) on other ports, including London, Newcastle upon Tyne and Liverpool.

There were a number of factors underlying the emergence of large-scale shipping lines organised on a more hierarchical basis. First, as the scale of demand increased in line with the growth of world trade and development, the provision of a regular service became more viable. Second, regularity permitted the establishment of a permanent bureaucracy performing repeated tasks that could be routinely monitored. Third, the growing use of steam power freed voyage times from the vagaries of the elements and made adherence to a strict timetable increasingly feasible. Fourth, improvements in communications technology, particularly the telegraph and then the telephone, made it possible to maintain continuous links with overseas offices, reducing the need for initiative on the part of employees and allowing improved monitoring of performance. Similar developments occurred across a broad range of sectors from the late nineteenth century, often initially in the United States, and this forms one of the major themes of modern economic history (Chandler, 1977, 1990).

The large-scale shipping lines that emerged by the early twentieth century can thus be seen as a competing organisational form to the entrepreneurial tramping network and as an early manifestation of the trend towards the industrialisation of services.[3] The early lines were

Notes to Table 8.10 (*cont.*)

(see RV and SV); V = 'various': shares held by persons who have several purchases, but no repeat investments in ships managed by any one managing agent, partner or network; RV = 'repeat and various': shares held by investors who have repeat purchases in one or more networks (and may have SV shares in other networks); RV refers to the repeat purchases only; SV = 'special various': shareholder has repeat purchases in a network (OR or RV) but has single purchases in another network (SV); OFV = 'owner's family various': purchases of shares by an owner's family member in other non-family networks; I = 'individual': shares owned by a person who has only one transaction.

Source: Boyce (1995: 52–3).

---

[3] Kirkaldy (1914: 167) traces an organisational lineage to the nineteenth-century shipping lines through the chartered companies of the seventeenth and eighteenth centuries, but,

Table 8.11 *Concentration in the German shipping fleet, 1914*

A. Tonnage owned by the major lines	
Firm	Thousand gross tons
Hamburg America Line	1,093
North German Lloyd	716
Hamburg South America Line	268
Hansa Line	339
German Australian Line	264
Kosmos Line	179
Roland Line	75
German East Africa Line	105
Woermann Line	112
Hamburg-Bremen-Africa Line	43
Total of above	3,194
Total German fleet	5,098
B. Concentration ratios (%)	
	%
CR3	42.1
CR8	60.3

Source: UK Board of Trade (1918: 95, 140).

often linked with postal contracts, usually with government subsidies. However, they soon became popular in the passenger business, particularly on the North Atlantic routes, where, as seen in table 8.7, the German shipping lines had considerable success. Aldcroft (1968a: 347) notes that the Hamburg America Line and the North German Lloyd already accounted for about 30% of westbound traffic on the North Atlantic routes by the early 1880s, and rapidly became the largest shipping companies in the world. By 1914, as table 8.11 shows, the eight largest German shipping companies owned 60.3% of the German-tonnage, while the three-firm concentration ratio was 42.1%. The liner sector was not confined to mail and passenger traffic, however, with freight forming an important part of the business.

To the extent that Britain's dominance of world shipping was based on the exploitation of a system of entrepreneurial tramping networks,

although the latter sometimes operated large fleets, they accounted for only a small proportion of British tonnage overall (Boyce, 1995: 26).

Table 8.12 *Consolidation among British shipowners, 1880–1920*

Period	Number of consolidations	Period	Number of consolidations
Before 1880	6	1900–1904	10
1880–1884	10	1905–1909	5
1885–1889	2	1910–1914	12
1890–1894	12	1915–1919	0
1895–1899	14	After 1920	5

Source: Boyce (1995: 78)

the emergence of the large-scale shipping lines organised on a hierarchical basis can be seen as an adverse development, from a British viewpoint. Seen in this light, the subsequent decline of British shipping becomes more understandable, and less of a mysterious missed opportunity than suggested by writers such as Sturmey (1962). Although a British liner sector emerged between 1870 and 1914, it did so in a way that retained many features of the network form of organisation, as Boyce (1995: 59–71) notes. Furthermore, the tramping sector continued to account for a larger share of total tonnage in Britain than in other countries.

Table 8.12 shows a process of consolidation among British shipowners, particularly during the 1880s and 1890s. Among a large sample of shipowners assembled by Boyce (1995: 78), fifty-one out of seventy-five undertook consolidations, including merging individual ventures into multiple shipowning firms, merging entire fleets and adopting limited liability. Table 8.13 shows the extent of concentration that had emerged in British shipping by the early twentieth century, with the largest eight enterprises accounting for 18.5% of all tonnage in 1910, rising to 42.5% by the end of World War I. Based on a contemporary estimate that 40% of the fleet consisted of liner tonnage, this means that the concentration ratio in the liner fleet (CR8*) was substantially higher at 44.6% in 1910, rising to 100% by the end of World War I.[4] Part C of table 8.13 shows the size distribution of tonnage for a sample of the British fleet, which provides further evidence of a much higher degree of concentration in the liner sector, and the continued dominance of small-scale enterprise in the tramping sector.

---

[4] The estimate that liners accounted for 40% of the fleet is taken from UK Board of Trade (1918: 54).

Table 8.13 *Concentration in the British shipping fleet, 1910–1918/19*

A. Tonnage owned by the major lines (gross registered tons)

Firm (and subsidiaries)	1910	1914	1919
British India	488,952	(merged with P&O)	
P&O	431,992	1,112,775	1,762,428
Cunard	217,109	469,916	558,380
Ellerman	316,544	685,058	793,772
Furness Withy	340,018	1,090,242	781,451
RMS/P	669,197	1,670,209	1,899,273
Holt	447,936	632,390	498,740
Union-Castle	296,328	(to RMS/P)	
Clan		251,570	326,766
Harrison		297,133	300,094
Total of above	3,208,076	6,209,293	6,920,904
Total UK fleet	17,300,000	18,900,000	16,300,000

B. Concentration ratios (%)

	1910	1914	1918/19
CR3	9.3	20.5	27.3
CR8	18.5	32.9	42.5
CR8*	44.6	90.0	100.0

C. Size distribution of a sample of firms

Distribution	1910		1914		1919	
(000 GRT)	Liner	Tramp	Liner	Tramp	Liner	Tramp
>1,000			3		2	
500–1,000	1		2		3	
400–500	3		1		1	
300–400	2				2	
200–300	2		2			
100–200	6	1	3	2	1	1
50–100	3	7	2	12	1	9
<50	2	77	1	70	1	36
Sample percentage of UK fleet	32.0		46.5		50.0	

Source: Boyce (1995: 128–9).

The threat to the British position was much weaker in tramp shipping than in the liner sector before World War I. Aldcroft (1968a: 358), for example, drawing upon the evidence in the UK Board of Trade (1909b), notes that the bulk of German shipping was employed in the liner sector, with tramp tonnage forming a very small share of the German fleet. Comparing tables 8.11 and 8.13, by 1914 the eight largest German shipping companies owned 60.3% of the German tonnage, compared with 32.9% of the British fleet owned by the eight largest enterprises. Similarly, the three-firm concentration ratio was 42.1% in Germany, compared with 20.5% in Britain. The major competition for Britain in tramp shipping came from Scandinavia and Greece.[5] However, it can be seen in table 8.6 that, between 1870 and 1911, the combined share of the world fleet accounted for by Norway, Sweden, Denmark and Greece fell from 11.7% to 9.8%. In tramp shipping, Britain retained a competitive advantage based on an extensive system of networks (Ville, 1990: 85–6).

In one sense, then, British shipping appears to fit quite well into Chandler's (1990) characterisation of British companies as retaining an attachment to 'personal capitalism', while 'managerial capitalism' developed in the United States and Germany. In contrast with Chandler's view, however, the network form of organisation continued to be suitable for certain types of economic activity, particularly in flexible rather than routinised services such as tramp shipping. Boyce (1995: 198–220) goes further than this, however, seeing the continued organisation of the large-scale British lines on a network basis as a strength rather than a weakness.

For Boyce (1995: 199), the holding company structure adopted in Britain allowed the merging units to preserve the reputation, client information and other specialised knowledge of the subsidiaries. This was bought at some cost, however, since it often resulted in duplication of agents and offices overseas (Boyce, 1995: 205). Furthermore, the evolution of a cartel system after 1875 makes it difficult to infer efficiency simply from the retention of market share. The owners of the major British lines operated a conference system to fix freight rates collusively and to avoid costly rate wars. Boyce (1995: 159–74) follows the majority report of the UK Board of Trade (1909b) in viewing the conference system in a favourable light, seeing it as a network-based cooperative system, which worked to the benefit of merchants as well as shipowners by ensuring that rates were high enough to maintain a regular service of high-class tonnage. The system of deferred rebates acted to encourage merchants to stick to conference shippers and to deter intermittent competition from tramps (Boyce, 1995: 160–1). Nevertheless, other writers such as Deakin (1973) have followed the minority report of

---

[5] UK Board of Trade (1909b, Vol. III, *Minutes of Evidence*: 402–3, paras. 11230–6).

Table 8.14 *British share of entrances and clearances at ports in selected countries, 1880–1911 (%)*

	1880	1890	1900	1911
United Kingdom	70.4	72.7	63.7	58.9
Germany	38.1	35.4	26.9	23.0
Norway	11.8	14.6	10.9	9.8
Sweden	13.5	20.5	9.9	5.4
Denmark	11.4	11.5	7.8	5.1
Netherlands	49.8	52.3	41.7	30.5
Belgium	59.4	53.2	44.6	44.1
France	40.6	44.0	40.6	36.1
Italy	34.3	49.4		28.7
Portugal	63.0	53.5	56.8	47.6
United States	51.7	52.8	52.8	50.1
Argentina	37.8	42.2	29.3	33.5
Chile	79.9	47.1	50.1	50.7
Japan			38.9	30.5
Canada	65.4	51.6	61.0	69.9
New Zealand	88.0	87.4	91.8	96.8
South Africa	85.6	87.9	89.8	80.0
India	79.1	82.4	79.0	76.6

Source: UK Board of Trade (1913b: 20–45).

the *Royal Commission*, adopting a more critical stance that focuses on attempts to deter entry and abuse market power.

The first conference was established among British shippers on the UK–Calcutta trade in 1875, and the system soon spread to other routes (Kirkaldy, 1914: 187). As competition from other European shippers grew, however, it became necessary to extend the conferences to include shippers from other countries. This affected the geographical structure of British shipping, with market-sharing agreements leading to a growing concentration on empire markets at the expense of European markets. Hence, table 8.14 shows a low and declining British share of entrances and clearances at most European ports, but a continued strong British showing on empire routes. In shipping, as in many other sectors, Britain was beginning to retreat from direct competition with the other major industrialised countries.

8.2.3 *Railways: penalties of an early start*

The modern railway age, with iron rails and steam locomotives, began in Britain during the 1820s. With three waves of investment, peaking in

Table 8.15 *Length of railway line open, 1831–1911 (miles)*

	Great Britain	Germany	United States
1831	140		95
1841	1,775	424	3,535
1851	6,266	3,817	10,982
1861	9,446	7,144	31,286
1871	13,388	13,342	51,455
1881	15,734	21,364	103,530
1891	17,328	26,984	168,403
1901	18,870	32,893	197,237
1911	20,015	38,513	243,979
Percentage increase 1871–1911	49.5	188.7	374.2

Sources: Great Britain – Mitchell (1988: 541); Germany – Mitchell (1975: table F1); United States – US Department of Commerce (1975: 728–31).

1839, 1847 and 1865 respectively, the British railway network was relatively mature by 1870, with a tight grid of branch lines built around the earlier trunk routes (Mitchell, 1964; Langton and Morris, 1986: 89). The pattern of growth of the railways in Britain, the United States and Germany is shown in table 8.15, which illustrates two important points. First, the British rail network was relatively complete by about 1870, increasing by only about 50% over the next forty years or so, compared with an increase of 188.7% in Germany and 374.2% in the United States. Second, there is an enormous geographical difference between Britain and Germany on the one hand and the United States on the other hand in terms of distances between major conurbations, which shows up in the much greater mileage of the US rail network.[6] This has important implications for productivity because the terminal handling element bulks proportionately much larger on short-haul journeys.

It is possible to construct indices of output, inputs and productivity for the British railway sector over the period 1871–1911. The first step is to obtain an index of output from the railway operating statistics in table 8.16. It is conventional to use ton-miles and passenger-miles as measures of output in the freight and passenger sectors respectively and to combine them together using passenger and freight revenues as weights. Here, however, the official data are available only on the numbers

---

[6] The population differences between the three countries are much less extreme. For example, the population of Great Britain in 1911 was 40.8 million, compared with 64.9 million in Germany and 92.0 million in the United States (Mitchell, 1975; 1988; US Department of Commerce, 1975).

Table 8.16 *Railway operating statistics, Great Britain, 1871–1911*

	Passenger journeys (million)	Freight loaded (million tons)	Average distances (miles)		Receipts (million pounds)	
			Passenger	Goods	Passenger	Goods
1871	360	166	10.0	30	19.4	25.5
1881	608	241	9.5	31	26.3	35.6
1891	823	306	9.0	30	33.4	41.8
1901	1,146	411	9.5	27	44.6	51.3
1911	1,296	517	10.0	28	51.7	61.2

Sources: Passenger journeys, freight loaded and receipts – Mitchell (1988: 546–7); average distances – freight: Cain (1980: 16); passengers: derived from Hawke's (1970: 51) estimates for 1870 and 1890 and Munby and Watson's (1978: 106) estimate for 1920, with linear interpolation.

of passengers carried and on the tonnage of freight hauled. Rough estimates of average distances can nevertheless be obtained from other sources. For passengers, Hawke (1970: 51) estimates average distance at 10 miles in 1870 and 9 miles in 1890, while Munby and Watson (1978: 106) find a figure of 10.5 miles in 1920. Using linear interpolation, this produces the pattern of average distances shown in table 8.16. For freight, Cain (1980) provides estimates of the average haul length in England and Wales for the period 1871–1911. Indices of ton-miles and passenger-miles are combined using revenue weights to obtain the index of output presented in table 8.17. With output growing at 2.9% per annum and labour growing at 3.4% per annum, labour productivity actually declined over the period. However, since capital was growing more slowly, TFP growth was just about positive at some 0.3% per annum. This was a dismal productivity growth performance on the railways, substantially slower than in the economy as a whole.

The sluggish productivity performance on Britain's railways contrasts with the rapid productivity advance on the US railroads at this time. Fishlow's (1966) figures, reproduced here in table 8.18, show labour productivity growth of 2.0% per annum and TFP growth of 2.1% per annum during the period 1870–1910. Hence, it can be seen in table 8.1 that, whereas in 1870 Britain had higher labour productivity on the railways than did the United States, by 1910 a substantial US labour productivity lead over Britain had opened up in this sector.

The poor productivity performance fed through to a deterioration in the operating ratio (working costs as a proportion of gross revenue), which rose from 51% in 1870–1874 to 63% in 1905–1909 (Gourvish,

Table 8.17 *Productivity trends on British railways, 1871–1911*

A. Indices of output, inputs and productivity (1911 = 100)

	Output	Labour	Capital	Labour productivity	TFP
1871	31.4	25.7	50.9	122.2	90.5
1881	48.4	42.4	64.2	114.2	95.1
1891	60.6	57.1	76.8	106.1	93.1
1901	80.0	85.8	90.6	93.2	91.0
1911	100.0	100.0	100.0	100.0	100.0

B. Growth rates of output, inputs and productivity (% per annum)

	1871–1911
Output	2.9
Labour	3.4
Capital	1.7
Labour productivity	− 0.5
TFP	0.3

Sources: Output – derived from table 8.16; labour – Mitchell (1988: 104); capital – Feinstein (1988: table XI).

Table 8.18 *Productivity trends on US railroads, 1870–1910*

A. Indices of output, inputs and productivity (1911 = 100)

	Output	Labour	Capital	Labour productivity	TFP
1870	6.0	13.5	16.6	44.4	43.4
1880	13.8	24.5	31.5	56.3	53.2
1890	32.8	44.1	61.9	74.4	66.5
1900	54.8	59.9	72.3	91.5	86.7
1910	100.0	100.0	100.0	100.0	100.0

B. Growth rates of output, inputs and productivity (% per annum)

	1870–1910
Output	7.0
Labour	5.0
Capital	4.5
Labour productivity	2.0
TFP	2.1

Note:
TFP calculation takes account of fuel as an additional input.
Source: Fishlow (1966: 626).

1980: 42). Although some early writers, such as Paish (1902), attributed this poor British performance to lack of enterprise, other potential explanations have been suggested in the literature, including (1) the nature of demand together with the competitive and regulatory structure of the industry, and (2) the disadvantage of the early start in Britain.

Although Aldcroft (1968b: 47) reaffirms the case for entrepreneurial failure, seeing railway leaders as devoting too much effort to empire building at the expense of efficient operation, most recent writers have preferred to emphasise the constraints faced by British railways. Ashworth (1960: 120–5) and Gourvish (1980: 44) argue that demand growth was concentrated in sectors with low margins, such as short-haul bulk traffic and third-class passengers, and, with existing facilities fully stretched by about 1870, further traffic growth required substantial capital investment. Furthermore, railway companies were in no position to refuse this extra business because of the dual threat of competition from other companies and growing regulatory pressure (Ashworth, 1960: 121).

A disadvantage of the early start in Britain was that the system was geared around technology that was becoming increasingly obsolete. Given the interrelatedness of the capital stock, this meant that piecemeal investments were often unable to embody best practice. As Clapham (1938: 350) notes, the size of locomotives, coaches and wagons was limited by 'bridges in congested towns, the short radius of curves and the whole lay-out of stations, docks and staiths'. The example of what Veblen (1915: 130) described as the 'silly little bobtailed' wagons for moving coal on British railways has been used by Frankel (1955) in his formalisation of the problem of technical interrelatedness and investment in a mature economy. In fact, van Vleck (1997: 140) has recently disputed this particular case, arguing that the wagons were small because this provided flexibility and substituted for the more expensive means of delivering coal by road. Nevertheless, even if this point is conceded, the general argument remains valid for other types of rolling stock and locomotives.

Both the above vindications of British railway performance raise issues concerning the efficiency of decentralised decision making. To the extent that the regulatory regime prevented mergers, and competition forced the railways to take on high-cost business that worsened productivity performance, there existed potential gains from amalgamation. Also, to the extent that amalgamations would have concentrated investment decisions in a world of technical interrelatedness, these potential gains would have been larger. However, if Chandler (1977) is to be taken seriously, it is possible to go even further than this. For him, it was the

The 'golden age' of British commerce, 1870–1914   169

pioneering of effective large-scale managerial hierarchies on the US railroads that provided the template and the human capital for the rise of American managerial capitalism more generally. Hence, it could be argued that one of the most significant effects of the fragmented structure of British railways was the failure to develop an effective managerial hierarchy.

To what extent, then, were there potential gains from amalgamation on the British railways before 1914? Dodgson (1993) provides some evidence on this by estimating a cost function from data on sixty railway companies, taken from the UK Board of Trade (1913a). Total costs (C) are related to passenger-train-miles (PTM), freight-train-miles (FTM), traffic density (DEN) and a vector of other variables (Z):

$$C = f(PTM, FTM, DEN, Z) \qquad (8.1)$$

Dodgson (1993: 163–4) uses the translog functional form, which is more flexible than the Cobb–Douglas specification commonly used. Returns to scale (RTS) are measured by the inverse of the sum of the elasticities of total costs with respect to passenger-train-miles (ε_{PTM}) and freight-train-miles (ε_{FTM}):

$$RTS = \frac{1}{\varepsilon_{PTM} + \varepsilon_{FTM}} \qquad (8.2)$$

Dodgson's (1993: 169) finding of constant returns to scale ($RTS \cong 1$) is consistent with Foreman-Peck's (1987: 709) results based on a sample of forty-six companies in 1865. Dodgson concludes that there were no significant cost reduction benefits to be achieved by amalgamation per se. Furthermore, the elasticity of cost with respect to traffic density was not significantly different from zero, although Dodgson (1993: 169) argues that working in terms of train-miles rather than ton-miles and passenger-miles may understate the overall effect of economies of density, since it ignores the effect of increased train loads.

Finally, to what extent did the fragmented structure of British railways slow down the development of an effective managerial class in Britain? In fact, there are good reasons to be sceptical here. First, as Channon (2001: 22–8) points out, drawing on the work of Wardley (1991, 1999), the 'Big Four' British railway companies of the pre-1914 period (the London and North Western Railway, the Great Western Railway, the Midland Railway and the North Eastern Railway) employed comparable numbers of workers to the four largest US railroads. In Britain, as in the United States, service sector companies, and particularly railway companies, played a leading role in the emergence of large-scale enterprise. Channon (2001: 28–50) also argues that British railways adopted integrated hierarchical management structures. The problem was not so much that Britain failed to follow US organisational methods on the railways as that the adoption of these methods in Britain did not lead to the same gains in productivity.

8.2.4 Telecommunications: new technology and organisational change

New technology brought about some dramatic changes in communications during the nineteenth century. Two of the most important new technologies were the telegraph and the telephone, which dramatically reduced the isolating effects of distance. This was bound to have an effect on asymmetries of information and the possibility of monitoring agents, and hence to have important effects on the organisation of business as well as social life (Perry, 1977). The impact of developments in communications on the 'industrialisation' of shipping services has already been noted, and later sections will explore the impact on distribution and finance. This section, however, concentrates on organisational issues arising in the telecommunications sector. As with the railways, the telegraph and telephone systems required large bureaucratic organisation to reap system-wide economies of scale. In the British case, a decentralised competitive telegraph system emerged before nationalisation in 1870, and nationalisation of the telephone system occurred only in 1912 (Ashworth, 1960: 117). Foreman-Peck and Millward (1994) see nationalisation as a response to market failure. However, it is by no means clear that performance improved under public ownership.

Figures on the key telecommunications services are given in table 8.19. The number of telegrams sent grew rapidly after nationalisation in 1870, peaking in the early years of the twentieth century. However, from the end of the nineteenth century there was more rapid growth in the telephone service. Turning to comparative data in table 8.20, Britain had a substantially higher number of telegraph messages per 1,000 persons than either Germany or the United States, although the margin of the lead over France was rather smaller by 1913. In table 8.21, by contrast, the picture was rather different in the diffusion of telephones, with both Germany and the United States showing higher densities than Britain in 1913. This inverse relationship between the use of the telegraph and the diffusion of the telephone has led some commentators to suggest that the behaviour of the British Post Office acted to retard the development of the telephone, which was seen as a threat to the revenue position of the telegraph (Brock, 1981: 132–6). It is true that the Post Office enforced its monopoly over communication by

Table 8.19 *Telecommunications statistics, United Kingdom, 1871–1913*

	Telegrams sent (million)	Telephone calls made		Number of telephones (thousand)
		Trunk (million)	Local (million)	
1871	8.6			
1881	29.9			
1891	66.5			
1901	89.6	9.0		3
1911	86.7	30.2		122
1913	88.5	36.0	797	731

Source: Mitchell (1988: 566).

Table 8.20 *Telegraph messages per 1,000 persons, 1851–1913*

	1851	1868	1913
United Kingdom	3.6	203	1,939
United States		166	1,159
Germany	1.5	146	960
France	0.2	148	1,688

Source: Derived from Foreman-Peck and Millward (1994: 55, 71, 109).

Table 8.21 *Telephones per 100 population before World War I*

	1913
United Kingdom	1.6
United States	9.1
Germany	1.9
France	0.7

Source: Foreman-Peck and Millward (1994: 109).

electricity, collecting royalties on the earnings of private telephone companies, and initially limited the size of exchange areas to preserve long-distance communications for the telegraph system. However, Perry (1977: 81–2) argues that some of the blame for the slow diffusion of

Table 8.22 *Labour productivity in the telegraph service, circa 1868*

	Messages per employee
United Kingdom	1,206
Germany	1,493
France	1,441
Belgium	1,754
Switzerland	2,255
Denmark	2,691
Italy	818
Russia	587

Source: Foreman-Peck and Millward (1994: 72).

the telephone must be borne by the private companies, since there was a general lack of consensus on the structure of the telephone service. Without consensus on whether the industry should be competitive, a private monopoly or a public monopoly, it is hardly surprising that expensive infrastructure investments were delayed.

Figures on productivity performance in telecommunications are difficult to obtain because the Post Office did not keep separate accounts for its different activities. Nevertheless, figures in table 8.22 for the telegraph system just before nationalisation suggest that Britain's labour productivity performance was poor. Labour productivity was about 20% higher in Germany and France, and more than twice as high in Denmark, with only Italy and Russia having lower labour productivity than Britain. This evidence suggests that, as with the railways, Britain did not excel in a sector in which the efficient form of organisation was a large-scale bureaucracy.

It is one thing to argue that British productivity performance was not particularly good in a sector in which Britain operated a decentralised private system and other countries operated a centralised state-controlled system. However, it is another thing to show that nationalisation improved matters in Britain. Indeed, Foreman-Peck and Millward (1994: 76–8) argue that, although nationalisation provided gains from system integration, these gains were more than offset by the removal of pressures for efficiency inherent in the move from private enterprise to state bureaucracy. Separate cost functions are estimated from time series data for the private enterprise period (1851–1868) and the post-nationalisation period (1871–1894). The cost function takes the basic form

$$C = f(Q, W, T) \tag{8.3}$$

where C is working cost, Q is the volume of messages sent, W is a factor price index and T is an index of technology. A dynamic error correction specification is estimated, allowing the derivation of a long-run elasticity of costs with respect to the volume of messages. The inverse of this elasticity gives the returns to scale. During the private enterprise period the long-run elasticity of costs with respect to the volume of messages for the Electric and International Telegraph Company (EITC), the largest operator, was 0.33, suggesting strongly increasing returns to scale. For the period after nationalisation, however, the long-run elasticity of costs with respect to the volume of messages was higher, at 0.47, suggesting rather more modest increasing returns to scale than during the private enterprise period (Foreman-Peck and Millward, 1994: 113–14). Too much should not be read into the results, since there are some severe measurement problems and the number of observations is small. Indeed, the possibility that there may have been an intrinsically lower rate of technical progress in the later period, independent of organisational form, cannot be ruled out. Nevertheless, the least that can be said is that the results do not support any 'grandiose claims for the superiority of a unitary state organization over a private firm' (Foreman-Peck and Millward, 1994: 77).

8.3   Distribution

8.3.1   Introduction

Table 8.23 sets out the data on output, inputs and productivity in the British distribution sector. While labour in the distribution sector grew at more than twice the rate of labour in the economy as a whole, output in distribution grew only slightly more rapidly. Hence, labour productivity in distribution actually shows a small negative rate of growth over the period as a whole. The capital data are for distribution and other services, and hence should be treated with some caution as an indicator of capital trends within the distribution sector only. Taken at face value, they show capital in distribution growing at a slightly faster rate than labour, so that TFP growth was a little more negative than labour productivity growth. This clearly represents a disappointing productivity growth performance.

Turning to international comparisons of labour productivity levels in table 8.24, the British performance clearly looks less worrying. Although the United States overtook Britain during the late nineteenth century, by 1911 the US lead was still only 20%. As Field (1996) notes, labour productivity growth in the US distribution sector was slow in

Table 8.23 *Productivity in the British distribution sector, 1871–1911*

A. Indices of output, inputs and productivity (1911 = 100)

	Output	Labour	Capital	Labour productivity	TFP
1871	47.7	42.7	41.0	111.7	113.8
1881	57.4	52.8	53.9	108.7	107.7
1891	71.0	66.7	63.7	106.4	108.6
1901	86.0	80.9	82.7	106.3	105.3
1911	100.0	100.0	100.0	100.0	100.0

B. Growth rates of output, inputs and productivity (% per annum)

	1871–1911
Output	1.9
Labour	2.1
Capital	2.2
Labour productivity	−0.2
TFP	−0.3

Note:
Capital data for distribution and other services.

Sources: Output – Feinstein (1972: table 53); labour – Feinstein (1972: table 60); capital – Feinstein (1988: table XI).

Table 8.24 *Comparative US/UK and Germany/UK labour productivity levels for the distribution sector, 1871–1911 (UK = 100)*

	US/UK	Germany/UK
1871	66.9	70.7
1881	107.9	38.6
1891	97.0	45.9
1901	107.1	49.7
1911	120.0	52.5

Notes:
Germany/UK comparison based on distribution and finance. US/UK dates of comparison are 1869/71, 1879/81, etc.

Source: Tables 3.1, 3.3.

comparison to the economy as a whole after 1869, but starting from a relatively high level. The comparison with Germany is complicated by the fact that the figures combine distribution and finance (in both countries), but the scale of the British lead is such as to suggest that

Britain must have been substantially ahead in the larger distribution sector.

8.3.2 Retailing and wholesaling for the home market

The most important changes in distribution for the home market tended to work in opposite directions. First, growing urbanisation and dependence on imported foodstuffs meant that fewer people lived within easy reach of the producers of their main items of consumption, such as fresh foodstuffs. This tended to lengthen the supply chain, with more intermediaries between producers and consumers. But, second, improved communications and standardisation made it feasible in some cases to shorten the chain of intermediaries (Jefferys, 1954: 9–10). Ashworth (1960: 129–30) argues that, on balance, the outcome was a reduction in the number of wholesalers, but an increase in their average size and the functions that they performed. As retailers needed to carry a greater variety of goods and ensure quality to their urban customers, the final stages of preparation were passed back from the retailer to the wholesaler (e.g. curing hams, blending teas, compounding medicines, skeining silks). However, particularly in the two decades before World War I, large-scale retailers increasingly bought direct from producers, bypassing the wholesaler. In the cotton trade, for example, Chapman (1992: 185–90) paints a picture of the home trade houses squeezed by such forces from the 1880s.

Clapham (1938: 238–51) emphasises the growth of large-scale enterprise in British retailing during the late nineteenth century, in the form of Co-operative Societies, department stores and multiple shops. However, quantification of these developments by Jefferys (1954: 1–39) suggests that they should not be exaggerated. By the outbreak of World War I large-scale retailers still accounted for only about one-fifth of total retail sales. By and large, the changes in the distributive trades that occurred before 1914 remained consistent with small-scale retailing enterprise.

The growth of the Co-operative Retail Societies can be charted quantitatively from 1881, and table 8.25 presents figures on the growth of membership and retail sales. The movement was strongest in the industrial north of England and Scotland, but the overall growth figures are quite impressive, with membership increasing at an annual rate of 5.3% between 1881 and 1915. Retail sales grew at about the same pace, so that growth came from the addition of new members rather than additional sales per member. Working in constant prices does not overturn the long-run stability of sales per member, although it does have

Table 8.25 *Membership and retail sales of Co-operative Societies, Great Britain, 1881–1915*

	Membership (hundred)	Current price sales (£ million)	Current price sales per member (£)	Real sales per member (£ in 1913 prices)
1881	547.2	15.4	28.14	27.86
1885	746.8	19.9	26.65	29.94
1890	961.6	26.9	27.97	32.15
1895	1,275.0	33.9	26.59	32.83
1900	1,707.0	50.1	29.35	32.98
1905	2,153.0	61.1	28.38	31.53
1910	2,541.7	71.9	28.29	30.10
1915	3,264.8	102.6	31.43	25.98

Sources: Derived from Jefferys (1954: 461); retail price index: derived from Feinstein (1972: table 65).

some effect on the short-run fluctuations. Although each society was autonomous, with its own board of management, it was also part of a wider organisation through the Co-operative Union and links with the two Co-operative Wholesale Societies. Hence, individual societies retained a good deal of independence while obtaining the advantages of large-scale buying through the centralisation of purchasing (Jefferys, 1954: 17–18).

A similar rationale underpins the growth of the multiple shop form of organisation, but within a capitalist rather than a mutual framework of ownership. Multiple shop retailing emerged in Britain during the 1850s, when W. H. Smith and Son and J. Menzies built up chains of bookstalls and the Singer Manufacturing Company established a chain of retail outlets (Jefferys, 1954: 21). Only in the 1870s did multiple shop retailing emerge in the main consumer goods trades, with particularly strong growth until the 1890s in footwear, grocery and provisions, meat and household stores (Jefferys, 1954: 24). From the mid-1890s to World War I growth continued, but at a slower pace, and spreading into new trades such as men's outfitting and tailoring (e.g. John Hepworth of Leeds) and chemists' goods (e.g. Jesse Boot). In this period some multiple shop retailers succeeded in establishing national chains; for example, the meat retailers Eastmans and James Nelson and Sons had over 1,000 branches each, while the Home and Colonial Tea Company, the Maypole Dairy Company, Lipton Ltd. and the Boots Pure Drug Company had over 500 branches each (Jefferys, 1954: 25–6; Mathias,

Table 8.26 *Number of multiple shop firms and branches in the United Kingdom, 1875–1915*

	10 or more branches		25 or more branches	
	Firms	Branches	Firms	Branches
1875	29	978	10	725
1880	48	1,564	15	1,093
1885	88	2,787	25	1,926
1890	135	4,671	47	3,468
1895	201	7,807	73	6,017
1900	257	11,645	94	9,256
1905	322	15,242	118	12,386
1910	395	19,852	149	16,462
1915	433	22,755	168	18,985

Source: Jefferys (1954: 22).

1967: 96–147, 165–91). The figures in table 8.26 show that, over the period 1875–1915, the number of multiple retailers with at least ten branches grew at an annual rate of 6.8%, while the number of firms with at least twenty-five branches grew at an annual rate of 7.1%. The growth rates are even higher for the number of branches. As well as economies of scale in buying, multiple shop retailers obtained economies of specialisation in administration and economies of standardisation in selling. With their low prices, cash transactions and rigorous advertising, multiple retailers can be seen as catering for the mass market (Jefferys, 1954: 27–8).

The other form of large-scale enterprise emphasised by Clapham (1938: 241–3) was the department store, which really came into being in its modern form only after the middle of the nineteenth century, as a number of drapery and clothing shops extended the range of their goods, adopted limited liability status and expanded. Until the 1880s department stores tended to trade on the basis of low prices, but from the 1890s a new emphasis began to emerge, stressing the attractiveness and amenities of shopping in a large store, together with the opportunity to examine a wide range of products (Jefferys, 1954: 20).

Jefferys (1954: 34) sees the emergence of large-scale retailing in late nineteenth-century Britain as dependent on the existence of a large, steady and consistent demand from a relatively homogeneous urban working class. The contrast here is most obvious with respect to Germany, for in the United States most writers have stressed the homogeneity of

Table 8.27 *Estimated maximum shares of large-scale retailers in the total retail trade of the United Kingdom, 1900–1915 (%)*

A. By economic types				
	1900	1905	1910	1915
Co-operative societies	7.0	7.5	8.0	9.0
Department stores	2.0	2.5	3.0	3.0
Multiple shop retailers	4.5	5.5	7.5	8.5
Total large-scale retailers	13.5	15.5	18.5	20.5
B. By main commodity groups				
	1900	1905	1910	1915
Food and household stores	13.5	16.0	19.0	22.0
Confectionery, reading and writing material, tobacco	4.5	5.0	5.5	6.0
Clothing and footwear	16.0	18.5	21.5	24.5
Other goods	7.5	9.5	11.0	14.0
All commodities	13.5	15.5	18.5	20.5

Source: Jefferys (1954: 29–30).

demand, even among the rural population. Whereas the mail-order store provided cheap, homogeneous goods to the rural consumer in the United States, this occurred on a much more limited scale in Germany (Chandler, 1990: 59, 420).

Considering the three forms of large-scale enterprise together, we can see in part A of table 8.27 that, as late as 1915, large-scale retailers accounted for at most 20.5% of total retail trade. Reliable figures are only available from 1900, but show that, during the period 1900–1915, the fastest growth was in multiple shop retailing. Although department stores increased their market share rapidly between 1900 and 1910, this was starting from a low base. Co-operative Societies still had the largest market share of the three types of large-scale retailing in 1915, but multiple shop retailing was catching up. Part B of table 8.27 shows the growth of large-scale retailing enterprise during the period 1900–1915, broken down by main commodity groups. Here we see that large-scale retailing was concentrated in particular areas, especially clothing and footwear, and food and household stores.

It is important, then, not to exaggerate the importance of large-scale retailing before World War I. The majority of retail outlets remained

Table 8.28 *Number and density of residential shops in Great Britain, 1869/72–1909/11*

	Number of shops	Number of shops per 10,000 population
1869/72	177,000	68
1879/82	230,000	77
1889/92	249,000	76
1899/02	293,000	79
1909/11	310,000	76

Note:
Figures relate to shops with a value of at least £20 assessed under the Inhabited House Duty.
Source: Jefferys (1954: 15).

small, often independent family businesses, catering for local markets. Although there are no comprehensive data on such shops, Jefferys (1954: 15) does present figures on the number of residential shops assessed under the Inhabited House Duty, and these figures are reproduced here in table 8.28. There are a number of problems with these figures, including: first, residential shops below the £20 limit are excluded; second, 'lock-up' shops are excluded; and, third, producer/retailers may not be classified consistently. Nevertheless, even these highly imperfect figures show the number of small shops more than keeping pace with the growth of population.

Many of the main developments within retailing, then, turned out to be consistent with small-scale enterprise, at least in the period before World War I. These developments included: first, the growing importance of fixed shops, replacing pedlars and fairs; second, the adoption of openly declared prices to replace haggling; and, third, the introduction of branding and packaging (Ashworth, 1960: 131–2). Most fixed shops remained relatively small, residential premises, while the adoption of declared prices, together with branding and packaging, led to experimentation with resale price maintenance, which protected small retailers from undercutting (Yamey, 1952). Nevertheless, large-scale retailing had gained a foothold, and would become more important after World War I.

8.3.3 Wholesale merchants and external trade

International trade played a very important part in the transformation of Victorian Britain, with Britain assuming a distinctive role in the

Table 8.29 *Visible trade of the United Kingdom, 1871–1911*

A. Values at current prices (£ million)

	Total imports	Domestic exports	Re-exports
1871	331.0	223.1	60.5
1881	397.0	234.0	63.1
1891	435.4	247.2	61.9
1901	522.0	280.0	67.8
1911	680.2	454.1	102.8

B. Shares of GDP at market prices (%)

	Total imports	Domestic exports and re-exports
1871	27.1	23.2
1881	30.5	22.8
1891	29.0	20.6
1901	25.9	17.2
1911	29.4	24.0

Sources: Trade data – Mitchell (1988: 453); GDP data – Feinstein (1972: table 3).

international division of labour. Under a free trade regime, Britain allowed her agriculture to shrink and specialised in the export of a limited range of staple manufactures (Saul, 1960: 43–64). This section is concerned with the activities of the merchants who organised this 'visible' trade in commodities. The quantitative dimensions of the trade are summarised in table 8.29. Between 1871 and 1911 total imports accounted for around 25 to 30% of GDP at market prices, while domestic exports and re-exports together accounted for around 20 to 25%.[7] The sizeable deficit on visible trade was balanced by a surplus on invisible items such as business services, emigrant funds and interest and dividends, yielding a surplus on the current account of the balance of payments, which can be taken as a measure of net investment abroad (Imlah, 1958: 42–81; Feinstein, 1972: table 8.15).

Volume measures of total imports, domestic exports and re-exports are available in table 8.30, and suggest that international trade grew substantially faster than aggregate output over the period 1871–1911.

---

[7] In a national income accounting framework it is usual to net out the entrepôt trade and to focus on retained imports, defined as total imports minus re-exports. However, they are included here because the import and re-export of overseas produce was an important part of the business of the distribution sector.

Table 8.30 *Volume of visible trade, United Kingdom, 1871–1911*

A. Volume indices (1911 = 100)

	Total imports	Domestic exports	Re-exports
1871	37.6	38.2	52.5
1881	49.3	49.4	60.3
1891	66.0	57.1	74.6
1901	86.2	64.9	82.4
1911	100.0	100.0	100.0

B. Average annual growth rates (%)

	Total imports	Domestic exports	Re-exports
1871–1911	2.4	2.4	1.6
1871–1881	2.7	2.6	1.4
1881–1891	2.9	1.4	2.1
1891–1901	2.7	1.3	1.0
1901–1911	1.5	4.3	1.9

Source: Imlah (1958: 97–8, 207).

Table 8.31 *Price indices for exports, imports and the aggregate output of the United Kingdom, 1871–1911 (1911 = 100)*

	Price of visible domestic exports	Price of visible retained imports	GDP deflator	Net barter terms of trade
1871	128.5	132.4	103.4	97.1
1881	104.4	121.6	96.1	85.9
1891	95.3	100.0	92.6	95.3
1901	95.1	90.7	97.7	104.9
1911	100.0	100.0	100.0	100.0

Sources: Imlah (1958: 97–8), Feinstein (1972: table 61).

Whereas real GDP grew at an annual rate of 1.7% during the period 1871–1911, real total imports and real domestic exports grew at 2.4% per annum, and re-exports at 1.6% per annum. Since trade as a share of nominal GDP (in table 8.29) remained essentially stationary, this implies that there was a downward trend in the relative price of both retained imports (total imports minus re-exports) and domestic exports. This can be seen in table 8.31, which provides price indices for retained imports, domestic exports and aggregate output. The table charts what happened to the net barter terms of trade, calculated as the ratio of the domestic export price index to the retained import price index. Although the terms of trade were stationary over the period as a whole, this reflected a worsening during the 1870s and 1900s and an improvement during the 1880s and 1890s. Returning to the volume indices in table 8.30, there is evidence of a negative relationship between the terms of trade and export growth and a positive relationship between the terms of trade and import growth. Exports boomed and imports slumped as the price of exports declined relative to the price of imports in the 1870s and 1900s, while exports slumped and imports boomed as the price of exports rose relative to the price of imports during the 1880s and 1890s.

Table 8.32 shows the principal items in which shipping merchants had to deal. Figures have been included in the table where a commodity accounted for at least 3% of total imports or 3% of domestic exports plus re-exports in 1871 or 1911. On the import side, the key commodities were raw cotton and grain and flour, with the bulk of British imports consisting of food and raw materials. On the export side, the key item was cotton goods. Although woollen goods had also been very important in 1871, they accounted for a smaller share of exports by 1911. Iron and steel remained important despite the growth of strong international competition, while coal, machinery and chemicals were all growing in importance.

Turning to the geographical composition of trade, table 8.33 provides a breakdown of visible imports and exports by continent. On the import side, the shares of Europe and America remained stable over the period 1871–1911. The biggest changes were the rise in Australasia's share and the corresponding decline in Asia's share. On the export side, the shares of Europe and North America declined, while South America's share remained stable. Britain became increasingly reliant for export markets on Australasia, Africa and Asia. This all led to the pattern of multilateral payments noted by Saul (1960: 45, 59–60), with Britain earning a surplus on trade with the primary producing countries of Africa, Asia, South America and Australasia to offset a deficit with the industrial countries of Europe and North America. Another important aspect of the geographical composition of trade is the role of the British Empire. In table 8.34 the share of the empire in British trade remained fairly stationary over the period 1861–1911, accounting for about a quarter of imports and about a third of exports. The drop in the empire share of exports between 1861 and 1871 was a temporary phenomenon, occasioned by a rise in exports to the United States and

Table 8.32 *Principal visible imports and exports of the United Kingdom, 1871–1911*

A. Principal imports

	Current values, c.i.f. (£ million)		Shares of total imports (%)	
	1871	1911	1871	1911
Grain and flour	42.7	71.7	12.9	10.5
Sugar, refined and unrefined	18.2	26.6	5.5	3.9
Tea	11.6	13.0	3.5	1.9
Meat and animals	10.4	49.7	3.1	7.3
Butter and margarine	6.9	27.1	2.1	4.0
Timber	12.3	25.9	3.7	3.8
Raw cotton	55.9	71.2	16.9	10.5
Raw wool	18.4	34.5	5.6	5.1
Oil, oilseed, gums, resins, tallow, etc.	18.6	29.4	5.6	4.3
Non-ferrous metals and manufactures	5.9	24.2	1.8	3.6
Total of above	200.9	373.3	60.7	54.9

B. Principal exports

	Current values, f.o.b. (£ million)		Shares of total exports and re-exports (%)	
	1871	1911	1871	1911
Coal	6.2	38.4	2.2	6.9
Iron and steel	25.5	44.8	9.0	8.0
Machinery	6.0	31.0	2.1	5.6
Cotton goods	72.8	120.1	25.7	21.6
Woollen goods	33.3	31.8	11.7	5.7
Chemicals	6.2	20.1	2.2	3.6
Total of above	150.0	286.2	52.9	51.4

Notes:
Imports – figures shown for commodities account for at least 3% of total imports in 1871 or 1911; exports – figures shown for commodities account for at least 3% of exports plus re-exports in 1871 or 1911.
Source: Mitchell (1988: 475–8, 482–3).

central Europe as a result of the civil war in North America and the railway boom and the Franco-Prussian war in Europe (Schlote, 1952: 90). Throughout the period 1861–1911, however, the settler colonies that were to be granted dominion status in the 1930s increased their

Table 8.33 *UK visible imports and exports by continent, 1871–1911 (%)*

A. Imports

	1871	1881	1891	1901	1911
Europe	41.3	38.4	43.3	42.7	41.4
Africa	7.5	5.0	5.0	4.4	6.4
Asia	16.1	14.9	13.3	9.7	12.8
North America	21.4	29.0	27.0	31.0	22.1
South America	9.2	5.9	4.1	5.4	8.8
Australasia	4.5	6.8	7.3	6.8	8.5

B. Exports

	1871	1881	1891	1901	1911
Europe	43.7	35.7	35.6	36.5	35.3
Africa	5.5	5.9	6.9	11.8	10.5
Asia	15.8	22.1	22.0	23.6	22.4
North America	19.5	17.1	14.8	10.1	11.1
South America	11.0	10.0	10.3	8.3	11.6
Australasia	4.5	9.2	10.4	9.7	9.1

Source: Schlote (1952: 156–60).

Table 8.34 *The role of the British Empire in British visible trade, 1871–1911 (%)*

A. Shares of British possessions in British trade

	1861	1871	1881	1891	1901	1911
Total imports	24.2	22.0	23.1	22.8	20.2	25.2
Domestic exports	33.8	23.0	33.9	34.8	37.4	35.0
Re-exports	8.4	7.1	11.6	11.9	12.3	12.7

B. Dominions' share of British trade with the empire

	1861	1871	1881	1891	1901	1911
Total imports	32.3	36.6	47.7	50.4	57.1	53.8
Domestic exports	38.7	40.0	46.4	47.4	49.9	51.1
Re-exports	49.1	47.2	56.3	60.8	71.5	71.1

Source: Schlote (1952: 161–2).

share of British trade with the empire. Here, however, note that the links with Australia, New Zealand and South Africa were growing more strongly than the links with Canada and Newfoundland (Schlote, 1952: 93, 168–9).

Although there is a large literature on merchants during the 'long' nineteenth century, much of it is essentially historical narrative based on the activities of a specific individual or company. However, the major study by Chapman (1992) offers a more general treatment based on wide coverage and a thematic approach. For the period after 1870 Chapman's main theme is the response to improved communications. With the introduction of the telegraph and the telephone, the possibility of instant communications had arrived, greatly reducing asymmetry of information and allowing much closer monitoring of agents. Chapman (1992: 193–230) examines the response of merchants to these developments in the cotton trade, the grain trade and a group of 'innovative trades' such as oil, rubber, meat and bananas. In general, the effects of the improved communications were to put pressure on the scale of commissions and the length of the supply chain. Nevertheless, there were important differences between trades.

In the cotton trade, we need to consider the import of raw cotton as well as the export of yarns and cloth. In the early nineteenth century the chain of middlemen involved in bringing raw cotton from America to Britain involved merchants in the southern United States, shippers, merchants in the British ports, cotton brokers in Liverpool, cotton dealers in Manchester and other Lancashire spinning centres, and buying brokers to represent the spinners (Chapman, 1992: 195; Edwards, 1967: 107–25). By the mid-nineteenth century the railway system was such that Lancashire spinners could make a weekly visit to Liverpool to buy cotton, and the trade was dominated by Liverpool merchants (Farnie, 1979a: 58–9). Continental European producers also used the Liverpool market. After about 1870, however, the position of Liverpool's merchants was undermined by a number of developments. First, the opening of the Suez Canal in 1869 meant that continental European producers could import cotton direct from India via continental ports. Second, the organisation in 1870 of the New York cotton market exclusively for futures trading meant that cotton could now be bought easily in standard quantities and qualities for delivery up to a year ahead. And, third, the relaying of the Atlantic cable in 1872 extended the influence of New York to continental Europe (Farnie, 1979a: 60).

However, Liverpool fought back, in particular with the organisation of its own futures market. Chapman's (1992: 197) figures on capital in a number of major US and UK merchant houses in the early twentieth

Table 8.35 *Capital of some major US and UK raw cotton merchants in the early twentieth century*

A. Major US houses

Merchant house	Base	Overseas partners or branches	Capital (£ thousand)	Date
Sprunt	Wilmington, NC	Liverpool; Bremen	300	1907
Weld	Montgomery, AL	Liverpool; Bremen	250	1907
Anderson Clayton	Houston, TX	Liverpool	200	1914
McFadden	Philadelphia, PA	Liverpool; Bremen; Le Havre	75	1904

B. Major UK houses

Merchant house	Base	Overseas partners or branches	Capital (£ thousand)	Date
Smith, Edwards and Co.	Liverpool	Calcutta	500	1904
Alexander Eccles	Liverpool		250	1906
W. H. Midwood and Co.	Liverpool	Augusta, GA	210	1911
Dennistoun, Cross and Co.	Liverpool	New York	200	1904
Muir, Duckworth and Co.	Liverpool	Alexandria; Savannah, GA	200	1906
A. Stern and Co.	Liverpool	St Louis, MO; Dallas, TX; Oklahoma City, OK	200	1908
J. Taylor and Sons	Liverpool		150	1911
Williams, Wilson and Co.	Liverpool	Fort Worth, TX; San Antonio, TX; Oklahoma City, OK	100	1908

Source: Chapman (1992: 197).

century, reproduced here in table 8.35, suggest that Liverpool merchants had not been overtaken by their American rivals. Indeed, the case of Welds, whose capital base shrank from £1,000,000 to £250,000 between 1899 and 1907, suggests that, if anything, the dynamic was in the other direction (Chapman, 1992: 198). Nevertheless, care must be taken not to over-interpret these figures on a few large firms such as Smith, Edwards and Company. Membership of the Liverpool Cotton Brokers Association was large, with a high turnover of firms. Of the 202 firms in 1885, fewer than a half were in business in 1905, but membership had risen to 220. Although Heylin (1913: 113–16) thinks that manufacturers could get a better deal by cutting out the middlemen and puts the survival of the Liverpool market down to ill-specified 'vested interests', it seems clear that the Liverpool market formed an

Table 8.36 *Merchants in the Lancashire cotton export trade, 1860–1911*

	Subscribers to the Manchester Royal Exchange	Members of the Manchester Chamber of Commerce		Merchants listed in *Slater's Directory of Manchester and Salford*	
		Cotton merchants	Cotton merchant-producers	Cotton shipping merchants	Grey cloth merchants and agents
1860	4,209	159	11		
1871	6,350				
1881	6,858				
1891	7,320				
1900	7,877	353	22	727	222
1901	8,040				
1911	9,921			773	226

Sources: Farnie (1979b: 101), Redford (1956: 299); Broadberry and Marrison (2002: 73).

important part of the atomistic Lancashire cotton industry, characterised by external economies of scale. Those weekly visits to Liverpool enabled spinners to reduce stocks to a minimum and to mix precisely the grades of cotton that they required (Mass and Lazonick, 1990: 15).

Turning to the export of cotton goods, improved communications put pressure on the chain of intermediaries between producers and retailers. The emergence of large-scale retailing, the growing importance of ready-made clothing and the rise of advertising all encouraged direct links between manufacturers and their customers. As merchants were squeezed, competition intensified, with a lengthening of credits and increased use of travellers in export markets as well as in the home market (Chapman, 1996: 87). As in the raw cotton trade, however, merchants continued to dominate the export trade in cotton goods, with manufacturers engaging in direct selling only reluctantly. Chapman (1996: 85) notes, for example, that Tootal Broadhurst Lee opened a New York office in 1888 only after it became apparent that the New York importers were abandoning the trade in plain and white goods, so that direct sales to major retailers had grown dramatically between 1882 and 1887. Rylands and Horrockses also made some experiments in dealing direct with retailers, but in general Lancashire producers continued to rely on the merchant system (Chapman, 1996: 85–6).

There is no single agreed measure of the scale of the merchant community engaged in the cotton export trade, but table 8.36 provides a number of indicators that tell a consistent story. The first column lists the number of subscribers to the Manchester Royal Exchange, which is where most of the export trade was conducted. This provides a continuous measure of the number of individuals engaged in the business, and is presented by Farnie (1979b) as an index of commercial activity for the cotton trade. It suggests a doubling of the size of the merchant community between 1860 and 1900, which is broadly consistent with Redford's (1956) data on the cotton merchant members of the Manchester chamber of commerce. The numbers are much lower in the case of the chamber of commerce because they represent corporate rather than individual membership, and because the membership was less representative of the industry as a whole (Farnie, 1979b: 97). Farnie's index also shows merchant numbers continuing to grow during the Edwardian boom, something which is also apparent from the number of merchant firms in *Slater's Directory of Manchester and Salford*, taken from Broadberry and Marrison (2002). As with the Liverpool merchants involved in the import of raw cotton, the Manchester merchants involved in the export of cotton goods provided important external economies of scale that helped to sustain Lancashire's dominant position in the world cotton industry. Copeland (1912: 371) praises the flexibility of the Manchester merchant system thus:

The tentacles of the Manchester trade reach out to all corners of the world, and whatever form of manufactured cotton is sought, whatever accommodation is desired, some one can be found in Manchester ready to accept the commission. Of all the assets which make it possible for the cotton industry to attain its largest dimensions in a country which does not produce the raw material, and which consumes only ten or twenty per cent of the yarn and cloth manufactured in its mills, none is more significant than the adaptability of the commercial organization.

The grain trade underwent major changes during the nineteenth century as Britain became increasingly dependent on imported grain. Table 8.37 shows that, as wheat imports more than doubled between 1873–1877 and 1910–1914, the geographical composition of trade shifted decisively away from the Baltic to the Atlantic as first the United States, then Argentina, then Canada became major suppliers of wheat to Britain. India and Australia also became important sources of supply. There was thus a decline in the importance of grain merchants engaged in trade with Russia and a corresponding rise in the fortunes of newer merchant houses based in Liverpool and engaged in the Atlantic trade. However, Chapman (1992: 205–8) notes that the three leading Liverpool merchant houses, Balfour Williamson, Ross T. Smyth and S. Sanday and Co., remained small players in the world grain trade, compared with Continental houses such as Bunge and Born and Louis

Table 8.37 *Principal sources of UK imports of wheat, 1873–1914 (Five-year annual averages, million cwt.)*

	1873–1877	1878–1882	1883–1887	1888–1892	1893–1897	1898–1902	1903–1905	1905–1909	1910–1914
Russia	9.0	6.7	8.0	16.2	16.4	4.5	21.8	15.2	13.7
Germany	3.7	3.0	1.8	1.7	0.8	0.7			
Canada	3.3	3.4	2.5	2.1	3.3	6.6	7.8	12.7	21.1
United States	21.4	34.5	25.6	21.4	30.0	37.8	12.6	18.1	22.4
Argentina			0.3	2.2	7.7	9.3	19.6	23.2	14.0
India	2.5	4.4	10.2	10.4	4.6	6.0	21.8	14.3	18.6
Australia	1.4	2.7	3.0	2.2	2.0	3.8	7.0	8.5	12.6
Total imports	47.2	57.2	55.2	61.5	70.0	70.2	94.5	95.3	104.5

Sources: Rees (1972: 129), Mitchell (1988: 225–6, 230–1).

Dreyfus and Co. Following Morgan (1979: 73), Chapman (1992: 211) argues that an important factor here was the role played by British millers such as Ranks, who took a direct role in the trade and reduced the role for middlemen.

Chapman (1992: 209) notes that British merchant houses were more successful in a number of new trades, including oil (Marcus Samuel and Bowrings), rubber (Harrison Crosfields and Heilbut Symons), meat (Vesteys and Borthwicks) and bananas (Fyffes). The first general conclusion that Chapman (1992: 211) draws from his survey of the cotton, grain and innovative trades is that British merchants tended to succeed in trades characterised by atomistic organisation. In trades such as cotton textiles, where the minimum efficient scale of manufacturing remained relatively small, merchants provided access to industry-wide or external economies of scale. In more concentrated trades, such as grain milling, however, large-scale producers could trade more directly and reduce the chain of middlemen. However, Chapman (1992: 223–8) goes on to draw a second general conclusion, that British merchant houses were more successful when they retained a decentralised organisational form, and generally foundered when a tight system of centralised control was imposed. In other words, relations within merchant houses needed to mirror the network form of relations between merchant houses in the wider merchant community.

Chapman (1992) deals mainly with trade in standardised products with a low transaction frequency and concentrates on imports into

Table 8.38 *Shares of world exports of manufactures, 1881–1913 (%)*

	United Kingdom	United States	Germany	France	Italy
1881–1885	43.0	6.0	16.0	15.0	2.0
1899	34.5	12.1	16.6	14.9	3.8
1913	31.8	13.7	19.9	12.8	3.5

Source: Matthews et al. (1982: 435).

Britain. However, there is another literature which concentrates on exports of more specialised products. As transaction frequency increased, brand loyalty was used to differentiate products, and advertising and product promotion were required, while for some goods, after-sales service was required (Nicholas, 1984: 498–501). In such cases, German and American manufacturers are typically seen as quickly establishing direct marketing organisations, while British manufacturers are seen as conservatively sticking with the outmoded form of merchant organisation (Allen, 1959: 13–14; Landes, 1969: 337; Kirby, 1981: 8). The decline in Britain's share of world manufactured exports seen in table 8.38 is usually cited in this context as evidence of poor marketing overseas. Yet it is scarcely credible that Britain could have maintained 43% of the world market as other countries industrialised.

Many of the dismal accounts of British overseas marketing techniques are based on an uncritical acceptance of contemporary consular reports, yet, as Nicholas (1984: 492–3) notes, American consuls were just as critical of American firms. In fact, Nicholas (497–505) goes on to note that the British merchant system was also capable of innovation and adaptation to the new circumstances. For example, in many cases a merchant house became sole agent for a particular manufacturer, hence being effectively converted into a direct representative (498–9). In other cases, British manufacturers did set up overseas branch sales offices or commence local production (500–2).

Jones (2000) looks at another business strategy of the British merchant houses during the pre-1914 period: expansion through diversification. Faced with improved communications putting pressure on the scale of commissions and the length of the supply chain, profits could be maintained by diversification. In particular, Jones (45–83) highlights the role of investment in related activities, such as a wool merchant house investing in farming, shipping and insurance. He finds that the post-tax return on net capital employed for a sample of eight merchant companies fluctuated around an average of roughly 10% between 1895

The 'golden age' of British commerce, 1870–1914 191

and 1914, considerably higher than in most of the industrial sectors analysed by Arnold (1999: 60) for the same period.

It would be a mistake, then, to view the merchant system simply as an anachronistic hangover from the past. First, it must be remembered that Britain's comparative productivity performance was better in distribution than in most other sectors. Second, for standardised products with low transaction frequency, the merchant system in its traditional form continued to work very well. Third, for new products requiring special attention, the traditional merchant system was capable of innovation and adaptation, and via the managing agency system, the merchant house could be converted to direct selling. As Nicholas (1984: 497, 506) notes, the US Department of Commerce regarded the network of British merchants as affording the British manufacturer an advantage over his American rival, reducing uncertainty and providing information and credit.

8.4 Financial services

8.4.1 Introduction

Data on output, labour inputs and labour productivity in the British financial services sector before World War I are shown in table 8.39. Output in financial services grew at more than three times the rate of output in the economy as a whole, but, since labour inputs also grew rapidly, labour productivity growth was only very slightly higher than in the economy as a whole. Capital stock data are unavailable on a separate basis for the financial services sector, which Feinstein (1988) presents together with data on distribution and other services, as noted earlier. Hence, it is not possible to calculate total factor productivity growth for financial services in this period. Turning to international comparisons of labour productivity, it is not possible to provide time series projections as with the other market service sectors, because of the unavailability of consistent time series data for financial services in the United States and Germany over this period. However, benchmark estimates are available for the US/UK comparison at 1870, 1890 and 1910 from Broadberry (1997b: 10), reproduced here in table 8.1. These estimates show Britain with a large productivity lead in 1870, but the United States closing the gap and pulling slightly ahead by 1910.

To gain an overview of the sector, it is helpful to examine the data on the balance sheets of UK financial institutions in table 8.40, based on the work of Sheppard (1971). Part A sets out the total assets (equal by definition to total liabilities) of UK banks, showing strong growth in

Table 8.39 *Productivity in the British financial services sector, 1871–1911*

A. Indices of output, inputs and productivity (1911 = 100)

	Output	Labour	Labour productivity
1871	12.2	17.4	70.1
1881	22.0	30.4	72.4
1891	34.1	47.8	71.3
1901	58.5	65.2	89.7
1911	100.0	100.0	100.0

B. Growth rates of output, inputs and productivity (% per annum)

	1871–1911
Output	5.3
Labour	4.4
Labour productivity	0.9

Sources: Output – Feinstein (1972: table 53); labour – Feinstein (1972: table 60).

the joint-stock banks of England and Wales, slower growth in the Irish and Scottish joint-stock banks, and decline in the consolidated balance sheets of *The Economist's* private bank series, the Co-operative Wholesale Society banks and the Yorkshire Penny Bank. Part B sets out the total assets of non-bank financial intermediaries, with rapid asset growth in the insurance companies, the Post Office Savings Bank and National Savings Bonds, and more modest growth in trustee savings banks and building societies. Part C shows that by 1911 banks accounted for 57.6% of the assets of all financial institutions, and non-bank financial intermediaries for 42.4%. Of the latter, the most important were the insurance companies, accounting for 25.3% of the assets of all financial institutions. The price level did not change much between 1881 and 1911, so that trends in real assets are not very different from the trends in nominal assets seen in table 8.40. Using Feinstein's (1972: table 61) GDP deflator to convert to real terms, and splicing the bank data at 1891, real assets of banks and non-bank financial institutions grew at an annual rate of 2.8% between 1881 and 1911. This compares with nominal asset growth of 2.9% per annum over the same period.

With population growth of 0.9% per annum between 1881 and 1911, British real per capita asset growth over the same period was 1.9% (Feinstein, 1972: table 55). In fact, it seems likely that this overstates real asset growth, since the proportion of financial institutions included in the statistical record became more complete over time. Thus, for

Table 8.40 *Total assets and total liabilities of UK financial institutions, 1881–1911*

A. Banks' total assets (£ million)

	Joint-stock banks, England and Wales	Joint-stock banks, Ireland	Joint-stock banks, Scotland	Private and CWS banks, Yorkshire Penny Bank	Combined UK banks
1881	296.0	56.8	99.8		452.6
1891	470.0	56.3	115.1		641.4
1891	470.0	56.3	115.1	83.8	725.2
1901	674.2	67.2	134.4	63.1	938.9
1911	836.3	84.8	140.2	56.7	1,118.0

B. Non-bank financial intermediaries' total assets (£ million)

	Insurance companies	Post Office Savings Bank	Trustee savings banks	Building societies	National Savings Bonds	Total non-bank financial intermediaries
1881	159.9	36.7	47.5	59.0	0.7	303.8
1891	217.5	72.9	48.3	67.1	5.1	410.9
1901	321.3	135.3	58.0	60.9	12.8	588.3
1911	491.3	176.6	67.2	63.5	24.8	823.4

C. Contribution to total financial institutions' assets and liabilities in 1911 (%)

Banks	57.6
Insurance companies	25.3
Post Office Savings Bank	9.1
Trustee savings banks	3.4
Building societies	3.3
National Savings Bonds	1.3
Total	100.0

Note:
The break in 1891 is due to the availability for the first time of data on private and CWS banks and the Yorkshire Penny Bank.

example, Capie and Webber (1985: 40–1) are able to show that UK nominal bank deposits, the major component of bank liabilities, grew at an annual rate of 2.2% between 1881 and 1911, rather than at 2.9%, as suggested by Sheppard's (1971) data.[8] Even ignoring this, however, the

---

[8] Although Capie and Webber (1985) provide revised data for UK bank deposits, they do not provide new figures for total liabilities and assets, since their interest is in obtaining new money supply data.

British figure compares unfavourably with the real per capita growth of assets of financial intermediaries in the United States during the second half of the nineteenth century. Goldsmith's (1958: 62) figures show US real per capita asset growth of 4.8% per annum over the period 1880–1900 and still 3.1% per annum over the longer period 1850–1900, which includes the Civil War.

8.4.2 Domestic banking

The key trend in domestic banking between 1870 and 1914 was the growth in the scale of enterprise. Table 8.41 shows that, whereas in 1825 all commercial banks in England and Wales were private, by 1900 private banks were outnumbered by joint-stock banks. The decline of the private bank is even more obvious if we consider the number of branches. The share of deposits in England and Wales accounted for by the five largest banks rose from 25% in 1870 to 43% by 1910 and 80% by 1920 (Capie and Rodrik-Bali, 1982: 287). Indeed, after the mergers of 1917/18, domestic banking was dominated by the 'Big Five' London clearing banks: Barclays, Lloyds, National Provincial, Midland and Westminster (Collins, 1988: 79). There were a number of factors underlying this growth of concentration, including legal changes which permitted joint-stock banking and limited liability, as well as economic and technological factors which encouraged amalgamations among banks.

Dealing first with the legal environment, the Bank of England held a monopoly of joint-stock banking in England and Wales until 1826, although joint-stock banks already had a strong position in Scotland, and had also been permitted in Ireland from the early 1820s (Collins, 1988: 66). Greater access to capital allowed the joint-stock banks to increase turnover and achieve economies of scale, particularly through the development of branch banking. By contrast, as can be seen in table 8.41, the private banks operated comparatively few branches. However, joint-stock banking did not immediately supplant private banking, which continued to be successful on the basis of local information networks. Not until after the company legislation of 1858 and 1862, which extended limited liability to banking, did joint-stock banks come to a clear position of dominance in banking in England and Wales (Cottrell, 1979: 53).

However, the emergence of large-scale enterprise in banking depended on more than just changes in the legal environment. The changes in communications technology that played such an important role in the organisation of distribution also had their effects in banking. Indeed, Nishimura (1971: 77–9) puts the introduction of the telegraph at the

Table 8.41 *Number of banks and branches, England and Wales, 1825–1913*

	Joint-stock banks		Private banks	
	Banks	Branches	Banks	Branches
1825	0	0	650	650
1850	99	576	327	518
1875	122	1,364	236	595
1900	83	4,212	81	358
1913	41	6,426	29	147

Note:
Branches of private banks in 1825 estimated on the assumption of one branch per bank.
Source: Collins (1988: 52).

centre of his study of changes in the banking system in the second half of the nineteenth century, with the switch from a locally based merchant network system, financed through the inland bill of exchange, to a modern branch banking system financed through the overdraft. He is critical of King (1936: 273) for treating the emergence of large-scale branch banking as exogenous, and using it to explain the decline of the inland bill of exchange. Rather, both reflected the improved communications, leading to a fundamental change in the conduct of the business of banking. As in other sectors of the economy, hierarchy could be substituted for network given the improvements to information flows and monitoring possibilities. Note that it was the emergence of joint-stock banks with national coverage that was important here, with small, local, joint-stock banks continuing to trade on the basis of local information networks.[9]

The growth in scale of the British banking system was accompanied by an increase in stability. To some extent, the greater stability was a result of the greater scale, since large banks had a greater potential than small banks for pooling risks (Collins, 1988: 64). However, Collins (1988: 85) argues that the growing professionalisation of banking also played a role, as banking firms that also conducted other businesses gave way to specialist bankers. The appearance of textbooks and banking journals to encourage good business practices was followed in the 1870s by the establishment of professional bodies. Bodies such as the Institute of Bankers in Scotland, founded in 1875, and the English Institute of

---

[9] See, for example, Newton's (1996) account of bank–industry relations in mid-nineteenth century Sheffield.

Bankers, established in 1879, offered advice on the education and training of staff and supervised professional examinations (Collins, 1988: 86). The City of Glasgow Bank failure in 1878 was the last major bank failure, although Barings needed to be rescued by the Bank of England and a consortium of banks in 1890 (Collins, 1988: 83). The Barings Crisis illustrates another factor behind the growing stability of the British banking system: the emergence of the Bank of England as a central bank, prepared to act as a lender of last resort (Collins, 1988: 86).

The emergence of a stable oligopoly in banking, however, raised the possibility of collusion and the avoidance of interest rate competition. Griffiths (1973: 5–6) traces the origin of restrictive practices in the City back to growing cooperation among English banks from the 1860s, leading to an agreement to pay one percentage point below Bank Rate on current accounts, before interest payments on current accounts were abolished altogether in 1877 as Bank Rate fell below 2%. A fixed rate of 1.5 percentage points below Bank Rate was agreed on deposit accounts in 1866, so long as Bank Rate remained between 2 and 5% (Griffiths, 1973: 6). Griffiths (1973: 11–14) suggests that the Treasury and the Bank of England acquiesced in these collusive agreements because they found it easier to implement interest rate policy when dealing with a small number of cartelised banks.

To what extent did this emergence of restrictive practices in banking adversely affect productivity performance? Campbell-Kelly (1998) shows the existence of conservative attitudes to new technology in the Post Office Savings Bank (POSB) before 1914. Thus, the POSB resisted the introduction of the typewriter before 1914 on the grounds that, given the scale of operations, pre-printed standard responses were cheaper, with more than 550 standard replies in use by 1885, rising to around 1,000 by 1914 (Campbell-Kelly, 1998: 22). Similarly, the POSB rejected the use of calculating machines because the bank had developed an accounting system that required balances to be calculated only at the end of the year, when interest calculations were made. Furthermore, interest computations could easily be made manually since the interest rate of 2.5% corresponded to an exact halfpenny per pound per month, and interest was paid only on whole pounds for whole months. The objection to loose-leaf filing depended on a perceived threat to security, since it was almost impossible to lose an account or to create a phantom account by inserting a fresh page in a bound ledger book. In this latter case, the nature of the business set limits to the diffusion of modern office technology. In all three cases, therefore, it could be argued that conservative attitudes to new technology were consistent with economic efficiency. Again, it is important to note that, in financial services, the

Table 8.42 *Combined balance sheets of UK banks, 1881–1911 (£ million)*

A. Assets

	Cash, money at call and short notice	Total discounts	Loans and advances	Total investments	Other assets	Total assets
1881	81.8	62.5	222.3	76.5	9.5	452.6
1891	121.2	62.8	307.4	137.1	12.9	641.4
1891	139.2	64.2	342.2	164.5	15.1	725.2
1901	204.3	66.1	442.9	203.1	22.5	938.9
1911	269.0	100.1	510.9	212.7	25.3	1,118.0

B. Liabilities

	Deposits and other accounts	Notes in circulation	Paid-up capital and reserves	Acceptances and endorsements	Miscellaneous liabilities	Total liabilities
1881	360.1	14.0	75.0	22.2	3.5	452.6
1891	523.8	13.9	92.5	19.5	11.2	641.4
1891	594.8	14.4	104.8	22.1	11.2	725.2
1901	796.9	15.0	114.2	29.0	12.8	938.9
1911	977.6	14.6	114.5	55.1	11.3	1,118.0

Note:
Acceptances and endorsements are excluded from total liabilities. The break in 1891 is due to the availability for the first time of data on private and CWS banks and the Yorkshire Penny Bank.
Source: Sheppard (1971: 116).

United States had only just pulled ahead of Britain in productivity terms by World War I. Here, however, it is worth remembering that the emergence of large-scale enterprise in banking in the United States was limited by regulation. In particular, regulations prevented the growth of inter-state banking, keeping concentration in US banking relatively low.

Table 8.42 provides the combined balance sheets of UK banks, which can be used to shed light on the conduct of banking in the decades before World War I (Sheppard, 1971; Goodhart, 1972). In a balance sheet, total assets (the claims by a bank on others) must be equal to total liabilities (the claims by others on a bank). On the asset side, banks needed to maintain sufficient liquid assets to meet the needs of customers, and this was met by holding cash and money at call and short notice. Over the period 1881 to 1911 this increased from the equivalent of 18.1% of total assets to 24.1%, with cash accounting for about a half of this category throughout the period (Sheppard, 1971: table A1.1). Total discounts accounted for a declining share of total assets. The key asset here was the bill of exchange, a form of commercial credit. For example, a cotton spinner from Manchester might pay a Liverpool cotton broker for his supply of raw cotton with a bill of exchange, drawn up for payment in three months' time (Collins, 1988: 107). The Liverpool broker would draw up the bill, and it would be signed by the Manchester spinner (the 'acceptor'). The Liverpool broker could hold the bill and collect the cash when it was due in three months' time, or he could sell ('discount') the bill. The latter involved the holder 'endorsing' the bill by signing his name on it, and transferring it to a new holder; the new holder then became entitled to the cash when it was due. The bill could be endorsed by another merchant or by a bank. Banks effectively provided short-term credit to business by routinely discounting bills in this way. As the nineteenth century wore on, the inland bill of exchange declined in importance, and foreign bills arising from overseas trade and finance became increasingly important from the 1870s (Nishimura, 1971: 65; Collins, 1988: 109). Also, from 1877 Treasury Bills issued to raise short-term finance for the government were discounted by banks, although they represented a mere 6.5% of total discounts in 1911 (Sheppard, 1971: table A1.1).

The most important item on the asset side of the balance sheet was loans and advances, which accounted for nearly a half of total assets. With the decline of the inland bill of exchange, short-term credit was increasingly provided for business customers through overdrafts (Nishimura, 1971: 55–64). However, it has often been argued that the banks failed to support British industry, particularly through the provision of medium- and long-term credit (Foxwell, 1917; Gerschenkron, 1962: 13–16; Kennedy, 1987: 121–2). The picture is not substantially altered if we include total investments, because banks held few industrial securities, preferring to concentrate on government securities (Collins, 1988: 113; Goodhart, 1972: 135). In the literature, a contrast is often drawn here with the German system of universal banking, which is seen as being highly supportive of German industry (Collins, 1998). In fact, it is important when considering the issue of bank finance for industry to maintain a distinction between two issues: first, the contrast between universal banking on the one hand and specialised credit and investment banking on the other hand; and, second, the support given to industry by specialised investment banks on the one hand and by universal banks on the other hand.

Although many writers have argued that a universal banking system is systematically more supportive of industry than a specialised system, the evidence in favour of this is often little more than the crude observation of faster industrial growth in Germany than in Britain, for which there could be many explanations (Collins, 1991: 10). In fact, on the general issue of universal versus specialised banking, it is necessary to compare the economies of scope from combining credit and investment banking in the large German universal banks with the economies of scale attained by the large British credit banks (more usually known as the commercial or clearing banks). Although some writers have argued in favour of universal banking on the basis of economies of scope, since the information on firms gained through credit banking can also be used to make decisions on long-term investment, others have taken universal banking as a sign of economic backwardness and the specialised English system as a sign of financial sophistication (Collins, 1998: 2–3; Gerschenkron, 1962). As with other services, finance was provided on a much greater scale in Britain than in Germany before World War I, permitting greater specialisation and sophistication. It is therefore perverse to criticise British banks for failing to develop along German lines as if the German system were the final stage on a development path (Collins, 1998: 18).

Once it is accepted that British commercial banks were part of a more specialised system, it becomes possible to view their behaviour in a more favourable light. As Collins (1998: 13) points out, it is unfair to criticise them for failing to make long-term investments in British industry, since that was not their function. It is fair, however, to assess how supportive they were of industry by examining their (short-term) lending behaviour, and here there is little evidence to suggest that British banks were any less supportive than their Continental counterparts. Examining a sample of 3,466 industrial accounts from 268 branches of twenty banks between 1866 and 1914, Capie and Collins (1996) find only 453 cases of banks refusing applications for loans, generally for good reasons. And, from the same sample, Baker and Collins (1999) find that of the 319 cases of industrial firms in distress between 1875 and 1914 banks were generally supportive, continuing to lend and lending for longer periods than normal, without altering the terms in their favour.

On the second issue, the degree of long-term support given to industry by banks, it has often been argued that the German universal banks provided a significant proportion of the long-term capital for German industry, while British investment banks favoured overseas assets at the expense of domestic industry. Here, again, the evidence to support the argument does not stand up to close scrutiny. On the German side, most industrial investment was financed from internal rather than external funds, just as in Britain (Edwards and Ogilvie, 1996). Also, to the extent that German banks were successful at directing funds into heavy industry, this meant that light industry was starved of funds (Neuburger and Stokes, 1974; Tilly, 1986). This point is reinforced by recent findings on Anglo-German labour productivity differences in the early twentieth century, with a German advantage in heavy industry offset by lower productivity in light industry (Broadberry and Burhop, 2005). And, on the British side, any lack of external finance for industry can be attributed more plausibly to lack of demand rather than lack of supply (Collins, 1991: 33–5). As Watson (1995) shows, when firms actively sought external finance, as in the brewing and iron and steel industries, they had little difficulty in obtaining it. The implication of this view is that, when investment banks made overseas issues, this was not the result of a systematic bias against domestic industry. Indeed, if such a market imperfection had existed, it would be expected to show up in rates of return, but Edelstein (1971) is able to show that no such bias existed; rates of return on domestic and overseas assets of the same risk (measured by the variance of returns) were not significantly different.

Turning to the liabilities side of the combined banks' balance sheet in table 8.42, by far the most important item was deposits, which accounted for 79.6% of total liabilities in 1881, rising to 87.5% in 1911. Although there is only scattered evidence on the precise breakdown of these deposits, there can be little doubt that the majority were in the form of current accounts that could be withdrawn immediately (Collins, 1988: 94–5). Although notes were never issued by the important London banks and many provincial banks in England and Wales, they were of some importance in Scotland and Ireland. For the system as a whole, they represented only a small part of total liabilities, but since they could be converted into coin or (in England and Wales from 1833) into Bank of England notes, they represented, like current deposits, a very liquid liability (Collins, 1988: 93). Paid-up capital and reserves represented a contingency fund which could be used by the proprietors to protect deposit holders and note holders in adverse circumstances, and could be important in maintaining confidence. The capital ratio was very high before World War I compared with more recent times; although it fell from 16.6% in 1881 to 10.2% by 1911, it would fall further across the two world wars to about 3% by the 1950s (Sheppard, 1971: table A1.1; Collins, 1988: 101).

The other identified item on the liabilities side of the balance sheet is acceptances and endorsements. This arose from the behaviour of banks in discounting bills, which has already been examined on the asset side of the balance sheet. In fact, banks did not have to retain the bills in their portfolio, but could rediscount them to other banks. This involved incurring a contingent liability, because, if the original acceptor failed to meet the debt, the successive endorsers of the bill would be required to meet it. Note, however, that this item should not be added to total liabilities, because the bills have already been included in the balance sheet on the asset side and the fact that banks rediscount to each other does not raise the liabilities of the system as a whole (Sheppard, 1971: 113). The overriding impression obtained from an examination of bank liabilities is their short-term nature, and this helps to explain the reluctance of banks to provide long-term loans to industry. However, it should also be remembered that the existence of large deposit liabilities readily convertible to cash reflected the success of the British banking system in mobilising savings and developing the cheque system (Collins, 1988: 112).

8.4.3 *International banking*

The clearing banks operated on a largely domestic basis, collecting deposits and making short-term loans in Britain. However, a crucial aspect of British banking in the decades before World War I was its international dimension, with Britain firmly at the centre of world trade and payments. These were the City of London's 'golden years' (Kynaston, 1995). The key institutions here were the merchant banks, which specialised in accepting overseas bills of exchange and issuing foreign loans (Cassis, 1994: 5). The discount houses were also heavily involved in this international business; although their business had grown up around the rediscounting of inland bills by domestic banks, the discount market internationalised as the inland bill of exchange declined from the middle of the nineteenth century, to be replaced largely by overseas bills, but also to a limited extent by Treasury Bills (King, 1936: 271–5). Another aspect of the City's international dimension was the overseas banks, which were headquartered in London but acted as clearing banks overseas, particularly in the empire (Cassis, 1994: 5). However, in a national accounting framework, these banks were clearly of greater quantitative significance to the overseas countries than to Britain.

Although many of these institutions were individually small, it is clear that together the City of London benefited from external economies of scale in classic Marshallian fashion. The large volume of business allowed a high degree of specialisation, which in turn allowed Britain to maintain a dominant position in world finance. It is also clear that, given information asymmetries, this was a business in which information networks were important. However appropriate Chandlerian

Table 8.43 *Capital of some leading London merchant banks, circa 1900*

	(£ million)
N. M. Rothschild and Sons, London	6.0
Marcus Samuel and Co.	2.0
Kleinwort, Sons and Co.	1.7
Chaplin, Milne and Co.	1.7
Glyn, Mills and Co.	1.5
J. H. Schröder and Co.	1.5
Baring Bros. and Co. Ltd	1.2
Lazard Bros.	1.2
R.Raphael and Sons	1.1
J. S. Morgan and Co.	1.0

Source: Chapman (1984: 200–1).

hierarchical management structures were in some other sectors, they were not appropriate for international finance before World War I. Sociologists have long analysed networks in banking from the point of view of barriers to social mobility, and this literature will be drawn on here to examine the economic workings of the City networks (Cassis, 1994).

Chapman (1984: 39) argues that a distinct group of specialists known as merchant bankers came into being between the financial crises of 1825 and 1837, strengthening their position in international finance and gradually withdrawing from international distribution. The early market leaders were Rothschilds and Barings, but Rothschilds grew more rapidly and the Barings Crisis of 1890 reinforced this divergence (Chapman, 1984: 17, 40). Barings had to be rescued by a consortium of bankers, led by the Bank of England, when a large proportion of their own capital became locked up in unsold Argentine stock (Chapman, 1984: 78; Kynaston, 1994: 422–37). By 1900 Rothschilds had pulled far ahead of Barings, which had also been overtaken by a number of other rival merchant banks. This is reflected in Chapman's (1984: 200–1) data on capital, reproduced here in table 8.43 for the ten largest merchant banks in the sample. However, it should be noted that the concept of capital used by Chapman seems to be based on the estimated wealth of the partners, a broader concept than the balance-sheet-based concept of paid-up capital and reserves used in the analysis of the domestic banks in table 8.41.[10] Nevertheless, it is clear that the capital of an individual

---

[10] Chapman (1984: 151) uses the same basis to estimate the capital of the London joint-stock banks in 1904/05 as £401 million, compared with Sheppard's (1971: 116–18)

merchant bank remained small relative to the capital of an individual joint-stock bank. These figures are more broadly comparable with the figures for capital employed by cotton merchants in table 8.35, also taken from the work of Chapman (1992), and suggest that the leading merchant banks outpaced those merchant enterprises that remained specialised in wholesale distribution.

The two main areas of merchant bank work involved the financing of world trade through the accepting of overseas bills of exchange and the organisation of long-term loans through new issues. Chapman (1984: 107–8) estimates that the volume of acceptances of overseas bills by London merchant banks in 1913 amounted to about £100 million, with the United States accounting for about a third of the total business, and Germany for a further quarter. International competition for acceptances was strong, especially from German banks, but British houses remained dominant in financing world trade before 1914 (Chapman, 1984: 124). Although some merchant banks never made new issues, for others it provided a sizeable, but risky, income. Foreign government loans became a staple after the 1818 Prussian loan, and were followed from the mid-1830s by railway loans and other infrastructure-related finance (Chapman, 1984: 82–98). The relatively small size of the merchant banks' capital did not act as a major obstacle, since they were able to make use of syndicates and borrowed capital from joint-stock banks and insurance companies. Here, again, it is possible to see the advantages of the network form of organisation in a highly customised line of business characterised by asymmetric information and difficulties of contractibility.

Turning to the overseas banks, Jones (1993: 52) also emphasises the advantages of the network form of organisation. He sees the avoidance of large and complicated managerial hierarchies as an important factor in the success of British overseas banks, despite the criticisms of this form of governance structure by Chandler (1990) and Wilkins (1989) in the context of industrial enterprise. The British overseas banks were able to build up a strong network-based system that capitalised on Britain's dominant role in world trade and the availability of City expertise in related areas, with the well-established domestic banking system providing an ideal source of management recruits (Jones, 1993: 57–61). As with so many aspects of British economic affairs from the late nineteenth century, there was a strong and growing link with the empire, particularly the 'white' dominions, and this is reflected in the data on the

estimate of only £81.8 million for the joint-stock banks of England and Wales and £115.4 million for all UK banks.

Table 8.44 *Geographical distribution of foreign branches of British overseas banks, 1860–1913 (%)*

	1860	1890	1913
Australasia	46	61	47
North America	9	5	8
Rest of Americas	11	6	7
Southern Africa	2	12	19
Rest of Africa	1	0	5
Middle East/North Africa	5	1	4
South Asia	14	6	4
South-east Asia	3	3	2
East Asia	6	3	2
Europe (excluding UK)	3	3	2
Total	100	100	100

Source: Jones (1993: 414).

geographical distribution of foreign branches of the overseas banks in table 8.44. Australia and New Zealand together accounted for about a half of the branches throughout the period, while South Africa grew rapidly in importance and most of the North American branches were in Canada. While the share of the four 'white' dominions rose from 57% in 1860 to 71% in 1913, the share of Continental Europe fell from 3% to 2%. As well as acting as clearing banks in the countries in which they operated, the British overseas banks often acted as government bankers and as currency agents, issuing the paper currency of a variety of countries (Jones, 1993: 109–19). They also helped to arrange loan issues for governments on the London capital market, although the merchant banks played a larger role in this area of business (Jones, 1993: 134).

Although the literature on international banking is littered with references to City networks, the amount of systematic empirical evidence on this issue is actually rather limited. The most convincing study is by Cassis (1994), who collects information on bankers and bank directors from ten private banks, twenty merchant banks, seven discount houses, thirteen joint-stock banks, fourteen overseas (colonial) banks and the Bank of England. Information was obtained on 460 individuals, representing 57% of the relevant population during the period 1890–1914. The sample includes forty-seven salaried general managers as well as partners and board members. Table 8.45 provides empirical evidence on the network links involving this group of bankers. Part A highlights the existence of strong intergenerational family ties, with 56% of the sample

Table 8.45 *City of London banking networks, 1890–1914*

A. Socio-economic class of fathers of bankers and bank directors (%)

	Bankers	Merchants, shipowners, company directors	Aristocrats, landowners	Professions, services, clergy	Other
Private bankers	87	0	11	2	0
Merchant bankers	87	3	0	7	3
Directors, joint-stock banks	44	20	23	8	5
Directors, colonial banks	10	27	27	20	16
Total sample	56	17	14	7	6

B. Education of bankers and bank directors (%)

	Public school and/or Oxbridge	Other type of education	Education unknown
Private bankers	72	6	22
Merchant bankers	50	17	33
Directors, joint-stock banks	50	15	35
Directors, colonial banks	36	38	26
Directors, Bank of England	67	16	17
Total sample	51	19	30

C. Proportion of bankers and bank directors who were Fellows of the Institute of Bankers (%)

Private bankers	45
Merchant bankers	8
Discount agents	9
Directors, joint-stock banks	27
Directors, colonial banks	11
Directors, Bank of England	92
General managers	77
Total sample	34

D. Number of boards on which bankers and bank directors had seats (%)

	No other board	1 or 2 boards	3 to 7 boards	8 or more boards
Private bankers, merchant bankers, discount agents	34	32	32	2
Directors, joint-stock banks and colonial banks	18	30	43	9
Directors, Bank of England	14	55	31	0
Managers	92	8	0	0
Total sample	22	34	39	5

Table 8.45 (*cont.*)

E. Socio-economic class of fathers-in-law of bankers and bank directors (%)

	Banker	Merchant	Aristocrat	Foreigner	Other	Unknown
Private bankers	13	6	38	2	32	9
Merchant bankers	16	10	16	19	14	25
Directors, joint-stock banks	6	6	24	3	25	36
Directors, colonial banks	8	8	13	4	18	49
Directors, Bank of England	12	24	18	6	37	3
Total sample	10	10	24	6	20	30

Source: Cassis (1994: 95, 100, 102, 151, 152, 204, 205, 281, 283).

being sons of bankers, and a further 17% the sons of merchants, shipowners or company directors. The intergenerational family tie was strongest among private bankers and merchant bankers, with 87% of the sample being sons of bankers, effectively running the family firm. The relationship was much weaker in the joint-stock banks, and weakest in the colonial banks, which offer the clearest example of networks extending beyond the family. Note that 14% of the sample had fathers who were aristocrats or landowners, illustrating the high degree of integration between banking and aristocratic circles noted by Cain and Hopkins (1993: 66–7).

Part B of table 8.45 shows the dominance of the public schools and Oxbridge in the education of the banking community, with the strongest link again being seen among private bankers and the weakest link among directors of the colonial banks. Part C shows the proportion of bankers and bank directors who were Fellows of the Institute of Bankers, the main professional body. The proportion was highest among the general managers, which is consistent with the Institute playing an important role in training as well as in networking. Part D investigates the idea that the banking elite were able to dominate industry through a network of interlocking directorships. In fact, more than a half of the sample had no more than two other directorships, and only 5% sat on eight or more boards.[11] Excluding the managers, private bankers were more likely than the others to sit on no other boards. Finally, part E returns to kinship ties

---

[11] Note that the figures refer to the number of boards sat on in one year, not the total lifetime membership of all boards.

via marriage. Not many bankers married daughters of bankers, despite a large proportion being sons of bankers. Rather, the most popular choice of bride for a banker seems to have been the daughter of an aristocrat, again confirming the links between aristocratic and banking circles.

The picture that emerges, then, is one which often appears in the literature on entrepreneurial failure: family firms, public school and Oxbridge education, marriage into the aristocracy, and empire links. And yet, this was a thriving part of the economy. Again, it must be emphasised that the network form of organisation continued to be well suited to international finance before World War I, however appropriate the hierarchical form of organisation may have been for some industrial sectors at this time.

8.4.4 Insurance

Insurance companies accounted for the largest share of non-bank financial intermediaries' assets throughout the period 1881–1911, as can be seen in table 8.40. Furthermore, the assets of insurance companies grew more rapidly than those of banks and all other non-bank financial intermediaries with the exception of the Post Office Savings Bank. Whereas the assets of all banks and non-bank financial intermediaries grew at an annual rate of 2.8% in nominal terms between 1881 and 1911, the assets of insurance companies grew at an annual rate of 3.7% in nominal terms, or 3.6% in real terms. The main areas of business remained fire, life and marine insurance, although accident insurance grew rapidly in importance. The other significant development was the growth of overseas business, with the result that insurance made a significant positive contribution to the balance of payments.

Table 8.46 sets out the basic data on fire insurance, with premium income growing at an annual rate of 3.5% in nominal terms or 3.4% in real terms between 1881 and 1913. The large jump in the number of fire offices after 1901 without a corresponding discontinuity in the premium income reflects the inclusion in the later statistics of a large number of offices with tiny premium incomes, as a result of a regulatory change. In fire insurance, the major companies had been cooperating on underwriting information, fire fighting services and agreed tariffs since the mid-1820s. Periodically, however, new companies entered when rates were high, as for example after the 1861 Tooley Street fire, a major warehouse conflagration in London, which led merchants to establish the Commercial Union and Mercantile companies (Raynes, 1964: 340–1; Liveing, 1961: 14–15). However, within a few years the new companies were cooperating with the 'tariff offices' and in 1868 a formal

Table 8.46 *Fire insurance business of UK offices, 1881–1913*

	Number of offices	Premium income (million pounds)
1881	50	9.5
1891	59	17.6
1901	52	20.3
1911	132	28.0
1913	131	29.2

Note:
The large jump in the number of offices after 1901 without a corresponding discontinuity in the premium income reflects the inclusion in the later statistics of a large number of offices with tiny premium incomes, as a result of a regulatory change.

Source: Supple (1970: 213).

constitution was adopted, establishing the Fire Offices' Committee (Cockerell and Green, 1994: 36). Cooperation among the fire offices spread into overseas business with the establishment in 1869 of a separate Fire Offices' Committee (Foreign) to supervise rates in overseas markets, an increasingly important source of premium incomes (Raynes, 1964: 343).

Although overseas business had been pioneered as early as 1782 by the Phoenix, the other major British fire offices were slower to move into foreign markets (Trebilcock, 1985: 166–8). Hence, overseas business remained a small part of total business in the mid-nineteenth century for the Sun and the Royal Exchange Assurance (REA), as can be seen in table 8.47. By the turn of the century, however, overseas business was the dominant source of premium income for all three companies. North America was an important market, with twenty-four British companies taking 24% of the US market in 1900, and with the nine largest companies earning over a half of their premium income there. In Canada, twenty-one British companies accounted for over two-thirds of the market (Cockerell and Green, 1994: 41). The position of British companies was strengthened by their ability to meet their commitments after major fires in Chicago, Boston and St John's during the 1870s (Cockerell and Green, 1994: 41). The reputation of the British companies was further strengthened after the San Francisco earthquake of 1906, when liabilities were met fairly and promptly, providing an important long-term advantage over many US competitors (Supple, 1970: 249–50).

The market for life assurance was still relatively small in mid-nineteenth-century Britain, with policy holders coming mainly from

Table 8.47 *Foreign premiums as a share of total premiums, three British fire offices, 1856–1910 (%)*

	Phoenix	Sun	REA
1856–65	34.8	8.9	4.1
1866–75	47.8	16.4	2.7
1880	51.0	17.1	3.0
1891	67.7	57.6	13.1
1900	70.2		54.2
1906	73.4		
1910			64.2

Note:
REA figures based on fire insurance only.
Source: Trebilcock (1985: 167).

Table 8.48 *Life assurance business of UK offices, 1850–1914*

A. Ordinary life assurance

	Number of offices	Premium income (£ million)	Sums assured (£ million)	Endowments as % of sum assured
1870	101	9.8	292.6	
1880	99	11.7	382.7	
1890	89	14.8	479.0	9.3
1900	85	21.8	676.0	24.4
1914	94	29.0	869.7	39.0

B. Industrial life assurance

	Premium income (£ million)
1850s	1.5
1905	11.5
1912	16.0

Source: Supple (1970: 219–21).

the prudent middle classes and, for credit purposes, the imprudent upper classes (Trebilcock, 1985: 522). However, the second half of the nineteenth century saw a widening of the market, with an extension of the system of agencies and branch offices and the introduction of endowment policies (Cockerell and Green, 1994: 64). The figures in part A of table 8.48 show premium income for ordinary life assurance growing at an annual rate of 2.5% in nominal terms and 2.4% in real terms between 1870 and 1914, with endowment policies accounting for a rapidly increasing share of the sums assured. However, the most important innovation was undoubtedly industrial life assurance, which enabled the insurance companies to enter the wage earners' market (Cockerell and Green, 1994: 67). Whereas ordinary life assurance required the payment of large premiums on an annual or quarterly basis, industrial life assurance collected premiums on a weekly basis, much better suited to the needs of weekly wage earners (Morrah, 1955: 25). The figures in part B of table 8.48 suggest that industrial life assurance business grew more rapidly than ordinary life assurance business. This brought the major industrial life assurance companies such as the Prudential into direct and sometimes fierce competition with friendly societies and burial societies, and, indeed, doorstep fights between rival agents of insurance companies and friendly societies were not unknown until the formation of the Industrial Life Offices Association in 1901 put a stop to the practice of transferring policies between societies (Cockerell and Green, 1994: 69).

As in fire insurance, the British life offices expanded into overseas markets, with the Pelican, the sister company of the Phoenix, pioneering sales of life policies abroad from 1798 (Trebilcock, 1985: 552–65). The major fire offices and the mutual Scottish life offices, in particular, developed a large overseas business in the United States and Canada, although restrictive legislation from the mid-nineteenth century led to the later withdrawal of many British offices from the North American life assurance market. Nevertheless, many British companies earned substantial profits in other overseas markets, with colonial business particularly successful in the late nineteenth century (Cockerell and Green, 1994: 70). Cooperation was not as strong as in fire insurance, although the Associated Scottish Life Offices and the Life Offices' Association provided a forum for the Scottish and English life offices, respectively, to discuss industry-wide issues. The growing professionalisation of the business was reflected in the formation of the Institute of Actuaries in 1848 and the Faculty of Actuaries in 1856, the latter dealing separately with Scotland.

Marine insurance was dominated by private underwriters operating through Lloyd's in London and local underwriting associations based in other major ports. The Royal Exchange Assurance and the London Assurance, which held a statutory monopoly of corporate insurance between 1720 and 1824, never accounted for more than a small part of the market, but the new joint-stock companies and partnerships admitted to the market after 1824 and the mutual associations of shipowners provided more serious competition for the private underwriters (Cockerell and Green, 1994: 6–10). Lloyd's responded to the pressure of strong competition during the 1860s with institutional reforms and the development of large syndicates. The institutional reforms aimed to increase security, with Lloyd's incorporating itself in 1871 so that there could be a Lloyd's policy underwritten only by Lloyd's members, and introducing compulsory deposits and guarantees between 1870 and 1887 to ensure that members met their commitments (Gibb, 1957: 142–3; Raynes, 1964: 317). In addition, the 1880s saw the emergence of large syndicates of underwriters (names), with one member writing for all in the syndicate, enabling private underwriters to compete with the companies in large volume business (Raynes, 1964: 318). Overseas business had been attracted to the London market on a substantial volume since the early eighteenth century, and marine insurance continued to make a substantial positive contribution to the balance of payments throughout the nineteenth century. There are no data on premium income for marine insurance, since large numbers of private underwriters have left no records. Nevertheless, Imlah (1958: 48) provides a rough estimate of the contribution of marine insurance to the balance of payments on the assumption that it was equivalent to about 2.5% of the value of Britain's foreign trade.[12] On this basis, marine insurance accounted for about 1% of GDP throughout the period between the end of the Napoleonic Wars and the beginning of World War I, a substantial contribution. Imlah's (1958: 70–5) net credit figures for the period 1841–1913 are presented in table 8.49. Whether measured in current price or constant price terms, it is clear that marine insurance made an increasingly positive contribution to the balance of payments as British shipping rose to dominance in world trade.

Accident insurance grew much more rapidly than the other major lines of insurance business, as can be seen from the data on premiums in table 8.50. The first wave of growth was based on personal accident insurance in the 1840s and 1850s, particularly with the increase in railway travel (Supple, 1970: 226–8). After the Employers' Liability Act of 1880, however, the major growth area was employers' liability insurance, which indemnified employers against claims of negligence when employees were injured at work (Supple, 1970: 228). The next wave of growth was motor insurance, which Supple (1970: 237) believes accounted for more than £1 million of premium income by 1914. With

---

[12] The original estimate was made by Giffen (1882: 207, 209, 221–2) and endorsed by Jenks (1927: 412).

Table 8.49 *Contribution to the UK balance of payments from marine insurance, 1841–1913 (£ million)*

	At current prices	At constant 1913 prices
1841	3.6	3.4
1851	4.9	6.2
1861	9.4	9.4
1871	15.4	15.5
1881	15.6	16.9
1891	16.8	18.8
1901	17.4	18.5
1911	24.7	25.6
1913	28.1	28.1

Sources: Balance of payments data at current prices from Imlah (1958: 70–5), converted to constant prices using the GDP deflator from Feinstein (1972: table 61) and the Rousseaux wholesale price index from Mitchell (1988: 722–3).

Table 8.50 *Accident insurance business of UK offices, 1884–1914*

	Premium income (£ million)
1884	0.5
1895	1.8
1905	5.2
1914	16.7

Source: Supple (1970: 228, 417).

personal accident premiums of £2.1 million and employers' liability premiums of £3.8 million, these three branches accounted for nearly £7 million of the £16.7 million total for accident premiums in 1914 (Supple, 1970: 237). On the eve of World War I, then, accident insurance was the most dynamic part of the insurance sector, but remained substantially smaller than the three main branches of fire, life and marine insurance.[13] Pearson (1997) argues that this late development of accident insurance in Britain reflected a generally poor innovation record in British insurance. However, his conclusion that this casts doubt on 'the

---

[13] It should be noted, however, that these figures do not include Lloyd's accident business, the volume of which is unknown (Supple, 1970: 417).

recent emphasis by Rubinstein, Cain and Hopkins, and others on the dynamism of the financial sector' surely goes too far (251). The British insurance sector may not have been particularly innovative, but it was highly successful on world markets.

Pearson's findings on innovation highlight the need to identify other sources of Britain's comparative advantage in insurance. The first point to note is that Britain, as a rich and highly urbanised society, could support a large service sector that reaped economies of scale from specialisation. Supple (1970: 114) notes, for example, that by 1852 life assurance cover amounted to over £5 per head of the population in Britain, compared with just two shillings in Germany and less than a shilling in France. This was clearly a transient advantage, which would disappear as other countries industrialised and urbanised. However, a more persistent underlying factor behind Britain's success in insurance was the form of organisation. Although it is clear that the nineteenth century saw the emergence of large-scale insurance companies, business continued to be organised on a fundamentally decentralised basis and dependent on individual enterprise.

The trend to large-scale enterprise can be seen in the rising concentration ratios in life and fire insurance. Supple (1970: 295–6) notes that, in life assurance, the largest ten firms accounted for 33% of premium income in 1881, rising to 43% in 1914, while in fire insurance the share of the largest nine firms increased from 54% in 1899 to 66% in 1904. Furthermore, a growing tide of amalgamations, particularly during the first decade of the twentieth century, led to the growth of composite insurers, offering policies across the full range of risks (Supple, 1970: 296–7). However, it would be too simplistic to see this growth of large-scale enterprise in insurance as a straightforward substitution of hierarchies for networks, mirroring developments in manufacturing. In fact, the growth of large-scale enterprise in insurance was dependent on a highly decentralised form of organisation, with sales conducted through agents, who were paid on a commission basis. In the 1880s, for example, Royal Exchange agents were paid a commission of 10% on new premiums and 5% on renewal premiums, with a 'procuration' fee of 10s. 6d. for each £500 of insurance (Supple, 1970: 286). Sometimes incentive schemes could be applied even to directors; at the Royal Exchange, for example, Supple (1970: 355) notes that attendance allowances were deducted from the directors' fees on a weekly basis and distributed in cash to those who turned up at the meetings. If decentralisation remained important in the large companies, it was the whole basis of operation at Lloyd's, which retained a strong position, particularly in marine insurance.

Furthermore, office mechanisation occurred only slowly in British insurance. Campbell-Kelly (1992) notes that at the Prudential Assurance Company, the largest British life insurer, it took from the 1870s to the 1930s to make the transition from manual data processing methods to the fully mechanised office. Although two primitive calculating machines were purchased in 1870, bound ledger books were replaced by loose-leaf manilla cards for recording policy details from 1871 and correspondence was centralised by the 1870s, the US office machinery boom of the 1890s and early 1900s largely passed by the Prudential. Campbell-Kelly (126) explains this partly in terms of resistance to the new office technology along similar lines to the resistance of workers in manufacturing to mass production technology. However, he also explains the slow adoption of modern office technology at the Prudential by the longevity of life assurance policies, which made it necessary to continue updating policies based on the old technology alongside new policies on any new system (132–3). This necessarily imparted a bias towards technological conservatism, with the nature of the business setting limits to the process of mechanisation. On this view, mechanisation occurred slowly but efficiently.

8.5 Conclusions

Britain had higher overall labour productivity than the United States or Germany in the late nineteenth century not because of high productivity in industry but because of high productivity in services and a relatively small agricultural sector. However, between the 1870s and World War I Britain began to lose that crucial productivity leadership in services as the United States and Germany also moved resources out of low-value-added agriculture and urbanised. Part of the faster productivity growth in services in the United States and Germany was therefore an inevitable part of the catching-up process. However, in addition to this, Britain was also facing the problem of adjustment to the 'industrialisation' of services. The growth of 'big business' in US services, with high volume, low margins and hierarchical management, mirrored the rise of 'mass production' in US industry. But Britain continued to do well in services where network forms of organisation remained dominant.

The sectoral studies in this chapter demonstrate a variety of experience. On the railways, where big business in services began, Britain was hampered by early development and technological lock-in, leading to the early emergence of a large US labour productivity lead. In shipping, although a more 'industrialised' liner section emerged, in which Britain faced strong competition from Germany, Britain continued to dominate the tramp shipping section on the basis of networks, and held on to market share in the liner section through the collusive ring system. Britain thus remained dominant in shipping before World War I, especially on empire routes, where network links were strongest. Although a substantial US labour productivity lead had already emerged by World War I in transport and communications as a result of the more successful industrialisation of these services, any US productivity lead in distribution or finance was small. In retailing, big business in the form of department stores, multiple shops and co-operatives still accounted for a small share of sales in both Britain and the United States, and, in wholesaling, Britain's network of merchant companies remained competitive abroad as well as at home. In finance, there was a contrast between domestic and international banking. In internationally oriented investment banking, Britain remained dominant before World War I, with the City of London acting like a 'Marshallian district', with many small specialised firms but the sector as a whole reaping external economies of scale. In domestic retail banking, by contrast, the process of 'industrialisation' was well under way, with the rise of joint-stock banks and growing concentration. However, there was still no substantial US productivity lead in this sector, since the 'industrialisation' of banking was inhibited in the United States by regulations limiting the growth of inter-state banking.

9 The collapse of the liberal world economic order, 1914–1950

9.1 Introduction

The period between 1914 and 1951 was highly disturbed, with only a short interlude between World War I and the Great Depression, and an even shorter interlude before World War II. Nevertheless, it is possible to identify trends in the comparative performance of the major market service sectors. Although productivity growth was faster in the United States than in Britain, the British market service sectors kept pace with their German counterparts. Since the United States had largely caught up with Britain by World War I in services, faster US productivity growth in these sectors after 1914 led to the United States forging ahead, although it was only in parts of the transport and communications sector that the US productivity lead became large, as can be seen from the benchmark estimates in table 9.1. Although Germany also had a substantial labour productivity lead over Britain on the railways in 1935, Britain had substantially higher labour productivity in communications and also in distribution and finance.

The US forging ahead in transport and communications, together with the absence of large Anglo-American productivity gaps in distribution and finance, is most easily explained by the increasing 'industrialisation' of much of the transport and communications sector in the United States, together with the continued suitability of large parts of the distribution and finance sectors for organisation on the basis of flexible networks, a traditional British strength. Furthermore, the continued employment of around 30% of the German labour force in agriculture between the wars meant that Germany's service sector remained underdeveloped, so that Britain continued to enjoy a substantial productivity advantage over Germany in most services.

The disruption to international economic relations caused by the two world wars and the increasingly protectionist and even autarkic environment of the inter-war period would be expected to have had a much greater impact on the highly globalised British economy than on either

Table 9.1 *Benchmark estimates of comparative labour productivity levels in market services, 1910–1950 (UK = 100)*

A. US/UK

	1910	1924	1930	1937	1950
Railways	215.5	342.2	447.9	390.6	620.7
Communications	143.5	136.1	166.5	270.0	144.6
Distribution	118.7			119.8	148.4
Finance	119.9	155.8	103.0	86.4	138.7

B. Germany/UK

	1935
Railways	178.9
Communications	34.5
Distribution and finance	54.3

Sources: tables 3.2, 3.4.

the domestically oriented US economy or the more highly protectionist German economy of the pre-1914 period. Nevertheless, growing integration within the British Empire to some extent cushioned the UK economy from the hostile international environment, providing secure supplies of vital food and raw materials in wartime and providing export markets on preferential terms. Although in the shortrun this clearly proved beneficial, and was at times perhaps even vital for survival, it seems likely that there were also some long-run costs. As the world economy reintegrated after World War II, trade with far-flung Commonwealth countries was bound to decline, and called for a major reorientation of marketing investments. Also, it may be argued that the strengthening of the Imperial Preference system had unfavourable effects for the economic and social system more generally, perpetuating incentives for rent-seeking at the expense of wealth creation.

The formalisation of collusive behaviour and restrictive practices in a number of British market service sectors during the Edwardian period was noted in chapter 8. These anti-competitive tendencies were strengthened during the inter-war period as protectionism limited international competition and as governments encouraged domestic collusion as a means to stabilise falling prices. As with Imperial Preference, it is possible to see these policies as having beneficial effects in the short run, but with adverse consequences in the long run. In the short run, preventing prices from falling helped to preserve employment by muting

Table 9.2 *Productivity in the British aggregate economy, 1911–1951*

A. Indices of output, inputs and productivity (1924 = 100)

	Output	Labour	Capital	Labour productivity	TFP
1911	93.9	101.3	85.0	92.7	98.5
1913	100.1	104.0	87.9	96.3	102.0
1924	100.0	100.0	100.0	100.0	100.0
1929	112.2	106.0	106.2	105.8	105.7
1932	106.8	102.0	109.7	104.7	102.1
1937	134.1	116.2	116.4	115.4	115.3
1951	161.4	128.4	134.6	125.7	123.7

B. Growth rates of output, inputs and productivity (% per annum)

	1911–1924	1924–1937	1937–1951	1911–1951
Output	0.5	2.3	1.3	1.4
Labour	−0.1	1.2	0.7	0.6
Capital	1.3	1.2	1.0	1.1
Labour productivity	0.6	1.1	0.6	0.8
TFP	0.1	1.1	0.5	0.6

Note:
Factor shares are 35% for capital and 65% for labour, based on 1937 figures.

Source: Output – Feinstein (1972: table 6); labour – Feinstein (1972: table 57); capital – 1911–1920: Feinstein (1988: table XI); 1920–1951: Feinstein (1972: table 44); factor shares – Matthews et al. (1982: 164).

real wage increases in the face of sticky nominal wages, but in the long run collusion also reduced competitive pressures for change, with adverse consequences for productivity growth.

As in chapter 8, it will be convenient to begin by setting out trends in productivity performance at the aggregate level, to provide a benchmark against which sectoral performance can be assessed. Table 9.2 provides indices of output, inputs and productivity in the United Kingdom between 1911 and 1951, together with growth rates calculated over the whole period and sub-periods. Since employment data for individual sectors are not available for the cyclical peak year 1913, productivity growth rates are calculated for 1911–1951 rather than for 1913–1951, but this makes little difference.[1] For the much shorter period covering World War I, although the use of 1911–1924 rather than 1913–1924

---

[1] For 1913–1951 output grew at an annual rate of 1.3%, while inputs grew at the same rates as for 1911–1951.

Table 9.3 *Comparative US/UK and Germany/UK productivity levels for the aggregate economy, 1911–1950 (UK = 100)*

A. US/UK		
	Labour productivity	TFP
1909/11	117.7	90.5
1919/20	133.3	108.2
1929	139.4	112.7
1937	132.6	105.9
1950	166.9	138.1
B. Germany/UK		
	Labour productivity	TFP
1911	75.5	75.4
1925	69.0	74.3
1929	74.1	78.5
1935	75.7	78.2
1950	74.4	76.2

Sources: Tables 6.1, 6.2.

does make more of a difference, it does not affect the basic findings that output growth and productivity growth were substantially slower than before or since.[2] The general pattern for the economy as a whole, then, was one of stagnating labour productivity across World War I, followed by a return to respectable productivity growth between the wars. Labour productivity growth of 1.1% per annum between the peak years of 1924 and 1937 compares favourably with the 0.9% achieved between 1873 and 1913. However, across World War II productivity growth slowed to about half the inter-war rate, at 0.6% per annum for labour productivity growth and 0.5% for TFP growth. The figures in table 9.3 place Britain's aggregate productivity performance in international perspective. Whereas the United States forged ahead, increasing the size of its labour productivity lead and pulling ahead in terms of TFP levels for the first time, Germany suffered a setback across World War I and did little more than make up the lost ground before another setback across World War II, so that, by 1950, Germany's comparative productivity position was about the same as in 1911, at roughly three-quarters of the British level.

[2] For 1913–1924 annual growth rates were 0.0% for output, −0.4% for labour, 1.2% for capital, 0.4% for labour productivity and −0.2% for TFP.

9.2 Transport and communications

9.2.1 Introduction

Table 9.4 provides data on output, input and productivity trends for the British transport and communications sector between 1911 and 1951. Output grew more rapidly than in the aggregate economy during both trans-war periods, but more slowly during the inter-war phase between 1924 and 1937. Inputs of both labour and capital grew more slowly than in the aggregate economy over the period as a whole, and in each sub-period, with the exception of labour across World War I. Consequently, labour productivity growth and TFP growth were substantially faster in transport and communications than in the aggregate economy over the period as a whole and in both trans-war phases. During the inter-war phase, however, both labour productivity growth and TFP growth were slightly slower in transport and communications than in the aggregate economy. To put the British performance into international perspective, table 9.5 shows the US labour productivity lead over Britain in transport and communications continuing to widen. However, the German labour productivity lead over Britain declined substantially as railways declined in relative importance.

9.2.2 *Shipping: the end of British hegemony*

World War I provided a major disruption to world shipping, from which the British shipping sector never really recovered. Although Britain lost a higher proportion of her merchant fleet than any other Allied or neutral country, this was not the major problem, since the lost tonnage was quickly replaced. The difficulties were caused by the fact that other countries built up their merchant fleets while British shipping was engaged in essential war work. Governments in these countries then pursued nationalistic shipping policies after the war, so that the markets could not be won back by the British (Sturmey, 1962: 54, 98–9). The excess supply of world tonnage was exacerbated by the general climate of protectionism, with the result that world trade did not grow as rapidly as world output. Tramp shipping, a particular British strength before 1914, suffered more severely than the liner business. This was partly because the large shipping lines were successful in limiting the decline of freight rates through the shipping conferences on the established liner routes (Deakin, 1973: 27–42). However, it also reflected the collapse of British coal exports, which had provided a major outward cargo for British tramp ships bringing grain and other bulk products home,

Table 9.4 *Productivity in the British transport and communications sector, 1911–1951*

A. Indices of output, inputs and productivity (1924 = 100)

	Output	Labour	Capital	Labour productivity	TFP
1911	79.1	97.7	91.1	81.0	83.0
1924	100.0	100.0	100.0	100.0	100.0
1929	112.6	103.0	106.0	109.3	108.3
1932	102.7	98.8	106.9	103.9	101.1
1937	122.0	107.9	107.7	113.1	113.2
1951	170.8	116.0	105.5	147.2	152.2

B. Growth rates of output, inputs and productivity (% per annum)

	1911–1924	1924–1937	1937–1951	1911–1951
Output	1.8	1.5	2.4	1.9
Labour	0.2	0.6	0.5	0.4
Capital	0.7	0.6	−0.1	0.4
Labour productivity	1.6	0.9	1.9	1.5
TFP	1.4	0.9	2.1	1.5

Sources: Output – Feinstein (1972: table 8); labour – Feinstein (1972: tables 59, 60), with adjustment for exclusion of the Irish Republic after 1920 from Mitchell (1988: 110); capital – 1911–1920: Feinstein (1988: table XI); 1920–1951: Feinstein (1972: table 44).

Table 9.5 *Comparative US/UK and Germany/UK labour productivity levels for the transport and communications sector, 1911–1950 (UK = 100)*

	US/UK	Germany/UK
1909/11	217.4	216.9
1919/20	250.6	140.0
1929	231.5	151.2
1937	283.4	132.4
1950	348.4	122.0

Sources: Tables 3.1, 3.3.

and which had enabled British tramps to undercut other European tramps. Carrying ballast rather than coal on the outward voyage, British ships were no longer able to compete with the lower crew costs of the Norwegian and Greek tramps. In the oil tanker business that largely

Table 9.6 *Output and productivity in British shipping, 1911–1951*

A. Indices of output, inputs and productivity (1924 = 100)

	Output	Labour	Capital	Labour productivity	TFP
1911	90.9	86.1	92.4	105.6	102.9
1921	83.1	92.3	98.0	90.0	88.1
1924	100.0	100.0	100.0	100.0	100.0
1929	108.2	95.6	104.8	113.2	109.6
1931	98.7	81.7	104.3	120.8	110.9
1932	93.9	78.4	101.9	119.8	109.3
1937	96.1	84.0	94.9	114.4	109.6
1951	104.9	58.4		179.6	

B. Growth rates of output, inputs and productivity (% per annum)

	1911–1924	1924–1937	1937–1951	1911–1951
Output	0.7	−0.3	0.6	0.3
Labour	1.1	−1.3	−2.6	−1.0
Capital	0.6	−0.4		
Labour productivity	−0.4	1.0	3.2	1.3
TFP	−0.2	0.7		

Sources: Output – derived from data on net tonnage of ships adjusted for improvements in speed and quality of service and capacity utilisation, as described in Lewis (1978: 259) for the period before World War I; labour – 1911–1921: census estimates from Mitchell (1988: 104–5); 1921–1937: Chapman (1953: 143); 1951: census estimate for 1951 from Mitchell (1988: 104–5) linked to 1931 estimate; capital – 1911–1920: Feinstein (1988: tables 15.11, 15.16, 15.17); 1920–1937: Feinstein (1965: tables 9.31, 9.32).

replaced the declining coal trade, it was indeed the Norwegian shipowners that came to dominate (Sturmey, 1962: 73–81).

In table 9.6, output is measured in the same way as before World War I, using the method of Lewis (1978: 259). Data on net tonnage are adjusted for trend improvements in speed and service at 0.5% per annum, and for capacity utilisation assuming trend growth between cyclical peaks in UK GDP from Feinstein (1972). On this basis, output stagnated throughout the period. Data on employment are available for the inter-war period from Chapman (1953) and can be extended back to 1911 and forward to 1951 using census data on the labour force. Over the whole period 1911 to 1951, labour productivity grew less rapidly in shipping than in transport and communications as a whole, but still more rapidly than in the aggregate economy. The most dramatic improvement of labour productivity in shipping occurred with the decline in the labour input across World War II, although labour productivity growth was also respectable during the period 1924 to 1937. For this period between the wars capital stock data can be obtained from Feinstein (1965), so it is possible to see that TFP growth was also respectable, but slightly slower than in the aggregate economy as well as in transport and communications as a whole.

World War I inevitably provided a major disruption to the business of the world's major shipping nation. However, British shipping companies were able to make good profits during the early stages of the war, since government controls were rather piecemeal before the formation of the Ministry of Shipping at the end of 1916. Although fixed 'Blue Book' rates were paid on requisitioned ships, much higher free-market rates could also be earned on ships that could avoid requisitioning (Salter, 1921: 24–9; Sturmey, 1962: 46–7). However, as shortages worsened with the adoption by Germany of unrestricted submarine warfare from late 1916, controls were tightened, and all ocean-going vessels were brought under control, including liners as well as tramps (Salter, 1921: 72). World War I was followed by a period of dislocation, during which shortages of tonnage and high market rates persisted. During this period there was a speculative frenzy, in which reserves built up from wartime profits were used to finance amalgamations and reflotations, to buy up old tonnage and to place orders for new ships at inflated prices. This was to have unfortunate consequences, since the new tonnage worsened the situation of excess supply, and shipping firms depleted reserves that might have been used later to finance modernisation (Sturmey, 1962: 55–60; Aldcroft, 1974: 134).

The biggest beneficiary from the British relative decline across World War I was the United States, as can be seen from the gross tonnage data in table 9.7. On the eve of World War I the US merchant marine carried only about 10% of US seaborne trade, which was severely disrupted by the withdrawal of foreign tonnage. This led to a major public shipbuilding programme through the US Shipping Board, which disposed of the ships after the war largely to US citizens, in such a way as to maintain the US merchant marine for strategic reasons (Sturmey, 1962: 37–8). Although the bulk of the German merchant fleet was redistributed to the Allies as reparations, the German fleet was quickly rebuilt to the pre-war tonnage and remained at this level until World War II.

The general state of excess supply throughout the inter-war period after the collapse of the immediate post-war boom is apparent in table 9.8. During the 1920s world shipping tonnage increased ahead of world seaborne trade, while during the 1930s tonnage remained stable as world trade collapsed during the Depression before recovering to the

Table 9.7 *World merchant fleet, 1913–1950*

A. Millions of gross tons

	1913	1920	1929	1939	1950
United Kingdom	18.3	18.1	20.0	17.9	18.2
United States	4.3	14.5	13.5	11.4	27.5
Germany	4.7	0.4	4.1	4.5	0.5
France	1.8	3.0	3.3	2.9	3.2
7 European countries	7.6	9.0	14.3	16.7	17.0
World total	43.1	54.0	66.4	68.5	84.6

B. Shares of world fleet (%)

	1913	1920	1929	1939	1950
United Kingdom	42.4	33.6	30.2	26.1	21.5
United States	9.9	26.9	20.3	16.6	32.5
Germany	11.0	0.8	6.1	6.5	0.5
France	4.2	5.5	5.0	4.3	3.8
7 European countries	17.7	16.7	21.5	24.3	20.1

Note:
The seven European countries are Italy, Netherlands, Sweden, Denmark, Norway, Greece and Spain.

Source: Svennilson (1954: 153).

Table 9.8 *World trade, shipping and freight rates, 1913–1938 (1913 = 100)*

	Seaborne trade	Shipping tonnage		Freight rates		
		Total	Active	United Kingdom	German liner	German tramp
1913	100	100	100	100	100	100
1920	83	122		439		
1921	82	132		158		
1924	106	134	126	113		103
1927	127	139	133	110	120	99
1929	135	145	141	97	114	100
1932	101	148	122	75	69	60
1933	103	145	123	73	66	49
1937	141	141	140	128	73	86
1938	135	144	142	98	77	64

Source: Sturmey (1962: 65).

1929 level at the end of the decade. Tonnage laid up peaked at 17.6% in 1932, but active tonnage was still in substantial excess supply at this time. UK freight rates in 1920 were still booming at more than four times the 1913 level, but crashed to 158% of the 1913 level in 1921 and continued to fall until 1933. The slump in freight rates was particularly bad in tramp shipping, as can be seen from the data on German freight rates, available separately for tramp and liner shipping. Since the price level was substantially higher during the 1920s and 1930s than in 1913, these freight rates suggest a substantial decline in real earnings from shipping.[3]

The inter-war period was marked by the growth of economic nationalism, which found expression in the world of shipping through the spread of postal subventions, operating subsidies, construction subsidies, indirect subsidies, state fleets and preferences (Sturmey, 1962: 101). Sturmey (100) identifies the countries that adopted practices which had a significant adverse effect on British shipping as the United States, Germany, France, Italy and Japan.[4] In all other cases, he argues, the fleet was too small or the subsidies too unimportant to have had a significant impact. The upshot for shares of seaborne trade carried in British ships can be seen in table 9.9. Whereas British ships continued to carry almost all seaborne trade on inter-imperial routes, Britain's share declined substantially on empire–foreign routes and precipitously on foreign–foreign routes. As in so many areas of economic life between the wars, Britain became increasingly dependent upon her network of imperial ties.

Superimposed upon the problems of excess capacity and nationalism in shipping was a technological shift away from steam power towards the motorship. As Svennilson (1954: 155), Sturmey (1962: 82–5) and others have noted, British shipowners lagged behind some of the more successful European countries in the adoption of the motorship. However, before this can be taken as evidence of entrepreneurial failure, it should be noted that the first commercial application of the diesel engine was in 1919, just as the British merchant fleet had returned to its peak tonnage, so that diffusion was limited by the rate of replacement (Henning and Trace, 1975: 378). Although Britain was slower to adopt the diesel engine than the Scandinavian countries with expanding

---

[3] Feinstein's (1972: table 61) GDP deflator takes a value of 270.8 in 1920, falling to 161.1 in 1934, before recovering to 174.2 by 1938.
[4] In the case of Japan, Sturmey (125) also stresses the importance of low wages, a factor that was to be of much greater significance after World War II with the decline of nationalism in shipping and the emergence of flags of convenience.

Table 9.9 *Shares of seaborne trade carried in British ships, 1912–1936 (%)*

	1912	1931	1936
Inter-imperial	95.6	94.4	93.2
Empire–foreign	60.8	52.6	47.2
Foreign–foreign	22.1	12.8	12.2
Total	47.6	39.3	39.4

Source: Leak (1939: 252).

Table 9.10 *Proportion of merchant tonnage using diesel propulsion, 1923–1939 (%)*

	1923	1925	1927	1929	1931	1933	1935	1937	1939
Norway	8.3	12.9	21.1	29.9	40.3	43.0	48.6	56.0	62.2
Denmark	16.0	18.1	22.2	29.2	35.9	39.5	41.9	48.7	52.2
Sweden	16.1	21.4	22.7	27.1	31.7	33.3	36.6	39.8	46.6
Netherlands	2.9	5.3	8.0	13.2	22.0	26.0	33.0	38.8	45.5
Japan	0.8	1.7	3.0	5.4	12.0	14.3	20.4	24.9	27.2
Germany	4.2	9.0	10.6	14.4	14.8	17.2	18.5	22.3	26.2
Great Britain	2.0	3.9	6.1	9.5	12.4	14.0	16.6	21.3	25.6
Italy	3.1	4.7	11.0	14.4	16.7	19.3	22.3	20.3	20.8
World	2.6	4.2	6.6	9.7	13.4	15.0	17.4	20.7	24.4

Source: Sturmey (1962: 84).

merchant marines, there was much less of a lag behind Germany and other countries that did not see growth in their merchant fleets, as can be seen in table 9.10. Nevertheless, in a paper which has many parallels with Harley's (1971) evaluation of the earlier switch from sail to steam, Henning and Trace (1975: 372) present calculations of annual net cash flow for motorships, oil-fired steamships and coal-fired steamships on the Europe–Australia route over the period 1922 to 1939. However, whereas Harley shows that British shipowners switched to steam when it was profitable to do so, Henning and Trace show that net cash flow was always highest for the motorship. They blame the slower adoption of motorships on this route by British shipowners than by other European shipowners on the strength of the coal lobby and pro-coal sentiment in Britain, together with the over-optimistic claims made by steam turbine machinery builders (385). However, it is only fair to note the loss of

Table 9.11 *Dividends of British shipping companies, 1932–1935 (% of nominal capital)*

	1932	1933	1934	1935
Harrisons	35.0	40.0	30.0	35.0
Holts	26.7	20.0	20.0	20.0
Booth	nil	nil	nil	3.0
Clan	1.8	4.5	5.4	3.5
Ellerman	3.0	n.a.	4.3	3.5
P&O	2.0	n.a.	2.0	2.0
Union Castle	nil	1.8	3.1	3.1
Tramp companies	1.1	0.9	1.0	1.5

Sources: Liner companies – Hyde (1967: 174); tramp companies – Jones (1957: 36).

financial reserves during the speculative boom of 1919/20, from which modernisation could have been financed, and the effect of the shipping conference system in removing competitive pressures on less efficient firms.

Profitability among British shipowners can be analysed using the data on dividends expressed as a percentage of nominal capital in table 9.11. As Hyde (1967: 173) notes, the figures must be treated with caution, since the more conservative older companies that had relied on self-financing often had nominal capitals that bore little relationship to the value of their capital assets. This applied in particular to Harrisons and Holts, both of which consistently provided very high returns to the small number of shareholders. Nevertheless, it is clear that the rate of return was substantially lower for the sample of tramp shipping companies, which accounted for about 3.5 million gross tons. At the end of 1933 a Special Committee on Tramp Shipping was set up by the Chamber of Shipping, and its recommendation was a government subsidy. This led to the 1935 British Shipping (Assistance) Act, providing an annual subsidy of up to £2 million until freight rates returned to their 1929 level, together with a 'scrap and build' scheme designed to assist shipbuilders as well as shipowners (Dyos and Aldcroft, 1969: 329). The subsidy provided a useful source of relief for the tramp owners, but the scrap and build scheme had only a limited impact, since its financial terms were not sufficiently attractive to encourage many takers (330). The shipping lines suffered less than the tramp owners, as freight rate falls were limited by the shipping conferences and the consolidated groups that had emerged by 1919 had access to greater resources. The industry was dominated between the wars by the 'Big Five', consisting

Table 9.12 *Net receipts of British shipping, 1913–1947 (£ million)*

	At current prices	At constant 1913 prices
1913	94	94
1920	340	126
1924	140	76
1929	130	74
1932	70	43
1937	130	77
1938	100	57
1947	196	67

Sources: 1913–1938 – Sayers (1976: appendix 32, table A); 1947 – Kendall (1950: 24), rearranged on the pre-war Board of Trade basis, converted to constant prices using the GDP deflator from Feinstein (1972: table 61).

of: BI/P&O (formed from British India and Peninsular and Oriental); Cunard; Ellerman; Furness Withy; and the Royal Mail Group. Significant tonnage was also owned by the 'Lesser Three', of Harrisons, Holts and Clan (Boyce, 1995: 128). Nevertheless, the liner section also had its difficulties, most notably the collapse in 1931 of the Royal Mail Group, which controlled some 2 million gross tons of shipping, about one-sixth of the British liner tonnage (Dyos and Aldcroft, 1969: 329). Nevertheless, government assistance to the liner owners was limited to a subsidy for Cunard on condition that it absorbed the White Star line, which had been taken over by the Royal Mail Group in 1927 (Pollard, 1992: 72). The subsidy took the form of a loan on easy terms to finance the building of two transatlantic liners, the Queen Mary and the Queen Elizabeth.

The value of total earnings from shipping was calculated on a detailed basis by the Board of Trade during the inter-war period, and the estimates are presented in table 9.12. Since visible imports were valued in the balance of payments c.i.f. (carriage including freight) while exports were valued f.o.b. (free on board), the earnings of UK ships from freight imports were included as an invisible credit. After World War II both imports and exports were valued f.o.b. in the balance of payments, so it was necessary to adjust the 1947 figure onto the pre-war basis. As Kendall (1948: 143) notes, the pre-war method 'measured both invisible exports and savings in invisible imports, whereas now it relates only to the former'. The post-war method has much to recommend it as a way of calculating the balance of payments, but for capturing the shrinking earnings of the shipping sector it is the pre-war method that is more appropriate. The estimates in table 9.12 are presented in both current and constant prices. The sharp increase in nominal earnings in 1920 translated into a much smaller rise in real earnings, and thereafter real earnings from shipping stagnated at about three-quarters of the 1913 level, with a further sharp fall during the Depression of the 1930s.

Returning to table 9.7, the UK share of the world merchant fleet declined across World War II, as across World War I, and, once again, what remained of the German fleet was confiscated as reparations. Other European countries also saw their shares of the world fleet decline. The United States was the main beneficiary across World War II, as across World War I, with the British dominions (principally Australia, Canada and India) the only other significant beneficiaries (Sturmey, 1962: 140–1). The impact of World War II on the finances of the shipping companies depended upon the rates paid for freight carried on requisitioned ships and the compensation received for lost tonnage. As during World War I, freight rates were more generous for ships from neutral countries, but the rates for British companies were set to allow a 5% profit (Sturmey: 143). Under the Government Tonnage Replacement Scheme, shipowners were compensated in cash for the depreciated historic cost in 1939, on the implicit assumption that the owners had the difference between this and the replacement cost as depreciation reserves. However, owners were credited with an additional amount reflecting the increase in insurance values of ships during the war, and this could be withdrawn when a ship was actually replaced (Sturmey: 144). Sturmey (145–7) argues that the liner companies held their own financially, but made no exorbitant gains, while the increase in the reserves of tramp companies was just sufficient to pay for the replacement of lost tonnage. The immediate post-war years saw a boom in freight rates and profits, but, in contrast to the speculative frenzy after World War I, shipowners adopted a cautious attitude towards replacement and fleet expansion (Sturmey: 156–8).

The period between 1914 and 1950 was a difficult one for British shipping, which lost its dominant role in world trade, and it is therefore tempting to be critical. It is true that, with the emergence of the concentrated group structure and adherence to the conference system, the nineteenth-century world of competing entrepreneurial networks had disappeared for good (Sturmey: 350–82). Nevertheless, productivity in shipping continued to grow at a respectable rate between the wars. Also, the performance during the two world wars is testimony to the continued strength and flexibility of the British merchant marine (and the service sector more generally) at this time. For, as Olson (1963: 132–47) notes, an impartial observer might have predicted success for the German submarine blockade of Britain rather than the British naval

230   Reassessing British market service performance

Table 9.13 *Length of railway line open, 1913–1950 (miles)*

	Great Britain	Germany	United States
1913	20,266	39,383	249,777
1920	20,312	35,758	252,845
1925	20,400	35,865	249,398
1930	20,265	36,151	249,052
1935	20,152	36,564	241,822
1939	19,982	38,490	235,064
1950	19,471	22,945	223,779

Note:
Germany subject to significant boundary changes across the two world wars. 1950 figure refers to Federal Republic of Germany only.

Sources: Great Britain – Mitchell (1988: 541–2); Germany – Mitchell (1975: table F1); United States – US Department of Commerce (1975: 728).

blockade of Germany, since Germany had retained a large agricultural sector through protection, while Britain had allowed her agricultural sector to shrink in the face of cheap grain imports from the New World. In Olson's view, it was the flexibility of Britain's sophisticated service sector that made the difference (146), and merchant shipping clearly played a critical role here.

9.2.3   Stagnation on the railways

The length of railway line open in Great Britain had reached 20,000 miles just before the outbreak of World War I, and remained at about this level until the end of World War II. As can be seen in table 9.13, this stagnation in the railway system occurred also in Germany and the United States. In Britain and elsewhere, new forms of transport, particularly on the roads, took business away from the railways, which entered a period of stagnation between the wars. Productivity stagnated along with output, as British railways struggled to cope with the new environment.

The main dimensions of output on the British railways are shown in table 9.14. Although there was a sharp decline in the number of passenger journeys from 1920, the decline in passenger-miles was less severe, as the average distance of journeys increased. Freight traffic declined from 1913 in terms of freight loaded, although net ton-miles followed a U-shaped pattern, with strong recovery across World War II. An important factor in the decline of freight traffic in the aftermath of World War I

Table 9.14 *Railway operating statistics, Great Britain, 1913–1951*

A. Passengers

	Passenger journeys (million)	Passenger-miles (million)	Average distance (miles)	Passenger receipts (£ million)
1913	1,550	15,500	10.0	54.5
1920	2,186	22,900	10.5	109.4
1924	1,747	21,300	12.2	95.1
1929	1,705	21,600	12.7	87.0
1932	1,557	18,900	12.1	73.5
1932	1,141	16,700	14.6	67.1
1937	1,295	21,000	16.2	75.2
1951	1,001	20,793	20.7	140.1

B. Freight

	Freight loaded (million tons)	Net ton-miles (million)	Average distance (miles)	Freight receipts (£ million)
1913	367	22,020	60	64.3
1920	320	19,173	60	126.9
1924	338	19,063	56	106.4
1929	332	18,855	57	106.7
1932	251	14,934	59	81.2
1937	299	18,384	61	94.6
1951	285	22,902	80	227.9

Note:
Freight loaded measured on the basis of carryings rather than loadings in order to eliminate duplication, so not directly comparable with pre-war figures; on the basis of loadings, the 1913 figure is 562 million tons. The 1913 figures on net ton-miles and passenger-miles are calculated on the basis of estimated average distances. Passenger figures from 1932 exclude railways operated by the London Passenger Transport Board.
Source: Munby and Watson (1978: tables A2, A11, A12, A17, A18).

was the low level of activity in Britain's heavy industries (Foreman-Peck and Millward, 1994: 241). The slump in the British coal industry was particularly serious, since coal and coke accounted for about a half of the ton-mileage of freight carried on Britain's railways (Munby and Watson, 1978: 86). The situation would have been even more serious for the railways had it not been for the deleterious effects of World War I on coastal shipping, which provided the main competition to the railways in the transport of coal (Ashworth, 1960: 338; Dyos and Aldcroft, 1969: 289). The data on passenger-miles and freight ton-miles from table 9.14 can be combined to provide an index of railway output in table 9.15.

Table 9.15 *Productivity trends on British railways, 1913–1951*

A. Indices of output, inputs and productivity (1924 = 100)

	Output	Labour	Capital	Labour productivity	TFP
1913	93.4	89.7	98.0	104.1	101.0
1924	100.0	100.0	100.0	100.0	100.0
1929	100.0	91.5	100.7	109.3	105.7
1932	82.9	85.4	101.0	97.1	91.5
1937	103.1	85.7	101.5	120.3	113.4
1951	115.6	91.0	99.4	127.0	123.1

B. Growth rates of output, inputs and productivity (% per annum)

	1913–1924	1924–1937	1937–1951	1913–1951
Output	0.6	0.2	0.8	0.5
Labour	1.0	−1.2	0.4	0.0
Capital	0.2	0.1	−0.1	0.0
Labour productivity	−0.4	1.4	0.4	0.5
TFP	−0.1	0.9	0.6	0.5

Sources: Output – derived from table 9.14; labour – Munby and Watson (1978: table A8.1); capital – 1913–1920: Feinstein (1988: table XI); 1920–1937: Feinstein (1965: table 9.10); 1937–1951: Feinstein (1972: table 44).

As in the period prior to World War I, revenues from passenger and freight trains are used to provide weights. Output grew at the very slow rate of 0.5% per annum during the 1913–1951 period as a whole. Since labour and capital inputs also stagnated, labour productivity growth and TFP growth were also 0.5% per annum over the period as a whole.

Labour productivity declined across World War I, with employment increasing more than output as a result of the 20% reduction in the length of the working week with the introduction of the eight-hour day in 1919 (Dowie, 1975: 441). For the inter-war period, 1924 to 1937, output virtually stagnated, but the number of employees declined, so that labour productivity grew at the respectable rate of 1.4% per annum, faster than in the economy as a whole. TFP growth of 0.9% per annum on the railways during this period was also respectable, but a little slower than in the economy as a whole. Nevertheless, the productivity performance over the period as a whole must be regarded as disappointing. This is particularly clear if an international comparative perspective is taken. Returning to table 9.1, the US labour productivity lead on the railways grew substantially across World War I and continued to grow during the 1920s. Although the gap narrowed slightly as the

Depression of the 1930s hit economic activity in the United States harder than in Britain, the gap increased again across World War II, and by 1950 US labour productivity on the railways had reached more than six times the British level. Although there was undoubtedly an element of geography in the large US lead, with terminal handling a much smaller element in transport over long distances, the scale of the German labour productivity lead in 1935 also suggests that not all the productivity gap can be explained in this way.

Aldcroft (1968c) has offered the most critical assessment of Britain's railways after 1914. Although the wartime traffic figures have never been published, Aldcroft argues (31) that the flow of traffic increased under government control during World War I despite the loss of labour to the forces and a cutting back on capital expenditure. The implication was that there were economies to be reaped from the integration of the system, so that a return to the fragmented pre-war system was unthinkable (Aldcroft, 1974: 120). Although nationalisation seemed a possibility for a while, the solution adopted in the Railways Act of 1921 was a reorganisation of the railways in private hands on the basis of four major groupings: the Great Western Railway (GWR), the Southern Railway (SR), the London and North Eastern Railway (LNER) and the London, Midland and Scottish (LMS). The limited productivity growth after 1924 suggests that any gains from amalgamation were at best modest, and it is this failure to produce a more dynamic performance that lies at the heart of Aldcroft's (1968c) criticisms.

Aldcroft (59–83) criticises the railways for unsystematic pricing policies, slowness to adopt electric or diesel traction, and the continued use of small wagons. On pricing policies, he argues (59–68) that the railway companies did not adjust prices to deal with the threat of road competition and also failed to relate prices to costs. There has always been some acknowledgement of the constraints imposed on pricing policy by government regulation in the form of the Railway Rates Tribunal established by the 1921 Railways Act. Bonavia (1981: 142–3) goes further than this, however, suggesting that the two criteria of costs and competition may have pulled in opposite directions, since costs were low on long-distance bulk freight, where there was little effective competition from road transport. However, his reliance on the views of managers such as the one who complains: 'I am quite sure that the railways have lost a very large quantity of traffic through fussing about costs and trying to calculate direct costs' does not inspire a great deal of confidence in railway management at the time (Bonavia: 67).

Although Aldcroft (1968c: 71–6) is also highly critical of the slow rate of adoption of electric or diesel traction on British railways, other writers are more equivocal on this issue. First, Southern Railways invested heavily in the electrification of their short-distance suburban routes, where the gains of electrification were greatest (Bonavia, 1981: 120). Second, the gains from main line electrification were far less clear, with the Weir Committee on Main Line Electrification in 1930 claiming only a modest 7% return, assuming no downturn (Foreman-Peck and Millward, 1994: 245). Third, railway electrification went as far in Britain as in other countries that lacked cheap hydro-electric power (Hannah, 1979: 166). In 1938 5.3% of British track was electrified, similar to Germany's 5.0% and France's 7.8%; the 73.8% in Switzerland and the 42.4% in Sweden were simply not relevant to British circumstances (Foreman-Peck and Millward, 1994: 246). Fourth, dieselisation had made only modest progress even on the US railroads in the 1930s, despite the cheapness of diesel fuel in America and the difficulties of supplying water for steam locomotives on some sections of line (Bonavia, 1981: 130).

Aldcroft (1968c: 81–3) is also critical of the continued use of small wagons on the British railways. As was noted for the pre-1914 period, it has been claimed that this reflected technological lock-in, due to the size and layout of the infrastructure (Frankel, 1955). However, van Vleck (1997) argues that the real reason for the continued use of the small wagon during the 1870–1914 period was that it provided flexibility, and this is echoed for the inter-war period by Bonavia (1981: 134), who notes that the transformation of freight handling that occurred in the 1960s and 1970s followed a massive transfer to road transport of the small 'retail' type of consignments. It seems likely, then, that the 'improvements' to freight handling that Aldcroft advocates for the railway managers of the 1930s would have hastened the movement away from rail, which could only have worsened their predicament.

Some of Aldcroft's specific judgements are undoubtedly too harsh and have the benefit of hindsight, as Bonavia (1981: vii) claims. Nevertheless, the poor productivity showing of British railways at this time remains to be explained. The perspective offered here is that the hierarchical form of organisation that was required to run the increasingly integrated railway system ran into difficulties in British conditions, largely because of the legacy of the past. This legacy was embodied in the experience or human capital of the workforce and management, which had a vested interest in the old ways of doing things. Furthermore, it was important that there was little pressure for change through competitive forces. Campbell-Kelly (1994: 70) notes, for example, a 1920 Office Appliances Committee report of the Railway Clearing House, which identified the possibility of calculating ton-mile statistics with six comptometers costing £100 16s. 0d. each. Since this would have allowed the replacement of seventy male clerks by six female clerks, it was calculated to lead to annual savings of £18,000 for a one-off total outlay of just over £600. Campbell-Kelly (1994: 71) notes that there were many similar examples, none of which elicited any critical comment from the Office Appliances Committee. He also notes that the inventory of office machinery remained pathetically small in 1930, with just sixty-four typewriters, seventy-three calculating machines and a sprinkling of duplicators and other office appliances for a staff of around 3,000 (71). It is important that the Railway Clearing House was effectively a monopoly, free from the competitive pressures that would have forced the adoption of the efficient technology.

To some extent, the inter-war railways took on many of the features of the poorly performing nationalised industries of the post-1945 period, with centralised management facing militant unions, and the government anxiously watching and intervening directly every so often. In this corporatist system, attempts to reduce labour costs concentrated more on downgrading posts than on improving operating procedures so as to reduce the amount of labour required, as Foreman-Peck and Millward (1994: 245) note. And, although union militancy in the early 1920s and the General Strike of 1926 was not repeated during the Depression of the 1930s, for some, at least, the bitterness remained (Bonavia, 1981: 48–9). It is also worth noting that organisational form varied between the four groups. Bonavia argues (10) that the Southern Railway, the best performer, was much more personally managed than the other companies, although this was also the smallest company. He also argues that, among the larger companies, the decentralised organisation of the LNER worked better than the highly centralised organisation of the LMS (12–13).

During World War II the railways were again brought under government control, and, as during World War I, there was an increase in the volume of traffic without any increase in inputs (Aldcroft, 1968c: 99). The Labour victory in 1945 and the financial weakness of the railway companies ensured that this time there would be no return to the private sector, and the Transport Act of 1947 brought the railways into public ownership on 1 January 1948 (Crompton, 1995: 138–41). By the end of the 1940s the British railway system was under unified control, with a centralised form of organisation that never worked well in British conditions.

9.2.4 *The rise of road and air transport*

The main factor behind the stagnation of the railways was the growth of road transport, which is considered now. Starting with an international

Table 9.16 *Motor vehicles per 1,000 inhabitants and motorisation indicator, 1922–1950*

A. Motor vehicles per thousand inhabitants

	Passenger cars			Commercial vehicles		
	United Kingdom	Germany	United States	United Kingdom	Germany	United States
1922	7.4	1.3	84.9	3.0	0.7	11.8
1926	16.9	3.4	163.7	6.0	1.6	24.1
1930	24.5	7.8	186.7	8.6	2.7	28.9
1935	33.0	12.7	176.8	10.4	4.1	29.4
1938	38.7	20.7	193.9	12.1	5.8	32.9
1950	46.2	12.6	260.7	20.9	12.0	57.8

B. Motorisation indicator

	Passenger cars			Commercial vehicles		
	United Kingdom	Germany	United States	United Kingdom	Germany	United States
1922	9.2	1.5	31.6	3.8	0.9	1.2
1926	23.0	4.0	63.4	8.2	1.8	9.3
1930	33.4	9.1	74.0	11.9	3.1	11.5
1935	45.2	15.2	71.3	14.4	4.8	11.8
1938	54.6	25.1	78.9	16.9	7.0	13.4
1950	66.6	17.5	114.7	30.1	16.7	25.5

Note:
For Germany the 1938 figure includes Austria and the Sudetenland, while the 1950 figure refers to the German Federal Republic only. Motorisation indicator obtained by dividing vehicles per inhabitant by geographical area.

Source: Svennilson (1954: 280).

perspective, the density of motor vehicle ownership in Britain, Germany and the United States is charted in table 9.16. Britain lagged behind the United States in terms of both passenger vehicle and commercial vehicle densities, but remained substantially ahead of Germany. To some extent the large US lead may be seen as reflecting geographical factors and, to counter this, Svennilson (1954: 148) provides an alternative indicator of motorisation, obtained by dividing vehicles per inhabitant by geographical area. On this basis, the United States retained a substantial lead in passenger vehicles, but not in commercial vehicles. These figures point to an important limitation of the data on road transport, which exclude

Table 9.17 *Output of the British public passenger road transport sector, 1911–1951*

A. Passenger journeys (million)

	Trams and trolleybuses
1911	3,008
1921	4,266

B. Passenger-miles travelled by final consumers (million)

	Trams and trolleybuses	Buses and coaches	Taxis and hire cars	Total
1921	7,987	3,451	1,645	11,438
1924	8,464	5,193	1,686	15,343
1929	9,494	11,307	929	21,730
1931	8,791	12,124	720	21,635
1932	8,328	12,545	667	21,540
1937	8,284	16,363	624	25,271

C. Passenger journeys (million)

	Trams and trolleybuses	Buses and coaches — Municipal	Buses and coaches — Total	Total
1937	3,962	2,040	6,664	10,626
1951	3,353	4,561	13,270	16,623

Sources: 1911–1921 – Munby and Watson (1978: table B6.1); 1921–1937 – Stone and Rowe (1966: 71); 1937–1951 – Munby and Watson (1978: tables B6.1, B6.2, B6.3).

the services of passenger cars. To the extent that individuals substituted private passenger journeys for journeys on public transport, the official figures will understate the growth of transport services (Ashworth, 1960: 339). There is also a problem with the measurement of road freight transport services, since vehicles owned by manufacturers or distributors are classified to those sectors rather than to road haulage (Feinstein, 1988: 319).

The output of the public passenger road transport sector is shown in table 9.17. For the period before 1920 data exist only on the number of journeys on trams and trolleybuses. Between the wars, however, Stone and Rowe's (1966) estimates of passenger-miles are available, obtained from data on revenue and average fares. As the tram and trolleybus sector stagnated, the more flexible bus and coach sector expanded rapidly, while taxis and hire cars provided a declining number of passenger-miles.

Table 9.18 *Output of the British road haulage sector, 1911–1951*

A. Traffic on Class I roads (tons per day)

Road		Census point	1911/12	1922
A57	Liverpool–Manchester–London	Sankey Bridge (Lancs.)	1,150	8,250
A24	London–Worthing	Near Findon (Sussex)	700	1,920
A1	London–Edinburgh	Framwellgate Moor (Durham)	650	3,350
A7	Edinburgh–Carlisle	Near Moorville (Cumberland)	650	1,920
A944	Mossat–Aberdeen	Loch of Skene (Aberdeen)	297	473

B. Mileage run by goods vehicles

	Million
1922	2,400
1928	4,000
1938	8,000

C. Ton-mileage of goods vehicles

	Million
1938	9,000
1952	19,000

Sources: 1911–1922 – UK Ministry of Transport (1931: 82); 1922–1938 – UK Department of Transport (1980: 4); 1938–1952 – UK Department of Transport (1980: 4, 1991: table 7.3).

Across World War II the data on journeys continue to show trams and trolleybuses stagnating while buses and coaches grew, with private operators accounting for the vast majority of journeys.

Turning to road freight, the highly fragmented nature of the sector means that estimates of output are more speculative (see table 9.18). Before the early 1920s only fragmentary road traffic survey data from the UK Ministry of Transport (1931: 82) exist, while between the wars there are some rough estimates of the mileage run by goods vehicles from the UK Department of Transport (1980: 4). Only from 1952 are reliable data available on ton-mileage, which can be linked to a rough estimate of ton-mileage for 1938. In fact, the index of output that can be derived from these figures moves broadly in line with the number of goods vehicles in use, provided in Mitchell (1988: 557–8).[5]

---

[5] This forms the basis of Feinstein's (1972: 209) index of road goods transport, since there is insufficient freight data to construct an annual index.

Table 9.19 *Productivity in British road transport, 1911–1951*

A. Indices of output, inputs and productivity (1924 = 100)

	Output	Labour	Capital	Labour productivity	TFP
1913	40.3	83.9	71.1	48.0	50.9
1921	75.9	87.8	89.9	86.4	85.8
1924	100.0	100.0	100.0	100.0	100.0
1929	146.2	131.6	115.0	111.1	116.5
1931	157.1	139.1	119.6	112.9	119.1
1932	163.0	140.9	120.7	115.7	122.1
1937	213.6	162.2	127.4	131.7	143.3
1951	414.8	143.5		289.1	

B. Growth rates of output, inputs and productivity (% per annum)

	1911–1924	1924–1937	1937–1951	1911–1951
Output	7.0	5.8	4.7	5.8
Labour	1.4	3.7	−0.9	1.3
Capital	2.6	1.9		
Labour productivity	5.6	2.1	5.6	4.5
TFP	5.2	2.7		

Sources: Output – derived from tables 9.17 and 9.18; labour – 1911–1921: census estimates from Munby and Watson (1978: table B4.1); 1921–1937: Chapman (1953: 143); 1951: census estimate for 1951 from Munby and Watson (1978: table B4.1) linked to 1931 estimate; capital – 1911–1920: Feinstein (1988: tables 15.3, 15.6, 15.8); 1920–1937: Feinstein (1965: tables 9.21, 9.23, 9.24).

The passenger and freight output data have been put together in table 9.19, using interpolation for the freight series where observations are missing, and using 1924 employment weights. Over the period as a whole, 1911–1951, output grew very rapidly at 5.8% per annum. With labour growing much more slowly, labour productivity grew at the impressive rate of 4.5% per annum. During the inter-war period, 1924–1937, data are available on capital as well as labour. With output growing at 5.8% per annum, labour productivity grew at an annual rate of 2.1% and TFP at 2.7%, substantially higher than in transport and communications as a whole or the aggregate economy.

These figures suggest that the road transport sector was a vibrant part of the British economy and effectively broke the monopoly of the railways between the wars, although this was more the case in passenger transport than in freight transport. Whereas by the late 1930s road transport supplied about 25 million passenger-miles compared with about 21 million passenger-miles on the railways, road transport accounted for only about 9 million freight ton-miles, compared with about 18 million ton-miles on the railways. The railways retained a strong position in the movement of freight over long distances, but could not match the flexibility of road transport over shorter distances (Aldcroft, 1968c: 55, 57).

It has been argued above that the growing integration of the railways led to the adoption of a centralised organisational form, which did not work well in British conditions. By contrast, motorised road transport remained highly competitive, with a decentralised form of organisation that has traditionally worked well in Britain. In fact, the structure was more concentrated in road passenger transport than in road freight transport, particularly after the tightening of the licensing system in the Road Traffic Act of 1930, which severely restricted new entry (Dyos and Aldcroft, 1969: 357). This can be seen partly as a response to genuine concerns arising from the adverse effects of cut-throat competition in the 1920s, with vehicles from different companies competing on the same routes in leap-frog fashion without regard to timetables or safety standards and issuing discount coupons. However, it should also be noted that the large municipal and private operators had a vested interest in restricting entry, and vigorously promoted their views to public bodies such as the Royal Commission on Road Transport (Dyos and Aldcroft, 1969: 341, 356). It should also be noted that the railways had substantial financial interests in bus companies, although the extent to which they used those interests to restrict the growth of road transport rather than to promote better road–rail coordination is open to question (Bonavia, 1981: 94–104). Nevertheless, as late as 1937 there were as many as 4,777 bus and coach operators in Great Britain, of which 3,763 operated fewer than five vehicles, although these operators accounted for only 14.3% of the number of vehicles (Munby and Watson, 1978: table B13.3). Although the Road and Rail Traffic Act of 1933 also established a licensing system in freight haulage, this part of the sector remained highly fragmented, with no equivalent of the large associated companies that emerged in passenger transport such as the Tilling, British Electric Traction (BET) and Scottish Motor Traction (SMT) groups (Savage, 1966: 124–8, 134–5).

Technical improvements to aircraft during World War I made civil aviation a commercial possibility, and a number of cross-channel services were started after the establishment of air navigation regulations in 1919 (Dyos and Aldcroft, 1969: 374–6). The British airlines got off to an uncertain start, however, due to technical difficulties, weak, highly seasonal demand, and heavily subsidised competition, particularly from

Table 9.20 *British civil aviation, 1920–1951*

	Aircraft mileage flown (million)	Number of passengers carried (thousand)	Passenger mileage (million)	Tons of cargo carried	Cargo ton-mileage (million)
1920	0.6	5.8		137	
1921	0.2	5.3		19	
1924	0.9	13.6		543	
1925	0.8	11.0	2.6	550	0.1
1929	1.2	28.5	7.1	927	0.3
1932	1.8	48.2	16.0	772	0.5
1937	10.8	244.4	49.7	3,961	4.7
1951	52.5	1,415.0	1,065.0	46,358	48.8

Sources: UK Board of Trade (*Statistical Abstract for the United Kingdom* various years), UK Central Statistical Office (*Annual Abstract of Statistics*, various years).

Table 9.21 *Aircraft flights and passengers carried between the United Kingdom and abroad, 1920–1951*

	Flights			Passengers carried		
	British aircraft	Foreign aircraft	Percent British	British aircraft	Foreign aircraft	Percent British
1920	2,854	768	78.8	5,799	584	90.9
1921	993	2,404	29.2	5,256	5,475	49.0
1924	2,794	2,044	57.8	10,456	7,402	58.6
1929	3,244	5,992	35.1	26,182	22,071	54.3
1932	2,757	6,221	30.7	41,609	29,122	58.8
1937	12,608	11,285	53.9	77,967	81,184	49.0
1951	47,000	48,100	49.4	706,300	880,900	44.5

Sources: UK Board of Trade (*Statistical Abstract for the United Kingdom*, various years), UK Central Statistical Office (*Annual Abstract of Statistics*, various years).

France. This uncertain start can be seen in table 9.20, with aircraft mileage and tons of cargo falling sharply in 1921. Furthermore, it is clear from table 9.21 that this was not simply the result of the recession, since flights by subsidised foreign-registered aircraft rose sharply at the same time. The British airlines were saved from extinction in 1921 only by the introduction of a government subsidy scheme, justified on strategic grounds (Lyth, 1995: 68). With the level of subsidy twice the revenue, competition between British airlines was seen as wasteful, and in 1924 the government encouraged the existing airlines to merge. A monopoly of subsidised air transport was granted to Imperial Airways for a ten-year period (Dyos and Aldcroft, 1969: 380).

Given the severe competition on west European services, Imperial Airways concentrated their expansion on empire routes, while British Airways, created in 1935 from a number of unsubsidised airlines, developed additional routes to South America and west Africa (Dyos and Aldcroft, 1969: 381, 386). British Airways also expanded the British presence on European routes with the help of government subsidies after the ending of Imperial Airways' ten-year monopoly of subsidised air transport (Lyth, 1995: 74–6). However, European routes remained dominated by more highly subsidised Continental airlines, so that British-registered aircraft rarely accounted for much more than a half of the flights and the number of passengers carried between Britain and abroad (table 9.21). On the cargo side, British airlines benefited from the mail contracts arising from the Empire Air Mail Scheme introduced in 1934 and the 'all-up' policy on first-class mail to Europe from 1936 (Dyos and Aldcroft, 1969: 382–3).

Nevertheless, by the end of the 1930s it was clear that civil aviation was still a long way from commercial viability. Along with an increase in subsidy, the government brought air transport under public ownership in 1939 with the formation of the British Overseas Airways Corporation (BOAC) from Imperial Airways and British Airways (Lyth, 1995: 76). The industry remained in public ownership under the post-war Labour government, but with three corporations serving different routes; British European Airways (BEA) on short-haul operations, British South American Airways (BSAA) on long-haul flights to South America, and BOAC on other long-haul operations (Lyth, 1995: 80–1). In the event, BSAA did not remain independent for long, merging with BOAC in 1948 after problems with its Tudor aircraft (Lyth, 1995: 81).

Attempts to establish air services on internal routes met with even more severe problems than on international routes, since there was initially little time saving compared with the railways (Dyos and Aldcroft, 1969: 389). The railways have been accused of stifling competition from an alternative mode of transport by acquiring financial control of a large proportion of the airline companies, although, as in the case of road transport, it is by no means clear to what extent the railway companies restricted the growth of air services as opposed to improving the co-ordination between rail and air transport (Bonavia, 1981: 106–17). Nevertheless, the fact that where Railway Air Services could not acquire a financial interest in competing airlines, they forced railway-accredited

Table 9.22 *Post Office mail traffic, United Kingdom, 1913–1951 (million)*

	Letters, postcards, packets, etc.	Parcels
1913	5,479	130.0
1924	5,585	126.4
1929	6,230	151.5
1932	6,540	158.1
1937	7,690	174.4
1951	8,500	232.7

Note:
Figures for 1913 include southern Ireland.
Source: Mitchell (1988: 564–5).

travel agents to refuse bookings for independent airlines suggests that, at the least, there is a case to answer (Lyth, 1995: 71).

9.2.5 Post and telecommunications

The volume of mail and telecommunications traffic is shown in tables 9.22 and 9.23. Mail traffic grew at an annual rate of 2.5% between 1924 and 1937, more or less in line with national income between the wars.[6] Over the same period the number of telegrams sent declined slightly, while the number of telephone calls grew rapidly, at an annual rate of 5.7%. Turning to table 9.24, although the telephone was more widely diffused in the United States, Britain did not lag behind other large European countries such as Germany or France. However, a number of smaller European countries (Sweden, Norway, Denmark and Switzerland) all had higher levels of telephone ownership.

The nationalisation of the telephone system in 1912 brought virtually the whole of the British post and telecommunications sector under the control of the Post Office (Ashworth, 1960: 117). Since data exist only for combined employment in the postal and telecommunications departments of the Post Office, it is natural to combine the comparative outputs of the different sectors using revenue weights, so as to obtain the comparative labour productivity position for the communications sector as a whole. The results are shown in table 9.1, and suggest a growing US labour productivity lead during the 1920s and 1930s, but

---

[6] GDP grew at an annual rate of 2.3% between 1924 and 1937, as can be seen in table 9.2.

Table 9.23 *Telecommunications statistics, United Kingdom, 1913–1951*

	Telegrams sent (million)	Telephone calls made		Number of telephones (thousand)
		Trunk (million)	Local (million)	
1913	89	36	797	731
1924	78	70	832	1,169
1929	72	111	1,155	1,768
1932	61	126	1,305	2,069
1937	72	101	1,882	2,827
1951	65	250	3,076	5,426

Note:
Figures for 1913 include southern Ireland. Telegram data for 1951 exclude telegrams sent via private cable companies. Telephone call data for 1937 and 1951 show all calls of fourpence or less as local, instead of twopence and under as previously.
Source: Mitchell (1988: 566–7).

Table 9.24 *Telephones per 100 population, 1913–1932*

	1913	1932
Great Britain	1.6	4.6
United States	9.1	14.3
Germany	1.9	4.6
France	0.7	3.0
Sweden	3.9	9.3
Norway	3.1	7.0
Denmark	4.2	9.8
Switzerland	2.3	8.5

Source: Foreman-Peck and Millward (1995: 253).

with Britain still maintaining a substantial labour productivity lead over Germany. Although the breakdown of employment by department in the British Post Office is not known, it seems likely that Britain's labour productivity position was better in the postal service than in telecommunications (Daunton, 1985: 234–6). This would certainly be the case if labour was allocated between departments on the basis of revenue, as suggested by Foreman-Peck and Millward (1994: 261–2). Given that wage rates were also much lower in Britain, however, prices were, if anything, slightly cheaper in Britain (Foreman-Peck and Millward, 1994: 255).

Chapter 8 has already shown that the nationalisation of the British telegraph system in 1870 did not lead to any dramatic improvement in performance, and it is difficult to avoid a similar judgement on the nationalisation of the telephone system in 1912. Any gains from system integration were offset by the removal of incentives for efficiency with the move from decentralised private or municipal ownership to centralised state bureaucracy. The detrimental effects of the centralised Post Office regime can be seen in the changing extent of telephone ownership in Hull compared to other English towns. Hull was the only part of the British telephone system to remain outside the nationalised Post Office system, retaining municipal ownership. As Foreman-Peck and Millward (1994: 257) note, whereas in 1893 Hull had 512 inhabitants per subscriber, compared with 147.8 in Newcastle, by 1937 Hull had half as many telephones again as Newcastle, despite having substantially less wealth as measured by rateable value. By estimating a simple regression equation linking the number of telephones to the rateable value in a sample of seventy-seven towns in 1937, Foreman-Peck and Millward (1994: 273) are able to predict what telephone ownership would have been in Hull under a Post Office regime. The regression equation predicts that telephone ownership in Hull under a Post Office regime would have been approximately half the level actually achieved under municipal ownership. If Post Office ownership was responsible for halving telephone ownership throughout the country, then in the absence of nationalisation Britain would have achieved telephone ownership density approximately equal to Scandinavian levels (Foreman-Peck and Millward, 1994: 257).

9.3   Distribution

9.3.1   Introduction

Indices of output, inputs and productivity in the British distribution sector are shown for the period 1911 to 1951 in table 9.25. Output grew much more slowly in distribution than in the aggregate economy over the whole period. However, this was largely due to the stagnation of distribution during the two trans-war periods. Between 1924 and 1937 output in distribution grew at an annual rate of 1.9% which was not so far behind the 2.3% annual growth rate in the aggregate economy. Although employment in distribution declined during both trans-war periods, the inter-war period saw very rapid employment growth, so that labour productivity in distribution declined during the 1924–1937 period. With the capital stock also growing quite rapidly between the

Table 9.25 *Productivity in the British distribution sector, 1911–1951*

A. Indices of output, inputs and productivity (1924 = 100)

	Output	Labour	Capital	Labour productivity	TFP
1911	93.9	107.8	85.9	87.1	94.3
1924	100.0	100.0	100.0	100.0	100.0
1929	108.5	122.1	106.7	88.9	93.1
1932	108.6	128.9	111.6	84.3	88.6
1937	127.4	139.6	120.4	91.3	96.1
1951	124.9	123.2	120.9	101.4	102.0

B. Growth rates of output, inputs and productivity (% per annum)

	1911–1924	1924–1937	1937–1951	1911–1951
Output	0.5	1.9	−0.2	0.7
Labour	−0.6	2.6	−0.9	0.3
Capital	1.2	1.4	0.0	0.9
Labour productivity	1.1	−0.7	0.7	0.4
TFP	0.5	−0.3	0.4	0.2

Sources: Output – Feinstein (1972: table 53); labour – Feinstein (1972: tables 59, 60), with adjustment for exclusion of the Irish Republic after 1920 from Mitchell (1988: 110); capital – 1911–1920: Feinstein (1988: table XI); 1920–1951: Feinstein (1972: table 44).

wars, total factor productivity in distribution also declined between 1924 and 1937. Despite the disappointing productivity growth performance in Britain, however, table 9.26 shows that there was no substantial deterioration in Britain's productivity position relative to the United States or Germany between the wars, and only a modest deterioration relative to the United States across World War II. This is consistent with the pattern of productivity growth in US distribution noted by Field (1996: 28). The Germany/UK comparison is complicated by the fact that the figures contain finance as well as distribution (in both countries). As for the pre-1914 period, however, the scale of the British lead is such as to suggest that Britain must have been substantially ahead in the larger distribution sector.

9.3.2 Retailing and wholesaling for the home market

Jefferys (1954: 11) argues that the changes in the channels of distribution before 1914 had worked on balance to strengthen the position of wholesalers. Between the wars, however, he sees developments as working to weaken the position of wholesalers (48). Although small-scale

Table 9.26 *Comparative US/UK and Germany/UK productivity levels for the distribution sector, 1911–1950 (UK = 100)*

A. US/UK

	Labour productivity
1909/11	120.0
1919/20	109.0
1929	121.9
1937	119.8
1950	135.2

B. Germany/UK

	Labour productivity
1911	52.5
1925	47.1
1929	50.3
1935	54.3
1950	50.7

Note:
Germany/UK comparison based on distribution and finance.
Source: Tables 3.1, 3.3.

producer-retailers continued to lose ground, sales by producers direct to retailers grew rapidly. This trend reflected the growing concern of producers with the marketing of their goods. As incomes rose, a larger share of the household budget was spent on branded, packaged goods, advertised in national media such as newspapers, radio and films. With such products, many of the functions traditionally performed by the wholesaler, such as packing, blending, breaking bulk, selecting and pricing, were transferred to the producer (Pollard, 1992: 83, 86–7). With the share of working-class expenditure on food falling from 60% in 1904 to 35% in 1937/38, the amount of discretionary income available for expenditure on such items rose considerably (Jefferys, 1954: 44). Furthermore, a number of manufactured foods had joined the list of heavily advertised products (Kaldor and Silverman, 1948: 144–7). For 1938, data on the relative importance of distribution channels show 4% of total retail sales accounted for by producer-retailers, 43% passing through one or more wholesalers (excluding the Co-operative Wholesale Societies) and 53% passing directly from the producer or importer to the retailer (Jefferys, 1950: 151).

Table 9.27 *Membership and retail sales of Co-operative Societies, Great Britain, 1910–1950*

	Membership (thousand)	Current price sales (£ million)	Current price sales per member (£)	Real sales per member (£ in 1913 prices)
1910	2,541.7	71.9	28.29	30.10
1915	3,264.8	102.6	31.43	25.98
1920	4,504.9	254.2	56.43	23.13
1925	4,911.0	183.6	37.39	21.61
1930	6,403.0	217.3	33.94	21.90
1935	7,483.9	220.4	29.45	21.04
1940	8,716.9	298.9	34.29	19.16
1945	9,404.9	361.1	38.39	16.99
1950	10,691.5	613.8	57.41	20.29

Sources: Derived from Jefferys (1954: 461); retail price index: Feinstein (1972: table 65).

As during the pre-1914 period, the Co-operative Societies, department stores and multiple shops gained market share at the expense of small retailers between the wars. Large-scale retailers increased their share of retail sales from about one-fifth before World War I to more than one-third by the mid-1930s (Jefferys, 1954: 73). The growth of the Co-operative Societies can be seen in table 9.27. Membership, which had reached about 3 million by the outbreak of World War I, continued to grow rapidly and passed the 10 million mark during the late 1940s. Although sales per member increased in nominal terms across World War I, this largely reflected wartime inflation. In real terms, sales per member declined by about one-third across World War I and then stagnated at about £20 per member in 1913 prices both throughout the inter-war period and into the period after World War II. The continued growth of the Co-operative Societies therefore depended on the spread of membership rather than the growth of sales per member, although the growth in trading membership is probably exaggerated by the figures due to the growing tendency for more than one member of a household to become a member (Jefferys, 1954: 55). The most important development here was the spread of geographical coverage beyond the traditional strongholds, in the industrial north of England and Scotland, and into the Midlands and the south of England. Whereas in 1914 the Midlands and south of England accounted for 23% of Co-operative sales, by 1939 this had risen to 44% (Jefferys, 1954: 56).

Table 9.28 *Number of multiple shop firms and branches in the United Kingdom, 1910–1950*

	10 or more branches		25 or more branches	
	Firms	Branches	Firms	Branches
1910	395	19,852	149	16,462
1920	471	24,713	180	20,602
1925	552	29,628	201	24,558
1930	633	35,894	258	30,594
1935	668	40,087	276	34,534
1939	680	44,487	303	39,017
1950	638	44,800	296	39,858

Source: Jefferys (1954: 61).

Although mergers and amalgamations led to a growing concentration of membership in the largest societies, other societies increased the scale of their buying and productive activities through the formation of federations, which gave many of the advantages of large scale while retaining a measure of independence (Jefferys, 1954: 56).

The most dynamic part of the distribution sector between the wars was multiple shop retailing. Whereas the Co-operative Societies remained heavily based in food retailing, multiple shop retailing also grew rapidly in non-food areas (Jefferys, 1954: 57–8, 72). Table 9.28 shows that the number of multiple shop firms and branches continued to grow, but less rapidly than before 1914.[7] As table 9.29 shows, however, the multiple shop retailers increased their share of total retail sales more rapidly than the Co-operative Societies or the department stores. These developments in multiple shop retailing reflected a number of factors, including amalgamations and mergers, the spread of multiple shop retailing into different trades, a shift of emphasis from competition on price to competition on service, the rise of variety chain stores and the integration of production and distribution.

First, amalgamations led to the emergence of giant firms such as the Home and Colonial Stores group, with over 3,000 branches in the grocery trade (Jefferys, 1954: 64; Mathias, 1967: 258–75). Second, although, before 1914, multiple shop retailing had been strong in groceries and provisions, footwear, chemists' goods, newspapers and books, and sewing machines, between the wars it also became strong in new

---

[7] Compare with table 8.26 in chapter 8.

Table 9.29 *Estimated maximum shares of large-scale retailers in the total retail trade of the United Kingdom, 1910–1950 (%)*

A. By economic types

	1910	1920	1925	1930	1935	1939	1950
Co-operative Societies	8.0	9.0	8.5	10.0	10.5	11.5	12.0
Department stores	3.0	4.0	4.0	5.0	5.5	5.5	6.0
Multiple shop retailers	7.5	10.0	11.5	14.0	17.0	19.5	20.5
Total large-scale retailers	18.5	23.0	24.0	29.0	33.0	36.5	38.5

B. By main commodity groups

	1910	1920	1925	1930	1935	1939	1950
Food and household stores	19.0	24.0	25.0	28.5	32.0	36.0	38.5
Confectionery, reading and writing material, tobacco	5.5	7.0	8.5	10.5	14.0	16.5	17.5
Clothing and footwear	21.5	25.5	32.0	38.5	43.0	50.0	54.0
Other goods	11.0	16.0	20.5	27.5	33.0	39.0	43.5
All commodities	18.5	23.0	24.0	29.0	33.0	36.5	38.5

Source: Jefferys (1954: 73–4).

areas, including milk, fish, baking, clothing, furniture and furnishings, electrical goods and radios, jewellery, wallpaper and paint, and pottery and glass (Jefferys, 1954: 66–7). Third, the shift of emphasis from competing on price to competing on quality of service partly reflected the growing prosperity of the nation, although it must also be considered within the context of the competitive structure of retailing and the growing importance of resale price maintenance. Fourth, variety chain stores such as Woolworths, British Home Stores and Littlewoods nevertheless continued to offer low prices with a minimum of service, but a wide range of products (Jefferys, 1954: 70).[8] Fifth, it was noted earlier that producers took a growing interest in distribution, particularly with branded, packaged goods. Similarly, it was open for retailers to integrate back into production, and many multiple shop retailers availed themselves of this opportunity, particularly where products were relatively standardised (Jefferys, 1954: 68).

---

[8] Jefferys (1954: 68) includes Marks and Spencer in this category, but, as Rees (1969: 114–15) points out, although they maintained a 5 shilling price limit, they drastically reduced the range and variety of merchandise, concentrating on clothing and food.

Department stores continued to increase their share of total retail sales between the wars, although not as rapidly as the multiple shop retailers, as can be seen in table 9.29. Jefferys (1954: 59) tentatively puts the number of department stores in 1914 at about 175 to 225, rising to about 475 to 525 stores in 1938, with many of the new stores opening in medium-sized provincial towns or the suburban shopping centres of the larger towns. Although Debenhams, United Drapery Stores, Great Northern and Southern Stores, and the John Lewis Partnership emerged as groups, financial integration was not accompanied by the centralised direction of individual stores (Jefferys, 1954: 60).

If the three forms of large-scale enterprise in retailing are considered together in part A of table 9.29, large-scale retailers accounted for at most 18.5% of total retail trade in 1910. By 1939, however, this had risen to 36.5% and by 1950 it had reached 38.5%. In some commodity groups, the share of large-scale retailers was substantially higher, as can be seen in part B of table 9.29. In clothing and footwear, for example, large-scale retailers accounted for up to 54% of retail sales by 1950. By contrast, confectionery, reading and writing material and tobacco remained dominated by small-scale retailers.

Despite the growing importance of large-scale retailing between the wars, then, small-scale retailing remained more important overall and continued to dominate overwhelmingly in some trades. There were a number of reasons for this. First, small-scale retailers were more flexible and better able to cater for small, local markets. Second, the widening in the range of goods regarded as essential and requiring frequent purchase in small quantities close to home, such as tobacco and cigarettes, sugar and chocolate confectionery, newspapers and magazines, and proprietary medicines, increased opportunities in such small, local markets. Third, small-scale retailers could offer a personal service, and in trades that remained highly skilled, such as butchery, the personal qualities of the owner had a significant effect on trade. Fourth, with the growth of branding, packaging and advertising by the manufacturer, together with the practice of resale price maintenance (RPM), it was possible in some areas for small-scale retailers to compete on an equal footing with large-scale retailers. The UK Board of Trade (1949: 1) estimates that, whereas in 1900 only 3% of consumers' expenditure had been on resale-price-maintained goods, by 1938 the proportion had risen to 30%.

Some writers have attempted to link the falling productivity in distribution between the wars to the decline in competition associated with the growth of large-scale retailing and the spread of RPM. Levy (1947: 221), for example, points to a widespread belief in the late 1940s that there were too many shops. However, whereas groups such as the retail trade associations and Political and Economic Planning favoured developing shopping centres according to a plan, Levy (224–5, 231) argued for a restoration of competition through action against restrictive practices such as resale price maintenance. His view was based on the belief that there were good reasons founded on consumer wants and needs to expect a multiplicity of retailers, many of them small, and no likelihood that the most efficient would be allowed to survive in a planned economy (Levy: 218). It was to be some time, however, before effective action was taken against restrictive practices (Yamey, 1966).

9.3.3 Wholesale merchants and external trade

This section considers the activities of the wholesale merchants who organised Britain's visible trade in commodities, beginning with an examination of the quantitative dimensions of the trade. Table 9.30 shows some dramatic changes in the degree of openness of the British economy to foreign trade, with a serious decline in the trade ratios between the wars, particularly during the 1920s and early 1930s. The share of total imports in GDP fell back from 29.4% in 1911 to just 16.4% in 1932, while over the same period the share of domestic exports plus re-exports in GDP fell from 24.0 to 9.7%.[9] This trend reflected general developments in the world economy, with world trade failing to keep pace with world income growth between the wars (Hilgerdt, 1945; Maizels, 1963). This was followed by a recovery in the degree of openness, particularly after World War II, but not to the high levels seen before World War I.

Turning to the volume of visible trade, in table 9.31, the most important development was the failure of domestic exports to regain their pre-1914 level until after World War II. Although domestic export values were higher during the 1920s than they had been before World War I, this reflected the higher prices resulting from wartime inflation.[10] Despite the collapse of domestic export volumes, total import volumes nevertheless remained above the pre-1914 level between the wars. To some extent this reflected an improvement in Britain's net barter terms of trade, defined as the ratio of the domestic export price index to the

---

[9] As noted in chapter 8, although it is usual in a national accounting framework to net out the entrepôt trade and to focus on retained imports, defined as total imports minus re-exports, we are interested here in the distribution sector because it handled the import and re-export of overseas produce.

[10] See table 9.30 for export values and table 9.32 for export prices.

Table 9.30 *Visible trade of the United Kingdom, 1911–1951*

A. Values at current prices (£ million)

	Total imports	Domestic exports	Re-exports
1911	680.2	454.1	102.8
1924	1,277.4	801.0	140.0
1929	1,220.8	729.3	109.7
1932	701.7	365.0	51.0
1937	1,027.8	521.4	75.1
1951	3,901.9	2,581.6	127.0

B. Shares of GDP at market prices (%)

	Total imports	Domestic exports and re-exports
1911	29.4	24.0
1924	28.9	21.3
1929	25.8	17.7
1932	16.4	9.7
1937	19.4	11.3
1951	27.1	18.8

Note:
Southern Ireland excluded from 1924 onwards.

Sources: Trade data – Mitchell (1988: 453–4); GDP data – Feinstein (1972: table 3).

retained import price index, and shown here in table 9.32. A given volume of exports bought a greater volume of imports between the wars than before 1914. However, the greater resilience of import volumes also reflected the fact that a greater proportion of Britain's foreign earnings was being spent on visible imports than before 1914, when a large proportion had been invested overseas (Ashworth, 1960: 349).

Table 9.33 shows the principal commodities in which British shipping merchants had to deal. Figures have been included in the table where a commodity accounted for at least 3% of total imports or 3% of domestic exports plus re-exports in 1911 or 1951. The key imports in 1911 were foodstuffs (such as grain and flour) and raw materials (such as cotton). During the inter-war period and across World War I these items remained important, but accounted for a smaller share of Britain's imports. Petroleum gained most in importance, but manufactured products such as textiles also increased their share. Turning to exports, the 'old staples' of coal, iron and steel and cotton goods declined in importance, while machinery, electrical goods, motor vehicles and aircraft and chemicals saw their shares rise (Kahn, 1946: 84–124).

Table 9.31 *Volume of visible trade, United Kingdom, 1911–1951*

A. Volume indices (1924 = 100)

	Total imports	Domestic exports	Re-exports
1911	86.7	118.3	101.7
1924	100.0	100.0	100.0
1929	110.5	106.8	108.9
1932	95.6	66.8	89.0
1937	114.5	86.0	87.3
1951	104.1	130.7	30.6

B. Average annual growth rates

	Total imports	Domestic exports	Re-exports
1911–1951	0.5	0.3	−3.0
1911–1924	1.3	−1.3	−0.1
1924–1929	2.0	1.3	1.7
1929–1937	0.4	−2.7	−2.8
1937–1951	−0.7	3.0	−7.5

Note:
The trade value data in current prices have been adjusted for the boundary change between 1911 and 1924 and converted to a volume basis using price deflators.

Sources: Trade data – Mitchell (1988: 453–4), Feinstein (1972: table 15); price deflators – Feinstein (1972: table 64).

Table 9.32 *Price indices for exports, imports and aggregate output of the United Kingdom (1924 = 100)*

	Price of visible domestic exports	Price of visible retained imports	GDP deflator	Net barter terms of trade
1911	50.3	63.2	52.2	79.6
1924	100.0	100.0	100.0	100.0
1929	85.2	86.5	95.1	98.5
1932	68.3	57.4	89.2	119.0
1937	75.7	70.3	91.9	107.7
1951	246.6	293.5	189.6	84.0

Source: Feinstein (1972: tables 61, 64).

Table 9.33 *Principal visible imports and exports of the United Kingdom, 1911–1951*

A. Principal imports

	Shares of total imports (%)		
	1911	1929	1951
Grain and flour	10.5	7.6	6.1
Sugar, refined and unrefined	3.9	1.9	2.7
Meat and animals	7.3	10.6	5.5
Butter and margarine	4.0	4.7	2.3
Timber	3.8	3.8	5.4
Raw cotton	10.5	6.3	6.6
Raw wool	5.1	5.0	6.4
Oil, oilseed, gums, resins, tallow, etc.	4.3	3.2	4.6
Rubber	2.7	1.4	4.1
Non-ferrous metals and manufactures	3.6	3.0	4.1
Paper-making materials	0.7	1.1	3.2
Petroleum	0.8	3.6	7.7
Textiles	0.0	4.7	4.0
Total of above	57.2	56.9	62.7

B. Principal exports

	Shares of total exports and re-exports (%)		
	1911	1929	1951
Coal	6.9	6.3	1.3
Iron and steel	8.0	8.1	4.0
Machinery	5.6	7.1	13.8
Electrical goods	0.5	1.6	5.2
Motor road vehicles and aircraft	0.6	2.2	10.0
Cotton goods	21.6	16.1	6.7
Woollen goods	5.7	6.0	4.0
Chemicals	3.6	3.2	7.1
Total of above	52.5	50.6	52.1

Notes:
Imports – figures shown for commodities accounting for at least 3% of total imports in 1911 or 1951. Exports – figures shown for commodities accounting for at least 3% of exports plus re-exports in 1911 or 1951.

Source: Mitchell (1988: 476–9, 483–5).

Table 9.34 *The role of the British Empire in British visible trade, 1911–1951*

	Shares of British possessions in British trade (%)		
	Imports	Exports	Re-exports
1911	25.2	35.0	12.7
1924 (old basis)	27.2	38.0	11.8
1924 (new basis)	30.2	41.7	18.9
1929	29.4	44.5	21.0
1932	35.4	45.3	22.6
1936	39.1	49.2	17.9
1951	43.5	55.1	15.5

Sources: 1911–1936 – Schlote (1952: 162–3); 1951–UK Board of Trade (*Annual Statement of the Trade of the United Kingdom*, various years), Vol. I, tables 13–14.

The most important shift in the geographical composition of Britain's trade was the growing importance of the empire, which can be seen in table 9.34. This reflected a policy of imperial economic integration which began to be implemented during World War I, although the 'Imperial Vision' had been an important political force before 1914 (Drummond, 1972: 36). During the 1920s, before the introduction of the British general tariff, international cartels played a part in stimulating trade within the empire, but the further growth of inter-imperial trade during the 1930s owed much to the policy of preferential tariff duties following the Ottawa Agreements of 1932 (Drummond, 1972: 20). The empire's share of British exports and imports continued to rise across World War II, due to the disruption of economic activity in Europe during the trans-war period. Note that more than 55% of Britain's exports went to 'British countries' by 1951.

There is not such a detailed secondary literature on the activities of wholesale merchants between the wars as for the pre-1914 period. A useful study by Political and Economic Planning (1937: 12–14), however, sets out the main trends affecting the merchant business. British merchant houses were hit by a number of adverse developments, which weakened their position in international trade. First, as the composition of international trade moved towards specialised goods requiring technical knowledge and after-sales service, large manufacturers increasingly adopted direct selling through marketing organisations abroad under their own control, while smaller manufacturers made use of the agency system. Second, British merchant houses faced growing competition from foreign firms. This particularly affected merchant houses domiciled in the countries with which they principally dealt; the merchant houses faced growing competition from local importing houses on the merchant side of their business and from emerging local banks on the financial side. Third, and probably most important, the growth of impediments to two-way trading hit the merchant business severely. The viability of merchant houses was based upon their ability to trade both ways, to keep their funds mobile. With the growth of protection abroad and in Britain, exchange restrictions, one-way export selling by large manufacturers, and state trading, opportunities for two-way trading were reduced severely.

One area in which the decline of the merchant house might be expected to show up is in the entrepôt trade. Despite the decline in the value of re-exports that Hurstfield (1944: 20) remarks on and that can be seen in table 9.30, however, table 9.31 demonstrates that the volume of re-exports declined less than the volume of exports during the 1920s and the 1930s. Only across World War II did re-exports cease to be an important part of Britain's international trade. Although the merchant system clearly took a battering between the wars, then, its decline should not be exaggerated. In some areas, at least, merchant enterprise remained viable. Indeed, Jones (2000: 84–115) charts the success of the main British trading houses in surviving the troubled wartime and interwar periods, noting that they remained giants of modern business enterprise on the China coast, in South-east Asia, in west Africa and in Chile and Peru, and expanded in east Africa.

The merchant system remained surprisingly resilient in the cotton cloth trade between the wars, despite the dramatic collapse in export volumes. Table 9.35 presents data on the membership of the Manchester Royal Exchange and the Manchester Chamber of Commerce, together with the number of firms listed in *Slater's Directory of Manchester and Salford*. As noted in Broadberry and Marrison (2002: 73), the classification for the cotton and associated trades in *Slater's Directory* remained unchanged between 1900 and 1939, which makes this a particularly valuable source for examining trends during this crucial period. For the period 1900–1911 there is broad agreement between the increase in the number of subscribers to the Royal Exchange and the number of merchant firms listed in *Slater's Directory*. Although the number of shipping merchants and grey cloth merchants and agents increased during the Edwardian boom, the increase was small given the scale of the export boom, with exports of cotton piece goods rising by 32.2% between 1900 and 1911. In fact, membership of the Royal Exchange peaked only in 1920, as if the Edwardian boom had merely been interrupted by the war. Similarly, *Slater's Directory* suggests that

Table 9.35 *Merchants in the Lancashire cotton export trade, 1900–1939*

	Subscribers to the Manchester Royal Exchange	Members of the Manchester Chamber of Commerce		Merchants listed in *Slater's Directory of Manchester and Salford*	
		Cotton merchants	Cotton merchant-producers	Cotton shipping merchants	Grey cloth merchants and agents
1900	7,877	323	22	727	222
1911	9,921			773	226
1913	10,371				
1920	11,539				
1921	11,223			1,007	293
1927	10,215			851	303
1929	9,368			823	284
1932	7,008				
1935	5,979	400	96		
1937	5,566			534	172
1939	5,062				

Sources: Manchester Royal Exchange – Farnie (1979b: 101); Manchester Chamber of Commerce – Redford (1956: 299); trade directories – Broadberry and Marrison (2002: 73).

there were more merchant firms in 1921 than in 1911. After the slump of 1920/21 membership of the Royal Exchange and the number of shipping merchants did decline, although the number of grey cloth merchants and agents did not begin to fall until after 1927. However, note that there were still more shipping merchants and grey cloth merchants and agents at the end of the 1920s than there had been at the height of the Edwardian boom. It is only with the further decline in merchant numbers during the 1930s that the dense merchant network at the heart of the specialised Lancashire system broke up. Thus, by 1935, membership of the Royal Exchange and the number of merchant firms had both declined to about three-quarters of their 1900 levels.

These trends fit closely with what we know from other sources. Chapman (1996: 89–90) comments that 'on the marketing side the old structure changed surprisingly little' and that '[i]t was only after the economic catastrophe of 1929–31 that this century-old system began to expire'. Thus, in the 1920s, Lancashire still benefited from a fairly stable merchant community with the requisite skills and experience to market abroad its product in an efficient and cost-effective manner. The fact that membership of the Chamber of Commerce was higher in 1935 than in 1900 suggests that a higher proportion of the cotton merchant firms was joining the chamber. One thing seems clear: given the continued existence of this dense merchant network, the Lancashire cotton industry could surely not have done better by adopting an internalised selling system along Japanese lines, as advocated by Mass and Lazonick (1990: 50).[11]

9.4 Financial services

9.4.1 Introduction

Whereas, before World War I, output in financial services grew more than three times as rapidly as in the economy as a whole, between 1911 and 1951 output in financial services grew at only about half the pace of the aggregate economy, as can be seen by comparing table 9.36 with table 9.2. Since employment in financial services continued to grow more rapidly than in the economy as a whole, labour productivity declined, particularly across World War I. This was the period when international financial leadership passed from London to New York, although London remained the pre-eminent European financial centre (Kindleberger, 1986: 289). Capital stock data are unavailable on a separate basis for the financial services sector, which Feinstein (1988) presents together with data on distribution and other services, so that it is not possible to provide estimates of total factor productivity in financial services.

Turning to international comparisons of labour productivity, it is not possible to provide time series projections as with the other market service sectors, because of the unavailability of consistent time series data for financial services in the United States and Germany over this period. However, benchmark estimates from Broadberry (1997b: 12) for the US/UK comparison and from Broadberry (1997c: 255) for the Germany/UK comparison are available in table 9.1. The United States pulled further ahead across World War I, but, with the collapse of the US financial system from 1929, Britain regained a small labour productivity lead during the 1930s. A clear US lead had been restored by 1950, however. For the Germany/UK comparison, the 1935 benchmark suggests a substantial British advantage, although this applies to distribution and finance combined.

The balance sheet data for UK financial institutions in table 9.37, taken from Sheppard (1971), help to provide an overview of the development of the financial services sector. Parts A and B set out the

---

[11] For a more detailed discussion of this issue the reader is referred to Broadberry and Marrison (2002).

Table 9.36 *Productivity in the British financial services sector, 1911–1951*

A. Indices of output, inputs and productivity (1924 = 100)

	Output	Labour	Labour productivity
1911	97.6	60.4	161.6
1924	100.0	100.0	100.0
1929	112.7	110.6	101.9
1932	104.2	113.0	92.2
1937	123.3	127.4	96.8
1951	133.6	123.6	108.1

B. Growth rates of output, inputs and productivity (% per annum)

	1911–1924	1924–1937	1937–1951	1911–1951
Output	0.2	1.6	0.6	0.8
Labour	3.9	1.9	−0.2	1.8
Labour productivity	−3.7	−0.3	0.8	−1.0

Sources: Output – Feinstein (1972: table 53); labour – Feinstein (1972: tables 59, 60), with adjustment for exclusion of the Irish Republic after 1920 from Mitchell (1988: 110).

growth of total assets (equal by definition to total liabilities) of UK banks and non-bank financial intermediaries, respectively, in nominal terms. Since substantial inflation occurred during both world wars, while prices fell for much of the inter-war period, part C also shows how nominal asset growth for banks and non-bank financial intermediaries combined was split between real asset growth and inflation, using Feinstein's (1972: table 61) GDP deflator to convert to real terms. Although nominal asset growth was faster during the two trans-war periods, real growth was substantially faster during the inter-war period, 1924–1937. Over the period 1911–1951 as a whole, real asset growth at 2.6% per annum outstripped the growth of GDP at 1.4% per annum. With population growth of 0.4% per annum between 1911 and 1951, British real per capita asset growth over the same period was 2.2% per annum (Feinstein, 1972: table 55). Although this is slower than the real per capita asset growth in US financial intermediaries of 2.8% per annum for the period 1900–1952, the US performance after 1929 was rather less impressive (Goldsmith, 1958: 62). US real per capita asset growth of 1.7% per annum between 1929 and 1952 compares unfavourably with the British figure of 2.7% per annum for the period 1929–1951.

Returning to parts A and B of table 9.37, note how the different parts of the British financial sector fared in relative terms. Amongst banks,

Table 9.37 *Total assets and total liabilities of UK financial institutions, 1911–1951*

A. Banks' total assets (£ million)

	Joint-stock banks, England and Wales	Joint-stock banks, Ireland	Joint-stock banks, Scotland	Private and CWS banks, Yorkshire Penny Bank	Combined UK banks
1911	836.3	84.8	140.2	56.7	1,118.0
1920	2,097.4	239.0	333.6	101.2	2,771.2
1920	2,097.4	71.9	333.6	101.2	2,604.1
1924	1,952.7	60.7	293.1	91.4	2,397.9
1929	2,059.6	59.9	304.9	111.4	2,535.8
1932	2,205.6	62.1	332.5	122.0	2,722.2
1937	2,496.4	58.3	390.3	168.2	3,113.2
1951	6,464.0	133.9	874.4	310.6	7,782.9

B. Non-bank financial intermediaries' total assets (£ million)

	Insurance companies	Post Office Savings Bank	Trustee Savings Banks	Building societies	National Savings Bonds	Friendly societies	Hire purchase societies	Total non-bank financial intermediaries
1911	491.3	176.6	67.2	63.5	24.8			823.4
1920	712.1	267.1	93.8	87.0	477.8			1,637.8
1920	712.1	267.1	93.8	87.0	477.8	118.1	1.0	1,756.9
1924	934.7	280.6	110.9	144.9	563.6	153.1	1.5	2,189.3
1929	1,252.0	285.0	130.1	312.7	552.0	212.9	4.3	2,749.0
1932	1,389.4	305.7	161.9	469.3	573.4	263.6	6.5	3,169.8
1937	1,744.7	470.5	235.0	710.4	556.0	363.5	16.0	4,096.1
1951	3,589.7	1,875.9	956.0	1,357.0	2,803.2	791.9	42.1	11,415.8

C. Nominal and real growth of assets, banks and non-bank financial intermediaries (% per annum)

	1911–1924	1924–1937	1937–1951	1911–1951
Nominal asset growth	6.9	3.5	7.0	5.8
Inflation	5.0	−0.6	5.2	3.2
Real asset growth	1.9	4.1	1.8	2.6

D. Contribution to total financial institutions' assets and liabilities (%)

	1920	1951
Banks	59.7	40.5
Insurance companies	16.3	18.7
Post Office Savings Bank	6.1	9.8
Trustee Savings Banks	2.2	5.0

Table 9.37 (cont.)

D. Contribution to total financial institutions' assets and liabilities (%)

	1920	1951
Building societies	2.0	7.1
National Savings Bonds	11.0	14.6
Friendly societies	2.7	4.1
Hire purchase societies	0.0	0.2
	100.0	100.0

Note:
From 1920 onwards data for Irish banks refer to Northern Ireland only.

Sources: Financial data – Sheppard (1971: appendix, sections 1–2), converted to real terms using Feinstein's (1972: table 61) GDP deflator.

total asset growth between 1911 and 1951 was 5.0% per annum in nominal terms, or 1.8% per annum in real terms. The joint-stock banks in England and Wales grew a little more rapidly, while the joint-stock banks in Ireland and Scotland and the private banks grew a little more slowly, though the differences were not large. Amongst the non-bank financial intermediaries, total asset growth between 1911 and 1951 was 6.4% per annum in nominal terms, or 3.2% in real terms. The insurance companies showed the slowest growth, while the fastest growth was shown by the National Savings Bonds. Whilst the growth of the National Savings Bonds was concentrated heavily in the two wartime periods, the rapid growth of the building societies was concentrated in the inter-war period. Hire purchase companies also showed rapid growth between the wars. Turning to part D of table 9.37, the upshot of these trends was a substantial decline in the share of banks in total financial institutions' assets, while most non-bank financial institutions saw their shares rise.

9.4.2 Domestic banking

The figures in table 9.38 on the number of banks and branches in Britain show a continuation of the pre-1914 trend towards high levels of concentration. After the mergers of 1917/18 domestic banking in England and Wales was dominated by the 'Big Five' London clearing banks (LCBs), Barclays, Lloyds, National Provincial, Midland and Westminster, which accounted for 80% of deposits by 1920 (Capie and Rodrik-Bali, 1982: 87). During the 1920s and 1930s the LCBs made acquisitions in Scotland and Northern Ireland and extended their overseas interests (Collins, 1988: 207–9). Concerns about a 'bankers'

Table 9.38 *Number of banks and branches, United Kingdom, 1911–1950*

	Joint-stock banks, England and Wales		All banks, United Kingdom	
	Banks	Branches	Banks	Branches
1911	44	5,410	75	7,314
1920	20	7,612	44	9,807
1920	20	7,612	38	9,156
1924	18	8,676	35	10,393
1929	16	9,815	34	11,704
1932	16	10,066	34	11,988
1937	15	10,097	32	12,245
1950	12	9,533	28	11,742

Note:
The first of the two rows for 1920 refers to the United Kingdom including the whole of Ireland, while the second row excludes southern Ireland.
Source: Sheppard (1971: 116–19).

trust', however, led to the establishment of a Treasury Committee on Bank Amalgamations in 1918, which obliged the clearing banks to seek an understanding with the Treasury on future amalgamations. This required banks to show that mergers would significantly extend geographical coverage or customer service, and effectively ruled out mergers between the Big Five banks until after World War II (Collins, 1988: 209–10). Sensitivity to allegations of a bankers' trust did not prevent the London clearing banks from operating a cartel, however, setting the normal deposit rate at two percentage points below Bank Rate from 1920. With price competition effectively suppressed, banks competed on the level of service, which helps to explain the continued growth in the number of branches during the 1920s, so that by 1929 banks were operating with about one branch per 4,000 of the population in England and Wales and one branch per 2,600 in less densely populated Scotland (Collins, 1988: 205–7). This was a much higher level of provision than in the United States, where the figure was about one branch per 9,800 in 1928 (Ackrill and Hannah, 2001: 108).

Table 9.39 provides the combined balance sheets of UK banks, which can be used to shed light on the conduct of banking in the period covering the two world wars. On the asset side, banks needed to hold sufficient liquid assets to meet the needs of their customers. This was met by holding cash and money at call and short notice, which had risen from 18.1% of total assets in 1881 to 24.1% in 1911. Across World War I this proportion fell back, to 21.2% in 1920, and then fluctuated around

Table 9.39 *Combined balance sheets of UK banks, 1911–1951 (£ million)*

A. Assets

	Cash, money at call and short notice	Total discounts	Loans and advances	Total investments	Other assets	Total assets
1911	269.0	100.1	510.9	212.7	25.3	1,118.0
1920	584.8	400.2	1,177.4	571.0	37.8	2,771.2
1920	551.5	392.9	1,115.3	508.2	36.2	2,604.1
1924	525.7	269.2	1,039.1	526.9	37.0	2,397.9
1929	571.6	253.1	1,222.7	439.8	48.6	2,535.8
1932	546.9	450.0	924.4	754.7	46.2	2,722.2
1937	635.9	294.3	1,124.0	1,005.1	53.9	3,113.2
1951	1,420.7	999.3	2,161.3	2,598.8	602.8	7,782.9

B. Liabilities

	Deposits and other accounts	Notes in circulation	Paid-up capital and reserves	Acceptances and endorsements	Miscellaneous liabilities	Total liabilities
1911	977.6	14.6	114.5	55.1	11.3	1,118.0
1920	2,537.7	54.3	163.6	110.9	15.6	2,771.2
1920	2,397.6	37.3	154.1	110.3	15.1	2,604.1
1924	2,194.2	27.2	163.2	142.5	13.3	2,397.9
1929	2,314.5	25.2	180.3	197.1	15.8	2,535.8
1932	2,509.6	24.3	178.1	107.7	10.2	2,722.2
1937	2,887.7	27.5	187.6	141.3	10.4	3,113.2
1951	7,464.8	82.8	213.4	536.8	21.9	7,782.9

Note:
Acceptances and endorsements are excluded from total liabilities.

Source: Sheppard (1971: 116–17).

this level during the rest of the inter-war period and across World War II. The LCBs published the ratio of cash to deposits monthly from 1921, although there was no uniformity across banks and 'window dressing' of the accounts was common, so that banks cannot be seen simply as 'slaves to the cash ratio' during this period (Balogh, 1947: 37–56; Collins, 1988: 240–2).

Total discounts fluctuated between about 10% and 15% of total assets during the period 1911–1951. However, whereas before 1914 commercial bills made up over 90% of this business, treasury bills became much more important during World War I and grew further in importance during the 1930s and across World War II. By 1951 treasury bills accounted for 80.4% of total discounts (Sheppard, 1971: 116–17). This trend reflected the decline of the bill of exchange, first the inland bill and subsequently the international bill, as well as the expansion of public expenditure and indebtedness (Balogh, 1947: 69). Cash and money at call and short notice, together with bills, qualified as liquid assets, and the London clearing banks published the ratio of liquid assets to deposits. As with the cash ratio, however, there was no requirement to maintain a particular liquidity ratio until 1951, when the Bank of England laid down guidelines that the LCBs should maintain a liquidity ratio of 28 to 32% with an absolute minimum of 25% (Collins, 1988: 243–7).

Before 1914 the most important item on the asset side of the balance sheet was loans and advances, which accounted for nearly a half of total assets. Although there was a decline in the importance of loans and advances across World War I, the pre-war level had been restored by 1929. Between 1929 and 1932, however, there was a sharp decline in loans and advances, and despite a subsequent recovery their share of total assets remained little more than one-third in the late 1930s. Across World War II there was a further decline in the importance of loans and advances, with their share of total assets falling to just 27.8% in 1951. To some extent the decline in advances and loans can be seen as reflecting a fall in demand, particularly in the depressed conditions of the 1930s (Balogh, 1947: 78). Another factor on the demand side may have worked through the effects of the decline in the general level of interest rates on the price of securities, enabling a realisation of industrial holdings of securities to provide an alternative source of liquid funds for industrial investment (Nevin, 1955: 250–1). On the supply side, however, it seems clear that the banks were uncompetitive and lost business to non-bank financial intermediaries, such as building societies. The operation of the cartel by the London clearing banks meant that bank advances were expensive, with a minimum charge of 5% for prime customers (Collins, 1988: 254).

The mirror image of the decline in advances and loans as a share of total assets was the increase in the share of investments. Whereas before World War I little more than a third of investments were in government bonds, by the 1920s this had risen to more than 80%, and after World War II to more than 95% (Sheppard, 1971: 116–17). It is clear from these trends, together with the growing importance of treasury bills in total discounts, that the banks became increasingly dependent on lending to the public sector during the period covering the two world wars (Collins, 1988: 250). This naturally raises the question of whether the banks neglected British industry, an allegation that was already made vigorously for the pre-1914 period and which has been considered in chapter 8.

Contemporary concerns that the banks were failing to provide adequate financial support to industry led to the establishment of the Committee on Finance and Industry in November 1929, under the chairmanship of a Scottish judge, H. P. Macmillan, KC, who became Lord Macmillan in 1930 (Sayers, 1976: 360). In fact, however, the UK House of Commons (1931) in its *Report of the Committee on Finance and Industry*, was not particularly critical of the clearing banks and largely endorsed the view that they played their part in the specialised British financial system. With merchant banks to assist in new issues and the finance of overseas trade, and the stock exchanges to provide markets for securities, it was reasonable for the clearing banks to focus in their relationship with industry on short-term loans and advances (Collins, 1988: 256).

Nevertheless, the *Report* (1931, para. 404) did identify what has come to be known as the 'Macmillan gap'. This referred to the capital needs of medium-sized firms seeking to borrow sums between about £50,000 and £200,000. These amounts were generally too large to be tied up as illiquid loans by banks, but too small to justify the fixed costs of a public issue (Collins, 1991: 85). The City responded during the mid-1930s with the formation of a number of institutions aimed at filling the Macmillan gap, including the Charterhouse Industrial Development Co. Ltd, Credit for Industry, and Leadenhall Securities Incorporation. The capital base of these institutions remained small, however, with a combined total of less than £1 million (Thomas, 1978: 119–20). The problem was not addressed on a sizeable scale until the formation of the Industrial and Commercial Finance Corporation Ltd in 1945, on the initiative of the Bank of England, with £15 million of share capital subscribed by the banks, with powers to borrow another £30 million (Thomas, 1978: 121).

For the pre-1914 period there is widespread agreement that the British banks confined themselves largely to short-term lending to industry within a highly specialised financial system, in contrast to the long-term investments made by the German universal banks in industry. For the period between the wars, however, the contrast is less clear (Collins, 1991: 68). While disruptions to the international economy forced City institutions in general to pay more attention to the domestic economy, the depressed state of trade made many industrial customers more dependent on their bankers. Holmes and Green (1986: 179), for example, point to the role played by the Midland Bank in providing extended credit and management time to major customers in the cotton industry, heavy engineering and motor vehicles during the 1920s. And the formation of the Bankers Industrial Development Company in 1930, under the leadership of the Bank of England, but with three-quarters of the share capital provided by the banks, led to further bank involvement in the problems of industry during the 1930s (Holmes and Green, 1986: 181).

Nevertheless, critics maintain that the more active role of the British banks in industrial finance between the wars still fell far short of what was needed. The most detailed criticism is offered by Tolliday (1987) in the context of bank involvement in the steel industry. He argues (177–9) that, although many steel firms became heavily indebted to their banks during the depressed conditions of the 1920s, the banks failed to use their leverage to bring about effective rationalisation, since they lacked expert knowledge and feared that, if they obtained a reputation for interfering in business decisions, their more profitable clients would switch banks. A similar argument is made in the case of cotton textiles by Bamberg (1988: 86). Best and Humphries (1986: 236) sum up the inter-war experience as the British banks responding passively to the difficulties of industry and failing to become a dynamic force for the rationalisation of British industry. Before accepting this critical assessment of the British banks, however, it is important to remember that a greater commitment by the banks to industrial restructuring would have made the banks' assets considerably less liquid, and this could have threatened the stability of the entire financial system. This is an issue of some importance, because, in contrast to the devastating collapse of the banking system that occurred in Germany, the United States and other countries, there were no important bank failures in Britain during the 1930s (Collins, 1998: 19–20). Indeed, the experience of the financial crisis after 1929 led the United States to insist on a clear separation between commercial and investment banking in the Glass–Steagall Act of 1933 (Carosso, 1970: 371).

It is important to remember that, in financial services, there was no substantial US productivity lead before World War II. Indeed, in domestic banking, it is clear that the United States was no more industrialised than Britain, due to restrictions on inter-state banking, which limited the possibilities of concentrated large-scale business. Ackrill and Hannah (2001: 72, 407) demonstrate that, after the merger wave of 1918–1920, the Big Five British clearing banks were larger than their US or German counterparts when their balance sheet assets are compared at contemporary official exchange rates. Wardley (2000: 83–9) argues that the British clearing banks were in the vanguard of office mechanisation in Britain between the wars, although he does not provide comparative data on the diffusion of office machinery, either across sectors of the British economy or between Britain and other countries. Although

Ackrill and Hannah (2001: 77) emphasise the slow diffusion of adding machines at Barclays, with the bank's overseas travellers commenting on the faster progress of mechanisation in the United States and Germany, it is not clear to what extent these observations apply to other banks.

Turning to the liabilities side of the combined banks' balance sheet, in table 9.39, the most important item was deposits, which accounted for 87.5% in 1911, rising to 95.9% by 1951. For the London clearing banks, the ratio of deposit accounts to the total of current and deposit accounts rose from 32.8% in 1919 to 50.5% in 1932, before falling back to 45.4% in 1938 (Balogh, 1947: 88). These trends are consistent with developments in aggregate economic activity and interest rates, with the transactions demand for money growing sharply during the recovery of the 1930s and the opportunity cost of holding money in current accounts falling with interest rates during the era of 'cheap money' from 1932 (Collins, 1988: 236). Although the issuing of notes had effectively ceased among English and Welsh banks by the early twentieth century, it remained important in Scotland and Ireland, with notes accounting for 8.8% of the liabilities of Scottish banks in both 1920 and 1951 (Collins, 1988: 228; Sheppard, 1971: 122–3). Given the dominance of the English and Welsh banks in the combined banks' balance sheet, notes rarely accounted for more than about 1% of liabilities throughout the period. Paid-up capital and reserves continued to decline in importance, falling from a little more than 10% of total liabilities in 1911 to about 6% during the inter-war period, and less than 3% by 1951. The most important factor here was wartime inflation, which increased the nominal value of deposits. However, this did not threaten the solvency of the banks, since they had significant undeclared reserves, which also rose in value with wartime inflation, and since their asset position was highly liquid if an emergency arose (Collins, 1988: 237–8). As for the pre-1914 period, acceptances and endorsements are not added to total liabilities because of the fact that banks rediscounting to each other does not raise the liabilities of the system as a whole (Sheppard, 1971: 113).

9.4.3 *International banking*

Although the clearing banks had operated largely on a domestic basis before World War I, the inter-war period saw them move into the field of international acceptance and other short-term credit (Balogh, 1947: 244). The key players in international banking nevertheless remained the merchant banks, which issued long-term foreign loans as well as offering short-term credit through acceptances. Whilst the merchant banks dealt largely with overseas business outside the empire, the colonial banks continued to play an important role within the empire (Ellinger, 1940: 360). Although the clearing banks had grown to dominate the domestic retail banking market and had adopted a cartel to suppress interest rate competition, international banking remained organised on a small-scale basis, with a large number of small institutions generating the external economies of scale that characterised the City of London. The network form of organisation remained appropriate in this branch of business, dominated as it was by information asymmetries.

International banking clearly suffered a series of major setbacks with the disruption of World War I, the financial crisis in many countries following the demise of the restored gold standard in 1931 and the further disruption of World War II. Amidst the chaos, financial leadership passed from London to New York. However, this should not necessarily be seen as indicating poor performance by the British financial services sector. Rather, it reflected the growing importance of the US economy in the world as both population and per capita national income grew more rapidly than in Britain, together with the differential effects of the two world wars on national wealth. While Britain ran down her external wealth to finance the war effort, the United States prospered as the 'arsenal of democracy' (Broadberry, 1988: 28–33; Broadberry and Howlett, 1998: 66–71, 2005). Although Britain continued to generate a current account surplus during the 1920s it was insufficient to offset the long-term capital outflows that the merchant banks re-established, and, as a result, Britain accumulated short-term liabilities (Drummond, 1987: 38). Given doubts about the sustainability of the sterling exchange rate at the pre-war parity of $4.86, this was a highly vulnerable position, and Britain was forced off gold in 1931 (Eichengreen, 1995: 280). Although the establishment of the sterling bloc (later formalised as the Sterling Area) propped up the role of sterling as a reserve currency during the 1930s, London never regained its pre-1914 status as the centre of the international financial system (Cairncross and Eichengreen, 1983: 23–6).

The scale of activity in the acceptance business is shown in table 9.40. At the end of the 1920s, although the value of overseas discounts had risen above the pre-war level in nominal terms, this represented a decline in real terms. Given the weakness of demand as world trade stagnated and the sterling bill of exchange declined in importance, the increased competition from clearing banks acted to squeeze margins in the acceptance business. Balogh (1947: 245) notes that the commission on acceptances, which had typically been between 1 and 1.5% before World War I, fell to between 0.5 and 1% during the 1920s. When the defaults following the 1931 crisis in central Europe left London institutions liable

Table 9.40 *Commercial bills outstanding in the London market, 1913/14–1936/37*

	Current prices (£ million)			Constant prices (£ million 1913)		
	Inland	Overseas	Total	Inland	Overseas	Total
1913/14	181.8	336.2	518.0	181.8	336.2	518.0
1928/29	211.8	540.0	751.8	120.5	307.2	427.7
1936/37	131.8	143.0	274.8	74.7	81.0	155.7

Note:
Current price figures converted to constant prices using GDP deflator from Feinstein (1972: table 61).

Source: Ellinger (1940: 374).

for £54 million of outstanding acceptances, failures were avoided only as a result of a complex series of 'standstill agreements' negotiated between private bankers, central bankers and politicians (Sayers, 1976: 503–12). After this crisis the international acceptance business declined rapidly, leaving outstanding bills on the London market in the late 1930s at a fraction of their pre-war level in real terms, as can be seen in table 9.40.

The value of new capital issues on the London market is shown in table 9.41. Although there was a revival of overseas issues during the mid-1920s, the peak pre-war levels were not regained, even in nominal terms. The decline would be even greater if Simon's (1968: 39) figure for overseas issues of £206.6 million were preferred to Hobson's (1914: 219) figure of £149.7 million. The decline in the real value of overseas issues was thus substantial, and can be seen as resulting from effective official control on foreign issues based on 'moral suasion' backed up by the power of the Bank of England (Balogh, 1947: 268–9). As a result, the share of overseas issues in total issues fell from more than 80% in 1913 to less than 20% in 1937.

The favourable conditions which British overseas banks had enjoyed before 1914 disappeared with the outbreak of World War I. Supplying financial services such as trade finance and exchange operations to the primary-commodity-producing settler colonies of Australia, New Zealand and South Africa proved a difficult specialisation when the terms of trade moved against primary commodities and tarrifs and exchange controls proliferated (Jones, 1993: 137). Nevertheless, Britain's overseas banking network remained intact during the period covering the two world wars. The value of total assets increased substantially

Table 9.41 *New capital issues in the United Kingdom, 1913–1937*

A. Current prices (£ million)						
	1913	1920	1924	1929	1932	1937
Home	36.0	324.6	89.3	159.4	83.8	138.8
Overseas	149.7	59.7	134.2	94.3	29.2	32.1
Total	185.7	384.2	223.5	253.7	113.0	170.9
B. Constant prices (£ million 1913)						
	1913	1920	1924	1929	1932	1937
Home	36.0	119.9	48.4	90.8	50.9	81.9
Overseas	149.7	22.0	72.7	53.7	17.8	18.9
Total	185.7	141.9	121.1	144.5	68.7	100.8
C. Proportions of total issues (%)						
	1913	1920	1924	1929	1932	1937
Home	19.4	84.5	39.9	62.8	74.1	81.2
Overseas	80.6	15.5	60.1	37.2	25.9	18.8

Note:
Current price figures converted to constant prices using GDP deflator from Feinstein (1972: table 61).

Sources: Hobson (1914: 219), Balogh (1947: 249–50).

across both world wars, in real terms as well as in nominal terms, as can be seen in table 9.42. During the 1930s, however, the value of total assets declined slightly, in both real and nominal terms. The geographical orientation became ever more firmly based on the empire, as can be seen in table 9.43. Australasia and southern Africa accounted for approximately two-thirds of all branches in 1913, rising to three-quarters between the wars. The strongest growth was in South Africa, with North America and Latin America declining in importance. The banks continued to be run on the basis of networks, with recruitment based on social background rather than university education or specific skills (Jones, 1993: 169–70). The system nevertheless coped well with the difficulties of war and depression, and, as in other parts of the British financial system, no major crisis occurred.[12]

---

[12] Jones (1993: 239–44) credits the Bank of England with helping to prevent any minor difficulties from turning into major crises, particularly in the case of the collapse of the Anglo-South American Bank in 1931.

Table 9.42 *Total assets of British overseas banks, 1890–1955*

	In current prices (£ million)	In constant prices (£ million 1913)
1890	236	263
1913	366	366
1928	803	456
1938	767	440
1955	2,567	618

Note:
Current price figures converted to constant prices using GDP deflator from Feinstein (1972: table 61).
Source: Jones (1993: 416).

Table 9.43 *Geographical distribution of foreign branches of British overseas banks, 1913–1955 (%)*

	1913	1928	1938	1955
Australasia	47	45	42	40
North America	8	0	0	0
Rest of Americas	7	5	4	3
Southern Africa	19	29	33	37
Rest of Africa	5	5	5	7
Middle East/North Africa	4	5	5	4
South Asia	4	3	3	3
South-east Asia	2	2	2	2
East Asia	2	2	2	1
Europe (excluding United Kingdom)	2	4	4	3
Total	100	100	100	100

Source: Jones (1993: 414–15).

9.4.4 Building societies

The share of building societies in total financial institutions' assets and liabilities increased dramatically between the wars, as can be seen in table 9.37. Whereas building societies accounted for 2.0% of total assets in 1920, this had risen to 9.9% by 1937, before falling back to 7.1% in 1951. This can be analysed on the liabilities side of the balance sheet in terms of the attractiveness of building society interest rates compared with other forms of saving. However, as Humphries (1984) and

Table 9.44 *Interest rates on British building society shares and the yield on consols, 1922–1938*

	Building society interest rate on shares (% per annum)	Standard rate of tax in the pound (s./d.)	Building society interest rate grossed up (% per annum)	Yield on consols (% per annum)
1922	4.4	6/-	6.29	4.4
1928	4.5	4/-	5.63	4.5
1932	4.5	5/-	6.00	3.7
1935	3.6	4/6	4.68	2.9
1938	3.3	5/-	4.40	3.4

Source: Humphries (1984: 332)

Broadberry (1987) note, it is also important to examine the asset side of the balance sheet, which reveals the positive steps taken by the building societies to expand mortgage advances.

An important factor in explaining the relative attractiveness of placing savings in building societies between the wars was the favourable tax treatment of interest payments. Since many building society savers had incomes below the income tax threshold before World War I, rather than deduct tax at source, and face the administrative burden of refunding the tax, the Inland Revenue agreed that the building societies should make a tax payment based on the average liability of taxpayers and non-taxpayers (Humphries, 1984: 330). As the proportion of taxpayers rose, the tax liability of building societies remained based on the low proportions of the past. As a result, building society rates became very attractive relative to other forms of saving. Table 9.44 shows how, although the building society interest rate on shares was the same as the yield on consols during the 1920s, the building society interest rate was much more attractive when grossed up to take account of the standard rate of income tax. The situation became even more favourable to building societies during the early 1930s, as building society rates fell more slowly than the yield on consols and other saving rates. At this point building societies took steps to limit the inflow of funds, since they did not want to become too dependent on short-term flows of 'hot money' in search of arbitrage opportunities (Cleary, 1965: 191).

This illustrates the point that the growth of building societies cannot be explained solely in terms of interest differentials attracting savings. Growth also depended on the building societies increasing advances, and here Humphries (1984: 338–42) points to a number of innovations, which together helped to underpin the building boom of the inter-war period. Building societies increased the repayment period, which extended the option of home ownership to more borrowers on lower incomes. The proportion of the purchase price of a house that societies were prepared to lend was also increased, particularly through the device of the builders' pool. This involved the builders providing security for advances in excess of 80% of the purchase price, drastically reducing the size of the deposit that purchasers needed to find. As Broadberry (1986: 62) notes, the context of this innovative activity was the emergence of national building societies from local societies, and a struggle for market share, which led to the temporary breakdown of the building society cartel during the mid-1930s.

9.4.5 Insurance

Insurance companies continued to account for the largest share of non-bank financial intermediaries' assets throughout the period 1911 to 1951, although asset growth was more rapid in other non-bank financial intermediaries. Whereas the assets of all non-bank financial intermediaries grew at an annual rate of 6.4% in nominal terms between 1911 and 1951, or 3.2% in real terms, the assets of insurance companies grew at an annual rate of 5.0% in nominal terms, or 1.8% in real terms (table 9.37). To some extent this slower growth of insurance companies than other non-bank financial institutions simply reflected the explosive growth of National Savings Bonds during the two world wars, but the faster growth of building societies and hire purchase societies was concentrated in the years between the wars. The period 1924 to 1937 nevertheless saw an impressive growth of insurance company assets at an annual rate of 4.8% in nominal terms, or 5.4% in real terms. Of the main areas of business, fire and marine insurance stagnated, while life and accident insurance expanded rapidly. Overseas business remained important, with British insurers continuing to play an important role in the world economy.

Fire insurance was the most mature branch of the insurance business, in that its function was the most straightforward and the most widely used. Future growth depended on rising insurable values in the home market and further penetration of overseas markets (Supple, 1970: 426). As a result of the difficult general business climate between the wars both at home and abroad, premium income stagnated in real terms, as can be seen in table 9.45. Furthermore, the relationship between high unemployment, idle plant and high fire wastage meant that fire insurance

Table 9.45 *Fire insurance business of UK offices, 1911–1951*

	Fire premiums	
	Current prices (£ million)	Constant prices (£ million 1913)
1911	28.0	29.1
1924	58.3	29.2
1929	58.4	31.6
1932	50.8	33.3
1937	49.8	29.4
1951	190.5	54.5

Note:
Current price figures converted to constant prices using GDP deflator from Feinstein (1972: table 61).

Sources: Supple (1970: 213, 427), Sheppard (1971: 160–1).

Table 9.46 *Life assurance business of UK offices, 1911–1951*

	Current prices (£ million)		Constant prices (£ million 1913)	
	Ordinary life premiums	Industrial life premiums	Ordinary life premiums	Industrial life premiums
1911	31.9	14.1	14.1	14.6
1924	58.8	34.1	34.1	18.5
1929	78.0	42.0	42.0	23.9
1932	86.4	46.4	46.4	28.2
1937	99.7	55.8	55.8	32.9
1951	232.4	108.2	108.2	30.9

Note:
Current price figures converted to constant prices using GDP deflator from Feinstein (1972: table 61).

Source: Sheppard (1971: 160–1).

did not prove very profitable. At the Phoenix, for example, fire loss rates exceeded the conventional safe limit of 50% of premium income in six years between 1921 and 1930 (Trebilcock, 1997: 124). Overseas business remained important for the British offices, accounting for more than a half of total fire premium income, with the United States alone accounting for 42% in 1918 and 34% in 1928 (Supple, 1970: 427).

By contrast with the stagnation of fire insurance, life assurance business grew rapidly in real terms between the wars, as can be seen in table 9.46. Ordinary life premiums grew at an annual rate of 4.1% in real terms between 1924 and 1937, while industrial premiums grew even more rapidly at 4.4% per annum. One factor behind the rapid growth of life business was the rise of group life and pension plans, as people 'invented' retirement (Hannah, 1986). A second factor was the innovative use of endowment assurances to provide a range of insurance 'consumer' services, such as financing house purchase, protecting family income or paying school fees (Trebilcock, 1997: 131). A third factor was the general decline in interest rates, which reduced the attractiveness of alternative forms of saving and encouraged individuals to pass the burden of investment on to the insurance companies (Supple, 1970: 436–7). Also, as Trebilcock (1997: 130) notes, life assurance policies were tax-efficient; during the 1920s it was even possible for an individual to borrow the money for a single-premium endowment policy from the insurance company, obtain tax relief on the premium and then repay the loan when the endowment matured.[13]

After a profitable boost during World War I marine insurance faced a bleak outlook between the wars, as world trade failed to keep pace with world income growth, particularly during the intensification of protection during the 1930s (Lewis, 1949: 58). British insurance companies saw marine premiums fall from £21 million in 1922, itself a bleak year after the collapse of the post-war boom, to an average of less than £11 million between 1931 and 1937 (Supple, 1970: 437).[14] Although there is a lack of data on premium income for the non-corporate sector, it is clear that Lloyd's remained an important player in marine insurance (Supple, 1970: 437). Profits on marine business were kept low by high losses on luxury liners as well as by competition amongst underwriters for the limited business (Trebilcock, 1997: 126).

Accident business, like life assurance, exhibited strong growth between the wars, as can be seen in table 9.47. However, this was largely the result of the growth of motor insurance, since premium income from the more traditional employers' liability and personal accident business stagnated in real terms. During the 1920s the spread of motor insurance occurred on a voluntary basis, but from 1931 third-party liability insurance became compulsory (Supple, 1970: 431). Attempts were made to boost accident business via 'coupon' insurance, in cooperation with

---

[13] This rather blatant tax scam was brought to an end with the Finance Act of 1930.
[14] That represents a fall of approximately 47.6% in nominal terms, or 22.9% in real terms.

Table 9.47 *Accident insurance business of UK offices, 1914–1951*

	Current prices (£ million)		Constant prices (£ million 1913)	
	Employers' liability and personal accident premiums	Motor and miscellaneous premiums	Employers' liability and personal accident premiums	Motor and miscellaneous premiums
1914	5.8	10.9	5.8	10.8
1924	8.8	40.8	4.8	22.1
1929	9.8	56.3	5.6	32.1
1932	8.7	53.4	5.3	32.5
1937	11.1	64.5	6.5	38.1
1951	36.5	193.0	10.4	55.2

Note:
Current price figures converted to constant prices using GDP deflator from Feinstein (1972: table 61).
Sources: Supple (1970: 417, 427), Sheppard (1971: 160–1).

newspapers during the 1920s, but with mixed results. The Phoenix, for example, underwrote a scheme for the insurance of *Daily Mail* readers against personal accident. However, the newspaper sought to encourage claims, so that they could achieve maximum publicity and sell more papers, which severely limited the usefulness of the scheme to the insurance company (Trebilcock, 1998: 575–8).[15]

Building upon the mergers of the first decade of the twentieth century, a series of amalgamations early after World War I led to the establishment of a structure of insurance companies that was to remain familiar until the late 1950s (Supple, 1970: 439). The main feature of these amalgamations was the acquisition of new types of business rather than further increasing concentration within each established field. In fire insurance, indeed, the degree of concentration actually declined, with the share of the ten largest companies falling from 81% of premium income in 1914 to 75% in 1928 and 73% in 1938 (Supple, 1970: 438). The composite structure of the insurance market was strengthened by developments such as the links established between Norwich Union Life and Norwich Union Fire in 1925, as well as by continued growth of the

---

[15] In the first ten months of the scheme nearly a quarter of the claims were fraudulent or misguided. One man was even tried for attempting to murder his wife so as to make a claim, with the resulting court case providing excellent copy for the newspaper (Trebilcock, 1998: 577).

established composite insurers such as the Royal Exchange Assurance (Supple, 1970: 439). It is tempting to see the emergence of the concentrated composite structure as evidence of Chandlerian economies of scale and scope. However, as Trebilcock (1997: 140–2) points out, the pressure for selling different types of insurance over a single counter came largely from the customer. There were few gains for the insurers in terms of cost reduction, since the different types of insurance were supplied using very different skills and institutional systems. What the concentrated structure did facilitate, however, was collusion. This was already long established in fire insurance, with tariffs set by the Fire Offices Committee from the late nineteenth century, and the approach was extended into motor insurance in 1913/1914 via the Accident Offices Association, which had been established in 1906 (Supple, 1970: 237; Westall, 1997: 55).

Despite the emergence of 'big business' in the form of the composite insurers, Campbell-Kelly (1992) points to the slow adoption of modern office technology in British insurance, which limited the extent to which the sector should be seen as 'industrialised' at this time. At the Prudential, Britain's largest life insurance company, it took about sixty years to make the transition from manual data processing, starting in the 1870s, to the fully mechanised office of the 1930s. There were, nevertheless, substantial productivity gains, with the expense ratio (the fraction of premium income consumed by administration, collection and actuarial expenses) declining from 40.5% in 1920 to 22.46% in 1939 (Campbell-Kelly, 1992: 132). Campbell-Kelly thus attributes (133) the slowness of the adoption of modern office technology at the Prudential, at least in part, to the longevity of life assurance policies, which made it necessary to continue updating policies based on the old technology alongside processing new policies on any system. In this case, the nature of the business can be seen as setting limits to the process of mechanisation, which therefore occurred slowly but efficiently.

9.5   Conclusions

Between 1911 and 1950 the United States pulled ahead of Britain in terms of total factor productivity as well as labour productivity, and in services as well as in the economy as a whole. A key factor here was the 'industrialisation' of services, with the move to a high-volume, low-margin approach to business and hierarchical management leading to substantial labour productivity growth in the United States. Although British services also saw amalgamations, they did not have similar results for labour productivity. In many sectors, there were at best weak competitive pressures for the adoption of the new technology that underpinned the high-volume approach to business.

Nevertheless, performance varied across sectors. Transport and communications witnessed the earliest adoption of new forms of organisation in the United States, especially on the railways. Britain's railways amalgamated into a four-company structure after World War I, but failed to reap substantial economies of scale. This led to the emergence of a very large productivity gap in this sector. Although it is possible to point to regulatory constraints, other factors including bad industrial relations and the slow adoption of new technologies, such as electrification, diesel locomotives, large wagons and office technology, point to a familiar problem of poor British performance in businesses requiring large scale, centralised control and hierarchical management. In shipping, Britain's pre-war strength lay in the tramping sector, with defensive rings already emerging in the liner sector. Further consolidation in the liner sector led to emergence of the 'Big Five', but slow adoption of modern technology shows up in the delayed switch from steam to the motorship. However, the British share of world shipping was undoubtedly also constrained by the nationalistic shipping policies pursued by other countries.

The 'industrialisation' of distribution proceeded at a slower pace than in transport and communications, with the growth of large-scale retailing limited in the domestic market by the willingness of consumers to accept standardisation and the shoring up of small-scale retailers by the widespread acceptance of resale price maintenance. In international wholesaling, British merchant companies retained a significant presence, organised on a network basis appropriate for this type of business. The scale of the US productivity lead was thus substantially smaller in distribution than in transport and communications.

The 'industrialisation' of financial services did not occur at a significantly faster rate in the United States than in Britain, so no substantial US/UK labour productivity gap appeared in this sector. Indeed, with the Great Depression hitting the US financial sector more severely than its British counterpart, Britain regained a small productivity lead during the 1930s. Restrictions on inter-state banking in the United States meant that banking remained more fragmented than in Britain, where the emergence of a 'Big Five' in domestic banking led to the establishment of an interest rate cartel. In international banking, business remained suited to entrepreneurial business networks, and British banks continued to do relatively well. However, the sector faced severe difficulties due to the disruptions of the international economy.

There was no trend deterioration in Britain's productivity position relative to Germany between 1911 and 1950, either in services or in the economy as a whole. Britain retained a substantial labour productivity lead over Germany in services largely as a result of the continued overcommitment to agriculture in Germany, which resulted in the underdevelopment of German services. The railways are an exceptional case, since they were developed as part of the modernised sector in Germany, along with heavy industry. As the railways became less important, Germany's productivity lead in transport and communications declined. Note also that the literature on the supposed superiority of German universal banking goes silent on the inter-war period, as problems of illiquidity with long-term involvement in heavy industry came to the fore.

10 Completing the industrialisation of services, 1950–1990

10.1 Introduction

By the early 1950s the US labour productivity lead over all European countries, including both Britain and Germany, had reached its peak. This was true in market services as well as in the economy as a whole, and reflected in part, at least, the much greater degree of disruption caused by World War II in Europe. Between 1950 and 1990 Britain narrowed the productivity gap with the United States, in services and in the economy as a whole, but at a slower pace than Germany. As a result, Germany overtook Britain in terms of labour productivity during the mid-1960s, again in both services and the economy as a whole.

As during the inter-war period, Britain's performance was generally poorer in sectors suitable for standardised, high-volume, low-margin business with hierarchical management, such as the railways, and rather better in sectors that remained suitable for customised, low-volume, high-margin business organised on the basis of networks, such as parts of the financial service sector. This is reflected to some extent in the benchmark estimates in table 10.1. However, general technological trends continued to favour standardisation and large-scale organisation, and more and more services became increasingly industrialised. Britain had little choice but to embrace these developments, but the transition to industrialised services was difficult, since social capabilities remained oriented towards the network form of organisation.

In considering the contrasting performances of the British, American and German economies after World War II, it is important to consider the institutional framework. During the early post-war period, there was a strong contrast between a 'corporatist' institutional framework in Britain and Germany on the one hand and a 'competitive' framework in the United States on the other hand. The corporatist framework in Europe was centred on a post-war settlement involving unions, employers' organisations and government. However, the system was much better at encouraging the accumulation of human and physical capital in

Table 10.1 *Benchmark estimates of comparative labour productivity levels in market services, 1950–1993 (UK = 100)*

A. US/UK			
	1950	1968	1993
Railways	620.7	395.0	370.3
Road transport		167.2	
Shipping		170.0	
Air transport		152.0	
Communications	144.6	302.0	152.9
Distribution	148.4		143.6
Finance	138.7		117.7

B. Germany/UK			
	1968	1973	1993
Railways	108.2		107.2
Road transport	129.8		
Shipping	190.0		
Air transport	113.0		
Communications	106.4		67.7
Distribution		127.0	112.1
Finance			109.9

Sources: tables 3.2, 3.4.

Germany, where unions and employers' organisations were centralised, than in Britain, where the equivalent labour market organisations were highly fragmented and decentralised. In the accumulation of human capital, Germany's more centralised framework was also better able to solve the free-rider problem of the poaching of skilled workers than Britain's decentralised framework. While Germany was able to establish an effective system of vocational training in services after World War II, Britain's apprenticeship system went into decline even in industrial sectors. Although a similar poaching problem existed in the United States, this was offset by the greater reliance on general education than vocational training. Turning to physical capital accumulation, again the more centralised German unions and employers' organisations were better able to deliver on agreements concerning investments in new technology and wage restraint than the more fragmented British labour market organisations.

There was, however, a major change of direction in Britain during the 1980s, with the adoption of a more vigorous anti-trust policy, the

Table 10.2 *Productivity in the British aggregate economy, 1951–1990*

A. Indices of output, inputs and productivity (1973 = 100)

	Output	Labour	Capital	Labour productivity	TFP
1951	55.5	92.1	46.7	60.4	71.6
1960	69.9	96.9	58.5	72.1	81.9
1968	87.0	99.2	81.0	87.7	92.3
1973	100.0	100.0	100.0	100.0	100.0
1979	107.0	101.4	120.3	105.5	101.1
1985	115.1	97.5	136.5	118.1	108.5
1990	133.8	108.6	156.6	123.2	112.4

B. Growth rates of output, inputs and productivity (% per annum)

	1951–1973	1973–1979	1979–1990	1951–1990
Output	2.7	1.1	2.0	2.2
Labour	0.4	0.2	0.6	0.4
Capital	3.5	3.1	2.4	3.1
Labour productivity	2.3	0.9	1.4	1.8
TFP	1.5	0.2	1.0	1.1

Note:
Factor shares are 25% for capital and 75% for labour, based on 1973 figures.

Sources: Output – UK Central Statistical Office (*National Income and Expenditure*, various years); labour – 1951–1965: Feinstein (1972); 1965–1990: UK Central Statistical Office (*Annual Abstract of Statistics*, various years), OECD (*Labour Force Statistics*, various years); capital – 1951–1965: Feinstein (1972); 1965–1990: UK Central Statistical Office (*National Income and Expenditure*, various years).

privatisation of a number of important services in the transport and communications sector, a policy of deregulation, particularly in financial services, and legislation to limit the immunities of trade unions. By the end of the 1980s the major contrast in the institutional frameworks was therefore between the competitive approach of Britain and the United States on the one hand and the corporatist approach of Germany on the other hand. After more than a century Britain's relative economic decline began to be stemmed, if not yet decisively reversed.

As with the earlier periods, it will be convenient to set out trends in productivity performance at the aggregate level, to provide a benchmark against which sectoral performance can be assessed. Table 10.2 provides indices of output, inputs and productivity in the United Kingdom between 1951 and 1990, together with growth rates calculated over the whole period and sub-periods between the cyclical peaks of 1951, 1973,

Table 10.3 *Comparative US/UK and Germany/UK productivity levels for the aggregate economy, 1950–1990 (UK = 100)*

	Labour productivity		TFP	
	US/UK	Germany/UK	US/UK	Germany/UK
1950	166.9	74.4	138.1	76.2
1960	167.9	94.5	139.6	95.1
1968	164.2	107.1	143.8	102.5
1973	152.3	114.0	137.7	108.6
1979	145.5	126.5	135.7	118.9
1985	134.8	120.9	128.4	113.3
1990	133.0	125.4	125.3	116.5

Sources: tables 6.1, 6.2.

1979 and 1990. During the period 1951 to 1973 output growth surged to its highest ever sustained rate. Since there was little growth of the labour force, this also translated into a historically unprecedented labour productivity growth rate of 2.3% per annum. The capital stock also grew rapidly, but this still allowed TFP growth of 1.5% per annum, well above the previous peak of 1.1% per annum between 1924 and 1937. There is a paradox here, in that the period of Britain's fastest growth rate was also the period of Britain's most serious relative economic decline, with most western European countries overtaking Britain in terms of aggregate labour productivity. This relatively poor British performance is reflected in table 10.3 by the German overtaking during the 1960s, and the relatively slow narrowing of the gap with the United States.

The period between 1973 and 1979 was little short of disastrous, with Britain's labour productivity growth falling to 0.9% per annum and TFP growth slumping as low as 0.2% per annum. The Thatcher years, 1979–1990, saw a return to respectable rates of output and productivity growth, although not quite as rapid as during the 1951–1973 period. By the end of the 1980s Britain's relative economic decline had been halted, but not decisively reversed.

10.2 Transport and communications

10.2.1 Introduction

Output, input and productivity trends in the British transport and communications sector during the period 1951–1990 are shown in table 10.4.

Table 10.4 *Productivity in the British transport and communications sector, 1951–1990*

A. Indices of output, inputs and productivity (1973 = 100)

	Output	Labour	Capital	Labour productivity	TFP
1951	55.0	112.7	66.5	48.8	55.7
1960	65.4	107.6	73.7	60.8	66.8
1968	80.0	103.8	85.6	77.1	80.9
1973	100.0	100.0	100.0	100.0	100.0
1979	110.2	98.2	108.2	112.2	109.5
1985	119.5	88.4	105.1	135.2	129.5
1990	152.7	93.8	108.9	162.8	156.8

B. Growth rates of output, inputs and productivity (% per annum)

	1951–1973	1973–1979	1979–1990	1951–1990
Output	2.7	1.6	3.0	2.6
Labour	−0.5	−0.3	−0.4	−0.5
Capital	1.9	1.3	0.0	1.3
Labour productivity	3.2	1.9	3.4	3.1
TFP	2.7	1.5	3.3	2.7

Sources: Output – UK Central Statistical Office (*National Income and Expenditure*, various years); labour – 1951–1965: Feinstein (1972); 1965–1990: UK Central Statistical Office (*Annual Abstract of Statistics*, various years), OECD (*Labour Force Statistics*, various years); capital – 1951–1965: Feinstein (1972); 1965–1990: UK Central Statistical Office (*National Income and Expenditure*, various years).

Comparing with trends in the whole economy in table 10.2, output in transport and communications grew at the same rate as in the whole economy before 1973, but more rapidly than in the economy as a whole after 1973. Since employment in transport and communications declined over the whole period, labour productivity growth in transport and communications was more rapid than in the whole economy both before and after 1973. Given the relatively slow growth of capital in transport and communications, TFP growth was substantially higher in this sector than in the economy as a whole. Table 10.5 places this productivity performance in international perspective. Compared with the United States, British productivity levels in transport and communications were relatively low, but the gap narrowed over time. Compared with Germany, there was a small productivity gap, which remained quite stable over time. Hence, transport and communications did not contribute directly to the worsening of Britain's productivity performance overall.

Table 10.5 *Comparative US/UK and Germany/UK labour productivity levels for the transport and communications sector, 1950–1990 (UK = 100)*

	US/UK	Germany/UK
1950	348.4	122.0
1960	318.8	117.0
1968	336.8	130.0
1973	303.3	119.5
1979	302.7	135.0
1985	294.8	132.7
1990	270.5	125.7

Sources: tables 3.1, 3.3.

10.2.2 Shipping

Following the stagnation of the inter-war period, the British merchant fleet returned to growth after World War II, as can be seen by the gross tonnage data in part A of table 10.6. In fact, the size of the British merchant fleet reached its all-time peak of 31.2 million gross tons in 1975 (Mitchell, 1988: 538). This was followed, however, by steady decline during the second half of the 1970s and dramatic collapse during the 1980s. Although absolute decline was visible only after 1975, relative decline occurred throughout the period, as can be seen by the data on shares of the world fleet in part B of table 10.6. The general context was one in which the previously dominant merchant marines of the developed countries lost ground to later-developing countries and flags of convenience. Within Europe the established maritime powers lost ground to Greece, while outside Europe the biggest advances were recorded by the rapidly developing Japan and the lightly regulated Liberia. The decline of shipping in the established maritime countries accelerated markedly in the 1980s as international organisations encouraged a more liberal approach to trade in services as well as commodities, and as governments reduced subsidies and companies withdrew from unprofitable activities (Kappel, 1989).

In table 10.7, an index of output has been constructed from data on freight and passenger movements presented in the UK Central Statistical Office's *Annual Abstract of Statistics*, following the method described in Deakin and Seward (1969: 17–41). The freight data, which are available on a ton-mile basis for most of the period, distinguish between tanker and dry cargo business in international trade and coastal shipping. Passenger data relate only to the number of journeys. Output in

Table 10.6 *World merchant fleet, 1950–1990*

A. Millions of gross tons

	1950	1960	1970	1980	1990
United Kingdom	18.2	21.1	25.8	27.1	6.7
West Germany	0.5	4.5	7.9	8.4	4.3
France	3.2	4.8	6.5	11.9	3.8
Italy	2.6	5.1	7.5	11.1	8.0
Greece	1.3	4.5	11.0	39.5	20.5
Norway	5.5	11.2	19.3	22.0	23.4
United States (inc. Great Lakes)	27.5	24.8	18.5	18.5	21.3
Panama	3.4	4.2	5.6	24.2	39.3
Japan	1.9	6.9	27.0	41.0	27.1
China	0.8	0.4	2.0	6.9	13.9
Liberia	–	11.3	33.3	80.3	54.7
World total	84.6	129.8	227.5	419.9	423.6

B. Shares of world fleet (%)

	1950	1960	1970	1980	1990
United Kingdom	21.5	16.3	11.4	6.5	1.6
West Germany	0.5	3.5	3.5	2.0	1.0
France	3.8	3.7	2.8	2.8	0.9
Italy	3.1	3.9	3.3	2.6	1.9
Greece	1.6	3.5	4.8	9.4	4.8
Norway	6.5	8.6	8.5	5.2	5.5
United States (inc. Great Lakes)	32.5	19.1	8.1	4.4	5.0
Panama	4.0	3.3	2.5	5.8	9.3
Japan	2.2	5.3	11.9	9.8	6.4
China	1.0	0.3	0.9	1.6	3.3
Liberia	–	8.7	14.6	19.1	12.9

Source: United Nations (*Statistical Yearbook*, various years).

shipping grew a little more slowly than in the economy as a whole before 1973, before going into moderate absolute decline during the 1970s and rapid collapse during the 1980s. Employment in shipping has declined throughout the whole post-war period, while capital in shipping has declined since 1973. Because of the declining inputs, labour productivity and TFP have grown more rapidly in shipping than in the economy as a whole. Nevertheless, the estimates of comparative labour productivity levels available in table 10.1 suggest that, by the late 1960s, Britain lagged behind both Germany and the United States. Although the productivity gap was smaller than in many other parts of the economy

Table 10.7 *Productivity in British shipping, 1951–1990*

A. Indices of output, inputs and productivity (1973 = 100)

	Output	Labour	Capital	Labour productivity	TFP
1951	58.1	150.6	64.9	38.6	47.6
1960	74.6	140.2	73.0	53.2	62.6
1968	85.2	118.4	73.8	72.0	81.0
1973	100.0	100.0	100.0	100.0	100.0
1979	96.5	85.1	86.3	113.4	113.0
1985	75.1	42.5	41.9	176.7	177.5
1990	70.3	39.1	18.1	179.8	217.6

B. Growth rates of output, inputs and productivity (% per annum)

	1951–1973	1973–1979	1979–1990	1951–1990
Output	2.4	−0.6	−2.9	0.5
Labour	−1.9	−2.7	−7.1	−3.4
Capital	2.0	−2.5	−10.3	−3.3
Labour productivity	4.3	2.1	4.2	3.9
TFP	3.3	2.0	5.9	3.9

Sources: Output – derived from the UK Central Statistical Office (*Annual Abstract of Statistics*, various years); labour – UK Department of Employment (1978, *British Labour Statistics Yearbook*, various years); capital – UK Central Statistical Office (*National Income and Expenditure*, various years).

in the US/UK case, it was larger than in most other parts of the economy in the Germany/UK case.

After the disruption and destruction of World War II the major British shipping companies began to rebuild their cargo liner fleets, continuing also to focus on the old routes to Commonwealth countries. Given the post-war shipping shortage and the conference system to maintain freight rates, this at first proved a profitable strategy for the major British shipping companies (Turner, 1969: 287–8). Peninsular and Oriental (P&O), Ocean (based on the Holts' Blue Funnel Line) and British and Commonwealth (formed in 1956 from a merger of the Clan Line and Union Castle) all earned reasonable rates of return as late as 1957 (Channon, 1978: 135–8; Turner, 1969: 288; Sturmey, 1962: 373). Profits were also good for the tramp shipping companies during the early 1950s (Sturmey, 1962: 182).

From the late 1950s, however, it became increasingly apparent that the world shipping market had changed fundamentally, and rates of return on capital declined seriously for the British shipping lines. By

Table 10.8 *Freight rates and the general price level in Britain, 1948–1969 (1948 = 100)*

	Tramp rates	Liner rates	GDP deflator		Tramp rates	GDP deflator
1948	100.0	100.0	100.0	1959	79.5	155.2
1949	82.3	101.5	103.0	1960	82.1	157.9
1950	84.0	110.0	103.6	1961	87.6	162.9
1951	173.7	131.8	111.3	1962	73.1	168.5
1952	110.6	136.3	121.3	1963	89.5	171.8
1953	85.7	133.0	125.0	1964	92.0	175.2
1954	95.2	132.0	127.6	1965	103.8	181.6
1955	141.2	136.0	132.2	1966	93.1	187.7
1956	173.6	154.0	140.5	1967	98.9	194.5
1957	124.6		146.2	1968	101.6	200.1
1958	74.2		152.8	1969	96.4	207.1

Sources: Tramp rates – UK Central Statistical Office (*Annual Abstract of Statistics*, various years); liner rates – McLachlan (1958: 61–2); GDP deflator – UK Central Statistical Office (*National Income and Expenditure*, various years).

1961 P&O's rate of return had fallen to 0.4% from almost 9% in 1957 (Turner, 1969: 288). Similarly, rates of return declined for the tramp shipping companies (Sturmey, 1962: 182). The first threat to profitability arose from increased competition, which affected both the tramp and liner sectors. Freight rates were more stable in the liner sector during the period 1948 to 1956, due to the conference system, as can be seen in table 10.8. Even here, however, there were pressures from national lines operated by governments, pressing for the conferences to keep freight rates down for balance of payments reasons (Turner, 1969: 288). In the tramp sector, where we have data on British freight rates until 1969, freight rates turned down seriously after 1956, never to regain this peak level, even in nominal terms. Freight rates are presented in table 10.8 along with the GDP deflator, and show tramp rates more than halving in real terms between 1948 and 1969. Henceforth, it would be extremely difficult for British shipping companies to obtain sufficient revenue to cover the high wage costs of British crews. A second problem was that, throughout the 1950s, demand for shipping services was moving strongly in favour of tanker business, which the British shippers were reluctant to embrace (Sturmey, 1962: 161–9). Third, from the early 1960s there was a move towards containerisation within the dry cargo business, with dramatic changes in operating methods.

The growth of the tanker trade and containerisation implied increases in both scale and standardisation, and may be expected to have run into difficulties in a British context, where the industrialisation of services generally created organisational problems. As Turner (1969: 290) notes, P&O had been run on a highly decentralised basis, with the original companies retaining a great deal of independence after merging. After building up the tanker business and investing in a container joint venture with Ocean and with British and Commonwealth, P&O were forced to address the issue of organisation after a fiercely contested takeover bid from the building and property development company Bovis in 1968 (Howarth and Howarth, 1986: 186–90). Although the Bovis bid was fought off, P&O were forced to implement a reorganisation plan drawn up by McKinsey, and adopted a multi-divisional structure in classic Chandlerian style (Channon, 1978: 136–7; Chandler, 1977). Following a strategy of diversification, Ocean also adopted a multi-divisional form in 1972 with the help of the Boston Consulting Group (Channon, 1978: 138–9; Falkus, 1990: 354). This represented a dramatic change of managerial strategy for Ocean, where hierarchical structures had previously been very flat, with the eleven managing directors sharing a common management room, or quarterdeck, and the senior director merely *primus inter pares* (Turner, 1969: 293). Although P&O and Ocean diversified, they remained committed to shipping. British and Commonwealth, on the other hand, were content to concentrate on other interests, such as airlines, insurance broking, hotels and vehicle component manufacturing. Accordingly, British and Commonwealth adopted a holding company structure (Channon, 1978: 139).

Despite the declining importance of the Commonwealth, the companies which were based on the old imperial routes (P&O to India and the Far East, Ocean to Australia, and British and Commonwealth to South Africa) survived better than companies such as Cunard, which depended on the North Atlantic trade (Turner, 1969: 283). Cunard's chief problem was that passenger traffic was responsible for more than a half of its revenue in 1956, just as jet travel was about to transfer most of the North Atlantic passenger business from ships to aircraft (Turner, 1969: 290). After making substantial losses between 1961 and 1967, Cunard was taken over by Trafalgar House Investments in 1968 (Channon, 1978: 136).

To what extent was the decline of British shipping inevitable? Sturmey (1962) considers (1) differences in crew costs, (2) unfair overseas competition based on subsidies and discrimination and (3) other exogenous factors, including the declining relative importance of Britain in world trade, the effects of war, the burden of taxation and government restrictions. Although he accepts that these factors may have played some role, he considers the most important constraints on the growth of British shipping to have been internal, arising from 'the attitudes of shipowners to changing circumstances' (394). In particular, he cites six examples of entrepreneurial failure amongst British shipowners in the early post-war period: (1) the neglect of tankers; (2) the slow replacement of steam tonnage by diesel; (3) the neglect of speed as a competitive factor; (4) the continued ordering of ships from high-cost British shipyards; (5) the neglect of ship standardisation; and (6) a tendency for shipowners to blame others.

Sturmey explains this alleged entrepreneurial failure by the structure of the industry. With tramps accounting for only 15.5% of total tonnage in 1960, the industry was dominated by the large shipping lines (50). Since the conference system made new entry into the liner sector very difficult, the established lines were heavily shielded from competitive pressures in the short run (381). However, since freight rates were set to protect the weaker members, the long-run competitive position of the conferences was undermined (Deakin, 1973: 207). Nevertheless, writing before the general collapse of shipping in the industrialised countries, it seems likely that Sturmey was too critical of the British shipowners. For example, when playing down the importance of cost differences, he compares British crew costs only with those of other industrialised countries (Sturmey, 1962: 314). The later *Report of the Committee of Inquiry into Shipping* (UK Board of Trade, 1970), chaired by Lord Rochdale, was much less critical. Indeed, in paragraph 1278, the committee appears to think the unthinkable and encourage British disinvestment, noting that

unless a shipping company is able in future to achieve a higher return on its capital assets than have most over the last 20 years, it would only be acting in the best interests of its shareholders if it decided to run down its investment of shipping activities.

In fact, encouraged by investment subsidies, the British shipowners had made substantial new investments in the late 1960s, and the British fleet continued to expand until 1975.[1]

Despite the dramatic collapse of the UK-registered merchant fleet during the 1980s, the decline in the UK-owned fleet and in the fleet on all British registers was far more muted, as noted in the official report *British Shipping: Challenges and Opportunities* (UK Department of Transport, 1990). The report presented figures on deadweight tonnage (dwt),

---

[1] The subsidies were designed to help British shipbuilders, but, as Hogwood (1979: 129) notes, 78% of grants paid out between 1967/68 and 1974/75 were used to buy ships built outside the United Kingdom.

Table 10.9 *UK-owned and British-registered shipping in 1989*

A. UK-owned

	Number	Thousand dwt
UK	491	4,151
Other British registers	164	8,198
Foreign registers	128	3,364
Total	783	15,713

B. British-registered

	Number	Thousand dwt
UK	537	4,485
Other British registers	623	25,855
Total	1,160	30,340

Source: UK Department of Transport (1990: 5).

which does not bear a simple relationship to gross tonnage. Whereas gross tonnage measures the volume of enclosed space, with a gross registered ton (grt) equal to 100 cubic feet, the deadweight is the weight in tons that brings a ship down from its light to its loaded draught line. As Stubbs et al. (1984: 163) note, passenger liners typically have a high gross tonnage relative to their deadweight tonnage, while the reverse is true of tankers. In 1989, when the gross tonnage of the UK-registered fleet was 6.025 million, the deadweight tonnage was 4.485 million, and, of this, 4.151 million dwt was UK-owned – as shown in table 10.9. However, the UK-owned deadweight tonnage was 15.713 million, with the bulk of the fleet that was not registered in the UK being flagged out to other British registers, primarily Crown Dependencies such as the Isle of Man and Dependent Territories such as Bermuda, Gibraltar and Hong Kong.[2] The deadweight tonnage on all British registers was higher still, at 30.34 million, of which 12.349 million was UK-owned.

One of the concerns behind the report was the perceived need, in the wake of the Gulf Crisis, to maintain a merchant fleet and a corps of highly trained officers and ratings that could be called on to serve British interests. Most of the report, however, concerned the economic contribution of shipping to the British economy, particularly through

---

[2] Hong Kong ceased to be a Dependent Territory in 1999.

the contribution to the balance of payments and through linkages to other international services provided in London (e.g. shipbroking, marine insurance, shipping finance, ship classification) and other activities in the UK economy (e.g. offshore, ports and harbours, shipbuilding and repair, equipment manufacture).

The overseas earnings of UK shipping and the contribution to the balance of payments are shown in table 10.10. In constant 1973 prices, UK shipping operators saw their real invisible exports and their contribution to the invisible trade balance peak in 1973/74. During the 1980s the invisible exports of UK shipping operators fell in current prices as well as in constant 1973 prices, despite the substantial rise in the general price level. Although invisible exports and the invisible trade balance of UK shipping operators have shown a clear negative trend in real terms, the overall balance of payments on shipping has fluctuated in a more cyclical manner. Nevertheless, there were more deficits than surpluses on shipping during the 1980s, whereas there had been more surpluses than deficits during the 1950s.

Shipping services, then, appear to conform to the product cycle model. As freight business became increasingly standardised with the growth of the tanker business and containerisation, shipping services were increasingly supplied by companies using cheap labour and flags of convenience. As trade in shipping services was liberalised, this inevitably meant a decline in the merchant fleets of the traditional maritime countries. British companies have nevertheless retained a sizeable presence in shipping, with the bulk of the UK-owned fleet now flagged out, particularly to other British registers, such as the Isle of Man and Bermuda.

10.2.3 Railways

The length of railway line open in Great Britain had remained stable between the two world wars, at approximately 20,000 miles, but during the 1950s a slow decline set in, as lines were closed in response to falling demand. Following the Beeching report of 1963, however, the pruning of the network was dramatically accelerated (British Railways Board, 1963). By the end of the 1960s the length of railway line open in Great Britain had fallen below 12,000 miles, as can be seen in table 10.11. By 1990, following further closures, it was little more than 10,000 miles. The length of railway line open also declined substantially in the United States, falling to little more than two-thirds of its 1950 level by 1990. In much of continental Europe, by contrast, the decline was much more muted. In West Germany, for example, between 1950 and 1990 the

Table 10.10 *UK shipping earnings and the balance of payments, 1952–1990 (£ million)*

A. At current prices

	UK shipping			Overseas shipping balance	Balance of payments on shipping
	Invisible exports	Invisible imports	Balance		
1952	510	295	215	81	+134
1960	562	476	86	120	−34
1968	917	745	172	137	+35
1973	1,825	1,439	386	491	−105
1979	3,187	2,173	1,014	887	+127
1985	2,452	1,745	707	1,004	−297
1990	2,858	1,567	1,291	1,302	−11

B. At constant 1973 prices

	UK shipping			Overseas shipping balance	Balance of payments on shipping
	Invisible exports	Invisible imports	Balance		
1952	1,244	720	524	198	+326
1960	1,083	917	166	231	−65
1968	1,325	1,077	248	198	+50
1973	1,825	1,439	386	491	−105
1979	1,305	890	415	363	+52
1985	604	430	174	247	−73
1990	529	290	239	241	−2

Note:
Invisible exports of UK shipping operators consist of freight services on UK visible exports and cross trades, overseas passenger revenue and time charter receipts from overseas. Invisible imports of UK operators comprise fuel and other goods purchased abroad. The balance of UK shipping operators is the difference between these invisible exports and invisible imports. The balance of overseas shipping operators is obtained as the difference between their receipts (UK invisible imports) and spending (UK invisible exports) in the United Kingdom. The receipts of overseas shipping operators are obtained from freight services on UK visible imports, UK coastal routes, UK passengers and chartering to UK residents, while their spending in the United Kingdom is on fuel and other supplies. The balance of payments on shipping is obtained as the difference between the balance of UK shipping operators and overseas shipping operators.

Source: UK Central Statistical Office (*United Kingdom Balance of Payments*, various years).

Table 10.11 *Length of railway line open, 1950–1990 (miles)*

	Great Britain	West Germany	United States
1950	19,471	22,945	223,779
1960	18,369	22,382	217,552
1970	11,799	20,512	205,782
1980	10,964	19,572	141,679
1990	10,305	18,722	151,622

Sources: Great Britain – Mitchell (1988: 542), UK Central Statistical Office (*Annual Abstract of Statistics*, various years); West Germany – Mitchell (1998a: table F1); United States – Mitchell (1998b: table F1).

length of railway line open fell only from around 23,000 miles to around 19,000 miles.

The decline of the railways largely reflected a loss of freight business with the growth of road haulage. This can be seen in table 10.12, which presents the basic railway operating statistics for Great Britain. Whereas net ton-miles of freight continued to trend downwards throughout the period, passenger-miles turned up from the late 1960s and surpassed the 1951 level by 1990. Whereas in 1951 freight had provided about two-thirds of total revenue, this had fallen to about one-third by 1990. Aggregating the passenger-miles and freight ton-miles using revenue weights yields the railway output series in table 10.13. This shows a negative trend in railway output throughout the period after World War II. Since labour and capital inputs also declined throughout the period, labour productivity and TFP both showed positive growth on the railways, but at a slower rate than in transport and communications as a whole, as can be seen by comparing table 10.13 with table 10.4. Comparing table 10.13 with table 10.2, however, note that productivity growth on the railways was faster than in the economy as a whole during the 1980s. The international comparisons in table 10.1 show the productivity performance of Britain's shrinking railway system in another light. Although the labour productivity gap with the United States remained large, it did decline substantially. The remaining gap may be seen as reflecting geographical differences, with the much larger distances in the United States meaning that terminal handling has been proportionally less important. Labour productivity on Britain's railways has been more or less on a par with Germany's railways during the post-war period.

Table 10.12 *Railway operating statistics, Great Britain, 1951–1990*

A. Passengers

	Passenger journeys (millions)	Passenger-miles (millions)	Average distance (miles)	Passenger receipts (£ million)
1951	1,001	20,793	20.7	140.1
1960	1,037	21,547	20.7	206.7
1968	831	17,835	21.5	243.2
1973	728	18,517	25.4	371.1
1979	748	19,884	26.6	930.5
1985	697	18,456	26.5	1,286.2
1990	779	21,190	27.2	2,044.9

B. Freight

	Freight loaded (million tons)	Net ton-miles (millions)	Average distance (miles)	Freight receipts (£ million)
1951	285	22,902	80	227.9
1960	248	18,650	75	261.4
1968	207	14,693	71	204.3
1973	195	15,603	80	198.5
1979	168	12,166	72	432.1
1985	121	9,418	78	596.2
1990	139	9,663	70	793.5

Sources: Mitchell (1988: 549), UK Central Statistical Office (*Annual Abstract of Statistics*, various years).

Despite this mixed productivity performance, the British railway system has been heavily criticised.[3] Critics of the performance of British Railways, such as Aldcroft (1968c) and Ashworth (1991), can point to the declining share of the railways in passenger and freight transport and the substantial financial losses incurred by the organisation. The figures on freight transport in table 10.14 show a particularly sharp drop in the share of freight moved by rail, mirrored by an increase in the share moved by road. In passenger transport, the share of passenger-miles accounted for by railways also declined substantially, although the biggest decline was in the share accounted for by public service road vehicles (i.e. buses and coaches). Table 10.15 presents the financial

---

[3] Foreman-Peck and Millward (1994: 300) make a similar point with regard to the nationalised fuel and transport sector as a whole.

Table 10.13 *Productivity trends on British railways, 1951–1990*

A. Indices of output, inputs and productivity (1973 = 100)

	Output	Labour	Capital	Labour productivity	TFP
1951	132.2	198.5	107.2	66.6	77.7
1960	118.9	171.2	107.2	69.5	78.1
1968	95.6	121.2	103.9	78.9	82.0
1973	100.0	100.0	100.0	100.0	100.0
1979	97.1	91.9	95.5	105.7	104.6
1985	84.7	73.7	87.0	114.9	110.3
1990	94.0	65.7	85.6	143.1	133.9

B. Growth rates of output, inputs and productivity (% per annum)

	1951–1973	1973–1979	1979–1990	1951–1990
Output	−1.3	−0.5	−0.3	−0.9
Labour	−3.1	−1.4	−3.1	−2.6
Capital	−0.3	−0.8	−0.9	−0.6
Labour productivity	1.8	0.9	2.8	1.9
TFP	1.1	0.7	2.2	1.4

Sources: Output – derived from the UK Central Statistical Office (*Annual Abstract of Statistics*, various years); labour – UK Department of Employment (1978, *British Labour Statistics Yearbook*, various years); capital – UK Central Statistical Office (*National Income and Expenditure*, various years).

results of British Railways on the basis used by the British Railways Board, in both current prices and constant 1973 prices. Based on these accounts, which informed public opinion at the time, British Railways earned a small financial surplus in the early post-war period before moving into deficit from the mid-1950s. With the deficit growing in nominal terms (although not in real terms) and remaining a permanent feature, a system of passenger support grants was introduced after 1968, with grants more or less offsetting the annual losses. As Gourvish (1986: 95–6) notes, however, these accounts do not give a true reflection of the plight of British Railways, due to the unsatisfactory treatment of capital costs. Putting depreciation and amortisation charges on a replacement cost basis rather than a historic cost basis, and correcting interest charges for the overvaluation of assets at the time of nationalisation, Gourvish (1986: 585) finds that in only a single year, 1952, was there a small surplus. Even then, once allowance is made for drawings on the abnormal maintenance fund set up to compensate for the disinvestment of the war years, this surplus disappears (96).

Table 10.14 *Passenger and freight transport by mode (%)*

A. Passenger-miles

	Public road	Private road	Rail	Air
1952	43.1	36.0	20.8	0.1
1960	27.7	56.4	15.6	0.3
1968	15.5	75.1	8.9	0.5
1973	11.5	80.3	7.7	0.5
1979	9.3	82.7	7.4	0.6
1985	9.0	83.7	6.6	0.7
1990	6.7	86.7	5.9	0.7

B. Freight ton-miles

	Road	Rail	Water	Pipeline
1953	37.7	43.7	18.4	0.2
1960	51.3	31.9	16.5	0.3
1968	60.8	18.5	19.0	1.7
1973	63.9	18.0	14.7	3.4
1979	64.1	12.5	17.0	6.4
1985	65.4	9.7	17.8	7.1
1990	71.6	8.3	14.3	5.8

Note:
A major change occurred in the water freight statistics from 1972, although statistics were also provided on the old basis until 1981. The figures on the new basis have been spliced to the old series at 1981.

Sources: Derived from UK Central Statistical Office (*Annual Abstract of Statistics*, various years), UK Department of Transport (*Transport Statistics Great Britain*, various years, *Transport Trends*, various years).

Some decline in the market share of the railways was inevitable, given the competition from road transport, but the decline was sharper in Britain than in other countries. One problem was the slow pace at which equipment and infrastructure was modernised in Britain, due to inadequate investment. This can be linked in turn to the financial losses and the reluctance of the government to fund improvements, coupled with the opposition of unions to the reduction in manning levels needed to make the investment pay. During the early post-war period it was hoped that modernisation would reverse the decline in demand, eliminate the losses and hence obviate the need for line closures. If higher prices were needed to finance the investment, however, it is difficult to see how the decline in demand could have been reversed (Aldcroft, 1968c: 144–5). A Modernisation Plan was published in 1955, which

Table 10.15 *Financial results of British Railways*

A. Current prices (£ million)

	Total working receipts	Total working expenses	Surplus/loss	Passenger grant support
1951	372.7	349.9	22.8	
1960	476.7	546.2	−69.5	
1968	456.5	547.1	−90.6	
1973	581.5	687.1	−105.6	91.4
1979	1,400.6	1,888.9	−488.3	522.5
1985/86	2,032.9	2,880.4	−847.5	895.9
1990/91	3,076.9	3,819.2	−742.3	699.9

B. Constant prices (£ million 1973)

	Total working receipts	Total working expenses	Surplus/loss	Passenger grant support
1951	986.0	925.7	60.3	
1960	918.5	1,052.4	−133.9	
1968	659.7	790.6	−130.9	
1973	581.5	687.1	−105.6	91.4
1979	573.5	773.5	−200.0	214.0
1985/86	497.2	704.4	−207.2	219.1
1990/91	560.6	695.8	−135.2	127.5

Note:
Current price figures converted to constant 1973 prices using GDP deflator from the UK Central Statistical Office (*National Income and Expenditure*, various years). Accounts presented on a financial year basis from 1985/86.

Sources: Mitchell (1988: 549), UK Central Statistical Office (*Annual Abstract of Statistics*, various years), UK Department of Transport (*Transport Statistics Great Britain*, various years).

envisaged investment of £1.24 billion over fifteen years (Gourvish, 1986: 256). Investment increased rapidly, over 60% of it on rolling stock, as the railways finally moved from the steam age to the diesel and electric age (Gourvish, 1986: 274–5). When this investment had failed to reverse the fortunes of the railways by the early 1960s, however, the equilibrium size of the network was reconsidered and Dr Richard Beeching was brought in from ICI to effect radical surgery on Britain's railways. His proposals, outlined in the report *The Reshaping of British Railways* (British Railways Board, 1963), envisaged the closure of more than 2,000 stations and 5,000 miles of track to bring the railway network down to a more sustainable size.

The return of a Labour government in 1964 brought a renewal of opposition to line closures, and a recognition of the need for subsidies to sustain the railways at a socially acceptable level of provision (Gwilliam, 1988: 267). Nevertheless, the 'Beeching axe' continued to fall, since the government was offering only short-term subsidies rather than providing the means for long-term survival (Gourvish, 1986: 452). By the late 1960s Beeching's cuts had largely been implemented, but the losses remained. A shortage of funds for investment remained a severe constraint during the 1970s, as governments discouraged fare increases as part of their anti-inflation strategy (Ashworth, 1991: 122–3; Gourvish, 1986: 474–86). Investment continued to suffer during the 1980s as Conservative governments used cash control to achieve short-term financial targets (Welsby and Nichols, 1999: 72). Nor does the privatisation of the mid-1990s appear to have made it easier to finance the modernisation of the railways and make up for the years of low investment during the period of public ownership (Welsby and Nichols, 1999: 72–5).

Investment was also held back by union militancy, which made it difficult to reap the benefits of modernisation (Pryke, 1981: 82–7). There was particularly strong opposition to any changes that encroached upon the autonomy of the footplate staff, most of whom belonged to the militant Associated Society of Locomotive Engineers and Firemen (ASLEF) and continued to be seen as an elite (Gourvish, 1986: 121). With the unions reluctant to dispense with firemen or guards, the benefits of moving from steam to diesel or electric power and the fitting of air brakes to wagons were correspondingly reduced (Pryke, 1981: 82–3).

Lack of investment clearly played a part in British Rail's difficulties. However, there were also problems arising from the institutional structures. For most of the post-war period Britain's railways were run on a highly centralised basis, which rarely worked well in Britain. Despite the fact that the institutional structures were frequently changed, this did little more than undermine morale and create a sense of uncertainty, until decentralisation was introduced on a sectoral basis in 1982, preparing the way for privatisation in the 1990s. At the time of nationalisation the railways had been seen as one part of an integrated inland transport system, with road haulage also being taken into public ownership. A British Transport Commission (BTC) was established, presiding over five executives, dealing with the railways; road haulage; London transport; hotels; and docks and inland waterways (Ashworth, 1991: 23). As Turner (1969: 183) puts it, 'an organisation employing 649,000 people had no separate management of its own, a patently absurd state of affairs'.

Following the election of a Conservative government in 1951 the idea of an integrated transport strategy was abandoned, and the 1953 Transport Act envisaged the BTC as providing railway services for the country as a whole and coordinated passenger services only in the London area (Channon, 1978: 214). The 1953 Act decreased the amount of coordination with other modes of transport, particularly as road haulage was denationalised, but it did not effectively decentralise management. Although the Railway Executive was abolished a number of its personnel were appointed to the BTC, so that power was retained in the centre rather than devolved to the area boards (Gourvish, 1986: 148, 156). In 1962, when the BTC was abolished, and the railways finally attained managerial independence under the British Railways Board (BRB), central control over the newly established regional boards was tighter than BTC control over the old area boards (Gourvish, 1986: 341).

The return of a Labour government in 1964 led to a second strategy for the integration of transport policy, resulting in the Transport Act of 1968 (Channon, 1978: 219). From the railway point of view, the key developments were a capital write-down and the distinction between 'commercial' and 'social' passenger services, with the latter being subsidised by grant aid (Gourvish, 1986: 365). A further round of organisational change in 1970 saw the BRB taking a largely non-executive role, spending more time on corporate planning and longer-term policy issues (Channon, 1978: 220). The 1974 Transport Act used European Commission regulations to underpin the idea of a social railway supported by a general grant rather than subsidies for specific services (Gwilliam, 1988: 268).

The most radical institutional change under public ownership, however, came in 1982 with the introduction of a more decentralised system of management, but on a sectoral rather than a regional basis. The railway business was broken into five major sectors (freight; parcels; InterCity passenger; provincial passenger; and London and South East), with all assets allocated to individual sectors (Gwilliam, 1988: 269). Where more than one sector used an asset, the secondary user was charged by the primary user, and each sector was set separate financial targets. As Joy (1998: 37) notes, this led to a dramatic improvement in locomotive utilisation rates. It also laid the foundations for future privatisation, by showing that the railways could be managed in small pieces (Joy, 1998: 38).

Privatisation during the mid-1990s led to a further major reorganisation of the railways in Britain. Rather than simply selling off the separate businesses established under the 1982 sectorisation, however, a more fragmented structure was chosen, with many train operating companies (TOCs) leasing rolling stock from rolling stock companies (ROSCOs) and track time from Railtrack, and with a rail regulator to oversee the system as a whole. Fears that the additional transactions costs of a more fragmented structure have not been offset by the introduction of genuine competition appear to have been borne out in practice (Welsby and Nichols, 1999: 70–2).

10.2.4 Road transport

A key factor behind the decline of the railways after World War II was the growth of road transport. On the passenger side, whereas during the inter-war period much of the growth of road traffic occurred on trams, buses and coaches, after World War II passenger-miles travelled on public service vehicles declined sharply. The sharpest growth of road passenger traffic was in private cars, which increased their share of passenger-miles from 36.0% in 1952 to 86.7% in 1990, as can be seen in table 10.14. Behind this growth of private motoring lay a dramatic rise in motor vehicle ownership, which is charted in table 10.16. Whereas in 1950 there was still a huge gulf in the density of car ownership between Europe and the United States, by 1990 the gap was much smaller. Since the official figures on the output of the road transport sector exclude the services of private cars, care must be taken in their interpretation. To the extent that individuals substituted private passenger journeys for journeys on public passenger transport, the official figures will understate the growth of transport services (Ashworth, 1960: 339). On the freight side, the growing share of road haulage in ton-miles mirrored the decline in the share of the railways (table 10.14).

As the volume of road traffic increased, pressure on the road network increased. Although governments have at times attempted to encourage greater use of the railways as part of an integrated transport policy, it is difficult to discern from the road mileage data in table 10.17 anything other than a clear policy of 'predict and provide' in the area of road provision. Whereas the total road mileage had remained fairly stable around 180,000 miles between the wars, the post-war period saw an expansion at an annual rate of 0.5%. Just as importantly, the network of trunk roads has been augmented since 1959 by an expanding motorway system.

The output of the public passenger transport sector since World War II shows a strong downward trend in table 10.18, with private road journeys displacing public passenger travel. Private passenger road-miles had already overtaken public passenger road-miles by the mid-1950s

Table 10.16 *Motor vehicles per 1,000 inhabitants, 1950–1990*

	Passenger cars			Commercial vehicles		
	United Kingdom	Germany	Unites States	United Kingdom	Germany	Unites States
1950	46.2	12.6	260.7	20.9	12.0	57.8
1960	107.5	84.2	340.7	29.1	14.0	67.6
1970	211.8	241.9	435.9	31.6	20.7	93.4
1980	275.9	377.4	534.7	34.2	26.3	150.1
1990	363.5	485.4	574.3	50.8	31.5	180.4

Sources: Society of Motor Manufacturers and Traders (various years), United Nations (*Statistical Yearbook*, various years).

Table 10.17 *Mileage of roads in Great Britain, 1950–1990*

	Motorways	Trunk roads	Other roads	Total
1950		8,176	175,645	183,821
1960	95	8,343	185,742	194,180
1970	657	8,352	191,373	200,382
1980	1,588	7,701	201,759	211,048
1990	1,908	7,876	212,699	222,483

Sources: Mitchell (1988: 555–6), UK Department of Transport (*Transport Statistics Great Britain*, various years).

Table 10.18 *Output of the British road transport sector, 1951–1990*

	Public passenger transport (billion passenger-miles)	Domestic freight transport (billion ton-miles)
1951	50.9	19.0
1960	43.9	30.1
1968	36.7	48.3
1973	32.9	55.3
1979	28.6	62.6
1985	30.4	63.2
1990	28.6	83.4

Sources: UK Central Statistical Office (*Annual Abstract of Statistics*, various years), UK Department of Transport (*Transport Statistics Great Britain*, various years, *Transport Trends*, various years), Munby and Watson (1978: table B7).

Table 10.19 *Productivity trends in the British road transport sector, 1951–1990*

A. Indices of output, inputs and productivity (1973 = 100)

	Output	Labour	Capital	Labour productivity	TFP
1951	68.1	114.7	68.2	59.4	67.6
1960	76.6	104.4	68.2	73.4	81.6
1968	94.1	110.1	81.8	85.5	92.1
1973	100.0	100.0	100.0	100.0	100.0
1979	105.9	93.9	121.6	112.8	105.7
1985	108.2	83.6	132.4	129.4	115.4
1990	132.9	86.1	132.4	154.4	138.6

B. Growth rates of output, inputs and productivity (% per annum)

	1951–1973	1973–1979	1979–1990	1951–1990
Output	1.8	1.0	2.1	1.7
Labour	−0.6	−1.0	−0.8	−0.7
Capital	1.7	3.3	0.8	1.7
Labour productivity	2.4	2.0	2.9	2.4
TFP	1.8	1.0	2.5	1.8

Sources: Output – derived from table 10.18; Labour – UK Department of Employment (1978, *British Labour Statistics Yearbook*, various years), UK Central Statistical Office (*Annual Abstract of Statistics*, various years); capital – UK Central Statistical Office (*National Income and Expenditure*, various years).

and continued to increase their dominance into the 1990s, as can be seen in table 10.14. Returning to table 10.18, note that, while public passenger transport saw a decline in output, domestic road freight business grew quite rapidly, at 4.9% per annum between 1951 and 1973, but slowing to 2.4% per annum after 1973. Combining the freight and public passenger data from table 10.18 using revenue weights yields the road transport sector output series in table 10.19. Given the importance of public passenger transport in the early period and the slower growth of road freight traffic after 1973, the growth of the road transport sector as a whole was relatively modest at 1.7% per annum over the period as a whole. Combined with a small decline in employment and a moderate growth of the capital stock, this modest growth of output in road transport resulted in labour productivity growth and TFP growth slightly below the average for transport and communications (table 10.4) but slightly above average for the economy as a whole (table 10.2). Putting the productivity performance of road transport in international perspective, the estimates of comparative labour productivity levels available in table 10.1 suggest that, by the late 1960s, Britain lagged behind both Germany and the United States. Although the productivity gap was smaller than in most other parts of the economy in the US/UK case, it was larger than in many other parts of the economy in the Germany/UK case.

As noted in the section on the railways, the 1947 Transport Act aimed to create an integrated transport system covering the railways, road haulage, buses and inland waterways, under the control of the British Transport Commission (Channon, 1978: 212). Focusing first on road haulage, the Road and Rail Traffic Act of 1933 had introduced a licensing system, distinguishing between A licences (required by general hauliers), B licences (required by carriers of their own goods who used spare capacity to carry other goods for payment) and C licences (required by carriers only of their own goods). Under the 1947 Transport Act, only holders of A and B licences operating over distances of more than twenty-five miles were nationalised, with holders of C licences carrying on more or less as before. By 1951 the BTC controlled 3,766 road undertakings, of which 3,289 had been acquired through compulsory purchase (Ashworth, 1991: 24).

The Conservative government elected in 1951 abandoned the idea of an integrated transport policy and set about returning the nationalised road haulage assets to the private sector. The 1953 Transport Act set up a disposal board to sell off the A- and B-licensed vehicles that had been acquired by the BTC (Barker and Gerhold, 1993: 69). By 1956, when the disposal board was wound up, about 9,000 of the 35,000 vehicles offered for sale remained unsold, and were vested in the newly created, publicly owned British Road Services (BRS) (Channon, 1978: 214). The industry continued to be highly regulated, however, with a reinstatement of the licensing system introduced by the 1933 Act. As Bayliss (1998: 119) notes, there was still a belief in the 1950s that the presence of a large number of firms with free entry was likely to destabilise the market rather than make it work efficiently, despite the analysis of Walters and Sharp (1953) showing that, prior to the 1933 Act, levels of bankruptcy had been lower in road haulage than in many other parts of the economy.

In 1962 the BTC was abolished and the commission's public road haulage interests passed to the newly created Transport Holding Company (THC), along with the commission's interests in road passenger transport, hotels and Thomas Cook, the travel agency (Channon, 1978: 217). The THC was the most successful British road haulage company, obtaining by 1968 a 7% share of the British market with a fleet of 27,000 vehicles, and expanding into continental Europe (Channon, 1978: 217). However, with the return of an integrated transport strategy under the 1968 Transport Act, the National Freight Corporation (NFC) was established, combining the road haulage interests of the THC with the road transport interests of British Rail and taking a controlling interest in Freightliners, the containerised rail freight system (Channon, 1978: 219). Whereas the Conservatives had retained the licensing system when denationalising road transport in 1953, Labour combined their policy of integration under the 1968 Transport Act with an important measure of deregulation (Bayliss, 1998: 123). The licensing system had been used to restrict entry, with existing hauliers opposing the granting of new A and B licences, and had done little to promote safety. The 1968 Transport Act removed most restrictions on capacity, apart from very large vehicles over sixteen tons, and focused on measures to improve safety (UK Department of Transport, 1978).

A study by Bayliss (1973) argues that, following deregulation, there was no evidence to suggest a large number of new entrants, a large number of bankruptcies or an increase of capacity out of line with demand. Furthermore, the level of profit margins was the same in 1971 as in 1965, costs and charges had risen in line with the general price level, and there was no evidence of a change in investment behaviour as a result of fears about the future. Similarly, the committee of inquiry established to investigate a number of exits from the industry after the oil crisis also failed to find any significant negative effects of deregulation (UK Department of Transport, 1978). Nevertheless, it is equally clear from the labour productivity data on the road haulage sector in table 10.20 that deregulation was not followed by any dramatic increase in productivity growth.

Turning to road passenger transport, apart from London Transport there was no compulsory nationalisation. However, the shareholdings of the railway companies in various bus operators, such as British Electric Traction, Scottish Motor Traction and Thomas Tilling, were retained by the BTC, and a small number of other bus companies were subsequently acquired by agreement (Channon, 1978: 212). By 1949 the road passenger transport assets of the BTC, which were initially looked after by the Road Haulage Executive, were significant enough to be granted their own Road Passenger Transport Executive (Ashworth, 1991: 24).

The idea of an integrated transport policy was abandoned under the Conservatives, and the executive structure of the BTC was abolished in 1953 (Channon, 1978: 214). However, whereas the bulk of the road haulage interests of the BTC were returned to the private sector, the road passenger interests remained a part of the BTC. When the BTC

Table 10.20 *Labour productivity in the British road transport sector, 1951–1990 (1973 = 100)*

	Public passenger transport	Domestic freight transport
1951	105.7	40.6
1960	106.2	64.2
1968	91.9	87.7
1973	100.0	100.0
1979	89.7	124.1
1985	114.8	132.8
1990	120.4	155.6

Sources: Derived from output data of table 10.18 and labour data underlying table 10.19.

was finally abolished in 1962, its road passenger transport interests passed to the Transport Holding Company (Channon, 1978: 215). The THC was the dominant provider on rural bus routes, and when British Electric Traction was brought under full public ownership in 1968, the THC had 42% of bus passenger service miles and 32% of bus passenger journeys (Channon, 1978: 218).

From 1968, as part of a return to an integrated transport policy, rural bus services were centralised under the National Bus Company (NBC), while passenger transport authorities (PTAs) were established in the major conurbations to coordinate bus and rail services (Channon, 1978: 219–20). The 1968 Transport Act also introduced a distinction on bus routes, as on the railways, between 'commercial' and 'social' services, with the latter eligible for operating subsidies (Channon, 1978: 222).

The next major institutional change came with the 1980 Transport Act, which aimed to introduce more competition in road passenger transport. Since the 1930 Road Traffic Act a prospective new entrant had been required to demonstrate a need for its service, which was usually opposed by existing operators. The 1980 Act required the Traffic Commissioners to grant a licence unless it was against the public interest (UK House of Commons, Transport Committee, 1995/96, para. 4). In express coaching, over distances of more than thirty miles, however, the 1980 Act went further and removed all regulations other than those relating to competence and safety (Davis, 1986). Coaching was dominated in 1980 by National Express, an operating division of the publicly owned NBC, and its Scottish counterpart, the Scottish Bus Group. Although National Express retained its dominant position, partly as a result of its privileged access to the major coach stations, fares fell sharply in real terms after deregulation (Davis, 1986: 158–60).

The 1980 Transport Act failed to have much of an impact on local bus services, however, as large operators were still in a position to object to the granting of new licences and to use their financial strength to defeat competition as it emerged. Since over 90% of local bus service operations were provided by the public sector, and since private sector costs were 30 to 40% lower than public sector costs, the government was keen to see effective competition emerge in this sector (UK House of Commons, Transport Committee, 1995/96, paras. 5, 7). The 1985 Transport Act extended the deregulation of express coaching to local bus services and led to the break-up of the NBC and the establishment of an arm's-length relationship between local authorities and local bus services (UK House of Commons, Transport Committee, 1995/96, paras. 11–13). Although the NBC was initially split into seventy-two companies, there was a period of consolidation, during which there were many allegations of predatory pricing and other anti-competitive practices (para. 21). As in express coaching, however, despite the continued high level of concentration, fares fell in real terms. Unfortunately, however, this did not attract more people to use the buses (para. 89). The positive effect of deregulation on labour productivity performance in the bus and coach sector is apparent in table 10.20, with labour productivity falling in public passenger road transport until the 1980s and rising thereafter.

While shipping and the railways have been in decline since World War II, road transport has expanded rapidly. On the freight side, road haulage has taken over from the railways as the main mode of transport. On the passenger side, however, although there has been a dramatic increase in passenger-miles travelled on the roads, most of these miles have been travelled in private cars and are not included as output in the national accounts. Buses have seen an even more severe decline than the railways. On a national accounting basis, then, output and productivity in the road transport sector have not grown as rapidly as might have been expected. Might performance have been better if the sector had been less regulated and subject to less frequent institutional changes? Productivity improvements and cost savings in express coaching and on the buses during the 1980s suggest that deregulation has been beneficial, although the picture is less clear in the road haulage sector, where there were no dramatic cost reductions or productivity improvements after the 1968 deregulation.

10.2.5 Air transport

The most rapidly growing part of the transport sector since World War II has been air transport. Figures on passenger-miles and freight short-ton-miles are shown in table 10.21. In addition to the strong

Table 10.21 *Traffic on UK airlines, 1951–1990*

	Million pasenger-miles		Million freight short-ton-miles
	Scheduled	Unscheduled	
1951	1,065		48.4
1960	3,959		112.7
1968	8,758	2,290	336.5
1973	16,272	7,763	621.3
1979	29,259	9,272	855.1
1985	31,963	15,533	1,209.6
1990	49,451	38,943	1,751.7

Source: UK Central Statistical Office (*Annual Abstract of Statistics,* various years).

growth of scheduled passenger business, there has been a dramatic increase in unscheduled passenger business since the 1960s, with the growth of package holidays. Freight business has also grown rapidly. Putting together the data on passenger and freight business from table 10.21 yields the series for output of the British air transport sector in table 10.22. Although labour and capital inputs have grown quite rapidly during the post-war period, there has also been rapid growth in both labour productivity and TFP. The period from 1951 to 1973 was the most impressive, but output and productivity growth have remained rapid since 1973. Britain has also fared relatively well in international comparisons of productivity in air transport. As can be seen in table 10.1, in the late 1960s labour productivity was only 13% higher in Germany and just over 50% higher in the United States.

Although there have been fluctuations in the share of traffic between the United Kingdom and abroad accounted for by British-registered aircraft, the average has been about 60% of flights and passengers since the 1950s, as can be seen in table 10.23. Turning to the contribution of UK-registered airlines to the balance of payments, in table 10.24, their invisible exports and contribution to the invisible trade balance have grown in real terms throughout the period since 1962, when detailed figures first became available. Since the invisible surplus of UK registered airlines exceeded the invisible deficit with overseas airlines between the early 1950s and the mid-1980s, civil aviation made a positive contribution to the current account of the balance of payments during this period. Since 1985, however, the balance of payments has moved into deficit on civil aviation. This largely reflects the fact that, while foreign airlines have attracted more UK passengers and hence contributed to invisible imports, the most rapid growth of UK civil aviation has been

Table 10.22 *Productivity trends in the British air transport sector, 1951–1990*

A. Indices of output, inputs and productivity (1973 = 100)

	Output	Labour	Capital	Labour productivity	TFP
1951	6.0	38.1	12.1	15.7	21.0
1960	20.2	57.1	60.6	35.4	34.8
1968	47.6	81.0	81.8	58.8	58.6
1973	100.0	100.0	100.0	100.0	100.0
1979	155.7	116.7	118.2	133.4	133.0
1985	197.0	107.1	99.0	183.9	188.2
1990	350.4	159.5	73.2	219.7	266.9

B. Growth rates of output, inputs and productivity (% per annum)

	1951–1973	1973–1979	1979–1990	1951–1990
Output	12.8	7.4	7.4	10.4
Labour	4.4	2.6	2.9	3.7
Capital	9.6	2.8	−4.4	4.6
Labour productivity	8.4	4.8	4.5	6.7
TFP	7.1	4.8	6.3	6.5

Sources: Output – derived from table 10.21; labour – UK Department of Employment (1978, *British Labour Statistics Yearbook*, various years), UK Central Statistical Office (*Annual Abstract of Statistics*, various years); capital – UK Central Statistical Office (*National Income and Expenditure*, various years).

Table 10.23 *Aircraft flights and passengers carried between the United Kingdom and abroad, 1951–1990*

	Flights			Passengers carried		
	British aircraft (thousand)	Foreign aircraft (thousand)	Percent British	British aircraft (thousand)	Foreign aircraft (thousand)	Percent British
1951	47.0	48.1	49.4	706.3	880.9	44.5
1960	146.7	78.4	65.2	3,459.2	2,597.7	57.1
1968	176.6	140.7	55.7	9,072.0	6,813.9	57.1
1973	252.8	168.5	60.0	19,160.2	11,905.6	61.7
1979	294.6	185.0	61.4	23,632.5	17,971.3	56.8
1985	367.0	212.3	63.4	30,383.3	22,479.4	57.5
1990	478.9	340.3	58.5	44,995.9	32,412.3	58.1

Source: UK Central Statistical Office (*Annual Abstract of Statistics*, various years).

Table 10.24 *UK civil aviation earnings and the balance of payments, 1952–1990 (£ million)*

A. At current prices

	UK airlines				Balance of payments on civil aviation
	Invisible exports	Invisible imports	Balance	Overseas airlines balance	
1952					0
1962	94	58	36	12	+24
1968	178	103	75	46	+29
1973	358	210	148	83	+65
1979	1,114	773	341	53	+288
1985	2,048	1,399	649	448	+201
1990	3,124	1,885	1,239	1,650	−411

B. At constant 1973 prices

	UK airlines				Balance of payments on civil avaition
	Invisible exports	Invisible imports	Balance	Overseas airlines balance	
1952					0
1962	168	104	64	21	+43
1968	257	149	108	66	+42
1973	358	210	148	83	+65
1979	456	316	140	22	+118
1985	505	345	160	110	+50
1990	579	349	230	306	−76

Note:
Invisible exports of UK airlines comprise the carriage of overseas passengers to, from or outside the United Kingdom, the carriage of UK visible exports and cross-trades, and charter receipts from overseas. Invisible imports of UK airlines consist of expenditure abroad on fuel, airport charges, crews' expenses and charter payments abroad. The balance of UK airlines is the difference between these invisible exports and invisible imports. The balance of overseas airlines is obtained as the difference between their receipts (UK invisible imports) and spending (UK invisible exports) in the United Kingdom. The receipts of overseas airlines are obtained from the carriage of UK passengers to or from the United Kingdom, UK visible imports, and chartering to UK residents, while their spending in the United Kingdom is on airport charges, fuel and other supplies. The balance of payments on civil aviation is obtained as the difference between the balance of UK airlines and overseas airlines.

Source: UK Central Statistical Office (*United Kingdom Balance of Payments*, various years).

in the non-scheduled business, ferrying UK passengers on package holidays, which does not contribute to invisible exports.

By and large, then, civil aviation should be seen as a success story in post-war Britain. Although for much of the period the scheduled passenger business was dominated by public corporations, this did not have the negative effects on Britain's comparative performance seen in many other sectors. There are a number of reasons for this. First, international air travel is a highly regulated business, with the 1944 Chicago Convention confirming national sovereignty over airspace, so that countries have had to bargain over the use of each other's airspace and landing rights at airports (Channon, 1978: 203). Publicly owned national airlines were thus quite normal in civil aviation. Second, British Airways, the publicly owned scheduled airline, was privatised during the 1980s and saw a substantial improvement in performance at a time when deregulation was leading to increased competition even on scheduled services (Green and Vogelsang, 1994). Third, however, there were also opportunities for enterprise outside the scheduled business sector, and Britain played a disproportionate role in this sector. Again, the Chicago Convention formalised the distinction between scheduled and non-scheduled business, with the former based on regular fixed price services and governed by the International Air Transport Association (IATA). Scheduled services were often subject to revenue pooling agreements as well as fixed prices (Channon, 1978: 203). Although civil aviation was dominated by scheduled services in the early post-war period, the high prices led to the rapid growth of non-scheduled services, particularly with the growing popularity of package holidays from the 1960s. And, as Johnson (1993: 213) notes, most of the European charter airlines have been based in Britain.

Civil aviation had been brought into public ownership in 1939, given the sector's lack of commercial viability during the inter-war period, and remained a public monopoly under Labour between 1945 and 1951. Although the new Conservative government encouraged the growth of private sector competition from 1952, British civil aviation continued to be dominated during the 1950s and 1960s by the publicly owned British Overseas Airways Corporation on long-haul routes and British European Airways on short-haul routes. BOAC's productivity performance was by no means poor, but the corporation did make substantial losses between 1947 and 1950 and again between 1957 and 1963 (Pryke, 1971: 157, 182). It seems likely that profitability was hit by BOAC's inheritance of the mantle of Imperial Airways, with its focus on developing and integrating air communications within the Commonwealth (Channon, 1978: 208). A further problem was the 'buy British' policy imposed on the corporation by the government, which saddled BOAC with high-cost British planes when cheaper American alternatives were available (Turner, 1969: 190; Pryke, 1971: 278). By contrast, on short-haul routes BEA avoided losses after 1953 (Pryke, 1971: 182). Although BEA also adhered to a 'buy British' policy, this imposed no real burden, since there was no marked American superiority in the size and range of planes operated by BEA (Turner, 1969: 189).

As the operating range of short-haul aircraft increased during the 1960s the separation between BEA and BOAC made less sense, and the two airlines were brought together in 1972 as British Airways (BA) (Channon, 1978: 210). Labour productivity growth slowed down during the 1970s, but remained respectable at BA, as in British civil aviation as a whole (Pryke, 1981: 137). Pryke (1981: 133–5) nevertheless argues that BA remained inefficient, particularly in comparison with the US scheduled airlines and other British non-scheduled carriers. Although the 'buy British' policy continued to affect costs, particularly through the decision to operate Concorde, profits remained substantial as a result of the limited nature of competition (Pryke, 1981: 132). On most routes BA was the only British scheduled carrier, although British Caledonian flew from Gatwick to some of the principal west European destinations, and Laker Airways launched the low-cost Skytrain on the North Atlantic route from 1977 (Pryke, 1981: 129, 136).

Although the privatisation of BA was announced in the Civil Aviation Bill of July 1979, a series of delays put back the process until January 1987. The delays were caused by (1) BA's move into losses during 1980/81 following the oil price rise at the end of 1979, coupled with strong price competition from Laker Airways on the previously lucrative North Atlantic route; (2) litigation over unfair practices following Laker's liquidation in 1984, which created uncertainty about the appropriate sale price; and (3) negotiations between Britain and the United States over transatlantic services, which affected the potential profitability of BA (Green and Vogelsang, 1994: 91–3). Green and Vogelsang (1994) nevertheless see the improvement in BA's profitability from 1982/83 as a 'turn-around anticipating privatisation'. This improvement in profitability continued after privatisation, rising to a peak in 1989/90, against a backdrop of losses and bankruptcy among many other large airlines (Green and Vogelsang, 1994: 94).

The improvement in BA's profits during the 1980s occurred during a period of deregulation following the 1980 Civil Aviation Act, which can be seen as building upon the 1977 US–UK air service agreement, which opened the way for Laker Airways, and the 1978 deregulation of domestic flights within the United States (Green and Vogelsang,

1994: 104–5). During the 1980s domestic flights were made almost completely free from regulation, apart from safety licensing, while a number of 'liberal bilateral' deals were made with other European countries, whereby any airline could fly between the two countries subject to approval from its home government and could offer any fare not vetoed by both governments (105–6). This was followed by a European Community policy of gradual multilateral liberalisation from 1987, so that by 1991 there was a commitment to allow EC airlines to compete freely in an open, integrated market (Stasinopoulos, 1993). The way in which BA gained from this process of deregulation may have owed something to the airline's dominant access to take-off and landing slots at Heathrow airport. For, as Green and Vogelsang (1994: 107) point out, Heathrow serves more international destinations than any other airport, and BA was the only airline that could serve both halves of most of the routes through the airport. However, it was not just profitability that improved, but also productivity. By 1990 BA had higher labour productivity as measured by revenue passenger-kilometres per employee than any other European airline (Johnson, 1993: 211).

The most enterprising part of British civil aviation during the 1980s, however, was in the non-scheduled business. By 1992, when BA flew 72.5 billion passenger-kilometres of scheduled business, British charter airlines flew 65.9 billion passenger-kilometres of unscheduled business. Whereas BA accounted for 27.0% of the scheduled business provided by EC airlines, British charter airlines accounted for 44.2% of the non-scheduled business (European Commission, 1994). The bigger British charter airlines, such as Britannia Airways, flew substantially more passenger-kilometres than a number of the smaller European scheduled airlines.

Air transport has expanded rapidly during the period since World War II, and in contrast to the situation in road transport, where much of the expansion took place in private vehicles, this is reflected in the national accounts. Although British productivity in the scheduled sector lagged behind the United States and Germany for much of the period, the gap was relatively small and there was a dramatic turnaround in BA's performance during the 1980s. This was combined with rapid growth in the non-scheduled sector, with Britain dominating the European charter airline sector.

10.2.6 Post and telecommunications

The volume of postal and telecommunications services is shown in tables 10.25 and 10.26. For most of the post-war period postal services

Table 10.25 *Postal services and television licences, United Kingdom, 1951–1990*

	Letters, postcards, packets, etc. (billion)	Parcels (million)	Postal orders issued (million)	TV licences (thousand)
1951	8.5	232.7	471.5	764
1960	10.2	234.7	706.7	10,470
1968	11.5	216.6	616.5	15,089
1973	10.8	194.3	361.7	17,125
1979	10.0	171.5	170.0	18,381
1985	11.4	205.5	58.6	18,716
1990	15.3	n.a.	42.3	19,645

Sources: Mitchell (1988: 565), UK Central Statistical Office (*Annual Abstract of Statistics*, various years).

Table 10.26 *Telecommunications statistics, United Kingdom, 1951–1990*

	Telegrams sent (million)	Telephone calls made		Number of telephones (thousand)
		Inland (million)	International (million)	
1951	65	3,326		5,426
1960	35	4,287		7,426
1968	31	7,947		12,009
1973	27	12,164	25	17,441
1979	17	19,122	87	24,760
1984	6	22,713	173	29,336
1984		22,686	173	19,812
1985		23,405	195	20,528
1990		28,529	358	24,797

Note:
Figures from 1984 relate to BT only. Number of telephones from 1984 refers to main lines only.

Sources: Mitchell (1988: 567), UK Central Statistical Office (*Annual Abstract of Statistics*, various years), UK Office of Telecommunications (various years).

stagnated, apart from a boost to the volume of non-parcel post during the late 1980s. As a guide to counter service activity in the Post Office, the number of postal orders issued declined sharply from the 1960s, while the number of television licences continued to increase after a

Table 10.27 *Telephones per 100 inhabitants, 1950–1990*

	United Kingdom	West Germany	France	United States	Japan
1950	10.6	5.0	5.7	28.4	2.0
1960	15.6	11.2	9.6	41.1	5.9
1970	25.0	23.3	17.3	58.7	19.2
1980	47.6	46.4	46.0	79.3	45.9
1990	44.3	47.4	49.8	54.5	44.1

Note:
1990 data refer to main lines only.

Source: United Nations (various years)

rapid surge during the 1950s and 1960s. Offsetting this stagnation in postal services was a dramatic growth in telecommunications. Although the telegraph system declined throughout the period and was eventually phased out during the 1980s, the number of telephones and the number of inland telephone calls grew at an annual rate of more than 5%, with international calls growing even more rapidly. Note that there was a structural break in the telecommunications statistics in 1984 with the privatisation of British Telecom (BT). Subsequent figures relate only to BT and the number of telephones from 1984 refers to main lines only.

The diffusion of the telephone in Britain is placed in an international perspective in table 10.27. The number of telephones in use per 100 inhabitants was substantially higher in the United States than in Europe or Japan in 1950, with Britain substantially ahead of France and Germany. By 1980 Germany, France and Japan had caught up with Britain, but a substantial gap with the United States remained. By 1990, using main lines only, the number of telephones per 100 inhabitants in Europe and Japan was quite close to the US level.

Putting together the volume indicators from the UK Central Statistical Office's *Annual Abstract of Statistics* yields the output index for communications shown in table 10.28. Communications output grew at an annual rate of 4.4% during the period as a whole, compared with output growth of 2.6% for transport and communications as a whole and 2.2% for the aggregate economy. Since employment in communications grew only slowly, labour productivity in communications grew at the rapid rate of 3.5% per annum. As the capital stock grew fairly rapidly in communications, TFP growth in communications was more modest at 2.5% per annum, but still more rapid than in the economy as a whole. Although output grew more slowly between 1973 and 1979 than before

Table 10.28 *Productivity trends in the British communications sector, 1951–1990*

A. Indices of output, inputs and productivity (1973 = 100)

	Output	Labour	Capital	Labour productivity	TFP
1951	38.7	75.6	31.0	51.2	64.0
1960	48.6	75.1	45.2	64.7	73.5
1968	76.7	92.4	69.8	83.0	89.1
1973	100.0	100.0	100.0	100.0	100.0
1979	120.1	94.8	128.4	126.7	117.4
1985	149.0	96.4	147.2	154.6	139.0
1990	202.3	101.1	180.2	200.1	173.2

B. Growth rates of output, inputs and productivity (% per annum)

	1951–1973	1973–1979	1979–1990	1951–1990
Output	4.3	3.0	4.7	4.4
Labour	1.3	−0.9	0.6	0.7
Capital	5.3	4.2	3.1	4.5
Labour productivity	3.0	3.9	4.1	3.5
TFP	2.0	2.6	3.5	2.5

Source: Output – derived from the UK Central Statistical Office (*Annual Abstract of Statistics*, various years); labour – UK Department of Employment (1978, *British Labour Statistics Yearbook*, various years), UK Central Statistical Office (*Annual Abstract of Statistics*, various years); capital – UK Central Statistical Office (*National Income and Expenditure*, various years).

or afterwards in communications, as in the aggregate economy, there was no reduction of productivity growth in communications. Table 10.1 provides some figures on comparative labour productivity in communications. For the US/UK case, the labour productivity gap widened substantially during the 1950s and 1960s before narrowing again during the 1970s and 1980s. For the Germany/UK case, the British improvement during the 1970s and 1980s is also clearly visible.

The comparatively poor British productivity performance in communications during the 1950s and 1960s and the subsequent improvements of the 1970s and 1980s are most easily explained by organisational factors. The poor performance occurred while the sector remained a state monopoly under centralised bureaucratic control, while the improvements occurred as telecommunications were first freed from Treasury restrictions and ultimately privatised.

Under the post-war Labour government, the centralised pre-war organisational and financial arrangements continued, with the power of strategic decision making resting in the hands of ministers. Although the Conservatives proposed a greater degree of financial independence for the Post Office in the *Report on Post Office Development and Finance* (UK House of Commons, 1955), the link with the Treasury was maintained and investment in telecommunications was held back (Channon, 1978: 254). When investment in exchange equipment was made, it continued to be in the old Strowger system, at a time when other countries were switching to the crossbar switching system developed in the United States and Sweden (Turner, 1969: 191). An attempt was made to leapfrog the crossbar system and move to an all-electronic exchange system, but this ended in fiasco when an exchange was opened and closed on the same day at Highgate Wood in 1962 (Channon, 1978: 254). Although the Post Office began to integrate crossbar equipment into the system from 1963, the technological delays made it more difficult to keep up with the rapidly increasing demand.

A series of reforms during the 1960s moved the Post Office towards corporation status. Under the Conservatives, the 1961 Post Office Act broke the links with the Exchequer and set financial targets for the Post Office in line with other nationalised concerns (Channon, 1978: 255). Under Labour, the Post Office was first brought under the scrutiny of the Select Committee on Nationalised Industries from 1965 and then changed into a public corporation from 1969. In the run-up to incorporation, separate product divisions were introduced for post and telecommunications, a marketing function and corporate planning were introduced and new, commercially oriented services, such as data processing, were introduced (Channon, 1978: 255).

In the postal service, incorporation was accompanied by the mechanisation of sorting and the introduction of a two-tier post (Daunton, 1985: 344–8). However, industrial relations problems meant that productivity continued to stagnate during the 1970s (Pryke, 1981: 149). With the prices of public corporations being held down as part of an anti-inflation policy, the postal service made substantial losses during the first half of the 1970s (Pryke, 1981: 159). Despite concluding that the postal service was inefficient, the UK Monopolies and Mergers Commission in its 1980 report *The Inner London Letter Post* stopped short of recommending removal of the Post Office's monopoly on the letter post. During the 1980s, however, the statutory monopoly was weakened, so that competition from private courier services was able to grow. In 1981 licences were granted to charities to deliver Christmas cards, while the market for time-sensitive mail with a minimum charge of £1 was opened up to private couriers. In 1982 private document exchanges were permitted, allowing firms to rent a box into which correspondents could deliver letters by hand (Estrin and de Meza, 1994: 209).

In telecommunications, the introduction of electronic switching equipment continued to be delayed during the 1970s, as attempts were made to develop a system domestically. The British-designed System X was introduced only in mid-1980, long after the availability of an American alternative (Pryke, 1981: 170). In fields other than switching, however, the Post Office's record was rather better, and productivity in telecommunications increased rapidly during the 1970s (Pryke, 1981: 172–3). During the 1980s productivity growth in telecommunications accelerated further as the rapid pace of technological progress was accompanied by wide-ranging organisational change.

In 1981 British Telecommunications was split from the Post Office and in 1984 became the first network-utility industry to be privatised (Armstrong and Vickers, 1994: 292–3). Given the natural monopoly element in any fixed-link network, the 1984 Telecommunications Act established a new regulatory framework with the Office for Telecommunications (Oftel). To avoid the perceived problems of US-style rate of return regulation, such as cost inefficiency, regulatory burden and vulnerability to 'capture', OFTEL adopted RPI-X price cap regulation. With prices rising by X% less than the retail price index, real price reductions were built into the framework, and, with X being increased from 3% in 1984 to 4.5% in 1989, these real price reductions were large (Armstrong and Vickers, 1994: 294–5, 300). However, although the fixed-link network is a natural monopoly, the provision of services on the network is not. Here, the limited nature of the competition allowed during the 1980s, restricted to a BT–Mercury duopoly, has been strongly criticised by Armstrong and Vickers (1994: 305–6). And yet, as Beesley and Laidlaw (1994: 310–12) point out, it is easy to forget how poor Britain's telephone service was at the beginning of the 1980s and how much it improved during the decade. By the early 1990s, as mobile phones, radio pagers, telex and fax machines, TV sets and computing equipment, as well as traditional telephones, were being connected to the public network, Britain's telecommunications sector was no longer characterised by technological backwardness and low productivity.

10.3 Distribution

10.3.1 Introduction

Indices of output, inputs and productivity in the British distribution sector are shown for the period 1951 to 1990 in table 10.29. For the

Table 10.29 *Productivity in the British distribution sector, 1951–1990*

A. Indices of output, inputs and productivity (1973 = 100)

	Output	Labour	Capital	Labour productivity	TFP
1951	55.0	77.8	29.7	70.7	89.9
1960	72.8	91.4	41.7	79.6	96.9
1968	86.0	90.3	70.2	95.2	101.4
1973	100.0	100.0	100.0	100.0	100.0
1979	100.0	106.0	140.4	94.3	88.0
1985	108.2	114.2	197.9	94.7	82.6
1990	130.0	124.6	287.7	104.3	84.6

B. Growth rates of output, inputs and productivity (% per annum)

	1951–1973	1973–1979	1979–1990	1951–1990
Output	2.7	0.0	2.4	2.2
Labour	1.1	1.0	1.5	1.2
Capital	5.5	5.6	6.5	5.8
Labour productivity	1.6	−1.0	0.9	1.0
TFP	0.5	−2.1	−0.3	−0.2

Sources: Output – UK Central Statistical Office (*National Income and Expenditure*, various years); labour – 1951–1965: Feinstein (1972); 1965–1990: UK Central Statistical Office (*Annual Abstract of Statistics*, various years), OECD (*Labour Force Statistics*, various years); capital – 1951–1965: Feinstein (1972); 1965–1990: UK Central Statistical Office (*National Income and Expenditure*, various years).

period as a whole output grew at the same rate as in the economy as a whole, although the slowdown of the 1970s and the acceleration of the 1980s were more pronounced in distribution, as can be seen by comparing table 10.29 with table 10.2. Since employment in distribution grew more rapidly than in the aggregate economy over the period as a whole, labour productivity also grew more slowly in distribution than in the aggregate economy. Given the very rapid growth of the capital stock in distribution, TFP growth was weak before 1973 and negative thereafter. Table 10.30 puts this apparently disappointing British productivity performance in international perspective. Although Britain continued to fall behind the United States in terms of comparative labour productivity levels, the gap remained smaller than in many other sectors, and it was not until the late 1970s that Britain was overtaken by Germany. It must be noted, however, that the Germany/UK comparison is complicated by the fact that the figures contain finance as well as distribution (in both

Table 10.30 *Comparative US/UK and Germany/UK labour productivity levels for the distribution sector, 1950–1990 (UK = 100)*

	US/UK	Germany/UK
1950	135.2	50.7
1960	143.2	64.2
1968	147.9	75.4
1973	153.8	88.0
1979	153.8	106.4
1985	177.3	109.2
1990	166.0	111.2

Note:
Germany/UK comparison based on distribution and finance.
Sources: tables 3.1, 3.3.

countries), although, before the 1980s, finance was much smaller than distribution.

10.3.2 Retailing and wholesaling for the home market

The position of wholesalers continued to weaken after World War II, as during the inter-war period. Pressure on wholesalers came from both retailers and producers. As large-scale retailing became more important, specialised buyers within retailing firms increasingly dealt directly with suppliers. And, as branded, packaged goods became more important in non-food as well as food retailing, producers took more responsibility for distribution and advertising (Stacey and Wilson, 1958: 86–93). Figures on wholesalers by method of trading are difficult to obtain on a consistent basis over time. Nevertheless, the figures in table 10.31, based on *Census of Distribution* data for 1950 and 1974, do show a substantial shift away from agents or brokers towards wholesalers buying outright and wholesaler-retailers. The growing openness of the British economy and the diminishing role of government purchasing after the reconstruction phase are also apparent in table 10.31.

The most dynamic part of the distribution sector was multiple shop retailing, continuing the trend of the inter-war period. In comparing the post-war statistics of table 10.32 with the inter-war statistics in chapter 9, it should be noted that the multiples are defined here as retailers with at least ten branches, including the department store groups that were categorised separately by Jefferys (1954) for the earlier period. Note also that table 10.32 refers to Great Britain only, so that the 1950 figures here differ slightly from the UK figures in chapter 9.

Table 10.31 *Wholesaling and dealing turnover in the United Kingdom by method of trading, 1950–1974 (%)*

	1950	1974
Wholesaler buying outright and selling in the United Kingdom	31.4	51.1
Wholesaler-retailer	1.4	6.7
Retailers' buying group	0.1	0.4
Manufacturers' wholesale organisation	6.9	5.8
Import and/or export merchant on own account	12.8	20.5
Agent or broker, home or export trade	28.4	5.3
Buying, selling or distributing for HM government	13.2	0.0
Purchasing organisation with head office abroad	0.8	1.2
Other wholesaling	5.0	9.0
Total wholesaling	100.0	100.0

Sources: UK Board of Trade (1953), UK Business Statistics Office (*Wholesaling and Dealing*, various years).

Table 10.32 *Shares of retail sales in Great Britain by form of organisation, 1950–1990 (%)*

	1950	1957	1961	1966	1971	1976	1980	1984	1990
Co-operative retailers	11.4	11.9	10.8	9.1	7.1	7.1	6.6	5.3	4.0
Multiple shop retailers	21.9	24.8	28.9	34.5	39.0	44.3	48.0	52.4	57.4
Independent retailers	66.7	63.3	60.3	56.4	53.9	48.6	45.4	42.3	38.6

Sources: UK Board of Trade (*Report on the Census of Distribution and Other Services*, various years), UK Business Statistics Office (*Retailing*, various years).

As can seen in table 10.32, although co-operative retailers increased their share of retail sales during the 1950s, this trend was reversed subsequently. By contrast, the multiples increased their share of retail sales continuously throughout the period, while the share of independents slumped from just over two-thirds in 1950 to less than 40% by 1990.

The productivity growth of the 1950s and 1960s was associated with a number of innovations, as the leading multiples broke free from the wartime and early post-war austerity of rationing, utility specifications and price fixing. A particular boost to labour productivity came from the spread of self-service, introduced to Britain at Tesco by Jack Cohen, after a visit to the United States in 1946 (Turner, 1969: 252). This development was encouraged initially by post-war labour shortages and later by the selective employment tax (SET), which taxed service sector employment in the mistaken belief that the expansion of industrial employment was the key to economic growth (Channon, 1978: 175). A second innovation was the growth of 'supermarkets' with large floor space, also inspired by the American experience (Anglo-American Council on Productivity, 1952; Hall et al., 1961: 92–5). A third development, underpinning the growth of the multiple chain, was the growing centralisation of a number of key functions, including buying, marketing and data processing, in which economies of scale permitted large savings (Turner, 1969: 245).

A fourth development, which facilitated the move to supermarkets with self-service, was the boom in the property market, as new suburban shopping precincts were developed and new towns constructed, and as town centres were rebuilt (Channon, 1978: 175). A fifth development was the gradual weakening of price fixing, partly as a result of the strategy of the more aggressive multiple retailers, and partly as a result of legal changes. Legal changes included the 1956 Restrictive Trade Practices Act, which outlawed the collective enforcement of resale price maintenance, and the 1964 Resale Prices Act, which outlawed RPM altogether, except in cases where a specific exemption had been granted (Yamey, 1966). However, before the legal changes occurred, the competitive strategy of supermarket chains such as Tesco and Sainsbury, and variety stores such as Marks and Spencer, British Home Stores, Woolworth, Boots and W. H. Smith, was already undermining RPM (Channon, 1978: 176–91). The strategy of firms such as these inspired the idea of a 'wheel of retailing', where new entrants provide price competition, then 'trade up', before becoming vulnerable themselves to price competition from further new entrants (Thorpe, 1990: 166–7). In this vein, Morelli (1998) interprets the opposition of the multiple food retailers to trading stamps in the early 1960s as an attempt to limit price discounts in the wake of the breakdown of RPM. Subsequent concerns over anti-competitive behaviour in the British retailing sector suggest that this issue had not gone away by the end of the 1980s (Moir, 1990).

The stagnation of the 1970s was followed by a return to buoyant growth of real retail sales during the 1980s, although strong employment growth limited the growth of labour productivity and combined with heavy capital investment to produce negative TFP growth (table 10.29). Bamfield (1988) sees this renewed dynamism as a result of a competitive struggle among the multiple retailers, triggered by Tesco's

'Operation Checkout' programme of price cuts in 1977. Stimulated by shortages of sites, rising property prices and a boom in share prices, the competitive struggle led to a series of amalgamations, culminating in the emergence of a number of mega-retailers such as Burton/Debenhams, Storehouse (Habitat/Mothercare/British Home Stores), Dee Corporation (Gateway/Carrefour/Fine Fare/Key Markets/International Stores) and Argyll (Presto/Lo-Cost/Allied Suppliers/Lipton/Safeway) (Bamfield, 1988: 19).

A number of important innovations occurred during this period, including the development of out-of-town shopping centres, increased store refurbishment, the introduction of electronic point of sale (EPoS) terminals and greater flexibility in opening hours. First, the development of out-of-town shopping centres occurred initially in groceries but spread to non-food areas such as department stores, DIY sheds and electrical discounting. This yielded benefits of convenience, particularly car parking, as well as economies of shop size (Bamfield, 1988: 19, 25–6). Second, at the same time, there was also a movement in marketing away from price appeal towards higher retail standards, the better presentation of goods, and improved store design and atmosphere, typified by 'lifestyle' retailers such as Habitat, Laura Ashley and Next. This all required increased spending on store refurbishment (Bamfield, 1988: 17, 23–4). Third, the introduction of EPoS terminals allowed improvements in stock control and automatic store replenishment. Furthermore, by yielding rapid feedback about sales, EPoS systems were increasingly used to aid marketing and decision-making in areas such as store design, space allocation, site evaluation and calculating the profitability of individual products (Bamfield, 1988: 22). Fourth, the lengthening of opening hours following deregulation in the mid-1980s has made it necessary for retailers to use more part-time employees to tailor the labour force to the amount of work available (Bamfield, 1988: 23).

Despite the decline of the co-operatives, large-scale retailers accounted for a rapidly growing share of retail sales, as a result of the dynamism of the multiple shop retailers. The share of retail sales accounted for by independent retailers thus fell from 66.7% in 1950 to 38.6% by 1990, as can be seen in table 10.32. Table 10.33 shows the share of large-scale retailers (co-operatives and multiples) in retail sales by main commodity groups. By 1990 large-scale enterprise had become very dominant in food and mixed retailing, was quite strong in clothing, footwear and leather goods and household goods, but was much weaker in drink, confectionery and tobacco and other non-food goods.

The growing concentration of retailing has led to concerns about the abuse of monopoly power. In particular, there have been allegations

Table 10.33 *Shares of large-scale retailers in retail sales in Great Britain by main commodity groups, 1950–1990 (%)*

	1950	1971	1990
Food	39.7	50.0	76.3
Drink, confectionery and tobacco	15.8	25.5	31.3
Clothing, footwear and leather goods	39.0	57.1	57.3
Household goods	28.1	33.7	45.3
Other non-food goods	28.2	28.9	26.0
Mixed retailing	42.3	67.6	81.1
Total retail sales	33.3	46.1	61.4

Sources: UK Board of Trade (*Report on the Census of Distribution and Other Services*, various years), UK Business Statistics Office (*Retailing*, various years).

that the large retailers are able to extract substantial discounts from manufacturers, making it difficult for small retailers to compete on price and hitting the profitability of small manufacturers. However, the UK Monopolies and Mergers Commission's 1981 report *Discounts to Retailers* generally supported the position of the retailers that the retail trade has remained highly competitive, concluding that, although the multiple retailers did extract significant discounts from manufacturers, these discounts resulted in lower prices to consumers. This view was also endorsed a few years later in the report *Competition in Retailing* by the UK Office of Fair Trading (1985).

The share of large-scale retailers in retail sales declined in only one category of table 10.33 during the 1970s and 1980s. This was in 'other non-food goods', which consists of: chemists; newsagents and stationers; booksellers; photographic goods retailers; jewellers; toys, hobby, cycle and sports goods retailers; florists, nurserymen and seedsmen; and retailers of other non-food goods not elsewhere specified. In all other sectors, the position of the independent retailer was seriously undermined. It is against this backdrop of a continued move towards large-scale enterprise that the continued deterioration of Britain's comparative productivity performance in distribution since 1973, charted in table 10.30, can be understood. This finding of poor British performance in large-scale hierarchically organised business is also apparent in the cross-sectional pattern of comparative productivity performance within distribution, with Britain's productivity gap in 1993 being larger in retailing than in wholesaling, which remained in the hands of smaller-scale enterprise. O'Mahony et al. (1998) report comparative US/UK labour productivity ratios of 146.1 in retailing but only 133.8 in wholesaling, while for the Germany/UK case the productivity ratios are 116.2 in retailing but 84.3 (a small British advantage) in wholesaling.

Although there have been attempts to break down the productivity gap by sector within retailing and wholesaling, these have been plagued by issues concerning market power. Thus, for example, O'Mahony (1997) finds British motor vehicle wholesaling highly productive relative to the United States and Germany, but motor vehicle retailing fairly unproductive. This conclusion is reached by comparing gross margins per person employed at the purchasing power parity (PPP) for motor vehicles. However, what this reflects is the fact that, in Britain in 1993, manufacturers exercised strong control over distribution through approved dealerships, so that margins were inflated within wholesaling, while normal margins within retailing were deflated by the high retail prices resulting from the restrictive practices of the car manufacturers (Rhys, 1993: 141–2; UK Monopolies and Mergers Commission, 1992). In food distribution, where market power rested largely with the retailers, the opposite picture emerged, with Britain looking relatively productive in food retailing but less productive in food wholesaling.

10.3.3 Wholesale merchants and external trade

As for previous periods, this survey of the activities of the wholesale merchants engaged in external trade begins with a quantitative survey of the main dimensions of Britain's trade in commodities. The shares of imports and exports in GDP at market prices, shown here in table 10.34, provide one measure of the degree of openness of the British economy. Note, however, that the figures for 1951 are exceptional, distorted by the effects of the rise in commodity prices associated with the Korean War. As a result, the share of imports shot up from 20.2% in 1950 to 27.1% in 1951, while the share of exports rose more modestly from 17.5% in 1950 to 18.8% in 1951. Apart from this blip, the 1950s look like a continuation of the inter-war position, with the shares of imports and exports well below their pre-1914 levels. Although trade ratios have increased with the growing liberalisation of the world economy since the early 1960s, on these measures the British economy in 1990 was still not as open as it had been prior to World War I.

Working in constant prices, in table 10.35, the volume of visible imports and exports both grew at about 3.5% per annum over the entire period 1951 to 1990, substantially faster than the volume of real GDP, which grew at an annual rate of 2.2% over the same period (table 10.2). Turning to table 10.36, however, the price of imports and exports

Table 10.34 *Visible trade of the United Kingdom, 1950–1990*

A. Values at current prices (£ million)		
	Imports	Exports (inc. re-exports)
1950	2,606.6	2,258.9
1951	3,901.9	2,708.6
1960	4,540.7	3,696.0
1968	7,897.5	6,433.9
1973	15,723.5	12,087.0
1979	46,924.9	40,637.0
1985	85,027.0	78,391.8
1990	126,086.1	103,692.4
B. Shares of GDP at market prices (%)		
	Imports	Exports (inc. re-exports)
1950	20.2	17.5
1951	27.1	18.8
1960	17.8	14.5
1968	18.2	14.8
1973	21.2	16.3
1979	23.7	20.5
1985	23.8	21.9
1990	22.9	18.8

Sources: Trade data – Mitchell (1988: 454), UK Board of Trade (*Overseas Trade Statistics of the United Kingdom*, various years); GDP data – UK Central Statistical Office (*National Income and Expenditure*, various years).

increased less rapidly than the price of aggregate output. This helps to explain why the share of exports and imports in GDP at current market prices did not increase more rapidly in table 10.34. Note also, from tables 10.2 and 10.35, that the extent to which the growth of imports and exports exceeded the growth of GDP was greater during the 1970s and 1980s than during the 1950s and 1960s, reflecting the slowness of the liberalisation of the world economy during the early post-war period. Returning to table 10.36, although the net barter terms of trade showed no trend during the post-war period as a whole, there was a cyclical movement in Britain's favour during the 1950s after the collapse of the Korean-War-induced bubble in commodity prices. The commodity price boom from the late 1960s created a temporary adverse movement in Britain's terms of trade, but this was reversed from the late 1970s as Britain became a net exporter of oil.

Table 10.35 *Volume of visible trade, United Kingdom, 1951–1990*

A. Volume indices (1973 = 100)

	Imports	Exports (inc. re-exports)
1951	49.5	48.3
1960	49.7	51.1
1968	71.2	72.1
1973	100.0	100.0
1979	119.2	134.6
1985	140.1	160.2
1990	194.1	198.2

B. Average annual growth rates (%)

	Imports	Exports (inc. re-exports)
1951–1990	3.5	3.6
1951–1973	3.2	3.3
1973–1979	2.9	5.0
1979–1990	4.4	3.5

Note:
The trade value data in current prices have been converted to a volume basis using price deflators.

Sources: Trade data – Mitchell (1988: 454); price deflators – UK Central Statistical Office (*National Income and Expenditure*, various years).

Table 10.36 *Price indices for exports, imports and the aggregate output of the United Kingdom, 1951–1990 (1973 = 100)*

	Price of exports	Price of imports	GDP deflator	Net barter terms of trade
1951	46.4	50.1	37.8	92.6
1960	59.8	58.1	51.9	102.9
1968	73.8	70.5	69.2	104.7
1973	100.0	100.0	100.0	100.0
1979	249.8	250.4	244.2	99.8
1985	404.8	385.9	405.8	104.9
1990	432.9	413.2	539.7	104.8

Sources: UK Central Statistical Office (*National Income and Expenditure*, various years).

The principal commodities shipped by wholesale merchants are shown in table 10.37 for imports and exports separately. The key development on the import side was the dramatic increase in the share of manufactured imports and a corresponding decline in the importance of food and raw materials. The strongest growth of imports occurred in machinery, road vehicles and aircraft, chemicals, and footwear, clothing, etc., while the largest decline occurred in raw cotton, raw wool, and grain and flour. These patterns reflected a general shift away from a pre-World-War-II division of labour within the international economy, whereby industrialised countries had sold manufactured exports to less developed countries in return for raw materials (Maizels, 1963: 79–110). The new, post-World-War-II pattern saw a dramatic growth of inter-industry trade, with industrialised countries increasingly exchanging manufactures with other industrialised countries (Batchelor et al., 1980: 16–30). On the export side, the chief developments were a movement away from textiles such as cotton and wool towards engineering products such as machinery, electrical goods, cars and aircraft, and the growing importance of chemicals. Petroleum and petroleum products also became more important with the discovery of North Sea oil, turning Britain into a net exporter of oil.

The most important shift in the geographical composition of Britain's trade was a reversal of the growth in the importance of the empire that had occurred during the first half of the twentieth century. Accompanying the decline in the importance of 'British countries' as export markets, shown here in table 10.38, was a growing importance of Europe, particularly the original six members of the European Economic Community (the EEC6). This reflected the growing importance of inter-industry trade in manufactures between industrialised countries noted above. This switch from empire to Europe created problems of adjustment for British manufacturers, discussed in detail in Broadberry (1997a) and Owen (1999).

The general strategy of the major British trading companies from the late nineteenth century had been diversification into related activities, such as agricultural estate management, shipping, insurance, finance and retailing. The lynchpin of this strategy had been the trade basis of a particular commodity or territory, and often both (Channon, 1978: 121–2). After World War II, however, control over this trade base was threatened by decolonisation, with independent governments often keen to wrest control of important commodities away from foreign interests. The most common strategy that the British trading companies adopted to deal with this threat was diversification into other commodities and into other territories where there was less political risk

Table 10.37 *Principal visible imports and exports of the United Kingdom, 1951–1990*

A. Principal imports

	Shares of total imports (%)		
	1951	1973	1990
Grain and flour	6.1	2.4	0.8
Meat and animals	5.5	4.9	1.7
Timber	5.4	2.9	1.1
Raw cotton	6.6	0.5	0.1
Raw wool	6.4	1.2	0.2
Oil, oilseed, gums, resins, tallow, etc.	4.6	1.5	0.5
Rubber	4.1	0.5	0.2
Non-ferrous metals and manufactures	4.1	4.0	2.4
Paper-making materials	3.2	1.3	0.6
Petroleum	7.7	10.7	5.0
Machinery	1.8	15.4	25.4
Road vehicles and aircraft	0.3	5.2	7.8
Textiles	3.9	3.3	3.1
Chemicals	2.7	5.5	8.6
Footwear, clothing, etc.	0.3	2.7	4.0
Total of above	62.7	62.0	61.5

B. Principal exports

	Shares of total exports and re-exports (%)		
	1951	1973	1990
Iron and steel	4.0	3.6	2.6
Machinery	13.8	21.4	18.6
Electrical goods	5.2	5.7	10.0
Motor road vehicles and aircraft	10.0	11.1	14.1
Cotton goods	6.7	0.5	0.3
Woollen goods	4.0	1.1	0.3
Chemicals	7.1	10.4	10.4
Petroleum and products	1.3	2.9	6.1
Total of above	52.1	56.7	62.4

Note:
Imports – figures shown for commodities accounting for at least 3% of imports in 1951 or 1990; exports – figures shown for commodities accounting for at least 3% of exports in 1951 or 1990.

Sources: Mitchell (1988: 477–80, 485), UK Board of Trade (*Overseas Trade Statistics of the United Kingdom*, various years).

Table 10.38 *Shares of British visible exports to 'British countries' and the 'EEC6', 1951–1990 (%)*

	British countries	EEC6
1951	55.0	10.4
1954	53.0	13.0
1958	49.3	13.1
1963	37.5	20.3
1968	31.2	19.3
1970	25.1	21.7
1980	20.1	34.6
1990	16.7	41.3

Note:
'British countries' includes the Irish Free State/Republic and the Republic of South Africa as well as the Commonwealth. 'EEC6' comprises the original six members of the EEC: Italy, France, West Germany, Belgium, Netherlands and Luxembourg.

Source: UK Board of Trade (*Annual Statement of the Trade of the United Kingdom*, various years).

(Channon, 1978: 122). Thus, for example, Booker McConnell, with traditional interests based on sugar trading in Guyana, diversified away from both Guyana and sugar after World War II, eventually focusing on engineering and food distribution in Britain (Jones, 2000: 151). An interesting contrast is provided by Lonrho, which started the post-war period as a relatively small company based on mining in Rhodesia. Under the controversial chief executive 'Tiny' Rowland, Lonrho acquired many of the interests being sold off by the other colonial trading companies and dealt with the problem of political risk by cultivating links with African governments and employing local managers. The strategy of diversification away from the traditional product and territory base in many companies led naturally to the adoption of a multi-divisional structure, although Lonrho retained a more entrepreneurial structure, with a highly personalised style of management under Tiny Rowland.

Jones (2000: 325–42) notes the apparent paradox that, although the major British merchant houses survived the difficult years of decolonisation from the 1950s to the 1970s, many disappeared during the apparently more favourable environment of the 1980s, as much of the developing world liberalised and became more open to foreign trade and investment. One factor which determined the fate of particular companies was the economic performance of their main host regions. Hence, for example, the United Africa Company, with extensive interests in Nigeria, was severely disadvantaged relative to Jardine Matheson and Swires, with their interests centred on Hong Kong. Nevertheless, the most important factor which decided the fate of the trading companies was the British capital market, which would not tolerate the low rates of return earned by conglomerates from the 1980s. Jardine Matheson and Swires were able to survive ultimately because they retained family control and were not at the mercy of shareholders interested only in the rate of return (Jones, 2000: 340–1).

10.4 Financial services

10.4.1 Introduction

Between 1951 and 1990 output in financial services grew more than twice as rapidly as in the economy as a whole, as can be seen by comparing table 10.39 with table 10.2. However, with employment also growing rapidly, labour productivity growth in financial services was a modest 1.1% per annum, compared with 1.8% in the economy as a whole. Although the national accounts do not provide separate estimates of the capital stock in financial services before 1972, table 10.39 provides data from O'Mahony (1999) on capital services for the pre-1973 period, derived from the underlying data on investment. This suggests a very rapid expansion of capital and a corresponding stagnation of TFP in financial services. However, it should be noted that the stagnation of TFP growth over the period as a whole masks negative TFP growth before 1979, followed by strongly positive TFP growth after 1979.

Turning to comparative levels of productivity, the benchmark estimates in table 10.1 suggest a relatively small US labour productivity lead in financial services in 1950, and an even smaller US lead in 1993. Germany also had a small labour productivity lead in financial services in 1993. As with previous periods, it has not proved possible to construct consistent time series estimates for financial services in the intervening years.

The balance sheet data for UK financial institutions in table 10.40 help to provide an overview of the development of the financial services sector. Several points should be noted concerning the presentation of the data. First, the total assets of the UK banking sector in part A are slightly different from the figures given in the previous chapter. This reflects the fact that Sheppard's (1971) estimates did not include foreign-owned banks, which later became enormously important. Second, separate figures for the London clearing banks, the Scottish clearing banks

Table 10.39 *Productivity in the British financial services sector, 1951–1990*

A. Indices of output, inputs and productivity (1973 = 100)

	Output	Labour	Capital	Labour productivity	TFP
1951	36.7	46.1	15.5	79.6	104.6
1960	54.8	57.2	32.0	95.8	110.7
1968	75.3	71.8	60.6	104.9	109.4
1973	100.0	100.0	100.0	100.0	100.0
1979	117.7	114.1	151.2	103.2	96.2
1985	168.1	142.3	219.8	118.1	106.0
1990	240.6	198.2	358.5	121.4	104.7

B. Growth rates of output, inputs and productivity (% per annum)

	1951–1973	1973–1979	1979–1990	1951–1990
Output	4.5	2.7	6.5	4.8
Labour	3.5	2.2	5.0	3.7
Capital services	8.5	6.9	7.8	8.1
Labour productivity	1.0	0.5	1.5	1.1
TFP	−0.2	−0.6	0.8	0.0

Sources: Output – UK Central Statistical Office (*National Income and Expenditure*, various years); labour – 1951–1965: Feinstein (1972); 1965–1990: UK Central Statistical Office (*Annual Abstract of Statistics*, various years), OECD (*Labour Force Statistics*, various years); capital – UK Central Statistical Office (*National Income and Expenditure*, various years), O'Mahony (1999).

and the Northern Irish banks were no longer published from 1981, due to difficulties with separating subsidiaries from parent banks following a spate of mergers, acquisitions and cross-holdings across the three groups (Bank of England, *Bank of England Quarterly Bulletin*, 1983: 562–3). However, the newly named 'retail banking' sector consisted largely of these three groups, providing a useful degree of continuity to the statistics. Third, 'national savings' includes the Post Office Savings Bank (later the National Savings Bank), the Trustee Savings Bank and National Savings Bonds, which were all enumerated separately in the previous chapter. Fourth, instead of friendly societies, which included 'superannuation and other trusts' and were of some importance in the pre-war period, 'pension funds' and 'investment and unit trusts' have been included for the post-war period.

Parts A and B of table 10.40 set out the growth of total assets (equal by definition to total liabilities) of UK banks and non-bank financial intermediaries, respectively, in nominal terms. However, given the rapid

Table 10.40 *Total assets and total liabilities of UK financial institutions, 1951–1990*

A. Banks' total assets (£ million)

	London clearing banks	Total UK retail banks	Total UK banking sector
1951	6,787	7,795	8,815
1960	8,259	9,419	11,567
1968	11,817	13,366	27,604
1973	21,688	24,478	99,034
1979	54,323	62,198	199,590
1985		181,455	589,880
1990		426,114	1,032,176

B. Non-bank financial intermediaries' total assets (£ million)

	Insurance companies	National savings	Building societies	Hire purchase companies	Investment and unit trusts	Pension funds	Total non-bank financial intermediaries
1951	3,590	6,094	1,357	42	307	760	12,150
1960	7,156	7,290	3,166	334	2,202	3,321	23,469
1968	14,832	8,619	8,298	756	6,932	7,480	46,917
1973	25,099	10,474	17,545	900	7,912	12,050	73,980
1979	52,456	13,464	45,789	1,872	11,888	42,348	167,817
1985	154,347	31,841	120,763	4,648	39,358	168,059	518,986
1990	274,759	37,577	216,148	9,832	65,499	302,714	906,529

C. Nominal and real growth of assets, banks and non-bank financial intermediaries (% per annum)

	1951–1973	1973–1979	1979–1990	1951–1990
Nominal asset growth	9.6	12.6	15.1	11.6
Inflation	4.4	14.9	7.2	6.8
Real asset growth	5.2	−2.3	7.9	4.8

D. Contribution to total financial institutions' assets and liabilities (%)

	1951	1990
Banks	42.0	53.2
Insurance companies	17.1	14.2
National savings	29.1	1.9
Building societies	6.5	11.2
Hire purchase companies	0.2	0.5
Investment and unit trusts	1.5	3.4
Pension funds	3.6	15.6
	100.0	100.0

inflation after World War II, part C shows how the nominal asset growth of banks and non-bank financial intermediaries was split between real asset growth and inflation, using the GDP deflator to convert to real terms. Real asset growth was strongly positive before 1973 and even more rapid after 1979. However, during the disturbed conditions of the 1970s real asset growth was significantly negative, as nominal interest rates and nominal asset growth failed to keep pace with inflation, creating a period of negative *ex post* real interest rates. With population growth of 0.3% per annum between 1951 and 1990, per capita real asset growth over the same period was 4.5% per annum, well above the 2.2% per annum achieved between 1911 and 1951.

Returning to parts A and B, it is possible to see how the different parts of the British financial services sector fared in relative terms. Amongst banks, total asset growth between 1951 and 1990 was 12.2% per annum in nominal terms, or 5.4% in real terms. The London clearing banks, and indeed the whole UK retail banking sector, declined in relative importance, particularly with the growth of foreign banks based in London. Whereas retail banks accounted for 88.4% of all bank assets in 1951, this had fallen to just 24.7% in 1973, before recovering to 41.3% by 1990. Amongst the non-bank financial intermediaries, total asset growth between 1951 and 1990 was 11.1% per annum in nominal terms, or 4.3% in real terms. Whereas the wartime period had seen a rapid expansion of national savings, the period from 1951 saw a real fall in this sector, which includes the Post Office Savings Bank (later the National Savings Bank), the Trustee Savings Banks and National Savings Bonds, which were all enumerated separately in the previous chapter. Part D thus shows the share of national savings in the total assets of banks and non-bank financial intermediaries declining from 29.1% in 1951 to just 1.9% by 1990. The share of insurance companies also declined a little. The sectors which gained the biggest shares were the pension funds and building societies, while investment and unit trusts and hire purchase companies also gained.

Figures on the contribution of financial services to the balance of payments are available from 1964, and are presented in table 10.41 in both current and constant price terms. The figures are available only on a net credit basis, with debits already subtracted from credits. Insurance

Notes to Table 10.40 (*cont.*)

Source: Financial data – Sheppard (1971: appendix, sections 1–2), UK Central Statistical Office (*Annual Abstract of Statistics*, various years), Bank of England (various years), Roe (1971), converted to real terms using GDP deflator from the UK Central Statistical Office (*National Income and Expenditure*, various years).

Table 10.41 *Balance of payments net credits of UK financial services, 1964–1990 (£ million)*

A. At current prices				
	Insurance	Banking	Other financial services	Total financial services
1964	36	18	49	103
1968	116	36	83	235
1973	217	107	277	601
1979	576	344	668	1,588
1985	2,178	1,105	904	4,207
1990	428	1,809	2,119	4,356
B. At constant 1973 prices				
	Insurance	Banking	Other financial services	Total financial services
1964	61	31	83	175
1968	168	52	120	340
1973	217	107	277	601
1979	236	141	273	650
1985	542	272	223	1,037
1990	79	335	393	807

Note:
'Other financial services' includes merchanting and brokerage.

Source: UK Central Statistical Office (*United Kingdom Balance of Payments*, various years).

has made a substantial positive contribution throughout the period, with Britain retaining a strong position in the world insurance market. The 1990 figure, however, reflects the crisis at Lloyd's, when a series of disasters led to huge underwriting losses to set against the continuing profitability of the corporate insurance sector. Banking and other financial services, including merchanting and brokerage, continued to make an increasingly positive contribution to the balance of payments. During the 1970s and the 1980s the invisible surplus earned by financial services was equivalent to around 1% of GDP at factor cost.

10.4.2 Clearing banks

During the inter-war period domestic retail banking in Britain was dominated by the 'Big Five' London clearing banks: Barclays, Lloyds, National Provincial, Midland and Westminster. These banks remained in a dominant position after World War II, but were prevented from further consolidation before the late 1960s by an understanding with the Treasury. This meant that further mergers would be permitted only if they significantly extended geographical coverage or customer service (Collins, 1988: 209–11). The interest rate cartel operated by the LCBs meant that price competition was effectively suppressed, and competition within this oligopoly occurred largely through the level of service.

One of the most striking features of table 10.40 is the declining relative importance of the London clearing banks, which accounted for 77.0% of total bank assets in 1951 but just 21.9% in 1973. To some extent this relative decline of the LCBs was just the flip side of the rapid expansion of overseas banks in London from the late 1950s. However, there were a number of other factors which hindered the position of the LCBs through to the 1970s (Collins, 1988: 412–20). First, the British banking system remained extremely compartmentalised by type of business until the late 1960s, with the clearing banks specialised in the relatively slow-growth business of domestic retail banking. Second, the interest rate cartel operated by the LCBs made them less competitive than other parts of the banking sector in attracting new business. The cartel operated with the approval of the monetary authorities, who welcomed the stability that it was seen as providing (Channon, 1978: 56–7). Third, when the monetary authorities wished to control the amount of credit in the economy they placed restrictions on the advances of the clearing banks, which were thus further disadvantaged in the competitive struggle with other financial institutions for new business. And, fourth, the operation of the tax system favoured segments of the market catered for largely by other financial institutions, such as building societies, insurance companies and pension funds.

After the early 1970s the relative decline of the clearing banks was reversed, with the LCB share of total bank assets rising back from 21.9% in 1973 to 27.2% by 1979. By this time, however, as a result of mergers and diversification, the published figures on the LCBs increasingly failed to reflect the fortunes of the parent companies. Accordingly, the monetary authorities decided to cease publishing separate figures for the LCBs, the Scottish clearing banks and the Northern Irish banks in 1981. Despite the absence of separate data on the LCBs, the continued recovery of the clearers can still be traced in the rising share of the retail banks, from 24.7% in 1973 to 41.3% in 1990. The recovery reflected a change in the strategy of both the monetary authorities and the clearing banks, which effectively removed the obstacles outlined above. First, beginning in the late 1960s a series of mergers and acquisitions allowed the clearing banks to diversify away from their traditional areas of specialisation. Second, the interest rate cartel was abolished with the 1971 monetary reforms known as Competition and Credit Control, allowing the clearers to compete more aggressively with other banks and non-bank financial institutions. Third, these reforms began a more even-handed approach to the treatment of different financial institutions, thus reducing the disadvantages faced by the clearers. Fourth, there was a phasing out of the favourable tax treatment of particular financial assets, although this was of less importance once the clearers had broken out of their traditional areas of specialisation.

The change of strategy appears to have been triggered by a report of the UK National Board for Prices and Incomes published in 1967, *Bank Charges*. The report expresses the view that amalgamations could reduce costs by closing down surplus branches, thus reducing bank charges. This signalled a relaxation of the policy that had been in place since 1918, that mergers would be allowed only if they significantly extended geographical coverage or customer service (Collins, 1988: 209–10). The relaxation produced a wave of merger proposals in 1968, beginning with the National Provincial and Westminster Banks combining to form the National Westminster Bank. This was followed by the amalgamation of the Royal Bank of Scotland, and the National Commercial Bank of Scotland, and the formation of Williams and Glyn's Bank from the new group's English subsidiaries. However, a proposed merger between Barclays, Lloyds and Martins Banks was barred by the Monopolies Commission, since the new group would have controlled about a half of all clearing bank business. Barclays was nevertheless allowed to acquire Martins (Channon, 1978: 57–8). Diversification in domestic business had occurred before 1968, with the clearers taking stakes in finance houses, but these were largely arms'-length investments and on a very limited scale. After 1968 the clearers expanded much more fully into other market segments, usually through subsidiaries. By 1975 most of the remaining clearers had active interests in merchant banking, unit trust management, factoring, leasing, insurance broking and underwriting, venture capital, computer services, travel services, credit finance, credit cards, personal tax and financial planning (Channon, 1978: 59–60). The development of international business by the clearers was a response to the growing competition from US and other multinational banks. This development was reflected in the growing participation by the clearers in the eurocurrency markets, and in the case of Barclays, at least, in the establishment of a direct presence overseas (Channon, 1978: 59–61).[4]

---

[4] The eurocurrency markets are discussed in the next section.

Before 1971 government regulation and controls on credit impacted disproportionately on the clearing banks. As well as being required to hold minimum proportions of their assets in cash and total liquid assets, the clearing banks bore the brunt of frequent attempts by the monetary authorities to restrict the growth of credit in the economy, via Bank of England requests to limit loans and advances. Other banks and non-bank financial institutions were not affected by these requests, apart from the finance houses, which were also partially owned by the clearing banks (Collins, 1988: 419–20). Hence, the 1971 Competition and Credit Control reforms not only abolished the clearing banks' interest rate cartel but also extended controls over assets and liabilities to all banks, although not to non-bank financial institutions (Collins, 1988: 420).

Until the late 1960s, then, the clearing banks can be seen as a cartel, maintaining a dominant position in traditional areas of specialisation, but missing out on the most rapidly growing parts of business. Capie and Billings (2001) show that the rate of return on capital earned by the clearers between 1948 and 1968 was about the same as in the rest of British business, but this is suggestive of the monopoly power of the cartel rather than efficiency. The clearing banks exhibit many of the characteristic problems of large-scale, hierarchical, centralised business in Britain during this period, making relatively slow progress in the adoption of labour-saving machinery and facing labour relations that were far from cordial.

The long period of limited competition between the 1920s and the late 1960s led to stagnation in strategy and bureaucracy in organisation, with most clearing banks run by a small group of general managers who were not main board members, and with largely non-executive main boards drawn from traditional banking families, peers, senior industrialists, former politicians and civil servants (Channon, 1978: 72; Holmes and Green, 1986: 247). Although most of the clearing banks had supplemented their centralised management systems with regional boards by the 1960s, Channon (1978: 77) sees this limited decentralisation as little more than an attempt to improve local image. However, with the increased competition from the late 1960s and the strategy of diversification, a more decentralised system of management could not be avoided and resulted in the adoption of a divisional structure. Nevertheless, Channon (78) argues that the divisional system did not work well, with the British clearing banks remaining over-bureaucratised compared with their American competitors, but at the same time being slow to make use of their extensive branch networks to integrate their new services with their conventional banking activities.

Mechanisation proceeded slowly, with the Midland Bank completing the mechanisation of branch bookkeeping only in 1959, having begun the process in the late 1920s (Holmes and Green, 1986: 248). Ackrill and Hannah (2001: 330–5) take a more positive view of the pioneering approach to computerisation at Barclays Bank, although the failure to have an effective bank-wide computer system installed in time for decimalisation in 1971 illustrates the potential costs of going for an over-ambitious system. With the growing routinisation of clerical work the proportion of females in the LCB labour force rose from 30% in 1948 to 52% in 1969, and pay differentials over other occupations were eroded (Nevin and Davis, 1970: 200). With bank employees continuing to work a six-day week when employees in many other industries had secured a five-day week, the clearing banks became fertile ground for collective action, culminating in unprecedented strike action by the National Union of Bank Employees (NUBE) in 1967, in support of their claim for recognition as well as in protest over pay and hours (Nevin and Davis, 1970: 201).

In the more competitive environment of the 1970s and 1980s, the clearing banks moved more quickly to adopt the new information and communications technologies that underpinned the improved productivity performance of the financial service sector after 1979, apparent in table 10.39. The clearers were quick to install a network of automated teller machines (ATMs), particularly 'through-the-wall' machines in branches, allowing customers access to services on a round-the-clock basis (Essinger, 1993: 12). Further innovations in customer service included the provision of remote banking services using telephones (and later, personal computers), and the issuing of debit cards and provision of an electronic funds transfer at the point of sale (EFTPOS) system (Essinger, 1993: 81–8). In addition, the computerisation of routine back-room data processing freed staff time for more interaction with customers, and the use of relational databases allowed the banks to retrieve data in a variety of configurations to improve the focus of marketing strategy (Essinger, 1993: 15–16).

The balance sheets of the LCBs in table 10.42 can be used to shed light on the conduct of the clearing banks in the period to 1973. From 1973, however, with the breakdown of the compartmentalisation of the British banking system, it is necessary to consider the balance sheets of all UK banks. Dealing first with the asset side of the balance sheets of the LCBs, clearing banks held a proportion of their assets in sufficiently liquid form to meet the needs of their customers. The most liquid assets were cash, money at call and short notice in the discount market, and bills, which could also be quickly converted to cash in the discount

Table 10.42 *Combined balance sheets of the London clearing banks, 1951–1973 (£ million)*

A. Assets

	Cash, money at call and short notice	Total discounts	Loans and advances	Total investments	Other assets	Total assets
1951	1,080	1,228	1,892	1,624	963	6,787
1960	1,150	1,149	3,195	1,407	1,358	8,259
1968	2,186	995	5,160	1,375	2,101	11,817
1973	2,883	722	13,604	1,487	2,992	21,688

B. Liabilities

	Deposits	Other liabilities	Total liabilities
1951	6,162	469	6,787
1960	7,236	745	8,259
1968	10,431	768	11,817
1973	19,708	202	21,688

Sources: Sheppard (1971: 116–17), UK Central Statistical Office (*Annual Abstract of Statistics*, various years).

market, where the Bank of England acted as lender of last resort. Before 1971 Bank of England regulation of the liquidity of the clearing banks took the form of requirements on the ratio of cash to deposits (the cash ratio) and the ratio of liquid assets to deposits (the liquidity ratio). From 1947 the clearing banks were required to maintain a cash ratio of 8%, while from 1951 they were also required to maintain a liquidity ratio of 28 to 30%, lowered to 28% in 1963 (Collins, 1988: 432–5). From 1971 the cash ratio and liquidity ratio were replaced by a new minimum 12½% ratio of eligible reserve assets to eligible liabilities. Furthermore, whereas the cash and liquidity ratios had applied only to the clearing banks, the eligible reserve asset ratio applied to all banks (Hall, 1983: 7). In the early post-war period the LCBs had a liquidity ratio well above the minimum requirement, largely as a result of a decline in the share of loans and advances with the dearth of commercial opportunities during the war. The share of liquid assets in total assets declined sharply in the late 1950s, and again after the introduction of Competition and Credit Control in 1971. Along with a decline in the share of liquid assets in total assets, there was also a change in the composition away from treasury bills. The importance of treasury bills in the early post-war period again reflected the effects of the war, with war finance dominating the balance sheets of the clearing banks. The declining relative importance of treasury bills from the 1950s reflected both the government policy of substituting long-term for short-term debt and the revival of private sector commercial bills (Collins, 1988: 435–6).

Turning to less liquid assets, the most important trend was an increase in the share of loans and advances in total assets, at the expense of total investments. Whereas loans and advances increased from 27.9% of total assets in 1951 to 62.7% by 1973, total investments declined from 23.9% to 6.9% over the same period. The low share of loans and advances and the high share of total investments in 1951 reflected the important role played by the clearing banks in war finance, since 96.1% of the investments were in the form of government bonds (Sheppard, 1971: 131). The growing share of loans and advances reflected the revival of commercial opportunities combined with the declining importance of government debt. However, it should be noted that the expansion of loans and advances did not proceed smoothly, since the lending of the clearing banks was subject to government restrictions. Indeed, the increase in loans and advances occurred largely in two sharp jumps: when controls were temporarily relaxed between 1958 and 1960, and after the introduction of Competition and Credit Control between 1971 and 1973 (Collins, 1988: 440–1). The other main development was a shift within loans and advances away from the traditional overdraft towards the provision of term loans, particularly to business customers (Collins, 1988: 443).

Despite the growing importance of loans to private business during the post-war period, there remained concerns about the willingness and ability of banks to provide adequate finance to industry. As noted in earlier chapters, this has been a persistent theme since the late nineteenth century, and the controversy still rages (Hutton, 1996). The issue was considered by a number of major official enquiries between the late 1950s and the late 1970s, which resulted in the *Report of the Committee on the Working of the Monetary System* (UK House of Commons, 1959), under the chairmanship of Lord Radcliffe, the *Report of the Committee of Inquiry on Small Firms* (UK House of Commons, 1971), under the chairmanship of J. E. Bolton, and the *Report of the Committee to Review the Functioning of Financial Institutions* (UK House of Commons, 1980), under the chairmanship of Harold Wilson. Like the Macmillan Committee in the 1930s, the Radcliffe, Bolton and Wilson Committees were not particularly critical of the banks.

The Radcliffe Report (UK House of Commons, 1959: 326) praised the role of the Industrial and Commercial Finance Corporation Ltd. (ICFC) in closing the 'Macmillan gap'. This had been identified by the Macmillan Committee as the difficulty faced by medium-sized firms in raising capital, since the amounts needed were too small to justify the fixed costs of a public issue but were also too large to be tied up as illiquid loans by banks. The ICFC had been set up in 1945 on the initiative of the Bank of England, but with share capital subscribed by the banks, specifically to address this problem (Thomas, 1978: 121). However, the Radcliffe Report (325–6) did suggest that more could still be done to help small firms, and encouraged the banks to switch from the system of renewable overdrafts to fixed-period loans.

The Bolton Report (UK House of Commons, 1971: 150–92) was largely satisfied with the role of the banks in providing finance to small firms. Although there was criticism of the way that quantitative restrictions on bank lending tended to hit small firms disproportionately, this was more a criticism of the monetary authorities than the banks (158–9). The Wilson Report (UK House of Commons, 1980) was also basically satisfied with the role of the banks, accepting that, given their short-term liabilities, long-term loans or equity stakes in firms could form only a small proportion of bank assets. Even the dissenting minority report focused not on the banks but, rather, on the alleged shortcomings of the insurance companies and pension funds in the provision of long-term finance for industry (274–87). The Wilson Report (222–3) noted that the banks had largely met the recommendation of the Radcliffe Report to reduce the importance of overdrafts and increase the use of fixed-period loans. The Wilson Report (62) noted further that, as the industrial and commercial companies sector moved from net surplus to net deficit during the deteriorating economic conditions of the 1970s, firms had turned increasingly to bank credit, which had become the main source of medium-term finance. The problem was not the role of the banks, then, but, rather, the decline in long-term industrial securities as a result of the uncertainty created by high inflation (225). With the return to lower inflation during the 1980s the equity market did recover, but bank lending continued to be the main source of external finance for industrial and commercial companies (Bank of England, *Bank of England Quarterly Bulletin*, 1985: 224–32).

The liabilities side of the LCB balance sheets exhibits a high degree of stability, with total deposits accounting for approximately 90% of total liabilities throughout the period 1951 to 1973. However, within the category of total deposits, there was an increase in the share of deposit accounts at the expense of current accounts. In the early 1950s the ratio of deposit accounts to the total of current and deposit accounts had been less than one-third, but by the early 1970s this ratio had risen to over 45%, back to the proportion of the 1930s (Collins, 1988: 427).

Table 10.43 *Combined balance sheets of all UK banks, 1973–1990 (£ million)*

A. Assets

	Cash and balances at Bank of England	Money at call	Total discounts	Loans and advances	Total investments	Other assets	Total assets
1973	1,237	2,548	1,426	87,574	1,962	4,287	99,034
1979	1,938	3,629	3,668	237,866	6,880	9,861	263,842
1985	3,063	6,414	5,701	675,417	47,696	23,460	761,751
1990	5,649	10,726	19,974	1,118,890	70,043	41,136	1,266,418

B. Liabilities

	Sterling deposits	Other currency deposits	Notes outstanding	Other liabilities	Total liabilities
1973	41,125	54,364	223	3,322	99,034
1979	76,915	169,497	498	16,932	263,842
1985	208,572	499,530	995	52,654	761,751
1990	528,160	637,435	1,678	99,145	1,266,418

Source: UK Central Statistical Office (*Annual Abstract of Statistics*, various years).

The high rates of inflation in the 1970s, in particular, made savers aware of the opportunity cost of holding money in accounts bearing no interest. Among the other liabilities, the Scottish and Northern Irish banks continued to issue their own notes, but the proportion of the liabilities of the banks accounted for by these notes declined from the 1950s (Collins, 1988: 426).

From 1973 the story has to be taken up via an analysis of the combined balance sheets of all UK banks, presented in table 10.43. The most liquid assets (the share of cash and balances at the Bank of England, money at call and bills discounted) continued to decline as a share of total assets. With loans and advances remaining stable at around 89% of total assets, the fall in the share of liquid assets was matched by a rise in the share of total investments. However, it is the liability side of the balance sheets that tells the more interesting story, with the growing share of non-sterling deposits until the mid-1980s reflecting the growing internationalisation of the business, but with a resurgence of sterling business during the boom of the late 1980s. This is, therefore, a convenient point at which to consider the merchant and overseas banks, traditionally the main actors in international banking.

10.4.3 Merchant banks, overseas banks and the wholesale money markets

The clearing banks maintained a vast branch network to facilitate the taking of deposits from small customers on a retail basis. Alongside the clearers, merchant banks had traditionally taken deposits from a smaller number of corporate customers or very rich individuals. In addition, banks could bid for funds in the wholesale money markets, which existed to channel funds between lenders and borrowers. Funds raised in this way could then be lent out, with the banks turning a profit on the differential between the interest paid and the interest received. The traditional wholesale money markets had been created by the discount houses, under the watchful regulatory eye of the Bank of England (Collins, 1988: 360–1). Deposits placed through the traditional money markets were thus secured, since the Bank of England acted as lender of last resort to the discount houses. From the 1950s, however, a number of parallel wholesale money markets emerged, operating outside the strict supervision of the monetary authorities. Of particular importance here were the eurodollar markets, in which holders of dollar funds outside the United States could place them on deposit with European banks to take advantage of higher interest rates and avoid restrictive US banking regulations (Tew, 1977: 154–7). The business was heavily based in London, building on the City's traditional expertise in international banking and taking advantage of the Bank of England's permissive attitude. The use of other currencies as well as dollars led to the use of the more general term 'Eurocurrency' rather than 'Eurodollar' markets (Collins, 1988: 374–6). Once established, the new services and the new financial instruments traded, such as certificates of deposit and interbank deposits, ensured the continuation of the parallel money markets long after the conditions that had brought them into being had receded (Collins, 1988: 365). The institutions involved in these parallel money markets, which included the merchant banks and overseas banks with offices in London, were labelled 'secondary banks' during the late 1960s (Revell, 1968).

London's role at the centre of the eurocurrency markets explains the explosive growth of the total UK banking sector compared with the UK retail banks in part A of table 10.40. It also explains the rapid growth of 'other currency deposits' compared with sterling deposits during the 1970s in part B of table 10.43. However, as well as stimulating the renewed growth of international financial activities, the merchant banks also played a key role in corporate finance from the 1950s. In particular, aggressive merchant banks such as Warburgs were instrumental in developing the contested takeover bid, acting as advisers to Tube Investments during their hostile bid for British Aluminium in 1957, which ushered in a new era of hostile takeovers (Channon, 1978: 63). The merger boom of the 1960s provided buoyant business for merchant banks offering advice on mergers and acquisitions, complementing the business of domestic new issues, in which merchant banks had become heavily involved between the wars.

The diversification of the clearing banks from the late 1960s blurred the distinction between merchant and clearing banks, and the distinction was further blurred by the diversification strategies of the merchant banks, moving into activities such as leasing and factoring services, insurance broking and underwriting, investment management and pension fund consultancy (Channon, 1978: 64–5). Unlike the clearers, however, the merchant banks became heavily involved in property development, which created problems during the secondary banking crisis of 1973–1975 (Collins, 1988: 381). An important principle of wholesale banking is to ensure a rough matching between assets and liabilities in terms of amount, period and currency, but this principle was neglected by some of the fringe banks during the monetary expansion following the introduction of Competition and Credit Control in 1971 (Reid, 1982: 27–8). As a number of fringe banks experienced difficulties from December 1973, the stability of the banking sector was threatened in a way not seen since the 1930s, or possibly even the Barings Crisis of 1890 (Reid, 1982: 193). The Bank of England, together with the clearing banks, established a Control Committee, known in City circles as the 'Lifeboat', to provide funds to beleaguered institutions. In addition to the £1.3 billion advanced by the Lifeboat, the Bank of England and other financial institutions had to provide exceptional finance to property companies and other businesses. Although much of the money was repaid, Reid (1982: 190–2) suggests that the rescue operation cost the Bank of England £100 million and the clearing banks £50 million in unrepaid loans.

The resurgence of London as the world's leading financial centre was based on international wholesale banking, which was the principal growth area in banking. Many of the banks involved in this business were based in London but foreign-owned. The growth of American and later Japanese multinational banking reflected the growing relative importance of these countries in the international economy and the strength of their currencies (Jones, 1993: 320–1, 370–1). By contrast, the British overseas banks, with their orientation towards retail banking in the former British Empire, went into relative decline. Although consolidation occurred, with six large multinational banking groups emerging by 1971, five of which had a multi-regional presence, attempts

Table 10.44 *Home ownership in Britain, 1914–1991*

	Rate of owner occupation (%)
1914	10.0
1939	33.0
1953	34.5
1961	44.4
1971	52.1
1981	58.6
1991	68.0

Source: Miles (1992: 66).

to diversify beyond traditional areas of expertise met with limited success (Jones, 1993: 262–72). Data from the Bank for International Settlements suggest that, by 1990, British-owned banks held just 4.6% of international bank assets, in sixth place behind Japan (35.5%), the United States (11.9%), Germany (10.1%), France (9.3%) and Italy (5.5%) (Jones, 1993: 321).

10.4.4 Building societies

The share of building societies in the assets of all financial institutions increased rapidly during the post-war period, as can be seen in table 10.40. While building societies accounted for 6.5% of total assets in 1951, this share had risen to 11.2% in 1990. In fact, the period of expansion occurred largely during the 1950s and 1960s, since the share of building societies had already reached 11.1% by 1968. As with the expansion of the inter-war period, it is necessary to consider both the liabilities and the asset sides of the building societies' balance sheets. On the liabilities side, the building societies continued to enjoy favourable treatment with regard to interest payments, being allowed to make a tax payment based on the composite tax liability of taxpayers and non-taxpayers (Cleary, 1965: 272–3). This enabled them to compete effectively for retail deposits. On the asset side, however, an important factor behind the expansion of building society advances was surely the massive extension of owner occupation, shown here in table 10.44. Since the building societies and the banks continued to operate in largely separate segments of the market during the 1950s and 1960s, this extension of home ownership naturally favoured the building societies, the traditional providers of mortgage finance, and this expansion should not be seen as evidence of particularly dynamic behaviour. Indeed, the building societies at this time operated a cartel, with interest rate adjustments being notoriously sticky, so that mortgage rationing was widespread (McKillop and Ferguson, 1993: 9–10).

Home ownership continued to grow rapidly during the 1970s and 1980s, but, with the breakdown of the traditional segmentation of British financial markets, this no longer favoured the building societies over the banks and other financial institutions, and the share of the building societies in the assets of all financial institutions stabilised. With banks breaking into their traditional territory, some building societies felt disadvantaged by the restrictive nature of building society regulations, and in 1989 the Abbey National, the second largest building society, became a publicly quoted bank, starting a trend towards building society demutualisation (McKillop and Ferguson, 1989: 20).

10.4.5 *Insurance*

Insurance companies accounted for the largest share of the assets of non-bank financial intermediaries between the 1960s, when they became more important than national savings, and the 1980s, when they were overtaken in size by pension funds. National savings accounted for the largest share of the assets of non-bank financial intermediaries in 1951, following a massive expansion to finance the war, but this part of the sector declined in real terms between 1951 and 1990, with nominal assets growing at an annual rate of 4.7% at a time when inflation averaged 6.8% per annum (table 10.40). The insurance companies experienced positive asset growth in real terms at a rate of 4.3% per annum, the same rate as for the non-bank financial intermediaries sector as a whole. The assets of pension funds grew at an annual rate of 8.6% in real terms.

By the start of the post-war period it had become conventional to classify the insurance market by making a distinction between long-term business and general business, with the former containing a large element of saving over a number of years and the latter focused largely on covering risks over a one-year period (Carter, 1988: 308). In table 10.45, long-term business is subdivided between ordinary and industrial life assurance in UK and overseas business. Note that, in comparing the inter-war and post-war classifications, the data in table 9.46 includes overseas business with ordinary life premiums. In table 10.46, general business has been broken down into the three main categories of (1) motor, (2) non-motor (fire and accident) and (3) marine (including aviation and transport), with each category covering UK and overseas

Table 10.45 *Life assurance business of UK offices, 1951–1990*

	Current price premiums (£ million)			Constant price premiums (£ million 1973)		
	Domestic ordinary	Domestic industrial	Overseas	Domestic ordinary	Domestic industrial	Overseas
1951	209	108	23	553	286	61
1960	468	161	61	902	310	117
1968	1,048	244	175	1,514	353	253
1973	2,224	356	394	2,224	356	394
1979	4,967	746	802	2,034	306	328
1985	13,714	1,198	2,341	3,380	295	577
1990	32,197	1,371	6,597	5,966	254	1,222

Note:
Current price figures converted to constant prices using GDP deflator from the UK Central Statistical Office (*National Income and Expenditure*, various years).

Sources: UK Central Statistical Office (*Annual Abstract of Statistics*, various years), Association of British Insurers (*Insurance Facts and Figures*, various years, *Insurance Statistics*, various years, *Insurance Statistics Year Book*, various years).

Table 10.46 *General insurance business of UK offices, 1951–1990*

	Current price premiums (£ million)			Constant price premiums (£ million 1973)		
	Motor	Non-motor (fire and accident)	Marine (including aviation and transport)	Motor	Non-motor (fire and accident)	Marine (including aviation and transport)
1951	119	303	68	315	801	180
1960	308	529	84	593	1,019	162
1968	605	961	161	874	1,389	233
1973	1,159	1,908	293	1,159	1,908	293
1979	2,545	4,449	515	1,042	1,822	211
1985	4,621	9,906	1,268	1,139	2,441	312
1990	8,549	15,378	1,564	1,584	2,849	290

Note:
Current price figures converted to constant prices using GDP deflator from the UK Central Statistical Office (*National Income and Expenditure*, various years).

Sources: UK Central Statistical Office (*Annual Abstract of Statistics*, various years), Association of British Insurers (*Insurance Facts and Figures*, various years, *Insurance Statistics*, various years).

risks. Note that, in comparing with the inter-war classification of chapter 9, in the post-war period motor insurance has been separated from other accident insurance, and non-motor accident has been combined with fire insurance.

Long-term business accounted for a growing share of the total premium income of insurance companies, with total life assurance premiums in table 10.45 growing at an annual rate of 5.4% in real terms, compared with a growth rate of 3.3% for general business premiums in table 10.46. This represented an increase in the growth rate of life assurance business compared with the inter-war period. However, in contrast to the inter-war period, growth was concentrated in ordinary business, with industrial business first slowing its rate of increase and then going into real as well as relative decline. Whereas industrial premiums accounted for 31.8% of long-term business in 1951, this had fallen to just 3.4% by 1990. The decline of industrial life assurance reflected growing prosperity, which reduced the market for the basic types of life assurance product sold by industrial life offices and the need for the payment of premiums on a weekly cash basis (Franklin and Woodhead, 1980: 43). The wider spread of bank accounts among the population, which accompanied growing prosperity, allowed the monthly or annual payment of premiums through banks. This was much more convenient for insurance companies that were keen to rationalise and mechanise administration. Overseas long-term business grew even more rapidly than domestic ordinary life assurance, with British companies playing an important role in the growth of trade in financial services, particularly during the 1980s.

Within general insurance business, the most rapidly growing segment was motor insurance, continuing a trend already established between the wars. Motor insurance premiums grew at an annual rate of 4.1% between 1951 and 1990, compared with 3.3.% in non-motor insurance and 1.2% in marine insurance (table 10.46). With non-motor insurance accounting for around 60% of general business throughout the period, motor insurance increased its share from around a quarter to a third, while marine insurance declined in relative importance.

The growing relative importance of motor insurance of course reflected the dramatic rise of road transport, as shown in the share of road transport in passenger-miles and freight ton-miles (table 10.14), the number of motor vehicles per thousand inhabitants (table 10.16) and the mileage of roads in Britain (table 10.17). Despite the rapid growth of premium income, however, the insurance companies were continually worried about the profitability of this business because of the number of accidents causing death and serious injury (Supple, 1970:

519). Although premiums could be raised by the 'tariff companies' which adhered to the cartel operated by the Accident Offices Association, and which controlled about two-thirds of the market in the 1950s, this risked losing business to non-tariff companies. As a response to their loss of market share, the tariff companies abandoned the common rate in 1968, and began offering substantial discounts to low-risk drivers (Channon, 1978: 104).

In non-motor (fire and accident), growth was achieved partly as a result of the spread of more traditional forms of insurance, such as personal accident, personal travel and burglary, to a wider segment of the population (Supple, 1970: 520). However, it was also partly achieved by the application of traditional forms to new areas of insurance, as with the widening of fire insurance to include damage against storms, frost, floods and other natural disasters, or with contractors' 'all risks' policies for large undertakings such as the erection of dams and nuclear power stations (Supple, 1970: 521–2). The problems for the insurance companies in this segment of the market included periodic natural disasters, with expensive damage claims, and a sustained increase in fire insurance claims, as a result of the increased use of open-plan structures and more electrical equipment (Supple, 1970: 522–3).

The slowest-growing segment of general insurance business between 1951 and 1990 was marine insurance, where the main innovation was the spread of cover to aviation and other transport risks. Despite the rapid growth of aviation business, this was not sufficient to drive rapid growth in the sector as a whole. Although these figures exclude Lloyd's marine business, which generated around the same amount of premium income as the insurance companies in the early post-war period, this affects the level of business more than the trend, which was similar in Lloyd's and the other companies (Supple, 1970: 523–4).

Although the UK insurance sector as a whole was dominated by composite insurers offering a full range of insurance products during the post-war period 1950 to 1990, the degree of competition varied in the life assurance and general business segments. Figures on the three-firm concentration ratio are presented in table 10.47, although care must be taken in comparing the data for 1984 with earlier years. Concentration was higher in life assurance than in general business in the 1950s, but the market leader in life assurance (the Prudential) saw its share of the market shrink from 24.3% in 1950 to 12.6% in 1972, and the other main companies also lost market share in the face of aggressive competition from other established composite insurers and new entrants (Channon, 1978: 95–7). Standard Life, a mutual company, had become the third largest provider of life cover by the early 1950s,

Table 10.47 *Three-firm concentration ratio in the UK insurance sector, 1950–1984 (%)*

	Life assurance	General business
1950	39.6	
1955		29.7
1960	30.9	37.5
1965	30.2	39.1
1970	28.7	47.9
1972	23.4	47.5
1984	21.5	33.6

Note:
Figures for 1950–1972 refer to the corporate sector only, while the 1984 figures include Lloyd's premium income and exclude industrial life assurance.
Source: Channon (1978: 97, 99), Carter (1988: 316).

and the mutual companies together managed to hold around 15 to 20% of the market through to the 1970s. The upshot of these trends was a substantial decline of the three-firm concentration ratio in life assurance, indicating an increase in competition.

In general business, by contrast, concentration first increased between 1955 and 1970, before declining during the 1970s and 1980s. The rising concentration ratio during the 1950s and 1960s resulted from a series of mergers amongst the composite companies. This merger boom might at first sight seem puzzling, since these companies operated cartels in each of the major categories of insurance. However, as Supple (1970: 530–1) points out, the high levels of profitability attracted new entrants, particularly in these areas. As a result, the tariff companies sought economies of scale in integrated operations, together with the defensive advantages of size in a hostile environment (Supple, 1970: 533; Channon, 1978: 99–101). The cartel in motor insurance was abandoned in 1968, and once this had happened the cartels in fire insurance and other categories came under increased pressure. Although the tariffs were abandoned fairly quickly in most areas, the fire tariff remained in force until 1985, despite a recommendation by the Monopolies Commission in 1972 that it should be terminated (Carter, 1988: 320; Westall, 1997: 57). Westall (57–61) argues that the period of regulated competition in general insurance through the organisational mediation of the tariff companies was brought decisively to an end only in the late 1980s, with the growth of direct marketing by companies such as Direct Line. This was a result of the revolution in ICT, and will be considered more fully in the next chapter. However, it is worth noting here that Direct Line, which was launched only in 1987, had already secured 12% of the UK private motor insurance market by 1990, rising to 25% by 1994 (Westall, 1997:57). This represented a considerable competitive threat to the established composite insurers.

The breakdown of the cartels in insurance put pressure on the profitability of underwriting, which, in turn, increased the importance of the investment performance of the companies. This growing importance of investment performance was reinforced by the need to cope with the rising inflation of the late 1960s and the 1970s. As a result of the massive issue of government debt during the war, the insurance companies, in common with other financial institutions, had very large holdings of British government securities in the early post-war period. During subsequent decades the main investment trends were away from government securities and into holdings of private equities and property (Channon, 1978: 105–7; Supple, 1970: 526–7).

Table 10.48 shows the overseas earnings of the UK insurance market. It should be noted that these earnings are greater than the contribution of insurance to the balance of payments as shown in table 10.41, which is limited to income from underwriting. Table 10.48 includes income from direct investment (i.e. profits from overseas subsidiaries) and from property and portfolio investment. The 1990 figures reveal the devastating impact of a series of disasters on Lloyd's, but the much smaller impact on companies and brokers. Overall, the UK insurance market continued to make substantial overseas earnings.

10.5 Conclusions

In the early 1950s the United States was at the zenith of its labour productivity leadership over Europe, in both the economy as a whole and in services. To some extent this situation reflected the much greater disruption that World War II caused in Europe, and between 1950 and 1990 Europe closed the productivity gap with the United States in line with the predictions of the convergence hypothesis. However, between the 1950s and the 1970s Britain was less successful than West Germany and other European countries in closing the productivity gap, and hence was overtaken by those countries. West Germany pulled ahead of Britain in the mid-1960s, in both services and the economy as a whole.

Why was West Germany more successful in catching up with the United States during the period between the beginning of the 1950s

Table 10.48 *Overseas earnings of the UK insurance market, 1965–1989* (£ million pounds)

A. At current prices

	Credits			Debits	Net earnings
	Companies	Lloyd's	Brokers		
1965	45	14	21		80
1968	90	74	36		200
1973	157	139	60	9	347
1979	522	424	228	16	1,158
1985	1,525	1,096	664	19	3,266
1989	1,677	660	721	131	2,927

B. At constant 1973 prices

	Credits			Debits	Net earnings
	Companies	Lloyd's	Brokers		
1965	72	23	34	–	129
1968	130	107	52	–	289
1973	157	139	60	9	347
1979	214	174	93	7	474
1985	376	270	164	5	805
1990	334	132	144	26	584

Note:
These figures differ from the contribution of insurance to the balance of payments in table 10.41, which are restricted to underwriting income; the figures in this table include income from direct investment (i.e. profits from overseas subsidiaries) and from property and portfolio investment.

Source: UK Central Statistical Office (*United Kingdom Balance of Payments*, various years).

and the end of the 1970s? The generally 'corporatist' institutional framework adopted in much of Europe as part of the post-war settlement, involving the establishment of a consensus between unions, employers' organisation and government, provided better incentives for the accumulation of human and physical capital in a country such as West Germany, where unions and employers' organisations were coherent and centralised, than in a country such as Britain, where the equivalent labour market institutions were fragmented and decentralised. In human capital accumulation, a centralised solution to the free-rider problem of poaching skilled workers encouraged the spread of apprenticeships into the service sector in West Germany, while, in the decentralised British setting, the apprenticeship system declined even in industry. In physical capital accumulation, the more centralised West German institutions were better able to commit credibly to agreements offering wage restraint in return for investments in new technology, or vice versa.

To some extent, the corporatist system was a natural accompaniment to the drive towards mass production in manufacturing and the industrialisation of services. General technological trends favoured standardisation and large-scale organisation, in services as well as in manufacturing, and the drive towards the industrialisation of services was more or less completed in this period. Britain had little choice but to embrace these developments, but the transition to industrialised services was difficult, since social capabilities remained oriented towards a more customised approach. Britain's performance remained rather better in sectors that remained suitable for customised, low-volume, high-margin business organised on the basis of networks, but this was a shrinking segment of the economy.

After a very unsuccessful performance during the 1970s Britain moved away from the corporatist institutional framework during the 1980s, in the direction of the more 'competitive' institutional framework of the United States. This involved a strengthening of anti-trust policy, privatisation, deregulation and limiting trade union immunities. Britain's relative economic decline was at least stemmed, but it was not yet decisively reversed. Only with the arrival of new technology in the 1990s, more suited to a customised approach to service provision and a decentralised form of organisation, has productivity growth in services been decisively better in Britain than in Germany and other European countries.

The sectoral variation in productivity performance illustrates these themes. In transport and communications, the industrialisation of services had already proceeded to a very high level by 1950, particularly on the railways and in post and telecommunications. Both British Railways and the Post Office operated as state monopolies with centralised bureaucracies, were starved of resources for investment, were slow to adopt new technologies even when resources were available and enjoyed less than cordial industrial relations with trade unions. Productivity performance between 1950 and 1973 was poor, but the situation improved during the 1970s and the 1980s in both sectors as Treasury restrictions were relaxed and decentralisation introduced. The privatisation of British Telecommunications in the 1980s and the introduction of competition provided a strong boost to productivity performance, although it is difficult to be so positive about the more ambitious privatisation of British Rail during the 1990s. Perhaps the most favourable response to the deregulation of the 1980s has been in air transport, which has seen explosive growth of non-scheduled air travel, and in passenger road transport, where deregulation has improved productivity on the buses.

Distribution in the domestic market became increasingly industrialised during the 1950s and 1960s, with the growth of large supermarkets and other multiple retailers offering self-service, and benefiting from scale economies in centralised functions such as buying, marketing and data processing. A further boost to scale came in the 1980s with the development of out-of-town shopping. Although Britain has followed US trends in organisation and technology in this highly 'industrialised' sector, the productivity outcomes have been disappointing. British performance has been rather better in merchant wholesaling and external trade, where Jones (2000) attributes the survival of British overseas trading companies in an unpromising period of decolonisation to the flexibility of the network form of organisation.

In financial services, the clearing banks between 1950 and the late 1960s exhibit many of the typical problems of large-scale, hierarchical, centralised business in Britain at this time, with slow progress in the adoption of labour-saving technology and uncordial labour relations. Sticking within the specialised niche of domestic retail banking, and operating a cartel, the clearing banks missed out on the rapidly growing parts of the sector. The abandonment of the cartel, decentralisation and aggressive expansion into other market segments saw an improved performance during the 1970s and 1980s. However, the real success story of British financial services is to be found in the more entrepreneurial institutions operating in the wholesale money markets. These 'parallel markets', operating outside the strict supervision of the monetary authorities, experienced an explosive growth that re-established London as the world's leading financial centre.

11 British services in the 1990s: a preliminary assessment

11.1 Introduction

To bring the story up to date, it is necessary to attempt a preliminary assessment of the performance of British services during the 1990s. No attempt will be made to provide a detailed assessment of individual services along the lines of the earlier chapters in this section, since historians have not yet had a chance to see the archival evidence that has informed judgments on earlier periods, and the literature is too sparse. Nevertheless, it is possible to provide the same quantitative information that has formed the backbone of earlier chapters, and hence bring the productivity trends up to date.

The most important development during this period has been in the area of technology. Whereas technological change for most of the twentieth century favoured standardisation, centralisation and large scale, the information and communications technology revolution of the 1990s has favoured customisation and decentralisation, but without sacrificing the high volume and high productivity of industrialised services. This trend mirrors the earlier retreat from mass production to flexible production that occurred in manufacturing during the 1980s (Edquist and Jacobsson, 1988; Milgrom and Roberts, 1990). Just as the trend towards standardisation and scale in services occurred unevenly between sectors in earlier periods, the information revolution of the 1990s has had an uneven impact on different sectors. Nevertheless, for services as a whole, these trends can be seen as favourable to Britain, where social capabilities remained adapted towards customisation and small scale rather than standardisation and large scale. Certainly, Britain began to catch up with continental European countries in services and in the economy as a whole during the 1990s, but, with the new technology and its applications being pioneered largely in the United States, Anglo-American productivity gaps have been slower to narrow, particularly since 1995 (O'Mahony and de Boer, 2002).

The key to understanding the impact of ICT on the organisation of services is the dramatic fall in the cost of information processing, by as much as 99.9% since the 1960s (Brynjolfsson and Hitt, 2000: 26). This has had a huge impact on efficient work practices, restoring autonomy to individual workers, but within an 'industrialised' environment characterised by the high-volume and low-margin provision of services. In the 'New Economy', many routine tasks have been automated, most workers perform their own clerical tasks using personal computers and email, and most workers have access through the use of networked computers and the internet to information that was previously only available centrally. The impact has been very large in the most technology-intensive parts of the service sector, such as financial and business services and transport and communications (O'Mahony and de Boer, 2002). However, the new technologies have not been adopted quite so extensively in other parts of the service sector, such as distribution.

11.2 Sectoral analysis of comparative productivity performance, 1990–2000

As in earlier chapters, it is helpful to begin by setting out Britain's recent productivity performance compared with the United States and Germany. However, from 1990 the German data refer to unified Germany, including the former German Democratic Republic, which has the effect of lowering overall German productivity. Hence, for a more representative picture of western Europe, data on France are also included.

Table 11.1 provides updated estimates from O'Mahony and de Boer (2002) for GDP per hour worked and GDP per capita for the US/UK, Germany/UK and France/UK comparisons. These authors focus on output per hour worked as the main measure of labour productivity, but, since hours worked per person and the proportion of the population in the labour force have varied quite substantially across the major economies considered here, data on GDP per capita are also provided. GDP per hour worked was nearly 40% higher in the United State in 1990, but by 1995 Britain had narrowed the gap to around 25 per cent. However, with the acceleration in US productivity growth after 1995, British catching up virtually ceased. Given high levels of labour force participation and long working hours, the US GDP per capita lead remained rather larger than the GDP per hour worked lead, at around 34% during the second half of the 1990s.

Turning to the comparison with western Europe, Britain has caught up steadily with France in terms of GDP per hour worked, but French labour productivity has remained substantially higher than in Britain, and close to US levels. In the unified Germany, GDP per hour worked

Table 11.1 *Comparative GDP per hour worked and GDP per capita, total economy, 1990–2001 (UK = 100)*

	1990	1995	2001
US/UK			
GDP per hour	138.4	124.4	123.9
GDP per capita	140.1	134.3	133.7
Germany/UK			
GDP per hour	123.5	118.7	117.0
GDP per capita	104.8	100.0	94.6
France/UK			
GDP per hour	139.1	128.0	122.3
GDP per capita	113.8	105.7	98.5

Note:
Data refer to unified Germany.
Source: Updated estimates from O'Mahony and de Boer (2002).

has also remained higher than in Britain, although the reunification pulled down German labour productivity relative to France. Note, however, that by the end of the 1990s the French and German labour productivity lead over Britain did not translate into higher GDP per capita. With higher labour force participation and longer hours of work, Britain has now eliminated the GDP per capita gap with much of western Europe.

If attention were to be confined solely to comparative levels of GDP per hour worked in table 11.1, it would be hard to understand why the recent literature on growth has been dominated by the idea of a productivity miracle in the United States, accompanied by chronic sclerosis in western Europe. The paradox can be explained partly by the inclusion of the data on GDP per capita, with the United States enjoying a substantial lead over all western European countries of the order of 30 to 40%. However, the differences in labour force participation and hours worked, which are the proximate source of this US per capita income lead, raise difficult issues concerning welfare. It could be argued, on the one hand, that Europeans are prevented from working longer hours by excessive taxation and labour market regulation or, on the other hand, that Americans are forced to work longer hours than they wish, due to external effects from the hours worked by others (Prescott, 2003; Layard, 2003). However, the popular perception of US dynamism and European sclerosis is also partly explained by the different growth trajectories of the two continents, particularly since 1995. Since the

Table 11.2 *Comparative labour productivity levels by sector: output per hour worked, 1990–2001 (UK = 100)*

	1990	1995	2001
US/UK			
Total economy	138.4	124.4	123.9
Agriculture	162.3	137.8	187.4
Industry	151.9	133.2	130.3
Services	133.1	121.4	120.6
Market services	*149.9*	*136.3*	*139.0*
Market economy	*148.8*	*134.0*	*136.9*
Germany/UK			
Total economy	123.5	118.7	117.0
Agriculture	37.4	39.6	46.9
Industry	126.1	105.0	103.8
Services	126.9	127.7	122.7
Market services	*145.5*	*141.1*	*131.1*
Market economy	*134.8*	*124.8*	*121.2*
France/UK			
Total economy	139.1	128.0	122.3
Agriculture	61.0	71.5	78.0
Industry	133.9	120.1	119.9
Services	152.2	137.7	127.2
Market services	*169.8*	*145.8*	*126.2*
Market economy	*142.6*	*129.3*	*120.7*

Note:
Data for Germany refer to unified Germany; 'market services' includes transport, communications, distribution, hotels and catering, financial and business services, and personal services; 'market economy' is defined as total economy excluding, health, education, public administration and real estate.

Source: Updated estimates from O'Mahony and de Boer (2002).

mid-1990s labour productivity growth has accelerated in the United States, whereas it has decelerated in the total EU15 and each of the three European countries included in table 11.1 (O'Mahony and van Ark, 2003). However, this concentration on the acceleration or deceleration of growth rates, popular in the literature, obscures the fact that labour productivity growth rates since the mid-1990s in the United States have not been much higher than in either Britain or Germany.

Table 11.2 shows comparative levels of output per hour worked for the usual sectoral division between agriculture, industry and services, but also shows figures for the market economy and market services. This deals with the increasingly problematic issue of the treatment of non-market services (health, education and public administration) in the national accounts as they have become more important. With output measured largely by inputs, national statistical offices have increasingly experimented with ways of allowing for productivity growth and quality improvements, but, as yet, no agreement has been reached on how to do this (O'Mahony and van Ark, 2003).

The basic picture was established in O'Mahony (1999), and table 11.2 provides updates for output per hour worked on a comparative basis, indexed on the UK = 100 basis. These data show a significant British labour productivity gap with all three countries in both industry and market services, and the United States also ahead of Britain in agriculture. Note that, since 1995, Britain has performed marginally better than the United States in industry but lost some ground in market services. Britain's productivity gap with Germany and France has narrowed in both industry and market services. By implication, table 11.2 shows the United States gaining some ground on Britain in market services and surging ahead of both Germany and France. Much of the literature on the recent US productivity experience has emphasised that the acceleration in US productivity growth was primarily due to market services, in particular those in which ICT is an important input (Triplett and Bosworth, 2003; O'Mahony and van Ark, 2003).

Table 11.2 also shows comparative labour productivity levels for the total market economy, which excludes non-market services and real estate. This shows a larger US lead over all three EU countries than is apparent from the aggregate economy figures, and, furthermore, this gap has been widening since 1995. Labour productivity growth in the non-market sector in the United States has been particularly poor over this time period, as shown in O'Mahony and van Ark (2003), and this broad sector represents a much larger share of aggregate economic activity in the United States than in the European countries. However, as discussed by Triplett and Bosworth (2003), part of the relatively poor US performance in non-market services, in particular in health, may be the result of measurement errors.

11.3 Sectoral productivity trends in Britain since 1990

11.3.1 *The aggregate economy*

As for the earlier periods, it will be convenient to set out trends in productivity performance at the aggregate level, to provide a benchmark against which sectoral performance can be assessed. Table 11.3 provides indices of output, inputs and productivity in the United Kingdom

Table 11.3 *Productivity in the British aggregate economy, 1990–1999*

A. Indices of output, inputs and productivity (1995 = 100)

	Output	Persons engaged	Capital	Output per person	TFP
1990	92.8	104.4	88.4	88.9	93.7
1995	100.0	100.0	100.0	100.0	100.0
1999	111.4	105.7	112.4	105.4	103.3

B. Growth rates of output, inputs and productivity (% per annum)

	1990–1995	1995–1999	1990–1999
Output	1.5	2.5	2.0
Persons engaged	−0.9	1.4	0.1
Capital	2.5	2.9	2.7
Output per person	2.4	1.1	1.9
TFP	1.3	0.8	1.1

Note:
Factor shares are 32% for capital and 68% for labour, based on 1995 figures.
Source: Derived from O'Mahony (2002).

between 1990 and 1999, together with growth rates calculated over the whole period and broken down into two sub-periods, 1990–1995 and 1995–1999. During the decade as a whole output growth continued at the high rate of the 1980s. Since there was little growth of the labour force, this also translated into a high rate of labour productivity growth, at 1.9% per annum. The capital stock also continued to grow rapidly, but this still allowed TFP growth of 1.1% per annum.

Breaking the decade down into the two sub-periods, there was an acceleration in the growth rate of output after 1995, as in the United States. However, in contrast to the United States, Britain exhibited a deceleration in productivity growth during the second half of the 1990s, with labour productivity growth declining sharply from 2.4 to 1.1% per annum and TFP growth falling from 1.3 to 0.8% per annum. It is this contrast between accelerating productivity growth in the United States and declining productivity growth in Britain and continental Europe during the second half of the 1990s that has given rise to a large literature talking of a productivity miracle in the United States and sclerosis in western Europe. However, it should be borne in mind that productivity growth rates in the United States were not much higher than in Britain or Germany, even during the second half of the 1990s.

Table 11.4 *Productivity in the British transport and communications sector, 1990–1999*

A. Indices of output, inputs and productivity (1995 = 100)

	Output	Persons engaged	Capital	Output per person	TFP
1990	85.0	112.8	80.3	75.4	84.0
1995	100.0	100.0	100.0	100.0	100.0
1999	130.7	106.9	130.0	122.3	114.8

B. Growth rates of output, inputs and productivity (% per annum)

	1990–1995	1995–1999	1990–1999
Output	3.3	6.7	4.8
Persons engaged	−2.4	1.7	−0.6
Capital	4.4	6.6	5.4
Output per person	5.7	5.0	5.4
TFP	3.5	3.5	3.5

Source: Derived from O'Mahony (2002).

11.3.2 Transport and communications

Output, input and productivity trends in the British transport and communications sector during the 1990s are shown in table 11.4. Comparing with the trends for the whole economy in table 11.3, output in transport and communications grew more rapidly than in the economy as a whole throughout the decade, but particularly after 1995. Both labour productivity and TFP in transport and communications grew very rapidly during this decade, reflecting the growing use of ICT in much of the sector (O'Mahony and de Boer, 2002). Note that, although there was a small decline in labour productivity growth during the second half of the decade, TFP grew equally rapidly before and after 1995.

11.3.3 Distribution

Table 11.5 provides data on output, input and productivity trends in the British distribution sector during the 1990s. For the period as a whole output grew at the same rate as in the economy as a whole although the boom of the second half of the 1990s was slightly more pronounced in distribution, as can be seen by comparing tables 11.5 and 11.3. Since

Table 11.5 *Productivity in the British distribution sector, 1990–1999*

A. Indices of output, inputs and productivity (1995 = 100)

	Output	Persons engaged	Capital	Output per person	TFP
1990	92.9	99.9	82.8	93.0	98.8
1995	100.0	100.0	100.0	100.0	100.0
1999	111.2	105.8	126.6	105.1	99.2

B. Growth rates of output, inputs and productivity (% per annum)

	1990–1995	1995–1999	1990–1999
Output	1.5	2.7	2.0
Persons engaged	0.0	1.4	0.6
Capital	3.8	5.9	4.7
Output per person	1.5	1.3	1.4
TFP	0.2	0.2	0.0

Source: Derived from O'Mahony (2002).

employment in distribution grew more rapidly than in the aggregate economy over the decade as a whole, labour productivity also grew more slowly in distribution than in the aggregate economy. Given the very rapid growth of the capital stock in distribution, TFP growth was essentially zero in this sector. Despite being a larger sector in terms of employment, distribution accounted for a smaller share of Britain's ICT capital than either transport and communications or financial and business services (O'Mahony and de Boer, 2002).

11.3.4 Financial and business services

During the 1990s output in financial and business services continued to grow more rapidly than in the economy as a whole, particularly after 1995, as can be seen by comparing table 11.6 with table 11.3. However, with employment also growing rapidly, labour productivity growth in financial and business services was slower than in the aggregate economy over the decade as a whole. TFP grew at the same rate in financial and business services as in the aggregate economy over the decade as a whole, although this was made up of a lower than average performance in the first half of the 1990s and a better than average performance after 1995. Financial and business services contained the second largest share of ICT capital after transport and communications.

Table 11.6 *Productivity in the British financial and business services sector, 1990–1999*

A. Indices of output, inputs and productivity (1995 = 100)

	Output	Persons engaged	Capital	Output per person	TFP
1990	91.0	96.5	86.7	94.3	97.6
1995	100.0	100.0	100.0	100.0	100.0
1999	126.9	116.3	121.7	109.1	107.5

B. Growth rates of output, inputs and productivity (% per annum)

	1990–1995	1995–1999	1990–1999
Output	1.9	6.0	3.7
Persons engaged	0.7	3.8	2.1
Capital	2.9	4.9	3.8
Output per person	1.2	2.2	1.6
TFP	0.5	1.8	1.1

Source: Derived from O'Mahony (2002).

11.4 The ICT boom of the 1990s

The second half of the 1990s saw an acceleration in the rate of economic growth in the United States, which was widely attributed to the diffusion of ICT. Early concerns about the lack of a productivity pay-off to ICT investments, known as the 'Solow paradox', began to give way to findings of positive returns to ICT spending at the firm level (Brynjolfson and Hitt, 1996). This was particularly true in market services, which were a very important part of economic activity by the 1990s. Eventually, even at the macro level, evidence emerged of a strong contribution of ICT to the acceleration of labour productivity growth through capital deepening (Jorgenson and Stiroh, 2000; Oliner and Sichel, 2000). Although researchers have also found evidence of some contribution to labour productivity growth from ICT capital deepening in European countries, the effect has been smaller (Colecchia and Schreyer, 2001; Inklaar et al., 2003; Cette et al., 2002; Oulton, 2001).

Table 11.7 decomposes the comparative labour productivity levels for market services in 1999 into the contributions of physical capital, skills and TFP. This shows that total capital, made up of both physical capital and skills, accounts for nearly all the German and French labour productivity lead over Britain. However, a substantial chunk of the US labour

Table 11.7 *Decomposition of comparative labour productivity levels in market services, 1999*

	US/UK	Germany/UK	France/UK
Market services			
Output per hour, comparative levels (UK = 100)	132	125	125
Percentage contributions:			
Physical capital	21	62	75
Skills	2	24	
TFP	77	14	25

Note:
Skills are included with TFP for France.

Source: O'Mahony and de Boer (2002).

productivity lead over Britain is the result of higher TFP. Although part of the mechanism by which ICT raises labour productivity is through capital deepening, there is a growing emphasis in the literature on TFP growth through the reorganisation of work practices in technology-intensive market service sectors (Brynjolfsson and Hitt, 2000). The importance of TFP to the US labour productivity advantage over Britain, and *a fortiori* over Germany and France, is consistent with this interpretation.

However, as Broadberry and O'Mahony (2004) note, there is a danger in jumping from this to the conclusion drawn by many economic commentators: that European economies have become too sclerotic and are in need of drastic reform along US lines (OECD, 2003; Gust and Marquez, 2002; UK Treasury, 2000). Although there may be dangers in sticking with tried and trusted methods when technological circumstances change, as Crafts (2004) points out, a historical perspective also suggests that there are good reasons to be cautious about an overenthusiastic embrace of the fashionable model of the day. The first point to note is that the differences between countries in both productivity levels and growth rates are relatively small. Part of the reason for the widespread enthusiasm about US growth rates after 1995 can be seen clearly in table 11.8, which shows the slowness of US growth in the period before 1995 while Europe was catching up (Field, 2004; Crafts, 2004). Any differences in productivity growth rates during the period since 1995 have been very small in comparison with the differences during the period 1950 to 1973, in market services as well as in the economy as a whole.

A second reason for caution about orienting policy too strongly towards the US model is that Europe is anyway moving in the direction of

Table 11.8 *Growth rates of real GDP per hour worked, 1950–2003 (% per annum)*

	1950–1973	1973–1995	1995–2003
United States	2.37	1.19	2.01
United Kingdom	2.66	2.18	1.98
Germany*	5.18	2.65	1.67
France	4.89	2.71	2.03

Note:
Former West Germany for the period 1950 to 1990; unified Germany thereafter.
Source: Broadberry and O'Mahony (2004).

adopting ICT, but in ways consistent with local circumstances. This view receives support from recent models of growth resulting from general-purpose technology (GPT) (Bresnahan and Trajtenberg, 1995; Helpman, 1998; Brynjolfsson and Hitt, 2000; Bresnahan et al., 2002; Basu et al., 2003). These models suggest that, when a GPT is first put in place, it might reduce measured output because it is correlated with unmeasured investments in complementary capital, such as training and reorganisation of the production process. Once these investments have been put in place, however, the impact of the GPT becomes positive. Basu et al. (2003), applying ordinary least squares (OLS) to a cross-section of US and UK industries, find that TFP growth is positively correlated with past investments in ICT, while it is negatively correlated with contemporaneous investments – consistent with GPT theory. They also suggest that there may be differences in the lag structures in the two countries. It is important to emphasise from historical experience that previous attempts by British governments to force the pace on the adoption of new technologies and their associated organisational changes have not been very successful. This probably shows up most obviously in the manufacturing sector during the post-war period, through the policy of encouraging mergers to bring about national champions with large enough market shares to justify investment in mass production technologies (Turner, 1969: 81–6; Cowling et al., 1980). The disastrous performance of a number of recent government ICT projects serves to underline this conclusion (UK House of Commons, Committee of Public Accounts, 2002, 2004).

A third point that can be made here concerns the impact on human capital. Broadberry (1997a) argues that the earlier embrace of the US industrial model in the 1950s and 1960s accelerated the decline of the apprenticeship system in Britain by downgrading the acquisition of intermediate-level skills. The return to fashion of flexible production from the 1970s did something to redress the imbalance and Britain began to make up its intermediate skills gap with the rest of continental Europe. There is a danger now that admiration for the US model is once again downgrading intermediate skills, with the government apparently preferring to concentrate on raising the proportion of school leavers going to university. This could be justified on the grounds that ICT requires the skills of university graduates, and that intermediate-level skills of the type that Germany has in abundance are no longer suitable for the world of modern technology (Crafts, 2004: 141–2). However, whilst it is clearly true that computers and related technologies were initially very complex to use, their widespread adoption has coincided with drastic simplification. Thus, it is unclear if the new technology will continue to be biased in favour of relatively expensive university graduates.

11.5 Conclusions

Britain's productivity performance relative to France and Germany, and to a lesser extent the United States, improved during the 1990s, particularly in market services. Britain's social capabilities were not well suited to the technological changes which drove the industrialisation of services during much of the twentieth century, and which required standardisation, centralisation and large scale. However, the widespread application of information and communications technology during the 1990s, with its emphasis on customisation and decentralisation, improved the situation, particularly in technology-intensive sectors such as financial and business services, and transport and communications.

The new technology has had a dramatic impact on the organisation of work, restoring autonomy to individual workers, but without sacrificing the productivity gains of the earlier industrialisation of services, brought about through high volumes and low margins. Many routine tasks have been automated, leaving most workers to provide a customised service, through access via networked computers and the internet to information that was previously only available centrally, and to perform their own clerical tasks using personal computers and email.

12 Summary and conclusions

This book tells the story of the role of services in Britain's productivity performance between the middle of the nineteenth century and the end of the twentieth century, with particular emphasis on how Britain compared with the United States and Germany. This is a vital missing part of most accounts of comparative productivity performance over the long run, since the overtaking of Britain by the United States and Germany cannot be explained by changing comparative productivity performance in industry, which has been surprisingly stationary over the last century and a half (Broadberry, 1997a, 1998).

A central part of the story involves the 'industrialisation' of market services, and the extent to which Britain was able to adapt to the technological and organisational changes that underpinned it, many of which originated in the United States. This involved the transition from customised, low-volume, high-margin business organised on the basis of networks to standardised, high-volume, low-margin business with hierarchical management. To the extent that some services remained unsuitable for industrialisation, Britain was able to retain a strong productivity position, even relative to the United States, and this helps to explain the moderate nature of Britain's relative economic decline. Nevertheless, Britain had already been overtaken by the United States in services, as in the economy as a whole, by the 1890s.

To the extent that conditions were even less favourable to the industrialisation of services in Germany before World War II, largely as a result of the much larger agricultural sector and the associated lower levels of urbanisation, Britain was able to retain a productivity lead over Germany. However, by the 1960s Britain had fallen behind Germany and many other western European countries, as well as the United States. Only with the information and communications technology revolution of the 1990s, with its return to customised service provision and more decentralised organisation, has Britain begun to narrow the productivity gap with Germany and other European countries in market services.

12.1 Measuring comparative productivity performance

Part I of the book is concerned with the measurement of comparative productivity performance, at the level of major sectors as well as for the economy as a whole. At the level of the aggregate economy, Britain had higher labour productivity than either the United States or Germany in the mid-nineteenth century, but was overtaken by the United States in the 1890s. The United States reached its peak labour productivity lead over both Britain and Germany in the early 1950s. Since then both countries have narrowed the productivity gap with the United States, but Germany did so more rapidly and overtook Britain in the 1960s. Germany continued to pull ahead of Britain until the 1980s. Only during the 1990s has Britain decisively narrowed the productivity gap with Germany and other western European countries.

Breaking the aggregate productivity performance down into the three main sectors of agriculture, industry and services, it is possible to show that services played a key role in these changing patterns of comparative aggregate productivity performance. Whereas comparative productivity in industry over the period 1870 to 1990 was stationary in both the US/UK and Germany/UK cases, comparative productivity trends in services mirrored trends in the economy as a whole. The main contribution of agriculture was through differential changes in the share of the labour force engaged in agriculture in the three countries. Since agriculture was a low-value-added sector, aggregate productivity was boosted as its share of the labour force declined. Agriculture already accounted for a precociously low share of employment in Britain by the mid-nineteenth century, so one way in which the United States and Germany were able to catch up on Britain was through the later shrinking of agricultural employment.

It is also possible to decompose comparative productivity trends in services into transport and communications, distribution, finance and other private services and government. In the key market services, British performance tended to be worst in transport and communications, best in finance, and somewhere in between in distribution. Part I is rounded off by the presentation of a complete sectoral data set for the United Kingdom, United States and Germany covering the period 1870 to 1990. Although the emphasis in the book is on comparative levels of productivity, the presentation of the data on this basis is complemented by an analysis of sectoral productivity growth rates in each country. This serves as a reminder that Britain continued to achieve substantial growth during its long period of relative economic decline, and has remained decisively part of the rich world.

12.2 Explaining comparative productivity performance

Part I of the book is about how, increasingly since the late nineteenth century, an economy could achieve high levels of aggregate labour productivity only by achieving high levels of labour productivity in services. Part II is about how, in turn, an economy was increasingly able to achieve high levels of labour productivity in services only by adopting a standardised, high-volume, low-margin approach to business, with hierarchical management. This approach to business, originating in the United States, replaced an earlier approach to business, based on the customised provision of low-volume, high-margin services, organised on the basis of networks. The transformation from the world of the 'counting house' to the world of the 'modern office' depended on technologies to improve information processing and communications. The adoption of these technologies in turn required sufficiently high levels of education and a willingness on the part of the labour force to accept the intensification of the labour process that the efficient utilisation of the new technologies required.

The new approach was first developed on the railways, before spreading rapidly to other parts of the transport and communications sector, and more slowly to distribution and finance. Factors delaying the increase in productivity in distribution included the limits to the degree of centralisation and standardisation that consumers found acceptable before the rise of mass personal transport, and restraints on competition which supported small retailers. The rise of a high-volume, impersonal, standardised approach in finance was also limited by regulatory restrictions on big business, although difficulties of overcoming asymmetric information problems in an automated, standardised business environment also played a role. The work of Bakker (2001) suggests that there is scope for applying this approach to other personal services such as entertainment, which also went through a process of 'industrialisation' during the twentieth century.

If Britain was slower than the United States to industrialise its service sector, Germany was slower still. The crucial factor before World War II was the much greater share of the labour force in Germany tied up in an agricultural sector characterised by very low productivity. With much of the population living in rural areas, and with relatively low per capita incomes, a high-volume service sector was inevitably slow to develop. The low degree of specialisation in the German service sector before World War II was reinforced by its domestic orientation compared with the highly cosmopolitan British service sector, reaping external economies of scale. The backwardness of the German service sector (with one or two notable exceptions) changed only after World War II with the sharp decline in the share of the labour force in agriculture.

The rest of Part II looks empirically at the proximate and more fundamental causes of the productivity differences identified in Part I. The key proximate sources of productivity differences are human and physical capital, and the key fundamental causes are competition and the institutional framework. Physical capital explains some of the labour productivity gaps, and data on sales of office machinery suggest that this was a crucial aspect of investment in high-volume service provision.

In human capital, it is important to distinguish between formal education and vocational training. In formal education, the United States had a significant advantage over Britain in primary education during the nineteenth century, in secondary education during the first half of the twentieth century, and in higher education during the second half of the twentieth century. Germany also lagged behind the United States in the provision of secondary education and higher education during the twentieth century. However, the apparent British and German disadvantage in formal education was offset by a much greater provision of vocational training than in the United States. Here, however, there was an important difference between Britain and Germany, with Britain leading in the provision of higher-level vocational training through professional associations, and Germany leading in the provision of intermediate-level training through apprenticeships. Putting together the formal education and the vocational training, it is likely that Britain suffered little human capital disadvantage relative to either Germany or the United States before World War II, especially in services. After World War II, however, any higher-level advantage that Britain had enjoyed from professional training was offset by the spread of mass higher education in the United States. For the comparison between Britain and Germany, the crucial development was the spread of intermediate-level vocational qualifications in German services, dramatically reducing the proportion of the workforce with 'low skills' and leading to the emergence of a substantial German human capital advantage by the 1970s.

Although the proximate sources of productivity differences are revealing, they leave unanswered the reasons for the different levels of physical and human capital accumulation. For a more fundamental explanation of these differences, it is necessary to consider the institutional framework. Whilst a full explanation of the evolution of the different institutional frameworks in Britain, the United States and Germany is beyond the scope of this book, it is possible to see a number of ways in which the competitive environment has affected productivity outcomes in the three countries. First, throughout the period studied here services have been more sheltered from competition than industry. British manufacturers that failed to keep up with productivity growth abroad were ultimately replaced by imports, but this could not happen to anything like the same extent in services. Hence, poor performance by service sector firms tends to show up in the productivity figures, while poor performance by industrial firms tends to show up in the sectoral composition of economic activity.

Second, the relative size of sectors has been affected more generally by different policy stances on competition in the three countries, with important implications for comparative productivity performance. Before World War II German tariff protection was designed to slow down the decline of agriculture and to promote the development of heavy industry. With unproductive workers retained in low-value-added agriculture, overall per capita incomes in Germany were depressed, and the concentration of the population in large cities was slowed down, all of which acted to limit the market for 'industrialised' services.

Third, the different institutional frameworks in the three countries affected the incentives to accumulate and innovate more generally. Since the emergence of big business in the late nineteenth century, US governments have usually taken a pro-competition stance, while British and German governments have been more equivocal. Before World War II Germany accepted cartels and British policy could at times be described more accurately as pro-trust rather than anti-trust. After 1945 'corporatist' post-war settlements in both Britain and Germany contrasted with the continuation of a more competitive institutional framework in the United States. However, the German framework was more centralised than the British, providing stronger incentives for the accumulation of both human and physical capital. For human capital, Germany's more centralised system was able to solve the free-rider problem of the poaching of skilled workers, spreading the apprenticeship system from industry into services. By contrast, Britain's apprenticeship system declined even in industry, where it had previously been strong. Although a similar poaching problem existed in the United States, it was less serious there because of the greater reliance on general education rather than firm-provided vocational training. For physical capital, greater centralisation made it easier for German trade unions and employers' organisations to deliver agreements involving wage restraint in return for investment in new technology than in Britain's fragmented system of industrial relations.

After Britain had fallen decisively behind most western European nations in terms of labour productivity levels during the 1970s, the

1980s saw a substantial movement away from the corporatist institutional framework, with a strengthening of anti-trust policy, privatisation and deregulation across much of the service sector, and substantial restrictions on trade union immunities. Britain's relative decline was stemmed, though not yet reversed. However, with the return to a more customised approach to service provision during the 1990s, based on the ICT revolution, Britain at last began to narrow the productivity gap with Germany and with many other western European countries in services and in the economy as a whole. With the new technology coming mainly from the United States, however, the Anglo-American productivity gap has remained substantial.

12.3   Reassessing the performance of British market services

Part III provides a reassessment of the performance of British market services since the mid-nineteenth century, in the light of the trends in productivity performance identified in Part I and the general framework of the industrialisation of services outlined in Part II. Chapter 8 begins with British commerce between 1850 and 1914. Although labour productivity grew more rapidly in the United States and Germany than in Britain in services and in the economy as a whole, this largely reflected catching up. Since services clearly made a very positive contribution to the British balance of payments, and the City of London dominated world trade and payments, and since productivity levels remained high, this period can be seen as the 'golden age' of British commerce.

However, Britain's position was already being threatened by the industrialisation of services that was beginning to occur in the United States, with the movement away from customised, low-volume, high-margin business organised on the basis of networks to standardised, high-volume, low-margin business organised on the basis of hierarchy. The process began on the railways and spread rapidly to other parts of the transport and communications sector, but more slowly to distribution and finance. British performance was better in the sectors which continued to be more suited to the network form of organisation. To the extent that British networks failed to adapt to the threat from more hierarchically organised overseas competitors, it became necessary to restrict competition. This was achieved by a growing focus on imperial integration and the cartelisation of markets. The worst British productivity performance occurred on the railways and in telecommunications, where large-scale hierarchical organisation was difficult to avoid. The best British performance was registered in tramp shipping, wholesale distribution, international banking and non-life insurance, where the network form of organisation remained efficient.

Labour productivity growth in services was as rapid in Britain as in Germany during the period 1914 to 1950, but the United States now forged ahead decisively, especially in services suited to further industrialisation. Hence, the US labour productivity lead became substantial in transport and communications, but remained much smaller in distribution and finance. Indeed, with the much greater negative impact of the Great Depression on the US financial system, Britain temporarily regained the labour productivity lead in financial services during the 1930s. The disruption caused by the breakdown of the liberal international economic system between 1914 and 1950 may be expected to have had a greater impact on Britain than on the United States, which was more oriented towards its large domestic market, or on Germany, which was more protectionist. Nevertheless, the negative effects were to some extent offset by an increasing reliance on integration within the British Empire. However, this had some long-run costs, since the major empire countries would not be natural British markets in the more integrated world economy which emerged after World War II. Similarly, the strengthening of collusive behaviour and restrictive practices which occurred during the inter-war period may have helped to stem the falling price level, and hence to prevent rising real wages and unemployment, but it also made adjustment to changed circumstances after World War II more difficult, by making the economy less flexible.

The period 1950 to 1990 saw the completion of the industrialisation process in services. Britain was slower than Germany and most other western European countries in closing the labour productivity gap with the United States, which peaked in the early 1950s in services as well as in the economy as a whole. As a result, Britain fell behind Germany during the 1960s. Both Britain and Germany adopted corporatist institutional frameworks after World War II, but the more centralised German system provided better incentives for the accumulation of human and physical capital, by solving the free-rider problem of poaching skilled workers and by facilitating a commitment to bargains involving wage restraint in return for investment in modern technology. As Britain's productivity performance continued to lag behind Germany's during the 1970s, pressures on the post-war corporatist system mounted, and during the 1980s Britain moved strongly towards a more competitive institutional framework with the privatisation and deregulation of many services, a strengthening of anti-trust policy, and restrictions on trade union immunities. Britain's relative economic decline was stemmed, but a reversal did not come before the technological changes of the 1990s. During the period 1950 to 1990 Britain's worst productivity performance in services occurred in large-scale, hierarchically organised sectors such as the railways, while the best performance was in sectors that remained more suitable for organisation on the basis of networks, such as parts of the financial service sector.

During the 1990s technological trends, which had previously favoured standardisation and large hierarchical organisation, now moved in favour of a greater degree of customisation and networks. The ICT revolution of the 1990s has, nevertheless, preserved the high volume and high productivity of industrialised services. Of course, the new technology has been easier to apply in some sectors than in others, as with the earlier industrialisation of services. However, the general trend has been an improvement in Britain's productivity performance in services and in the economy as a whole, so that Britain has begun to catch up with continental European economies. With most of the new technology originating in the United States, however, Anglo-American productivity gaps have been slow to narrow.

Bibliography

OFFICIAL PUBLICATIONS, REPORTS AND ARCHIVE SOURCES

Anglo-American Council on Productivity (1952), *Retailing*, London: Anglo-American Council on Productivity.

Association of British Insurers (various years), *Insurance Facts and Figures*, London: Association of British Insurers.

(various years), *Insurance Statistics*, London: Association of British Insurers.

(various years), *Insurance Statistics Year Book*, London: Association of British Insurers.

Bank of England (various years), *Bank of England Quarterly Bulletin*, London: Bank of England.

British Railways Board (1963), *The Reshaping of British Railways*, London: HMSO.

European Commission (1994), *Panorama of EU Industry*, Luxembourg City: European Commission.

Food and Agriculture Organisation (various years), *FAO Yearbook*, Rome: Food and Agriculture Organisation.

Kaiserliches Statistisches Amt (various years), Berufs- und Gewerbezählung, *Statistik des Deutschen Reichs*, Berlin: Kaiserliches Statistisches Amt.

(various years), *Statistisches Jahrbuch für das Deutsche Reich*, Berlin: Kaiserliches Statistisches Amt.

Königlichen Statistischen Bureau (various years), *Statistisches Handbuch für den Preussischen Staat*, Berlin: Königlichen Statistischen Bureau.

Länderrat des Amerikanischen Besatzungsgebiets (1949), *Statistisches Handbuch von Deutschland, 1928–1944*, Munich: Länderrat des Amerikanischen Besatzungsgebiets.

League of Nations (1939), *Statistical Yearbook of the League of Nations, 1938/39*, Geneva: League of Nations.

OECD (2003), *The Sources of Economic Growth in OECD Countries*, Paris: Organisation for Economic Co-operation and Development.

(various years), *Labour Force Statistics*, Paris: Organisation for Economic Co-operation and Development.

(various years), *Services: Statistics on International Transactions*, Paris: Organisation for Economic Co-operation and Development.

Slater, I. (various years), *Slater's Directory of Manchester and Salford*, Manchester: Isaac Slater.

Society of Motor Manufacturers and Traders (various years), *The Motor Industry of Great Britain*, London: Society of Motor Manufacturers and Traders.

Statistisches Bundesamt (1972), *Zenzus im Produzierenden Gewerbe, 1967*, Wiesbaden: Statistisches Bundesamt.

(1975), *Handels- und Gaststättenzählung, 1968*, Wiesbaden: Statistisches Bundesamt.

(1988), *Lange Reihen zur Wirtschaftsentwicklung*, Wiesbaden: Statistisches Bundesamt.

(1991), *Volkswirtschaftliche Gesamtrechnungen 1950 bis 1990*, Fachserie 18, Reihe S.15, Wiesbaden: Statistisches Bundesamt.

(various years), *Arbeits- und sozialstatistischen Mitteilungen*, Bonn: Statistisches Bundesamt.

(various years), *Der Aussenhandel der Bundesrepublik Deutschland*, Wiesbaden: Statistisches Bundesamt.

(various years), *Die Industrie der Bundesrepublik Deutschland*, Wiesbaden: Statistisches Bundesamt.

(various years), *Statistisches Jahrbuch für die Bundesrepublik Deutschland*, Wiesbaden: Statistisches Bundesamt.

Statistisches Reichsamt (1939), *Die Deutsche Industrie*, Berlin: Statistisches Reichsamt.

(various years), *Monatliche Nachweise über den auswärtiges Handel Deutschlands*, Berlin: Statistisches Reichsamt.

(various years), *Statistisches Jahrbuch für das Deutsche Reich*, Berlin: Statistisches Reichsamt.

(various years), Volks-, Berufs- und Betriebszählung, *Statistik des Deutschen Reichs*, Berlin: Statistisches Reichsamt.

UK Board of Trade (1908), *Report of an Enquiry by the Board of Trade into Working-Class Rents, Housing and Retail Prices, together with the Standard Rates of Wages Prevailing in Certain Occupations in the Principal Industrial Towns of the United Kingdom*, Cd. 3864, British Parliamentary Papers, CVII.

(1909a), *Report of an Enquiry by the Board of Trade into the Earnings and Hours of Labour of Workpeople of the United Kingdom*, London: HMSO.

(1909b), *Report of the Royal Commission on Shipping Rings*, Cd. 4668, London: HMSO.

(1911), *Report of an Enquiry by the Board of Trade into Working-Class Rents, Housing and Retail Prices, together with the Rates of Wages in Certain Occupations in the Principal Industrial Towns of the United States of America*, Cd. 5609, British Parliamentary Papers, LXXXVIII.

(1912), *Final Report of the First Census of Production of the United Kingdom (1907)*, London: HMSO.

UK Board of Trade (1913a), *Railway Returns for England and Wales, Scotland and Ireland, for 1912*, London: HMSO.

UK Board of Trade (1913b), *Tables Showing the Progress of Merchant Shipping in the United Kingdom and the Principal Maritime Countries*, Cd. 7033, British Parliamentary Papers, LX.

(1913c), *Report of an Enquiry by the Board of Trade into Working-Class Rents and Retail Prices, with the Rates of Wages in Certain Occupations in Industrial Towns of the United Kingdom in 1912*, Cd. 6955, British Parliamentary Papers, LXVI.

(1915), 'Report of an enquiry by the Board of Trade into the conditions of apprenticeship and industrial training in various trades and occupations of the United Kingdom', London: HMSO (printed but not published).

(1918), *Reports of the Departmental Committee Appointed by the Board of Trade to Consider the Position of the Shipping and Shipbuilding Industries after the War*, Cd. 9092, London: HMSO.

(1938), *Final Report on the Fifth Census of Production and the Import Duties Act Inquiry, 1935*, London: HMSO.

(1949), *Report of the Committee on Resale Price Maintenance*, London: HMSO.

(1953), *Census of Distribution and Other Services, 1950*, London: HMSO.

(1970), *Report of the Committee of Inquiry into Shipping*, Cmnd. 4337, London: HMSO.

(various years), *Annual Statement of the Trade of the United Kingdom*, London: HMSO.

(various years), *Census of Production: Final Report*, London: HMSO.

(various years), *Overseas Trade Statistics of the United Kingdom*, London: HMSO.

(various years), *Report on the Census of Distribution and Other Services*, London: HMSO.

(various years), *Statistical Abstract for the United Kingdom*, London: HMSO.

UK Business Statistics Office (various years), *Retailing*, Business Monitor SDA25, London: HMSO.

(various years), *Wholesaling and Dealing*, Business Monitor SDO26, London: HMSO.

UK Central Statistical Office (1956), *National Income Statistics: Sources and Methods*, London: HMSO.

(various years), *Annual Abstract of Statistics*, London: HMSO

(various years), *Economic Trends Annual Supplement*, London: HMSO.

(various years), *National Income and Expenditure*, London: HMSO.

(various years), *United Kingdom Balance of Payments*, London: HMSO.

UK Department of Education and Science (various years), *Education Statistics for the United Kingdom*, London: HMSO.

UK Department of Employment (1978), *British Labour Statistics: Historical Abstract, 1886–1968*, London: HMSO.

(various years), *British Labour Statistics Yearbook*, London: HMSO.

UK Department of Industry (1973), *Report on the Census of Production, 1968*, London: HMSO.

(1975), *Census of Distribution and Other Services, 1971*, London: HMSO.

(1979), *Report on the Census of Production, 1975*, London: HMSO.

UK Department of Transport (1978), *Road Haulage Operators' Licensing: Report of the Independent Committee of Inquiry*, London: HMSO.

(1980), *Report of the Inquiry into Lorries, People and the Environment*, London: HMSO.

(1990), *British Shipping: Challenges and Opportunities*, London: HMSO.

(1991), *Transport Statistics Great Britain*, London: HMSO.

380   Bibliography

(various years), *Transport Statistics Great Britain*, London: HMSO.

(various years), *Transport Trends*, London: HMSO.

UK House of Commons (1931), *Report of the Committee on Finance and Industry*, Cmd. 3897, London: HMSO.

(1955), *Report on Post Office Development and Finance*, Cmd. 9576, London: HMSO.

(1959), *Report of the Committee on the Working of the Monetary System*, Cmnd. 827, London: HMSO.

(1971), *Report of the Committee of Inquiry on Small Firms*, Cmnd. 4811, London: HMSO.

(1980), *Report of the Committee to Review the Functioning of Financial Institutions*, Cmnd. 7937, London: HMSO.

UK House of Commons, Committee of Public Accounts (2002), 'New IT systems for magistrates' courts: the Libra Project', *Treasury Minutes of the Forty-Third to the Forty-Sixth Reports for the Committee of Public Accounts 2001–02*, Cm 5393, London: HMSO.

(2004), 'The cancellation of the benefits payment card', *Treasury Minutes of the First to Third Reports for the Committee of Public Accounts 2002–03*, Cm 6105, London: HMSO.

UK House of Commons, Transport Committee (1995/96), *The Consequences of Bus Deregulation*, Vol. I, *Report and Minutes of Proceedings*, London: HMSO.

UK Ministry of Agriculture and Fisheries (1912), *Agricultural Output of Great Britain, 1908*, Cd. 6277, London: HMSO.

UK Ministry of Labour (1928), *Report of an Enquiry into Apprenticeship and Training for the Skilled Occupations in Great Britain and Northern Ireland, 1925–26*, London: HMSO.

UK Ministry of Transport (1931), *Final Report of the Royal Commission on Transport*, Cmd. 3751, London: HMSO.

UK Monopolies and Mergers Commission (1980), *The Inner London Letter Post*, London: HMSO.

(1981), *Discounts to Retailers*, London: HMSO.

(1992), *New Motor Cars*, London: HMSO.

UK National Board for Prices and Incomes (1967), *Bank Charges*, London: HMSO.

UK Office of Fair Trading (1985), *Competition in Retailing*, London: HMSO.

UK Office of Population Censuses and Surveys (various years), *Census of England and Wales*, London: HMSO.

(various years), *Census of Great Britain*, London: HMSO.

(various years), *Census of Scotland*, London: HMSO.

UK Office of Telecommunications (various years), *Report of the Director General of Telecommunications*, London: Office of Telecommunications.

UK Post Office (various years), *Telecommunications Statistics*, London: HMSO.

UK Treasury (2000), *Productivity in the UK: The Evidence and the Government's Approach*, London: HMSO, available at http://www.hm-treasury.gov.uk.

United Nations (various years), *Statistical Yearbook*, New York: United Nations.

US Congress (1893), *Wholesale Prices, Wages and Transportation: Report by Mr Aldrich from the Committee on Finance*, Washington, DC: GPO.

US Department of Commerce (1913a), *Thirteenth Census of the United States*, Vol. VIII, *Manufactures, 1909, General Report and Analysis*, Washington, DC: GPO.
  (1913b), *Thirteenth Census of the United States*, Vol. X, *Manufactures, 1909, Reports for Principal Industries*, Washington, DC: GPO.
  (1913c), *Thirteenth Census of the United States*, Vol. XI, *Mines and Quarries, 1909, General Report and Analysis*, Washington, DC: GPO.
  (1966), *Housing Construction Statistics, 1889 to 1964*, Washington, DC: GPO.
  (1975), *Historical Statistics of the United States: From Colonial Times to 1970*, Washington, DC: GPO.
  (1983), *National Income and Product Accounts of the United States, 1929–1982*, Washington, DC: GPO.
  (1987), *Fixed Reproducible Tangible Wealth in the United States, 1925–85*, Washington, DC: GPO.
  (various years), *Census of Manufactures*, Washington, DC: GPO.
  (various years), *Foreign Commerce and Navigation of the United States*, Washington, DC: GPO.
  (various years), *Statistical Abstract of the United States*, Washington, DC: GPO.
  (various years), *Survey of Current Business*, Washington, DC: GPO.

BOOKS AND ARTICLES

Abramovitz, M. (1986), 'Catching up, forging ahead and falling behind', *Journal of Economic History*, 46, 385–406.
Abramovitz, M., and P. A. David (1973), 'Reinterpreting economic growth: parables and realities', *American Economic Review*, 63, 428–39.
  (1996), 'Convergence and deferred catch-up', in R. Landau, T. Taylor and G. Wright (eds.), *The Mosaic of Economic Growth*, Stanford, CA: Stanford University Press, 21–62.
Ackrill, M., and L. Hannah (2001), *Barclays: The Business of Banking, 1690–1996*, Cambridge: Cambridge University Press.
Afton, B., and M. Turner (2000), 'The statistical base of agricultural performance in England and Wales, 1850–1914', in E. J. T. Collins (ed.), *The Agrarian History of England and Wales*, Vol. VII, *1850–1950*, Cambridge: Cambridge University Press, 1755–2140.
Aghion, P., and P. Howitt (1998), *Endogenous Growth Theory*, Cambridge, MA: MIT Press.
Aldcroft, D. H. (1968a), 'The mercantile marine', in D. H. Aldcroft (ed.), *The Development of British Industry and Foreign Competition, 1875–1914*, London: Allen and Unwin, 326–63.
  (1968b), 'The efficiency and enterprise of British railways, 1870–1914', *Explorations in Entrepreneurial History*, 5, 158–74.
  (1968c), *British Railways in Transition: The Economic Problems of Britain's Railways since 1914*, London: Macmillan.
  (1974), 'The decontrol of shipping and railways after the First World War', in D. H. Aldcroft, *Studies in British Transport History*, Newton Abbot: David and Charles, 117–43.

Allen, G. C. (1959), *British Industries and their Organization* (4th edn.), London: Longmans.
Allen, R. C. (1994), 'Real incomes in the English-speaking world, 1879–1913', in G. Grantham and M. MacKinnon (eds.), *Labour Market Evolution: The Economic History of Market Integration, Wage Flexibility and the Employment Relation*, London: Routledge, 107–38.
Anderson, G. (1976), *Victorian Clerks*, Manchester: Manchester University Press.
Armstrong, M., and J. Vickers (1994), 'Competition and regulation in telecommunications', in M. Bishop, J. Kay and C. Mayer (eds.), *The Regulatory Challenge*, Oxford: Oxford University Press, 283–308.
Arnold, A. J. (1999), 'Profitability and capital accumulation in British industry during the transwar period, 1913–1924', *Economic History Review*, 52, 45–68.
Ashworth, W. (1960), *An Economic History of England, 1870–1939*, London: Methuen.
  (1991), *The State in Business: 1945 to the Mid-1980s*, London: Macmillan.
Aubin, H., and W. Zorn (eds.) (1976), *Handbuch der Deutschen Wirtschafts- und Sozialgeschichte*, Stuttgart: Klett-Cotta.
Bain, G. S., and R. Price (1980), *Profiles of Union Growth: A Comparative Statistical Portrait of Eight Countries*, Oxford: Blackwell.
Bairoch, P. (1976), 'Population urbaine, et taille des villes en Europe, de 1600 à 1970', *Revue d'histoire économique et sociale*, 54, 304–35.
  (1989), 'European trade policy, 1815–1914', in P. Mathias and S. Pollard (eds.), *The Cambridge Economic History of Europe*, Vol. VIII, *The Industrial Economies: The Development of Economic and Social Policies*, Cambridge: Cambridge University Press, 1–160.
Baker, M., and M. Collins (1999), 'English industrial distress before 1914 and the response of the banks', *European Review of Economic History*, 3, 1–24.
Bakker, G. (2001), 'Entertainment industrialised: emergence of the international film industry, 1890–1940', Ph.D. thesis, European University Institute, Florence.
Balke, N. S., and R. J. Gordon (1989), 'The estimation of prewar gross national product: methodology and new evidence', *Journal of Political Economy*, 97, 38–92.
Balogh, T. (1947), *Studies in Financial Organization*, Cambridge: Cambridge University Press.
Bamberg, J. H. (1988), 'The rationalization of the British cotton industry in the interwar years', *Textile History*, 19, 83–102.
Bamfield, J. (1988), 'Competition and change in British retailing', *National Westminster Bank Review*, February, 15–29.
Barger, H. (1955), *Distribution's Place in the American Economy since 1860*, Princeton, NJ: National Bureau of Economic Research.
Barger, H., and H. H. Landsberg (1942), *American Agriculture, 1899–1939: A Study of Output, Employment and Productivity*, New York: National Bureau of Economic Research.
Barker, T., and D. Gerhold (1993), *The Rise and Rise of Road Transport, 1700–1990*, Cambridge: Cambridge University Press.

Basu, S., J. G. Fernald, N. Oulton and S. Srinivasan (2003), 'The case of the missing productivity growth: or, does information technology explain why productivity accelerated in the United States but not in the United Kingdom?', *NBER Macroeconomics Annual*, 18, 9–63.

Batchelor, R. A., R. L. Major and A. D. Morgan (1980), *Industrialisation and the Basis for Trade*, Cambridge: Cambridge University Press.

Batstone, E. (1986), 'Labour and productivity', *Oxford Review of Economic Policy*, 2 (30), 32–43.

Bayliss, B. (1973), 'Licensing and entry to market', *Transportation Planning and Technology*, 2, 41–7.

(1998), 'Regulation in the road freight transport sector', *Journal of Transport Economics and Policy*, 32, 113–31.

Bean, C., and N. F. R. Crafts (1996), 'British economic growth since 1945: relative economic decline . . . and renaissance?', in N. F. R. Crafts and G. Toniolo (eds.), *Economic Growth in Europe since 1945*, Cambridge: Cambridge University Press, 131–72.

Beesley, M., and B. Laidlaw (1994), 'The development of telecommunications policy in the UK, 1981–1991', in M. Bishop, J. Kay and C. Mayer (eds.), *The Regulatory Challenge*, Oxford: Oxford University Press, 309–35.

Best, M. H., and J. Humphries (1986), 'The City and industrial decline', in B. Elbaum and W. Lazonick (eds.), *The Decline of the British Economy*, Oxford: Clarendon Press, 223–39.

Blundell, R., R. Griffith and J. van Reenan (1995), 'Dynamic count data models of technological innovation', *Economic Journal*, 105, 333–44.

Bolino, A. C. (1989), *A Century of Human Capital by Education and Training*, Washington, DC: Kensington.

Bonavia, M. R. (1981), *Railway Policy between the Wars*, Manchester: Manchester University Press.

Booth, A. (2001), *The British Economy in the Twentieth Century*, Basingstoke: Palgrave.

Borenstein, I. (1954), *Capital and Output Trends in Mining Industries, 1870–1948*, New York: National Bureau of Economic Research.

Boyce, G. (1995), *Information, Mediation and Institutional Development: The Rise of Large-Scale Enterprise in British Shipping, 1870–1919*, Manchester: Manchester University Press.

Braverman, H. (1974), *Labor and Monopoly Capital: The Degradation of Work in the Twentieth Century*, New York: Monthly Review Press.

Bresnahan, T., E. Brynjolfsson and L. M. Hitt (2002), 'Information technology, workplace organization, and the demand for skilled labor: firm-level evidence', *Quarterly Journal of Economics*, 117, 339–76.

Bresnahan, T., and M. Trajtenberg (1995), 'General purpose technologies: engines of growth?', *Journal of Econometrics*, 65, 83–108.

Broadberry, S. N. (1986), *The British Economy Between the Wars: A Macroeconomic Survey*, Oxford: Blackwell.

(1987), 'Cheap money and the housing boom in interwar Britain: an econometric appraisal', *Manchester School*, 55, 378–91.

(1988), 'The impact of the world wars on the long-run performance of the British economy', *Oxford Review of Economic Policy*, 4 (1), 25–37.

(1993), 'Manufacturing and the convergence hypothesis: what the long-run data show', *Journal of Economic History*, 53, 772–95.

(1994), 'Comparative productivity in British and American manufacturing during the nineteenth century', *Explorations in Economic History*, 31, 521–48.

(1997a), *The Productivity Race: British Manufacturing in International Perspective, 1850–1990*, Cambridge: Cambridge University Press.

(1997b), 'Forging ahead, falling behind and catching up: a sectoral analysis of Anglo-American Productivity Differences, 1870–1990', *Research in Economic History*, 17, 1–37.

(1997c), 'Anglo-German productivity differences 1870–1990: a sectoral analysis', *European Review of Economic History*, 1, 247–67.

(1998), 'How did the United States and Germany overtake Britain? A sectoral analysis of comparative productivity levels, 1870–1990', *Journal of Economic History*, 58, 375–407.

(2003), 'Relative per capita income levels in the United Kingdom and the United States since 1870: reconciling time-series projections and direct-benchmark estimates', *Journal of Economic History*, 63, 852–63.

(2004a), 'Human capital and skills', in R. Floud and P. Johnson (eds.), *The Cambridge Economic History of Modern Britain*, Vol. II, *Economic Maturity, 1860–1939*, Cambridge: Cambridge University Press, 56–73.

(2004b), 'Explaining Anglo-German productivity differences in services since 1870', *European Review of Economic History*, 8, 229–62.

Broadberry, S. N., and C. Burhop (2005), 'Comparative productivity in British and German manufacturing before World War II: reconciling direct benchmark estimates and time series projections', University of Warwick, available at http://www2.warwick.ac.uk/fac/soc/economics/staff/faculty/broadberry/wp/.

Broadberry, S. N., and N. F. R. Crafts (1990), 'The impact of the depression of the 1930s on productive potential in the United Kingdom', *European Economic Review*, 34, 599–607.

(1992), 'Britain's productivity gap in the 1930s: some neglected factors', *Journal of Economic History*, 52, 531–58.

(2003), 'UK productivity performance from 1950 to 1979: a restatement of the Broadberry–Crafts view', *Economic History Review*, 56, 718–35.

Broadberry, S. N., and R. Fremdling (1990), 'Comparative productivity in British and German industry, 1907–37', *Oxford Bulletin of Economics and Statistics*, 52, 403–21.

Broadberry, S. N., and S. Ghosal (2002), 'From the counting house to the modern office: explaining Anglo-American productivity differences in services, 1870–1990', *Journal of Economic History*, 62, 967–98.

(2005), 'Technology, organisation and productivity performance in services: lessons from Britain and the United States since 1870', *Structural Change and Economic Dynamics*, 16, 437–66.

Broadberry, S. N., and P. Howlett (1998), 'The United Kingdom: victory at all costs', in M. Harrison (ed.), *The Economics of World War II: Six Great Powers in International Comparison*, Cambridge: Cambridge University Press, 43–80.

(2005), 'The United Kingdom during World War I: business as usual?', in S. N. Broadberry and M. Harrison (eds.), *The Economics of World War I*, Cambridge: Cambridge University Press, 206–34.

Broadberry, S. N., and D. A. Irwin (2006), 'Labor productivity in Britain and America during the nineteenth century', *Explorations in Economic History*, 43, 257–79.

Broadberry, S. N., and A. Marrison (2002), 'External economies of scale in the Lancashire cotton industry, 1900–1939', *Economic History Review*, 55, 51–77.

Broadberry, S. N., and M. O'Mahony (2004), 'Britain's productivity gap with the United States and Europe: a historical perspective', *National Institute Economic Review*, 189, 72–85.

Brock, G. W. (1981), *The Telecommunications Industry: The Dynamics of Market Structure*, Cambridge, MA: Harvard University Press.

Brown, J. (1987), *Agriculture in England: A Survey of Farming, 1870–1947*, Manchester: Manchester University Press.

Brynjolfsson, E., and L. M. Hitt (1996), 'Paradox lost? Firm-level evidence on the returns to information systems', *Management Science*, 42, 541–58.

(2000), 'Beyond computation: information technology, organizational transformation and business performance', *Journal of Economic Perspectives*, 14 (4), 23–48.

Brynjolfsson, E., T. Malone, V. Gurbaxani and A. Kambil (1994), 'Does information technology lead to smaller firms?', *Management Science*, 40 (12), 1628–44.

Cain, P. J. (1980), 'Private enterprise or public utility? Output, pricing and investment on English and Welsh railways, 1870–1914', *Journal of Transport History* (3rd series), 1, 9–28.

Cain, P. J., and A. G. Hopkins (1993), *British Imperialism: Innovation and Expansionism, 1668–1914*, London: Longman.

Cairncross, A., and B. Eichengreen (1983), *Sterling in Decline: The Devaluations of 1931, 1949 and 1967*, Oxford: Blackwell.

Calmfors, L., and J. Driffill (1988), 'Centralization of wage bargaining', *Economic Policy*, 6, 13–61.

Calomiris, C. W. (1995), 'The costs of rejecting universal banking: American finance in the German mirror, 1870–1914', in N. R. Lamoreaux and D. M. G. Raff (eds.), *Coordination and Information: Historical Perspectives on the Organization of Enterprise*, Chicago: University of Chicago Press, 257–315.

Campbell-Kelly, M. (1992), 'Large-scale data processing in the Prudential, 1850–1930', *Accounting, Business and Financial History*, 2, 117–39.

(1994), 'The Railway Clearing House and Victorian data processing', in L. Bud-Frierman (ed.), *Information Acumen: The Understanding and Use of Knowledge in Modern Business*, London: Routledge, 51–74.

(1998), 'Data processing and technological change: the Post Office Savings Bank, 1861–1930', *Technology and Culture*, 39, 1–32.

Capie, F. (1994), *Tariffs and Growth: Some Insights from the World Economy, 1850–1940*, Manchester: Manchester University Press.

Capie, F., and M. Billings (2001), 'Profitability in English banking in the twentieth century', *European Review of Economic History*, 5, 367–401.
Capie, F., and M. Collins (1996), 'Industrial lending by commercial banks, 1860s–1914: why did banks refuse loans?', *Business History*, 38 (1), 26–44.
Capie, F., and G. Rodrik-Bali (1982), 'Concentration in British banking, 1870–1920', *Business History*, 24, 280–92.
Capie, F., and A. Webber (1985), *A Monetary History of the United Kingdom, 1870–1982*, Vol. I, *Data, Sources, Methods*, London: Allen and Unwin.
Carlin, W. (1996), 'West German growth and institutions, 1945–90', in N. F. R. Crafts and G. Toniolo (eds.), *Economic Growth in Europe since 1945*, Cambridge: Cambridge University Press, 455–97.
Carosso, V. P. (1970). *Investment Banking in America: A History*. Cambridge, MA: Harvard University Press.
Carson, D. (1949), 'Changes in the industrial composition of manpower since the Civil War', in *Studies in Income and Wealth* no. 11, New York: National Bureau of Economic Research, 46–134.
Carr-Saunders, A. M., and P. A. Wilson (1933), *The Professions*, Oxford: Oxford University Press.
Carter, R. L. (1988), 'Insurance', in P. Johnson (ed.), *The Structure of British Industry*, London: Unwin Hyman, 308–31.
Cassis, Y. (1994), *City Bankers, 1890–1914*, Cambridge: Cambridge University Press.
Cette, G., J. Mairesse and Y. Kocoglu (2002), 'Croissance économique et diffusion des TIC: le cas de la France sur longue période (1980–2000)'. *Revue française d'économie*, 16, 155–92.
Chandler, A. D., Jr. (1977), *The Visible Hand: The Managerial Revolution in American Business*, Cambridge, MA: Harvard University Press.
  (1980), 'The growth of the transnational industrial firm in the United States and the United Kingdom: a comparative analysis', *Economic History Review*, 33, 396–410.
  (1990), *Scale and Scope: The Dynamics of Industrial Capitalism*, Cambridge, MA: Harvard University Press.
Channon, D. F. (1978), *The Service Industries: Strategy, Structure and Financial Performance*, London: Macmillan.
Channon, G. (2001), *Railways in Britain and the United States, 1830–1940*, Studies in Economic and Business History, Aldershot: Ashgate.
Chapman, A. L. (1953), *Wages and Salaries in the United Kingdom, 1920–1938*, Cambridge: Cambridge University Press.
Chapman, S. (1984), *The Rise of Merchant Banking*, London: Allen and Unwin.
  (1992), *Merchant Enterprise in Britain: From the Industrial Revolution to World War I*, Cambridge: Cambridge University Press.
  (1996), 'The commercial sector', in M. B. Rose (ed.), *The Lancashire Cotton Industry: A History Since 1700*, Preston: Lancashire County Books, 63–93.
Clapham, J. H. (1938), *An Economic History of Modern Britain: Machines and National Rivalries (1887–1914), with an Epilogue (1914–1929)*, Cambridge: Cambridge University Press.

Clark, C. (1951), *The Conditions of Economic Progress* (2nd edn.), London: Macmillan.
Cleary, E. J. (1965), *The Building Society Movement*, London: Elek.
Cockerell, H. A. L., and E. Green (1994), *The British Insurance Business: A Guide to its History and Records* (2nd edn.), Sheffield: Sheffield Academic Press.
Colecchia, A., and P. Schreyer (2001), 'ICT investment and economic growth in the 1990s: is the United States a unique case?', Paris: Organisation for Economic Co-operation and Development.
Collins, M. (1988), *Money and Banking in the UK: A History*, London: Croom Helm.
  (1991), *Banks and Industrial Finance in Britain, 1800–1939*, London: Macmillan.
  (1998), 'English bank development within a European context, 1870–1939', *Economic History Review*, 51, 1–24.
Conrad, J., L. Elster, W. Lexis and E. Loening (eds.) (1910), *Handwörterbuch der Staatswissenschaften*, Jena: Verlag von Gustav Fischer.
Copeland, M. T. (1912), *The Cotton Manufacturing Industry of the United States*, New York: Augustus Kelley Reprint [1966].
Cortada, J. W. (1993), *Before the Computer: IBM, NCR, Burroughs and Remington Rand and the Industry they Created, 1865–1956*, Princeton, NJ: Princeton University Press.
Cottrell, P. L. (1979), *Industrial Finance, 1830–1914: The Finance and Organization of English Manufacturing Industry*, London: Methuen.
  (1981), 'The steamship on the Mersey, 1815–80: investment and ownership', in P. L. Cottrell and D. H. Aldcroft (eds.), *Shipping, Trade and Commerce: Essays in Memory of Ralph Davis*, Leicester: Leicester University Press, 137–63.
Cowling, K., P. Stoneman, J. Cubbin, J. Cable, G. Hall, S. Domberger and P. Dutton (1980), *Mergers and Economic Performance*, Cambridge: Cambridge University Press.
Crafts, N. F. R. (1985), *British Economic Growth During the Industrial Revolution*, Oxford: Oxford University Press.
  (2004), 'Fifty years of economic growth in Western Europe: no longer catching up but falling behind?', *World Economics*, 5, 131–45.
Crompton, G. (1995), 'The railway companies and the nationalisation issue, 1920–50', in R. Millward and J. Singleton (eds.), *The Political Economy of Nationalisation in Britain, 1920–1950*, Cambridge: Cambridge University Press, 116–43.
Crouch, C. (1993), *Industrial Relations and European State Traditions*, Oxford: Clarendon Press.
Daunton, M. J. (1985), *Royal Mail: The Post Office since 1840*, London: Athlone.
David, P. A. (1996), 'Real income and economic welfare growth in the early republic', unpublished manuscript, All Souls College, Oxford and Stanford University, CA.
David, P. A., and G. Wright (1999), 'Early twentieth-century productivity growth dynamics: an inquiry into the economic history of "our ignorance"', unpublished manuscript, All Souls College, Oxford, and Stanford University, CA.

Davis, E. (1986), 'Express coaching since 1980: liberalisation in practice', in J. Kay, C. Mayer and D. Thompson (eds.), *Privatisation and Regulation: The UK Experience*, Oxford: Clarendon Press, 147–61.

Deakin, B. M. (1973), *Shipping Conferences: A Study of their Origins, Development and Economic Practices*, Cambridge: Cambridge University Press.

Deakin, B. M., and T. Seward (1969), *Productivity in Transport: A Study of Employment, Capital, Output, Productivity and Technical Change*, Cambridge: Cambridge University Press.

Denison, E. F. (1967), *Why Growth Rates Differ: Postwar Experience in Nine Western Countries*, Washington, DC: Brookings Institution.

Dodgson, J. S. (1993), 'British railway cost functions and productivity growth, 1900–1912', *Explorations in Economic History*, 30, 158–81.

Dowie, J. A. (1975), '1919–20 is in need of attention', *Economic History Review*, 28, 429–50.

Drummond, I. M. (1972), *British Economic Policy and the Empire, 1919–1939*, London: Allen and Unwin.

(1974), *Imperial Economic Policy, 1917–1939: Studies in Expansion and Protection*, London: Allen and Unwin.

(1987), *The Gold Standard and the International Monetary System, 1900–1939*, London: Macmillan.

Dyos, H. J., and D. H. Aldcroft (1969), *British Transport: An Economic Survey from the Seventeenth Century to the Twentieth*, Leicester: Leicester University Press.

Easterlin, R. A. (1981), 'Why isn't the whole world developed?', *Journal of Economic History*, 41: 1–19.

Edelstein, M. (1971), 'Rigidity and bias in the British capital market, 1870–1913', in D. N. McCloskey (ed.), *Essays on a Mature Economy: Britain After 1840*, London: Methuen, 83–105.

Edquist, C., and S. Jacobsson (1988), *Flexible Automation: The Global Diffusion of Technology in the Engineering Industry*, Oxford: Blackwell.

Edwards, A. M. (1943), *Comparative Occupation Statistics for the United States, 1870–1940*, Washington, DC: US Bureau of the Census.

Edwards, J., and S. Ogilvie (1996), 'Universal banks and German industrialization: a reappraisal', *Economic History Review*, 49, 427–46.

Edwards, J. D. (1978), *History of Public Accounting in the United States*, Tuscaloosa, AL: University of Alabama Press.

Edwards, M. M. (1967), *The Growth of the British Cotton Trade, 1780–1815*, New York: Augustus M. Kelly.

Eichengreen, B. (1995), *Golden Fetters: The Gold Standard and the Great Depression, 1919–1939*, Oxford: Oxford University Press.

(1996), 'Institutions and economic growth: Europe after World War II', in N. F. R. Crafts and G. Toniolo (eds.), *Economic Growth in Europe since 1945*, Cambridge: Cambridge University Press, 38–72.

Ellinger, B. (1940), *The City: The London Financial Markets*, London: Staples.

Essinger, J. (1993), *Managing Technology in Financial Institutions*, London: Pitman.

Estrin, S., and D. de Meza, (1994), 'Delivering letters: should it be decriminalized?', in M. Bishop, J. Kay and C. Mayer (eds.), *Privatization and Economic Performance*, Oxford: Oxford University Press, 208–24.

Falkus, M. (1990), *The Blue Funnel Legend: A History of the Ocean Steam Ship Company, 1865–1973*, London: Macmillan.
Farnie, D. A. (1979a), *The English Cotton Industry and the World Market, 1815–1896*, Oxford: Clarendon Press.
  (1979b), 'An index of commercial activity: the membership of the Manchester Royal Exchange, 1809–1948', *Business History*, 21 (1), 97–106.
Federico, G., and P. Malanima (2004), 'Progress, decline, and growth: product and productivity in Italian agriculture, 1000–2000', *Economic History Review*, 57, 437–64.
Feinstein, C. H. (1965), *Domestic Capital Formation in the United Kingdom, 1920–1938*, Cambridge: Cambridge University Press.
  (1972), *National Income, Expenditure and Output of the United Kingdom, 1855–1965*, Cambridge: Cambridge University Press.
  (1988), 'Sources and methods of estimation for domestic reproducible fixed assets, stocks and works in progress, overseas assets and land', in C. H. Feinstein and S. Pollard (eds.), *Studies in Capital Formation in the United Kingdom, 1750–1920*, Oxford: Oxford University Press, 257–471.
Field, A. J. (1996), 'The relative productivity of American distribution, 1869–1992', *Research in Economic History*, 16, 1–37.
  (2004), 'US productivity growth in the interwar period and the 1990s', available at http://www.unc.edu/depts/econ/seminars/Field.pdf.
Fishlow, A. (1966), 'Productivity and technological change in the railroad sector, 1840–1910', in D. S. Brady (ed.), *Output, Employment and Productivity in the United States after 1800*, Studies in Income and Wealth no. 30, New York: Columbia University Press (in association with the National Bureau of Economic Research), 583–646.
Flora, P. (1983), *State, Economy and Society in Western Europe, 1815–1975: A Data Handbook in Two Volumes*, Frankfurt: Campus Verlag.
Fohlin, C. (1999), 'Universal banking in pre-World War I Germany: model or myth?', *Explorations in Economic History*, 36, 305–43.
Foreman-Peck, J. S. (1985), 'Seed-corn or chaff? New firm formation and the performance of the interwar economy', *Economic History Review*, 38, 402–22.
  (1987), 'Natural monopoly and railway policy in the nineteenth century', *Oxford Economic Papers*, 39, 699–718.
Foreman-Peck, J. S., and R. Millward (1994), *Public and Private Ownership of British Industry, 1820–1990*, Oxford: Clarendon Press.
Foxwell, H. S. (1917), 'The financing of industry and trade', *Economic Journal*, 27, 502–22.
Frankel, M. (1955), 'Obsolescence and technological change in a maturing economy', *American Economic Review*, 45, 296–319.
Franklin, P. J., and C. Woodhead (1980), *The UK Life Assurance Industry: A Study in Applied Economics*, London: Croom Helm.
Fremdling, R. (1975), *Eisenbahnen und deutsches Wirtschaftswachstum, 1840–1879: Ein Beitrag zur Entwicklungstheorie und zur Theorie der Infrastruktur*, Dortmund: Gesellschaft für Westfälische Wirtschaftsgeschichte.

(1977), 'Railroads and German economic growth: a leading sector analysis with a comparison to the United States and Great Britain', *Journal of Economic History*, 37, 583–604.

(1988), 'German national accounts for the 19th and early 20th century: a critical assessment', *Vierteljahrschrift fuer Sozial- und Wirtschaftsgeschichte*, 75, 339–55.

(1991), 'Productivity comparisons between Great Britain and Germany, 1855–1913', *Scandinavian Economic History Review*, 39, 28–42.

(1995), 'German national accounts for the 19th and early 20th century', *Scandinavian Economic History Review*, 43, 77–100.

Fremdling, R., and R. Stäglin (2003), 'Die Industrieerhebung von 1936: Ein Input-Output-Ansatz zur Rekonstruktion der Volkswirtschaftlichen Gesamtrechnungen für Deutschland im 19. und 20. Jahrhundert – ein Arbeitsbericht', *Vierteljahrschrift für Sozial- und Wirtschaftsgeschichte*, 90, 416–28.

Friedman, M., and A. J. Schwartz (1982), *Monetary Trends in the United States and the United Kingdom: Their Relation to Income, Prices, and Interest Rates, 1867–1975*, Chicago: National Bureau of Economic Research.

Gallman, R. E. (1960), 'Commodity output, 1839–1899', in *Trends in the American Economy in the Nineteenth Century*, Vol. XXIV, *Studies in Income and Wealth*, Princeton, NJ: National Bureau of Economic Research, 13–71.

(1987), 'Investment flows and capital stocks: US experience in the nineteenth century', in P. Kilby (ed.), *Quantity and Quiddity: Essays in US Economic History*, Middletown, CT: Wesleyan University Press, 214–54.

Gerschenkron, A. (1962), *Economic Backwardness in Historical Perspective*, Cambridge, MA: Harvard University Press.

Gibb, D. E. W. (1957), *Lloyd's of London: A Study in Individualism*, London: Macmillan.

Giffen, R. (1882), 'On the use of import and export statistics', *Journal of the Statistical Society*, 45.

Gilb, C. L. (1966), *Hidden Hierarchies: The Professions and Government*, New York: Harper and Row.

Gilbert, M., and I. B. Kravis (1954), *An International Comparison of National Products and the Purchasing Power of Currencies*, Paris: Organisation for European Economic Co-operation.

Goldin, C. (1998), 'America's graduation from high school: the evolution and spread of secondary schooling in the twentieth century', *Journal of Economic History*, 58: 345–74.

(2001), 'The human-capital century and American leadership: virtues of the past', *Journal of Economic History*, 61, 263–292.

Goldin, C., and L. Katz (1996), 'Technology, skill, and the wage structure: insights from the past', *American Economic Review, Papers and Proceedings*, 86, 252–7.

Goldsmith, R. W. (1958), *Financial Intermediaries in the American Economy since 1900*, Princeton, NJ: Princeton University Press (in association with the National Bureau of Economic Research).

Goodhart, C. A. E. (1972), *The Business of Banking, 1891–1914*, London: Weidenfeld and Nicolson.

Gourvish, T. R. (1980), *Railways and the British Economy, 1830–1914*, London: Macmillan.
  (1986), *British Railways, 1948–73: A Business History*, Cambridge: Cambridge University Press.
Green, R., and I. Vogelsang (1994), 'British Airways: a turn-around anticipating privatization', in M. Bishop, J. Kay and C. Mayer (eds.), *Privatization and Economic Performance*, Oxford: Oxford University Press, 89–111.
Greif, A. (1989), 'Reputation and coalitions in medieval trade: Maghribi traders', *Journal of Economic History*, 49, 857–82.
  (2000), 'The fundamental problem of exchange: a research agenda in historical institutional analysis', *European Review of Economic History*, 4, 251–84.
Griffiths, B. (1973), 'The development of restrictive practices in the UK monetary system', *Manchester School*, 41, 3–18.
Grunzel, J. (1916), *Economic Protection*, Oxford: Clarendon Press (in association with the Carnegie Endowment for International Peace).
Guinnane, T. W. (2002), 'Delegated monitors, large and small: Germany's banking system, 1800–1914', *Journal of Economic Literature*, 40, 73–124.
Gust, C., and J. Marquez (2002), *International Comparisons of Productivity Growth: The Role of Information Technology and Regulatory Practices*, International Finance Discussion Paper no. 727, Board of Governors of the Federal Reserve System, Washington, DC.
Gwilliam, K. (1988), 'Rail transport', in P. Johnson (ed.), *The Structure of British Industry* (2nd edn.), London: Unwin Hyman, 257–80.
Habakkuk, H. J. (1962), *American and British Technology in the Nineteenth Century*, Cambridge: Cambridge University Press.
Hall, M. (1983), *Monetary Policy since 1971: Conduct and Performance*, London: Macmillan.
Hall, M., J. Knapp and C. Winsten (1961), *Distribution in Great Britain and North America: A Study in Structure and Productivity*, Oxford: Oxford University Press.
Halsey, A. H. (ed.) (1988), *Trends in British Society Since 1900: A Guide to the Changing Social Structure of Britain* (2nd edn.), London: Macmillan.
Handy, C., C. Gordon, I. Gow and C. Randlesome (1988), *Making Managers*, London: Pitman.
Hannah, L. (1974a), 'Managerial innovation and the rise of the large-scale company in interwar Britain', *Economic History Review*, 27, 252–70.
  (1974b), 'Takeover bids in Britain before 1950: an exercise in business prehistory', *Business History*, 16, 65–77.
  (1979), *Electricity before Nationalisation: A Study of the Development of the Electricity Supply Industry in Britain to 1948*, London: Macmillan.
  (1986), *Inventing Retirement: The Development of Occupational Pensions in Britain*, Cambridge: Cambridge University Press.
  (1994), 'The economic consequences of the state ownership of industry, 1945–1990', in R. Floud and D. N. McCloskey (eds.), *The Economic History of Britain Since 1700*, Vol. III, *1939–1992* (2nd edn.), Cambridge: Cambridge University Press, 168–94.

Harley, C. K. (1971), 'The shift from sailing ships to steamships, 1850–1890: a study in technological change and its diffusion', in D. N. McCloskey (ed.), *Essays on a Mature Economy: Britain After 1840*, London: Methuen, 215–34.

Hawke, G. R. (1970), *Railways and Economic Growth in England and Wales, 1840–1870*, Oxford: Oxford University Press.

Hayami, Y., and V. W. Ruttan (1971). *Agricultural Development: An International Perspective*, Baltimore: Johns Hopkins University Press.

(1985), *Agricultural Development: An International Perspective* (2nd edn.), Baltimore: Johns Hopkins University Press.

Helpman, E. (ed.) (1998), *General Purpose Technologies and Economic Growth*, Cambridge, MA: MIT Press.

Henning, F.-W. (1996), *Handbuch der Wirtschafts- und Sozialgeschichte Deutschlands*, Paderborn: Ferdinand Schöningh.

Henning, G. R., and K. Trace (1975), 'Britain and the motorship: a case of delayed adoption of new technology', *Journal of Economic History*, 35, 353–85.

Heston, A., and R. Summers (1993), 'What can be learned from successive ICP benchmark estimates?', in A. Szirmai, B. van Ark and D. Pilat (eds.), *Explaining Economic Growth: Essays in Honour of Angus Maddison*, Amsterdam: North Holland, 353–73.

Heston, A., R. Summers and B. Aten (2001), 'Price structures, the quality factor, and chaining', Organisation for Economic Co-operation and Development, Paris, available at http://www.oecd.org/dataoecd/23/40/2425050.pdf.

Heylin, H. B. (1913), *Buyers and Sellers in the Cotton Trade*, London: Griffin.

Hicks, J. R. (1935), 'Annual survey of economic theory: the theory of monopoly', *Econometrica*, 3, 1–20.

Hilgerdt, F. (1945), *Industrialization and Foreign Trade*, Geneva: League of Nations.

Hobson, C. K. (1914), *The Export of Capital*, London: Constable.

Hoffmann, W. G. (1965), *Das Wachstum der deutschen Wirtschaft seit der Mitte des 19. Jahrhunderts*, Berlin: Springer.

Hogwood, B. W. (1979), *Government and Shipbuilding: The Politics of Industrial Change*, Farnborough: Saxon House.

Holmes, A. R., and E. Green (1986), *Midland: 150 Years of Banking Business*, London: Batsford.

Homburg, H. (2000), 'The first large firms in German retailing – the chains of department stores from the 1920's to the 1970/80's: structures, strategies, management', *Jahrbuch für Wirtschaftsgeschichte*, 1, 171–98.

Howarth, D., and S. Howarth (1986), *The Story of P&O: The Peninsular Steam Navigation Company*, London: Weidenfeld and Nicolson.

Humphries, J. (1984), 'Inter-war house building, cheap money and building societies: the housing boom revisited', *Business History*, 29 (3), 325–45.

Hurstfield, J. (1944), 'The control of British raw material supplies', *Economic History Review*, 14, 1–31.

Hutton, W. (1996), *The State We're In* (rev. edn.), London: Vintage.

Hyde, F. E. (1967), *Shipping Enterprise and Management, 1830–1939: Harrisons of Liverpool*, Liverpool: Liverpool University Press.

Imlah, A. H. (1958), *Economic Elements in the Pax Britannica: Studies in British Foreign Trade in the Nineteenth Century*, New York: Russell and Russell.

Inklaar, R., M. O'Mahony and M. Timmer (2003), *ICT and Europe's Productivity Performance: Industry-Level Growth Accounting Comparisons with the United States*, Research Memorandum GD-68, Groningen Growth and Development Centre, Groningen, the Netherlands.

Irwin, D. A. (2002), 'Interpreting the tariff–growth correlation of the late 19th century', *American Economic Review, Papers and Proceedings*, 92, 165–9.

Jefferys, J. B. (1950), *The Distribution of Consumer Goods: A Factual Study of Methods and Costs in the United Kingdom in 1938*, Cambridge: Cambridge University Press.

(1954), *Retail Trading in Britain, 1850–1950*, Cambridge: Cambridge University Press.

Jenks, L. H. (1927), *The Migration of British Capital to 1875*, New York: Knopf.

Jeremy, D. J. (1991), 'The hundred largest employers in the UK: 1907, 1935, 1955', *Business History*, 33 (1), 93–111.

Jeremy, D. J., and D. A. Farnie (2001), 'The ranking of firms, the counting of employees, and the classification of data: a cautionary note', *Business History*, 43 (3), 105–18.

Johnson, P. (1993), 'Air transport', in P. Johnson (ed.), *European Industries: Structure, Conduct, Performance*, Aldershot: Elgar, 204–29.

Jones, E. L. (1968), *The Development of English Agriculture, 1815–1873*, London: Macmillan.

Jones, G. (1993), *British Multinational Banking, 1830–1990*, Oxford: Clarendon Press.

(2000), *Merchants to Multinationals: British Trading Companies in the Nineteenth and Twentieth Centuries*, Oxford: Oxford University Press.

Jones, L. (1957), *Shipbuilding in Britain: Mainly between the Two World Wars*, Cardiff: University of Wales Press.

Jorgenson, D. W., and K. Stiroh (2000), 'Raising the speed limit: US economic growth in the information age', *Brookings Papers on Economic Activity*, 1, 125–211.

Joy, S. (1998), 'Public and private railways', *Journal of Transport Economics and Policy*, 33, 27–49.

Kahn, A. E. (1946), *Great Britain in the World Economy*, New York: Columbia University Press.

Kaldor, N., and R. Silverman (1948), *A Statistical Analysis of Advertising Expenditure and the Revenue of the Press*, Cambridge: Cambridge University Press.

Kappel, R. (1989), 'Global trends in international shipping: over-capacities, liberalization and national state interference', in K. Wohlmuth (ed.), *Structural Adjustment in the World Economy and East–West–South Economic Co-operation*, Bremen: University of Bremen Institute of World Economics and International Management, 319–55.

Kendall, M. G. (1948), 'United Kingdom merchant shipping statistics', *Journal of the Royal Statistical Society*, Series A, 111, 133–44.

(1950), 'The UK mercantile marine and its contribution to the balance of payments', *Journal of the Royal Statistical Society*, Series A, 113, 9–29.

Kendrick, J. W. (1961), *Productivity Trends in the United States*, Princeton, NJ: National Bureau of Economic Research.

Kennedy, W. P. (1987), *Industrial Structure, Capital Markets and the Origins of British Economic Decline*, Cambridge: Cambridge University Press.

Kindleberger, C. P. (1967), *Europe's Postwar Growth: The Role of Labor Supply*, Cambridge, MA: Harvard University Press.

(1986), *The World in Depression, 1929–1939*, Harmondsworth: Penguin.

King, W. T. C. (1936), *History of the London Discount Market*, London: Routledge.

Kinghorn, J. R., and J. V. Nye (1996), 'The scale of production in western economic development: a comparison of official industry statistics in the United States, Britain, France, and Germany, 1905–1913', *Journal of Economic History*, 56, 90–112.

Kirby, M. W. (1981), *The Decline of British Economic Power Since 1870*, London: Allen and Unwin.

Kirkaldy, A. W. (1914), *British Shipping: Its History, Organisation and Importance*, London: Kegan Paul.

Kirner, W. (1968), *Zeitreihen für das Anlagevermögen der Wirtschaftsbereiche in der Bundesrepublik Deutschland*, Berlin: Duncker and Humblot.

Kohler, H., and H. Reyher (1988), *Arbeitszeit und Arbeitsvolumen in der Bundesrepublik Deutschland, 1960–1986: Datenlage-Struktur-Entwicklung*, Nuremberg: Institut für Arbeitsmarkt und Berufsforschung der Bundesanstalt für Arbeit.

Kopper, C. (2002), *Handel und Verkehr im 20. Jahrhundert*, Munich: Oldenbourg.

Kravis, I. B., Z. Kenessey, A. W. Heston and R. Summers (1975), *A System of International Comparisons of Gross Product and Purchasing Power*, Baltimore: Johns Hopkins University Press.

Kynaston, D. (1994), *The City of London*, Vol. I, *A World of its Own, 1815–1890*, London: Chatto and Windus.

(1995), *The City of London*, Vol. II, *Golden Years, 1890–1914*, London: Chatto and Windus.

Lamoreaux, N. R. (1994), *Insider Lending: Banks, Personal Connections, and Economic Development in Industrial New England*, Cambridge: Cambridge University Press.

Lancaster, K. (1973), 'The dynamic inefficiency of capitalism', *Journal of Political Economy*, 81, 1092–110.

Landes, D. S. (1969), *The Unbound Prometheus: Technological Change and Industrial Development in Western Europe from 1750 to the Present*, Cambridge: Cambridge University Press.

Langton, J., and R. J. Morris (eds.) (1986), *Atlas of Industrializing Britain, 1780–1914*, London: Methuen.

Layard, R. (2003), *Happiness: Has Social Science a Clue?*, Lionel Robbins Memorial Lectures, London School of Economics, 3–5 March, available at http://cep.lse.ac.uk/layard/.

Leak, H. (1939), 'The carrying trade of the British shipping', *Journal of the Royal Statistical Society*, 102, 213–57.

Lebergott, S. (1966), 'Labor force and employment, 1800–1960', in D. S. Brady (ed.), *Output, Employment and Productivity in the United States after 1800*,

Studies in Income and Wealth no. 30, New York: National Bureau of Economic Research, 117–204.
Levy, H. (1947), *The Shops of Britain: A Study of Retail Distribution*, London: Kegan Paul.
Lewis, W. A. (1949), *Economic Survey, 1919–1939*, London: Allen and Unwin.
  (1978), *Growth and Fluctuations, 1870–1913*, London: Allen and Unwin.
Lindert, P. H. (2004), *Growing Public: Social Spending and Economic Growth Since the Eighteenth Century*, Vol. II, *Further Evidence*, Cambridge: Cambridge University Press.
Liveing, E. (1961), *A Century of Insurance: The Commercial Union Group, 1861–1961*, London: Witherby.
Lockwood, D. (1958), *The Blackcoated Worker: A Study in Class Consciousness*, London: Allen and Unwin.
Lomax, K. C. (1959), 'Production and productivity movements in the United Kingdom since 1900', *Journal of the Royal Statistical Society*, Series A, 122, 185–210.
Lothian, J. R., and M. P. Taylor (1996), 'Real exchange rate behavior: the recent float from the perspective of the past two centuries', *Journal of Political Economy*, 104, 488–509.
Lucas, A. F. (1937), *Industrial Reconstruction and the Control of Competition: The British Experiments*, London: Longmans, Green and Co.
Lyth, P. J. (1995), 'The changing role of government in British civil air transport, 1919–49', in R. Millward and J. Singleton (eds.), *The Political Economy of Nationalisation in Britain, 1920–1950*, Cambridge: Cambridge University Press, 65–87.
McClelland, C. E. (1991), *The German Experience of Professionalization: Modern Learned Professions and their Organizations from the Early Nineteenth Century to the Hitler Era*, Cambridge: Cambridge University Press.
McCloskey, D. N. (1970), 'Did Victorian Britain fail?' *Economic History Review*, 23, 446–59.
  (1990), *If You're So Smart: The Narrative of Economic Expertise*, Chicago: University of Chicago Press.
McCloskey, D. N., and L. G. Sandberg (1971), 'From damnation to redemption: judgments on the late victorian entrepreneur', *Explorations in Economic History*, 9, 89–108.
McCraw, T. (1996), 'Competition and "fair trade": history and theory', *Research in Economic History*, 16, 185–239.
McKillop, D., and C. Ferguson (1993), *Building Societies: Structure, Performance and Change*, London: Graham and Trotman.
McLachlan, D. L. (1958), 'Index numbers of liner freight rates in the United Kingdom trades, 1946–1957', *Yorkshire Bulletin of Economic and Social Research*, 10, 50–62.
Maddison, A. (1964), *Economic Growth in the West*, London: Allen and Unwin.
  (1982), *Phases of Capitalist Development*, Oxford: Oxford University Press.
  (1987), 'Growth and slowdown in advanced capitalist economies: techniques of quantitative assessment', *Journal of Economic Literature*, 25, 649–98.
  (1991), *Dynamic Forces in Capitalist Development*, Oxford: Oxford University Press.

(1995), *Monitoring the World Economy, 1820–1992*, Paris: Organisation for Economic Co-operation and Development.

(2001), *The World Economy: A Millennial Perspective*, Paris: Organisation for Economic Co-operation and Development.

Maizels, A. (1963), *Industrial Growth and World Trade: An Empirical Study of Trends in Production, Consumption and Trade in Manufactures from 1899–1959 with a Discussion of Probable Future Trends*, Cambridge: Cambridge University Press.

Marshall, A. (1920), *Principles of Economics* (8th edn.), 1977, London: Macmillan.

Martin, R. F. (1939), *National Income in the United States, 1799–1938*, New York: National Industrial Conference Board.

Mass, W., and W. Lazonick (1990), 'The British cotton industry and international competitive advantage: the state of the debates', *Business History*, 32 (4), 9–65.

Mataja, V. (1910), 'Handel', in J. Conrad, L. Elster, W. Lexis and E. Loening (eds.), *Handwörterbuch der Staatswissenschaften*, Jena: Verlag von Gustav Fischer, 242–53.

Mathias, P. (1967), *Retailing Revolution: A History of Multiple Retailing in the Food Trades based upon the Allied Suppliers Group of Companies*, London: Longmans.

Matthews, D., M. Anderson and J. R. Edwards (1997), 'The rise of the professional accountant in British management', *Economic History Review*, 50, 407–29.

Matthews, R. C. O., C. H. Feinstein and J. C. Odling-Smee (1982), *British Economic Growth, 1856–1973*, Oxford: Oxford University Press.

Mayer, C., and O. Sussman (2001), 'The assessment: finance, law, and growth', *Oxford Review of Economic Policy*, 17, 457–66.

Miles, D. (1992), 'Housing and the wider economy in the short and the long run', *National Institute Economic Review*, 139, 64–77.

Milgrom, P., and J. Roberts (1990), 'The economics of modern manufacturing: technology, strategy and organisation', *American Economic Review*, 80, 511–28.

Mitch, D. F. (1992), *The Rise of Literacy in Victorian England: The Influence of Private Choice and Public Policy*, Philadelphia: University of Pennsylvania Press.

Mitchell, B. R. (1964), 'The coming of the railways and United Kingdom economic growth', *Journal of Economic History*, 24, 315–36.

(1975), *European Historical Statistics, 1750–1970*, London: Macmillan.

(1988), *British Historical Statistics*, Cambridge: Cambridge University Press.

(1998a), *International Historical Statistics, Europe, 1750–1993* (4th edn.), London: Macmillan.

(1998b), *International Historical Statistics, The Americas, 1750–1993* (4th edn.), London: Macmillan.

Moir, C. (1990), 'Competition in the UK grocery trades', in C. Moir and J. Dawson (eds.), *Competition and Markets: Essays in Honour of Margaret Hall*, London: Macmillan, 91–118.

More, C. (1980), *Skill and the English Working Class, 1870–1914*, London: Croom Helm.

Morelli, C. (1998), 'Constructing a balance between price and non-price competition in British multiple food retailing, 1954–64', *Business History*, 40 (2), 45–61.
Morgan, D. (1979), *Merchants of Grain*, New York: Viking.
Morrah, D. (1955), *A History of Industrial Life Assurance*, London: Allen and Unwin.
Munby, D. L., and A. H. Watson (1978), *Inland Transport Statistics: Great Britain 1900–1970*, Vol. I, *Railways, Public Road Passenger Transport, London's Transport*, Oxford: Clarendon Press.
Neale, A. D. (1960), *The Antitrust Laws of the United States of America: A Study of Competition Enforced by Law*, Cambridge: Cambridge University Press.
Neuburger, H. M., and H. H. Stokes (1974), 'German banks and German growth, 1883–1913: an empirical view', *Journal of Economic History*, 34, 710–31.
Nevin, E. (1955), *The Mechanism of Cheap Money: A Study of British Monetary Policy, 1931–1939*, Cardiff: University of Wales Press.
Nevin, E., and E. W. Davis (1970), *The London Clearing Banks*, London: Elek.
Newton, L. (1996), 'Regional bank–industry relations during the mid-nineteenth century: links between bankers and manufacturers in Sheffield, c.1850 to c.1885', *Business History*, 38 (3), 64–83.
Nicholas, S. J. (1984), 'The overseas marketing performance of British industry, 1870–1914', *Economic History Review*, 37, 489–506.
Nickell, S. J. (1996), 'Competition and corporate performance', *Journal of Political Economy*, 104, 724–46.
Nishimura, S. (1971), *The Decline of Inland Bills of Exchange in the London Money Market, 1855–1913*, Cambridge: Cambridge University Press.
O'Brien, P. K., and L. Prados de la Escosura (1992), 'Agricultural productivity and European industrialisation', *Economic History Review*, 45, 514–36.
Ó Gráda, C. (1994), 'British agriculture, 1860–1914', in R. Floud and D. McCloskey (eds.), *The Economic History of Britain Since 1700*, Vol. II, *1860–1939* (2nd edn.), Cambridge: Cambridge University Press, 145–72.
O'Mahony, M. (1992), 'Productivity levels in British and German manufacturing industry', *National Institute Economic Review*, 139, 46–63.
  (1996), 'Measures of fixed capital stocks in the post-war period: a five-country study', in B. van Ark and N. F. R. Crafts (eds.), *Quantitative Aspects of Post-War European Economic Growth*, Cambridge: Cambridge University Press, 165–214.
  (1997), *Comparative Productivity in Market Services: The Distributive Trades*, Discussion Paper no. 109, National Institute of Economic and Social Research, London.
  (1999), *Britain's Productivity Performance 1950–1996: An International Perspective*, London: National Institute of Economic and Social Research.
  (2002), 'National Institute sectoral productivity dataset', National Institute of Economic and Social Research, London, available at http://www.niesr.ac.uk/research/research.htm#4.
O'Mahony, M., and W. de Boer (2002), 'Britain's relative productivity performance: has anything changed?', *National Institute Economic Review*, 179, 38–43.

O'Mahony, M., N. Oulton and J. Vass (1998), 'Market services: productivity benchmarks for the UK', *Oxford Bulletin of Economics and Statistics*, 60, 529–51.

O'Mahony, M., and B. van Ark (2003), *EU Productivity and Competitiveness: An Industry Perspective. Can Europe Resume the Catching-up Process?*, Office for the Official Publications of the European Communities, Luxembourg City: Enterprise Publications.

O'Rourke, K. H. (1997), 'The European grain invasion, 1870–1913', *Journal of Economic History*, 57, 775–801.

(2000), 'Tariffs and growth in the late 19th century', *Economic Journal*, 110, 456–83.

O'Rourke, K. H., and J. G. Williamson (2000), *Globalization and History: The Evolution of a Nineteenth-Century Atlantic Economy*, Cambridge, MA: MIT Press.

Oliner, S., and D. Sichel (2000), 'The resurgence of growth in the late 1990s: is information technology the story?', *Journal of Economic Perspectives*, 14 (4), 3–22.

Olson, M. (1963), *The Economics of the Wartime Shortage: A History of British Food Supplies in the Napoleonic War and in World Wars I and II*, Durham, NC: Duke University Press.

(1982), *The Rise and Decline of Nations: Economic Growth, Stagflation, and Social Rigidities*, New Haven, CT: Yale University Press.

Oulton, N, (2001), *ICT and Productivity Growth in the United Kingdom*, Working Paper no. 140, Bank of England, London.

G. Owen (1999), *From Empire to Europe: The Decline and Revival of British Industry since the Second World War*, London: HarperCollins.

Paige, D., and G. Bombach (1959), *A Comparison of National Output and Productivity of the United Kingdom and the United States*, Paris: Organisation for European Economic Cooperation.

Paish, G. (1902), *The British Railway Position*, London: The Statist.

Pearson, R. (1997), 'Towards an historical model of services innovation: the case of the insurance industry, 1700–1914', *Economic History Review*, 50, 235–56.

Perkin, H. (1996), *The Third Revolution: Professional Elites in the Modern World*, London: Routledge.

Perkins, E. J. (1999), *Wall Street to Main Street: Charles Merrill and Middle-Class Investors*, Cambridge: Cambridge University Press.

Perry, C. R. (1977), 'The British experience 1876–1912: the impact of the telephone during the years of delay', in I. de Sola Pool (ed.), *The Social Impact of the Telephone*, Cambridge, MA: MIT Press, 69–96.

Pilat, D. (1994), *The Economics of Rapid Growth: The Experience of Japan and Korea*, Aldershot: Elgar.

Political and Economic Planning (1937), *Report on International Trade: A Survey of Problems Affecting the Expansion of International Trade, with Proposals for the Development of British Commercial Policy and Export Mechanism*, London: Political and Economic Planning.

Pollard, S. (1992), *The Development of the British Economy, 1914–1990* (4th edn.), London: Arnold.

Pollard, S., and P. Robertson (1979), *The British Shipbuilding Industry, 1870–1914*, Cambridge, MA: Harvard University Press.

Prais, S. J. (1981), *Productivity and Industrial Structure: A Statistical Study of Manufacturing Industry in Britain, 1909–70*, Cambridge: Cambridge University Press.

(1995), *Productivity, Education and Training: An International Perspective*, Cambridge: Cambridge University Press.

Prasada Rao, D. S. (1993), *Intercountry Comparisons of Agricultural Output and Productivity*, Economic and Social Development Paper no. 112, Food and Agriculture Organisation, Rome.

Prescott, E. (2003), *Why do Americans Work so much More than Europeans?*, Staff Report no. 321, Research Department, Federal Reserve Bank of Minneapolis, available at http://www.nber.org/confer/2004/si2004/efjk/prescott.pdf.

Pryke, R. (1971), *Public Enterprise in Practice: The British Experience of Nationalization over Two Decades*, London: MacGibbon and Kee.

(1981), *The Nationalised Industries: Policies and Performance since 1968*, Oxford: Martin Robertson.

Raynes, H. E. (1964), *A History of British Insurance* (2nd edn.), London: Pitman.

Reader, W. J. (1966), *Professional Men: The Rise of the Professional Classes in Nineteenth-Century England*, London: Weidenfeld and Nicolson.

Redford, A. (1956), *Manchester Merchants and Foreign Trade*, Vol. II, *1850–1939*, Manchester: Manchester University Press.

Rees, G. (1969), *St Michael: A History of Marks and Spencer*, London: Weidenfeld and Nicolson.

Rees, G. L. (1972), *Britain's Commodity Markets*, London: Elek.

Reid, M. (1982), *The Secondary Banking Crisis, 1973–75: Its Causes and Course*, London: Macmillan.

Revell, J. (1968), 'A secondary banking system', *The Banker*, 118, 798–812.

Rhys, G. (1993), 'Motor vehicles', in P. Johnson (ed.), *European Industries: Structure, Conduct and Performance*, Aldershot: Elgar, 126–53.

Ringer, F. K. (1979), *Education and Society in Modern Europe*, Bloomington, IN: Indiana University Press.

Ritschl, A. (2002), *Deutschlands Krise und Konjunktur 1924–1934: Binnenkonjunktur, Auslandsverschuldung und Reparationsproblem zwischen Dawes-Plan und Transfersperre*, Jahrbuch für Wirtschaftsgeschichte, Beiheft 2, Berlin: Akademie-Verlag.

(2004a), 'Spurious growth in German output data, 1913–1938', *European Review of Economic History*, 8, 201–23.

(2004b), 'How and when did Germany catch up to Great Britain and the US? Results from the official statistics, 1901–1960', paper presented to Economic History Society annual conference, Royal Holloway, University of London, 2–4 April.

Ritschl, A., and M. Spoerer (1997), 'Das Bruttosozialprodukt Deutschlands nach den amtlichen Volkseinkommens- und Sozialproduktstatistiken 1901–1995', *Jahrbuch für Wirtschaftsgeschichte*, 2, 27–54.

Roe, A. (1971), *The Financial Interdependence of the Economy, 1957–1966*, Cambridge: Chapman and Hall.

Rostas, L. (1948), *Comparative Productivity in British and American Industry*, Cambridge: National Institute of Economic and Social Research.

Rotella, E. J. (1981), *From Home to Office: U. S. Women at Work, 1870–1930*, Ann Arbor, MI: UMI Research Press.

Routh, G. (1965), *Occupation and Pay in Great Britain, 1906–1960*, Cambridge: Cambridge University Press.

Rubinstein, W. D. (1993), *Capitalism, Culture and Decline in Britain, 1750–1990*, London: Routledge.

Salter, J. A. (1921), *Allied Shipping Control: An Experiment in International Administration*, Economic and Social History of the World War (British Series), Oxford: Clarendon Press (in association with the Carnegie Endowment for International Peace).

Saul, S. B. (1960), *Studies in British Overseas Trade, 1870–1914*, Liverpool: Liverpool University Press.

Savage, C. I. (1966), *An Economic History of Transport* (rev. edn.), London: Hutchinson.

Sayers, R. S. (1976), *The Bank of England, 1891–1944* (2 volumes & appendices), Cambridge: Cambridge University Press.

Schlote, W. (1952), *British Overseas Trade: From 1700 to the 1930s*, Oxford: Blackwell.

Schumpeter, J. A. (1943), *Capitalism, Socialism and Democracy*, London: Allen and Unwin.

Sheppard, D. K. (1971), *The Growth and Role of UK Financial Institutions, 1880–1962*, London: Methuen.

Simon, M. (1968), 'The pattern of new British portfolio foreign investment, 1865–1914', in A. R. Hall (ed.), *The Export of Capital from Britain, 1870–1914*, London: Methuen, 15–44.

Smith, A. D., and D. M. W. N. Hitchens (1985), *Productivity in the Distributive Trades: A Comparison of Britain, America and Germany*, Cambridge: Cambridge University Press.

Smith, A. D., D. M. W. N. Hitchens and S. W. Davies (1982), *International Industrial Productivity: A Comparison of Britain, America and Germany*, Cambridge: Cambridge University Press.

Smolensky, E. (1972), 'Industrial location and urban growth', in L. Davis, R. A. Easterlin and W. N. Parker (eds.), *American Economic Growth: An Economist's History of the United States*, New York: Harper and Row, 582–607.

Soskice, D. W. (1991), 'The institutional infrastructure for international competitiveness: a comparative analysis of the UK and Germany', in A. B. Atkinson and R. Brunetta (eds.), *The Economics of the New Europe*, London: Macmillan, 45–66.

(1994), 'Reconciling markets and institutions: the German apprenticeship system", in L. M. Lynch (ed.), *Training and the Private Sector: International Comparisons*, Chicago: University of Chicago Press, 25–60.

Spoerer, M. (1997), 'Weimar's investment and growth record in intertemporal and international perspective', *European Review of Economic History*, 1, 271–98.

Stacey, N. A. H., and A. Wilson (1958), *The Changing Pattern of Distribution*, London: Batsford.

Stasinopoulos, D. (1993), 'The third phase of liberalisation in community aviation and the need for supplementary measures', *Journal of Transport Economics and Policy*, 27, 323–8.

Stigler, G. J. (1951), 'The division of labor is limited by the extent of the market', *Journal of Political Economy*, 59, 185–93.

Stiglitz, J., and A. Weiss (1981), 'Credit rationing in markets with imperfect information', *American Economic Review*, 71, 393–410.

Stone, R., and D. A. Rowe (1966), *The Measurement of Consumers' Expenditure and Behaviour in the United Kingdom, 1920–1938*, Vol. II, Cambridge: Cambridge University Press.

Stubbs, P. C., W. J. Tyson and M. Q. Dalvi (1984), *Transport Economics* (rev. edn.), London: Allen and Unwin.

Sturmey, S. G. (1962), *British Shipping and World Competition*, London: Athlone Press.

Summers, R., and A. Heston (1988), 'A new set of international comparisons of real product and price levels: estimates for 130 countries, 1950–1985', *Review of Income and Wealth*, 34, 1–25.

Supple, B. E. (1970), *The Royal Exchange Assurance: A History of British Insurance, 1720–1970*, Cambridge: Cambridge University Press.

(1994), 'Fear of failing: economic history and the decline of Britain', *Economic History Review*, 47, 441–58.

Svennilson, I. (1954), *Growth and Stagnation in the European Economy*, Geneva: United Nations

Tedlow, R. S. (1996), *New and Improved: The Story of Mass Marketing in America*, Boston: Harvard Business School Press.

Temin, P. (2002), 'The golden age of European growth reconsidered', *European Review of Economic History*, 6, 3–22.

Tew, B. (1977), *The Evolution of the International Monetary System 1945–77*, London: Hutchinson.

Thomas, W. A. (1978), *The Finance of British Industry, 1918–1976*, London: Methuen.

Thorpe, D. (1990), 'Economic theory, retail output and capacity in British retailing', in C. Moir and J. Dawson (eds.), *Competition and Markets: Essays in Honour of Margaret Hall*, London: Macmillan, 153–206.

Tilly, R. (1986), 'German banking, 1850–1914: development assistance for the strong', *Journal of European Economic History*, 15, 113–52.

(1991), 'Germany', in R. Sylla and G. Toniolo (eds.), *Patterns of European Industrialization: The Nineteenth Century*, London: Routledge, 175–96.

Tolliday, S. (1987), *Business, Banking and Politics: The Case of British Steel, 1918–1939*, Cambridge, MA: Harvard University Press.

Trebilcock, C. (1985), *Phoenix Assurance and the Development of British Insurance*, Vol. I, *1782–1870*, Cambridge: Cambridge University Press.

(1997), 'Phoenix: financial services, insurance, and economic revival between the wars', in P. Clarke and C. Trebilcock (eds.), *Understanding Decline: Perceptions and Realities of British Economic Performance*, Cambridge: Cambridge University Press, 123–44.

(1998), *Phoenix Assurance and the Development of British Insurance*, Vol. II, *The Era of the Insurance Giants, 1870–1984*, Cambridge: Cambridge University Press.
Triplett, J. E., and B. P. Bosworth (2003), 'Productivity measurement in service industries: "Baumol's disease" has been cured', *Federal Reserve Bank of New York Economic Policy Review*, 9 (3), 23–33.
Turner, G. (1969), *Business in Britain*, London: Eyre and Spottiswoode.
Tyack, D. (ed.) (1967), *Turning Points in American Educational History*, Lexington, MA: Xerox.
van Ark, B. (1992), 'Comparative productivity in British and American manufacturing', *National Institute Economic Review*, 142, 63–74.
van Vleck, V. N. L. (1997), 'Delivering coal by road and rail in Britain: the efficiency of the "silly little bobtailed" wagons', *Journal of Economic History*, 57, 139–60.
Veblen, T. (1915), *Imperial Germany and the Industrial Revolution*, New York: Macmillan.
Ville, S. P. (1987), *English Shipowning during the Industrial Revolution*, Manchester: Manchester University Press.
(1989), 'Patterns of shipping investment in the port of Newcastle upon Tyne, 1750–1850', *Northern History*, 25, 205–21.
(1990), *Transport and the Development of the European Economy, 1750–1918*, London: Macmillan.
von der Decken, H., and R. Wagenführ (1935), 'Entwicklung und Wandlung der Sachgüterproduktion', *Vierteljahrshefte zur Konjunkturforschung*, 11, 145–63.
Wagenführ, R. (1933), 'Die Industriewirtschaft: Entwicklungstendenzen der deutschen und internationalen Industrieproduktion 1860 bis 1932', *Vierteljahrshefte zur Konjunkturforschung Sonderheft*, 31, 3–70.
Walters, A. A., and C. S. Sharp (1953), *Report on Traffic Costs and Charges of Freight Transport in Great Britain*, Birmingham: Birmingham University Press.
Ward, M., and J. Devereux (2003), 'Measuring British decline: direct versus long-span income measures', *Journal of Economic History*, 63, 826–51.
(2004), 'Relative U.K./U.S. output reconsidered: a reply to Professor Broadberry', *Journal of Economic History*, 64, 879–91.
Wardley, P. (1991), 'The anatomy of Big Business: aspects of corporate development in the twentieth century', *Business History*, 33 (2), 268–96.
(1999), 'The emergence of Big Business: the largest corporate employers of labour in the United Kingdom, Germany and the United States c.1907', *Business History*, 41 (4), 88–116.
(2000), 'The commercial banking industry and its part in the emergence and consolidation of the corporate economy in Britain before 1940', *Journal of Industrial History*, 3, 71–97.
(2001), 'On the ranking of firms: a response to Jeremy and Farnie', *Business History*, 43 (3), 119–34.
Watson, K. (1995), 'The new issue market as a source of finance for the UK brewing and iron and steel industries, 1870–1913', in Y. Cassis, G. Feldman and U. Olsson (eds.), *The Evolution of Financial Institutions and Markets in Twentieth-Century Europe*, Aldershot: Scolar, 209–48.

Webb, S. B. (1980), 'Tariffs, cartels, technology, and growth in the German steel industry, 1879 to 1914', *Journal of Economic History*, 40, 309–29.

Welsby, J., and A. Nichols (1999), 'The privatisation of Britain's railways: an inside view', *Journal of Transport Economics and Policy*, 33, 55–76.

Westall, O. M. (1997), 'Invisible, visible and "direct" hands: an institutional interpretation of organisational structure and change in British general insurance', *Business History*, 39 (4), 44–66.

White, E. N. (2000), 'Banking and finance in the twentieth century', in S. L. Engerman and R. E. Gallman (eds.), *The Cambridge Economic History of the United States*, Vol. III, *The Twentieth Century*, Cambridge: Cambridge University Press, 743–802.

Wilkins, M. (1989), *The History of Foreign Investment in the United States to 1914*, Cambridge, MA: Harvard University Press.

Williamson, J. G. (1995), 'The evolution of global labor markets since 1830: background evidence and hypotheses', *Explorations in Economic History*, 32, 141–96.

Yamada, S., and V. W. Ruttan (1980), 'International comparisons of productivity in agriculture', in J. W. Kendrick and B. N. Vaccara (eds), *New Developments in Productivity Measurement and Analysis*, Chicago: Chicago University Press (in association with the National Bureau of Economic Research), 509–85.

Yamey, B. S. (1952), 'The origins of resale price maintenance: a study of three branches of retail trade', *Economic Journal*, 62, 522–45.

(1966), 'The United Kingdom', in B. S. Yamey (ed.), *Resale Price Maintenance*, London: Weidenfeld and Nicolson, 249–98.

Yates, J. (1989), *Control through Communication: The Rise of System in American Management*, Baltimore: Johns Hopkins University Press.

Index

Abramovitz, M. 7, 109
Accident Offices' Association 278
agriculture 3, 8, 12, 16, 24, 26, 27, 35, 38–9, 40, 41–3, 45–6, 47, 50, 51, 55, 66, 68, 71, 73, 76, 77, 81, 90–1, 93, 95, 130–2, 134, 142, 180, 214, 216, 280, 361, 370, 372, 373
air transport 29, 77, 240–3, 308–14, 355
Aldcroft, D. H. 151, 160, 162, 168, 223, 227, 231, 233–5, 240–2, 296, 298
apprenticeship 7, 14, 117–18, 128, 141, 282, 354, 367, 372, 373
Argyll 324
Ashley, Laura 324
Associated Scottish Life offices 210
Associated Society of Locomotive Engineers and Firemen (ASLEF) 300
automated teller machines (ATMs) 340

Bairoch, P. 90, 130
Balfour Williamson 188
Bank of England 82, 194–204, 265–70, 333–46
Bank Rate 196, 263
Bankers Industrial Development Company (BIDC) 266
banks *see* clearing banks, international banking, merchant banks, overseas banks
Barclays Bank 194, 262, 268, 336, 338, 340
Barings Bank 196, 202, 346
Beeching Report 293, 299, 300
Bill of Exchange 195, 198, 201, 269
Bolton Report 342–3
Bonavia, M. R., 233–42
Booker McConnell 331
Boot, Jesse 176, 323
Bowrings 189
British Airways (BA) 242, 312, 313
British and Commonwealth 288, 290

British Electric Traction (BET) 240, 306, 307
British Empire 11, 12, 83, 91, 148, 169, 182, 201, 203, 207, 215, 217, 225, 242, 256, 268, 271, 329, 346, 375
British European Airways (BEA) 242, 312
British Home Stores (BHS) 250, 323
British India (BI) 228
British Overseas Airways Corporation (BOAC) 242, 312
British Railways (BR) 296–306, 355
British Road Services (BRS) 305
British Shipping (Assistance) Act 227
British South American Airways (BSAA) 242
British Telecom (BT) 316, 319, 355
British Transport Commission (BTC) 300–6
Broadberry, S. N. 1, 5, 7, 9, 10, 13, 20, 21, 22, 24, 26, 38, 82, 83, 87, 93, 97, 118, 129, 130, 140, 188, 191, 200, 257, 259, 269, 272, 274, 329, 366, 367, 369
building societies 192, 265, 272–4, 335, 337, 347–8
Bunge and Born 188
Burton/Debenhams 324

calculating machine 85, 86, 113–14, 196, 214, 234, 235
see also comptometer, computer, tabulator
Campbell-Kelly, M. 85, 112, 138, 196, 214, 234, 235, 278
Capie, F. 93, 130, 193, 194, 199, 262, 339
capital 6–8, 9, 14, 43, 88, 90, 92–3, 96, 98, 109–26, 128, 132, 140, 141, 143, 151, 154, 156, 157, 166, 168, 173, 185, 190, 191, 194, 199, 200, 202–3, 204, 220, 223, 227, 232, 233, 239, 245, 259, 266, 267, 268, 269, 270, 281–2, 284, 285, 287, 288, 291, 295, 301, 304, 309, 316, 320, 323, 332, 338,

Index 405

339, 343, 354, 362, 364, 365–6, 367, 372, 373
see also human capital, physical capital
Carlin, W. 90, 128, 140, 141, 143
Cassis, Y. 82, 201, 204
Chandler, A. D. Jr. 6, 10, 70, 83, 84, 87, 88, 92, 95, 98, 147, 159, 163, 168, 178, 201, 203, 278, 290
Channon, D. F. 288–90, 301, 305–7, 312–13, 318, 323, 329, 337–9, 346, 351–2
Channon, G. 169
Chapman, S. 175, 185–9, 202–3, 258
Charterhouse Industrial Development Co. Ltd 266
Chicago Convention (1944) 312
City of Glasgow Bank 196
City of London 10, 82, 83, 147, 201, 215, 269
Civil Aviation Act (1980) 313
Clapham, J. H. 94, 168, 175, 177
clearing banks 92–4, 194, 199, 201, 204, 262–3, 264–5, 266, 267, 269, 336–44, 346, 356
Cleary, E. J. 273, 347
Collins, M. 12, 91, 93, 94, 194–201, 262–8, 337–46, 353
Committee of Inquiry into Shipping (1970) 291
Committee of Inquiry on Small Firms see Bolton Report
Committee on Finance and Industry see Macmillan Report
Committee on Resale Price Maintenance (1949) 251
Committee on the Working of the Monetary System see Radcliffe Report
Committee to Review the Functioning of Financial Institutions see Wilson Committee
competition 2, 6, 8–9, 11, 43, 84, 87, 88, 90, 91, 127–43, 148–9, 163–4, 168, 182, 187, 196, 203, 210, 211, 215, 217, 231, 233, 240–2, 249, 251–2, 256, 263, 269, 276, 289, 290, 298, 302, 307, 308, 312, 313, 318, 319, 323, 325, 337, 338, 339, 340, 346, 351–3, 355, 371, 372, 373, 374
see also protection, resale price maintenance
Competition and Credit Control (CCC) 338, 339, 341, 342
comptometer 234
computer 15, 86, 112, 338, 340, 358, 368

concentration 85, 140, 160, 161, 163, 194, 197, 213, 215, 249, 262, 277, 308, 324, 351–2
Co-operative Union 176
Co-operative Wholesale Societies 176
Co-operative Wholesale Society banks 192
Copeland, M. 188
Cottrell, P. L. 82, 159, 194
Crafts, N. F. R. 1, 9, 13, 26, 41, 87, 128, 129, 142, 143, 366, 368
Credit for Industry 266
Cunard 228, 290

Daily Mail 277
Daunton, M. J. 244, 318
David, P. A. 46, 109, 117
Deakin, B. M. 11, 129, 149, 163, 220, 286, 291
Debenhams 251, 324
Dee Corporation 324
demand 2, 6, 10, 35, 94, 98, 147, 159, 168, 177, 200, 240, 265, 268, 269, 289, 293, 298, 306, 318
Depression of the 1930s see Great Depression
distribution 4, 6, 10, 11, 12, 23, 28, 29, 31, 33–5, 39, 41, 45, 47, 49, 67, 70, 75, 77, 81, 83, 84, 87, 88, 94–5, 130, 134, 138, 148, 149, 173–91, 202, 216, 245–59, 319–32, 356, 363–4, 371, 374; see also retailing, wholesaling
domestic banking 194–201, 203, 262–8
Dreyfus, Louis and Co. 188
Drummond, I. 129, 256, 269
duplicator 85, 86, 235

Eastmans 176
economies of scale 6, 81–3, 90, 92, 96, 170, 177, 187, 188, 189, 194, 199, 201, 215, 269, 278, 279, 323, 352, 371
education 2, 5, 7–8, 14, 68, 71, 75, 81, 83, 88, 104, 106, 107, 114–17, 124, 148, 196, 206–7, 271, 282, 361, 371, 372, 373; see also human capital
Eichengreen, B. 9, 90, 128, 140, 269
Electric and International Telegraph Company (EITC) 173
Electronic funds transfer at the point of sale (EFTPOS) 340
electronic point of sale terminals (EPoS) 324
Ellerman 228
eurodollar 345

406 Index

Faculty of Actuaries 210
Farnie, D. A. 88, 185, 188
Feinstein, C. H. 36–76, 108, 125, 150, 180, 191, 192, 222, 223, 237, 259, 260
Field, A. J. 6, 84, 173, 246, 366
finance 4, 6, 12, 23, 28, 29–31, 33–5, 38, 39, 41, 47, 49, 55, 67, 70, 72, 75, 81, 82, 84–5, 87, 91, 92–4, 134, 139–40, 147, 191–214, 216, 223, 227, 228, 259–78, 298, 300, 318, 332–53, 364, 371, 374; *see also* building societies, domestic banking, insurance, international banking
Fire Offices' Committee 208, 278
Fohlin, C. 92, 140
Foreman-Peck, J. 88, 112, 169, 170, 172, 231, 234, 244, 245
Franco-Prussian War 183
Fremdling, R. 47, 50–1, 73, 76, 92, 93, 140
Furness Withy 228
Fyffes 189

General Strike 235
Gerschenkron, A. 12, 77, 91–3, 132, 140, 198, 199
Goldin, C. 7, 114–17
Gourvish, T. R. 166
Government Tonnage Replacement Scheme 229
Great Depression 11, 216, 229, 233, 235, 279, 375
Great Northern and Southern Stores 251
Great Western Railway (GWR) 169, 233
Greif, A. 82

Habitat 324
Hamburg America Line 160
Hannah, L. 111, 130, 140, 234, 263, 267, 276, 340
Harley, C. K. 154–7, 226
Hawke, G. R. 166
Hepworth, John 176
Heston, A. 44
hierarchies 2, 5, 10–11, 13, 14, 15, 16, 35, 81, 83–106, 147–9, 153, 159–61, 169, 170, 195, 201, 203, 207, 213, 214, 234, 278, 279, 281, 290, 325, 339, 356, 369, 371, 374, 376
Hoffmann, W. G. 46–94, 108, 126
Home and Colonial Tea Company 176
human capital 6–8, 9, 14, 15, 88, 107, 114–24, 128, 140, 141, 169, 234, 281–2, 354, 367, 372, 373; *see also* education, vocational training
Hyde, F. E. 227

ICT *see* information and communications technology
Imlah, A. H. 10, 82, 134, 147, 154, 180, 211
Imperial Airways 242, 312
Imperial Preference 13, 217
Industrial and Commercial Finance Corporation Ltd (ICFC) 266, 342
industrial relations 128, 140, 279, 318, 355, 373
industrialisation of services 2, 5–6, 10, 11, 12, 16, 35, 81–106, 117, 137, 138, 147–8, 149, 159, 170, 214, 215, 216, 278, 279, 281, 290, 355, 368, 369, 371, 374, 375, 376
information and communications technology 5, 10, 14–15, 81, 85–6, 148, 340, 352, 357–8, 361, 368, 369, 371, 374
Inhabited House Duty 179
Inquiry into Lorries, People and the Environment 238
Institute of Actuaries 210
Institute of Bankers in Scotland 195
insurance 11, 23, 85, 149, 192, 203, 207–14, 229, 262, 274–8, 290, 293, 329, 335, 343, 346, 348–53, 375
International Air Transport Association (IATA) 312
international banking 11, 85, 149, 201, 207, 215, 268–71, 279, 344–7, 375
international trade 47, 134–7, 179–85, 252–6, 257, 286, 326–9

Jardine Matheson 332
Jefferys, J. B. 94, 175–9, 246–51, 321
Jeremy, D. J. 88, 96
Jones, G. 84, 94, 190, 203–4, 257, 270–1, 331–2, 346, 356

Kendrick, J. W. 36–55, 108, 125
Kirkaldy, A. W. 164
Kopper, C. 95
Kynaston, D. 10, 147, 201, 202

labour productivity comparisons
aggregate economy 1–3, 21–7, 36–54
agriculture 3, 24–7, 36–54
distribution 4, 29–32, 67, 70, 75, 77
finance 4, 29–32, 67, 70, 72, 75

Index

industry 3, 24–7, 36–54
services 3, 24–7, 36–54
transport and communications 4, 28–32, 67, 69, 74
Laker Airways 313
Lamoreaux, N. 84
Lewis, John 251
Lewis, W. A. 154, 222, 276
Lindert, P. H. 114
Lipton Ltd 176, 324
Liverpool Cotton Brokers Association 186
Lockwood, D. 85, 86
Lloyd's 210–11, 213, 276, 336, 351
Lloyds Bank 194, 262, 336, 338
London Assurance 210
London and North Eastern Railway (LNER) 233, 235
London and North Western Railway (LNWR) 169
London, Midland and Scottish Railway (LMS) 233
Lonrho 331

Macmillan Report 266, 342
Maddison, A. 19–22, 38, 43–4, 108, 110
Maizels, A. 252, 329
Manchester Chamber of Commerce 188, 257
Manchester Royal Exchange 188, 257–8
manufacturing 1, 20–1, 24, 26, 38, 40, 47–9, 51–2, 55, 56, 66, 69, 73, 76, 77, 87, 112, 117, 118, 129, 130, 137, 138, 142, 214, 355, 357, 367
Marks and Spencer 323
Marshall, A. 82, 201, 215
Martins Bank 338
Mathias, P. 176, 249
Matthews, R. C. O. 108, 123
Maypole Dairy Company 176
McCloskey, D. N. 53, 109, 129
measurement problems 22–3, 28, 173, 237, 361, 370
Menzies, J. 176
merchant banks 82, 93, 201, 202–3, 204, 207, 266, 268–70, 338, 345–6
Mercury 319
Midland Bank 194, 262, 266, 336, 340
Midland Railway 169
Mitch, D. F. 114
Mitchell, B. R. 29, 56, 66–75, 114, 165, 238, 286
Monopolies Commission 338, 352
Monopolies and Mergers Commission 318, 325, 326
Munby, D. L. 69, 166, 231, 240

National Board for Prices and Incomes 338
National Bus Company (NBC) 307
National Commercial Bank of Scotland 338
National Express 307
National Freight Corporation (NFC) 306
National Provincial Bank 262, 336, 338
National Savings Bonds 192, 262, 274, 333, 335
National Union of Bank Employees (NUBE) 340
National Westminster Bank 338
nationalisation 129, 170–3, 233, 235, 243, 245, 297, 300, 301, 305, 306, 318
Nelson, James and Sons 176
networks 2, 5, 10, 11, 13, 14, 35, 81, 82–3, 84, 87, 97–106, 147, 149, 157–63, 189, 191, 194–5, 201–7, 213, 214–15, 216, 258–9, 269, 270, 279, 281, 355, 356, 369, 371, 374, 376
Next 324
Nishimura, S. 194, 198
North Eastern Railway 169
North German Lloyd 160
Norwich Union 277

Ocean 288, 290
Office for Telecommunications (Oftel) 319
office mechanisation 5, 7, 81, 85, 88, 107, 111–14, 137, 138, 196, 214, 234–5, 267, 278; *see also* calculating machine, comptometer, computer, duplicator, information and communications technology, tabulator, telegraph, telephone, typewriter, vertical filing system
Office of Fair Trading (OFT) 325
Olson, M. 9, 132, 141, 229
O'Mahony, M. 15, 77, 108, 325, 332, 357–66
O'Rourke, K. H. 11, 90, 130
overseas banks 201, 203–4, 270–1, 337, 345–7

Paige, D. 40, 72
Paish, G. 168
passenger transport authorities (PTAs) 307
Pearson, R. 212
Peninsular and Oriental (P&O) 228, 288, 290
Phoenix Assurance 208, 210, 275, 277
physical capital 6–7, 9, 14, 43, 90, 107–14, 126; *see also* capital
Pollard, S. 228, 247

Post Office 111, 170–2, 243, 245, 318, 355, 318–19
Post Office Savings Bank (POSB) 138, 192, 196, 207, 333, 335
post-war settlement 9, 14, 90, 128, 140–2, 143, 281, 353, 373
PPP *see* purchasing power parity
Prais, S. J. 7, 87, 107, 117, 120, 128
privatisation 9, 14, 282, 300, 301, 312, 313, 316, 317, 319, 355, 374, 375
professional associations 7, 107, 117, 118–23, 124, 148, 195, 206, 372
protection 8, 11, 12, 16, 35, 50, 81, 90–1, 106, 129, 130–4, 142, 216, 220, 230, 257, 276, 373, 375
Prudential Assurance Company 210, 214, 278, 351
Pryke, R. 300, 312–13, 318–19
purchasing power parity 22, 51, 68, 71, 73, 114

quality 113, 156, 175, 250, 361; *see also* measurement problems

Radcliffe Report 342–3
Railway Clearing House 234–5
Railway Rates Tribunal 233
railways 6, 10, 11, 12, 13, 29, 31, 34, 35, 49, 67, 69, 74, 77, 83, 85, 91, 92, 96, 106, 147, 150, 165, 215, 216, 220–30, 240–2, 279, 280, 293, 302, 308, 355
Railways Act (1921) 233
Ranks 189
Reader, W. J. 118
Redford, A. 188
resale price maintenance 84, 130–4, 179, 251, 279, 323, 249
Resale Prices Act (1964) 323
Restrictive Trade Practices Act (1956) 323
retailing 94–6, 175–9, 187, 215, 246–52, 279, 321–6, 329, 356
Ringer, F. K. 116
Ritschl, A. 51
Road and Rail Traffic Act (1933) 240, 305
Road Passenger Transport Executive 306
Road Traffic Act (1930) 240, 307
road transport 29, 235–40, 242, 302–8, 314, 350, 355
Rostas, L. 39, 47, 66–77
Rotella, E. J. 86, 137
Rothschilds Bank 202
Routh, G. 118, 137
Royal Bank of Scotland 338

Royal Commission on Shipping Rings 162, 163
Royal Commission on Transport 238
Royal Exchange Assurance (REA) 208, 210, 213, 278
Royal Mail Group 228
RPI-X 319
RPM *see* resale price maintenance
Rubinstein, W. D. 2, 91, 213

Samuel, Marcus 189
Sanday, S. and Co. 188
Saul, S. B. 180, 182
Sayers, R. S. 266, 270
Schlote, W. 11, 148, 183
Scottish Motor Traction (SMT) 240, 306
secondary banking crisis 346
Sheppard, D. K. 191, 193, 197–8, 200, 259, 265, 268, 332, 342
shipping 11, 29, 82, 97–8, 134, 151–64, 211, 215, 220–30, 231, 279, 286–93
Slater's Directory of Manchester and Salford 188, 257
Smith, A. D. 40, 72, 76–7
Smith, Edwards and Company 186
Smith, W. H. and Son 176, 323
Smyth, Ross T. 188
Soskice, D. W. 128, 140, 141
Southern Railway (SR) 233, 234, 235
Special Committee on Tramp Shipping 227
standardisation 2, 10, 13, 14, 35, 137, 81, 175, 189, 279, 281, 289, 293, 355, 357, 369
Sturmey, S. G. 161, 220–9, 288–91
Suez Canal 156, 185
Sun Insurance Office 208
Supple, B. 208–13, 274–8, 350–3
Svennilson, I. 225, 236
Swires 332

tabulator 86
telecommunications 170, 243, 314; *see also* telegraph, telephone
telegraph 6, 23, 67, 84, 85, 159, 170, 185, 194, 245, 316
telephone 6, 23, 67, 83, 85, 86, 98, 111, 159, 170, 185, 242, 316, 340
Temin, P. 50
Tesco 323
Thomas, W. A. 266, 343
Tilling Group 240, 306
Tilly, R. 91, 93, 140, 200
Tolliday, S. 94, 267
Tootal Broadhurst Lee 187

Index

Transport Act (1947) 235, 305
Transport Act (1953) 301, 305
Transport Act (1968) 306–7
Transport Act (1974) 301
Transport Act (1980) 308
Transport Act (1985) 308
transport and communications 4, 12, 28, 34, 49, 67, 69, 74, 77, 83, 92, 96, 138, 150–73, 216, 220–45, 284–319, 358, 363; *see also* air transport, railways, road transport, shipping, telecommunications
treasury bills 198, 201, 264, 265, 341
Treasury Committee on Bank Amalgamations (1918) 263
Trebilcock, C. 208–10, 275
Triplett, J. E. 361
Trustee Savings Bank (TSB) 192, 333, 335
Turner, G. 288–90, 300, 313, 318, 323, 367
typewriter 85, 112, 196, 235

United Africa Company 331
US Civil War 134, 194

van Ark, B. 72, 360, 361
van Vleck, V. N. L. 234
vertical filing system 85, 86

Ville, S. P. 82, 159, 163
vocational training 7, 9, 14, 90, 107, 117, 140, 282, 372; *see also* apprentices, professional associations

Ward, M. 22, 43–5
Wardley, P. 88, 96, 169, 267
Webb, S. 90, 132
Weir Committee on Main Line Electrification 234
Westall, O. M. 278, 352, 353
Westminster Bank 194, 262, 336, 338
White, E. N. 6, 85
wholesaling 84, 85, 94, 106, 175, 179, 203, 215, 246, 252, 279, 320, 326, 356
Wilkins, M. 203
Williams and Glyn's Bank 338
Williamson, J. G. 11, 45
Wilson Report 342, 343
Woolworth 250, 323
World War I 1, 11, 19, 24–7, 218, 219, 223, 232, 253, 265, 269
World War II 1, 13, 19, 24, 219, 229, 235, 253, 265

Yamey, B. S. 130, 179, 252, 323
Yates, J. 85–7
Yorkshire Penny Bank 192